GUNFIGHTERS HIGHWAYMEN & VIGILANTES

GUNFIGHTERS HIGHWAYMEN & VIGILANTES

VIOLENCE ON THE FRONTIER

ROGER D. McGRATH

University of California Press

Berkeley   Los Angeles   London

University of California Press
Berkeley and Los Angeles, California

University of California Press, Ltd.
London, England

©1984 by
The Regents of the University of
California

Library of Congress Cataloging in
Publication Data

McGrath, Roger D.
   Gunfighters, highwaymen, and
vigilantes.

   Includes bibliographical references
and index.
   1. Violence—California—Aurora—
Case studies.
2. Violence—California—Bodie—
Case studies. 3. Frontier and pioneer
life—West (U.S.)—History. 4. Mining
industry and finance—West (U.S.)—
History. 5. Violence—West (U.S.)—
Case studies.   I. Title.
HN80.A92M33 1984   978   83–6886
ISBN 0–520–05101–7

Printed in the United States of America

1 2 3 4 5 6 7 8 9

To Susan

For her understanding and love

"We pack six shooters
and derringers for
fear of the knave."

An Aurora miner, 1863

CONTENTS

ILLUSTRATIONS

ACKNOWLEDGMENTS

Any writer accumulates debts to a number of people and institutions that have affected his career. I am no exception. James M. Wood and Stanford Shaw early on demonstrated to me that history could be enormously exciting, and Fawn Brodie showed me that it could be excitingly written. Norris Hundley introduced me to the American West of the scholar, and Richard F. Logan to the perspective of the historical geographer; they both have offered continual encouragement—something most writers need in large doses—and Norris Hundley read the manuscript in all its stages chapter by chapter, never failing to provide incisive criticism and editorial suggestions.

The staffs of numerous libraries were helpful in my research, especially those at the Bancroft, the California State, the Huntington, and the UCLA Research libraries. Particularly valuable assistance was also rendered by the staffs of the California and Nevada historical societies and by Robert E. Stewart who, while serving as press secretary to the governor of Nevada, unearthed some important territorial correspondence and documents in the statehouse. I owe a special debt of gratitude to Ann Morgan, Elizabeth Nino, and Susan Cathleen McGrath for their patience and perseverance in typing the manuscript during its successive stages of production.

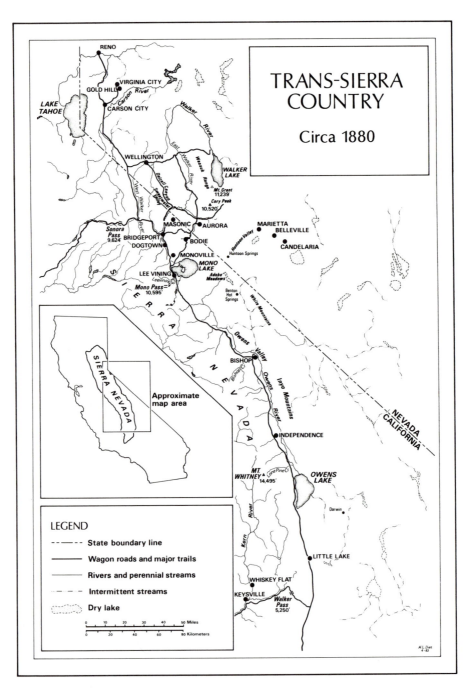

1.   By 1880 more than a dozen towns had been established in the trans-Sierra country. Most of the towns existed solely for the purpose of extracting the mineral wealth that lay buried in the earth. (Cartography by Noel Diaz)

PREFACE

The early morning hours of Thursday, 13 June 1878, found Patrick Gallagher's Shamrock saloon in Bodie crowded with men. Some stood at the bar drinking Irish whiskey, others at the chop counter eating fried steaks, while several huddled around the gambling tables playing faro. Suddenly two men began quarreling—Alex Nixon, the popular and powerfully built president of the Bodie miners' union, and Tom McDonald, twenty pounds lighter than Nixon but no small man himself. When McDonald claimed he was the better man, Nixon unleashed a vicious blow that caught McDonald in the eye and sent him tumbling to the floor.

The Shamrock's burly bartender and a deputy constable tried to separate the men and cool their tempers. But McDonald drew a gun and asked the bigger Nixon if he would give him "even chances." "Yes, by God," answered Nixon while pulling a revolver out of his hip pocket. Both men opened fire. Nixon's first shot missed McDonald by inches but McDonald's hit Nixon in the side. "My God, boys, I'm shot," exclaimed the big miner as he staggered back and fell to the floor. As he lay there with blood running out of a hole in his side, he fired two more shots at McDonald. They missed. McDonald returned the fire. The rounds tore holes in the wooden planks of the Shamrock's floor but left Nixon untouched. It hardly mattered. Less than two hours later Nixon died from the effects of McDonald's first shot.

It is popularly assumed that the frontier was full of Nixons and McDonalds—brave, strong, and reckless men who often resorted to violence—and that these men helped make the frontier a violent and lawless place. On the frontier, says conventional wisdom, a structured society did not exist and social control was largely absent; law enforcement and the criminal justice system had limited, if any, influence; and danger—both from man and from the elements—was ever present. This view of the frontier is projected by motion pictures, television, popular literature, and most scholarly histories (see the Appendix for a review of the scholarly literature). But was the frontier really all that violent? What was the nature of the violence that did occur? Were frontier towns more violent than cities in the East? Has America inherited a violent way of life from the frontier? Was the frontier more violent than the United States is today?

This book attempts to answer these questions and others about violence and lawlessness on the frontier and to do so in a new way. Whereas most authors have drawn their conclusions about frontier violence from the exploits of a few notorious badmen and outlaws and from some of the more famous incidents and conflicts, I have chosen to focus on two towns that I think were typical of the frontier—the mining frontier specifically—and to investigate *all* forms of violence and lawlessness that occurred in and around those towns.

The towns are Aurora and Bodie. Nestled high in the mountains of the trans-Sierra country, they were two of the most spectacular mining towns of the Old West and had widespread reputations for violence. During their boom years each boasted a population of more than five thousand, and together they produced gold and silver bullion valued in excess of $35 million—equivalent to some $700 million in today's dollars. Aurora had its heyday during the early 1860s and reflected the divisions created by the Civil War, whereas Bodie boomed in the late 1870s and early 1880s and was, as one prospector later called it, the last of the old-time mining camps. I have given slightly greater emphasis to Bodie, but only because of the greater number of extant sources—especially newspapers—for the town. Aurora and Bodie saw lawmen and outlaws, cowboys and Indians, highwaymen and petty thieves, prostitutes and gamblers, opium addicts and alcoholics, miners and claim-jumpers, brawlers and gunfighters, and vigilance committees and law-and-order associations. The towns were home to one of the most deadly gunfighters of the Old West, pistol-packing women, Chinese tongs and a Chinese badman, a gang leader who shot to death no fewer than seven men, and a brilliant one-armed lawyer who never lost a case.

Emerging from my investigation of Aurora and Bodie—an investigation that consumed several years and exhausted every available source—is a much fuller picture (possibly the first really representative view) of frontier violence as well as the stories of some of the most colorful characters and exciting events in the history of the Old West. Included with a goodly number of gunfights, stage robberies, and vigilante actions is a revealing look at the operation of the criminal justice system; the role that women and minorities played in the violence; and direct statistical comparisons of frontier crime with crime that occured contemporaneously in the settled East and with that which occurs in the United States today. The results say much about America's frontier heritage and offer some real surprises—several long-cherished notions about frontier violence are thoroughly repudiated while other widely held beliefs, long suspected of being mythical, are demonstrated to be well founded in fact.

1

THE
ESMERALDA
EXCITEMENT

Forgotten by most today, Aurora rivaled Virginia City as the West's most spectacular mining town during the early 1860s. Aurora was the urban center for the Esmeralda mining district, which spread over the hills that surrounded the town in the trans-Sierra country. With a population of over five thousand people and a yearly bullion production in the millions of dollars, Aurora attracted the attention of nearly every western miner during its heyday. Ironically, the discovery of Aurora's wealth was purely accidental.

One day in August 1860, three down-on-their-luck and weary miners, J. M. Corey, James M. Braly, and E. R. Hicks, stumbled upon the riches of Aurora.[1] Corey and Braly, residents of San Jose, had crossed over the Sierra Nevada during the spring of 1860 to prospect Washoe, as the area immediately east of Lake Tahoe was then known. They soon joined forces with Hicks, a part-Cherokee veteran miner, who had been prospecting the trans-Sierra country from Oregon southward. The three of them continued to drift southward until they reached Mono Lake. Turning back to the northeast, the three luckless prospectors passed through the Bodie, El Dorado, and Masonic mining districts and found themselves in the rugged Wassuk Range west of Walker Lake.

When days of climbing and searching brought them no closer to riches, they decided to head south again: first to Coso, just below the Owens Valley, and then on to Arizona and perhaps Mexico. On the morning of 22 August 1860 they reached Esmeralda Gulch. Finding good grass and water, they decided to set their stock out to graze and to lay over for a day or two. Hicks, the hunter of the party, started up craggy Esmeralda Hill to the west of their camp in search of game. Just over the crest of the hill, he stumbled upon some ledges of quartz. He laid down his rifle and broke off a few pieces. Curious blue streaks ran all through the rock. Hicks had discovered what soon became known as the Old Winnemucca Lode.[2]

With quartz samples in hand, Hicks returned to camp. Corey and Braly immediately recognized the blue streaks as sulfurets of silver and feverishly tested the

1.   J. Wells Kelly, *First Directory of Nevada Territory*, pp. 239–41.

2.   Kelly, p. 240. James M. Braly later claimed that it was he, not Hicks, who first discovered the quartz ledges. See Joseph Wasson, *Account of the Important Revival of Mining Interests in the Bodie and Esmeralda Districts*, p. 43.

quartz. It was exceedingly rich. All three now examined the surrounding hillsides, and by 25 August they had established four claims: Winnemucca, Esmeralda, Cape, and La Plata. These claims would make the three partners moderately wealthy men.[3] Hicks later sold out for $10,000 and returned to his native Arkansas; Corey and Braly eventually received $30,000 apiece for their shares and returned to the Santa Clara Valley. Somehow Hicks, Corey, and Braly managed to avoid the so-called curse that haunted discoverers of rich deposits of gold and silver in the Far West. Mining superstition had it that the discoverers of such deposits invariably came to untimely or violent ends.[4]

After posting notices on their claims, the three excited sourdoughs hurried off to Monoville, the nearest mining camp, and in the best tradition of prospectors, spread the news of the discovery. Some twenty miners from Monoville followed them back to their camp, and on 30 August 1860 a meeting was held to form a mining district.[5] The district was christened Esmeralda—Spanish for "emerald"—at the suggestion of Corey, who had remembered the name from Victor Hugo's *Notre Dame de Paris*. Dr. E. F. Mitchell was elected president of the district, and James Braly was chosen recorder. The choice of Braly was a good one. He refused to record a claim until he had personally inspected the ground and had made certain that it was correctly staked.[6] The potential for disputes over claims and for claim jumping—two important sources of violence in many mining camps—was thereby greatly reduced.

The day after the organization of the district, the Real Del Monte mine was located. The Del Monte would be one of the richest of Esmeralda's mines. By November 1860, just two months after the discovery, 357 claims had been recorded, and the mining district had spread over Silver, Middle, and Last Chance hills.[7] The rush to the Esmeralda "excitement" was on.

During the winter of 1860–1861, hundreds of hopefuls from Washoe and Visalia pushed their way through deep snow and over rutted roads and rock-strewn trails to reach Esmeralda.[8] Most of these prospectors were soon staking claims that would have to wait until spring to be worked. New silver leads were being discovered all the time, but it quickly became obvious that large capital investment would be required to develop the mines and to build quartz mills to crush the rock. Investors were cautious. A recent silver lead swindle in San Francisco had made some wary, and the uncertainty of property titles in Esmeralda prior to the official organization of the area (slated for 1 June 1861) inhibited others.[9]

Nevertheless, by the end of June 1861 the first quartz mill—the Pioneer Mill— was in operation in Willow Spring Gulch, just below some rich claims on Last Chance Hill.[10] Two more mills were crushing rock before the end of the year, and in 1862 eight

3. Wasson, *Account of Revival*, p. 44.

4. *Bodie Standard*, 3 May 1882.

5. Kelly, *First Directory*, p. 241; Wasson, *Account of Revival*, p. 44.

6. W. A. Chalfant, *Outposts of Civilization*, p. 55.

7. Wasson, *Account of Revival*, p. 44.

8. Visalia *Delta*, 19 Jan. 1861; Samuel Youngs's Journal, 19–25 Nov. 1860. The original Journal is in the possession of Robert E. Stewart, Carson City, Nevada. A highly edited version of the original is Ethel Zimmer, ed., "Colonel Samuel Youngs' Journal."

9. Visalia *Delta*, 11 and 30 May 1861.

10. Wasson, *Account of Revival*, p. 45; Myron Angel, ed., *History of Nevada*, p. 416.

more were built. Eventually, Esmeralda would have seventeen mills in operation.[11] The mills charged $50 a ton to process ore, but Esmeralda's rock, a high grade sulfuret of silver with a significant percentage of gold, assayed at $100 to $300 a ton.[12] A few mines, such as the Wide West, ran into fabulously rich veins and brought out ore worth nearly $3,000 a ton.

Almost all of Esmeralda's wealth lay near the surface. When the mine shafts reached a depth of seventy-five or one hundred feet, they moved through the richest ore and into a layer of barren quartz. The Wide West mine struck its bonanza within fifty feet of the surface. Edmund Green, the superintendent of the Wide West, noted that the mine's ore chamber was wide enough to "turn a wagon and horses in."[13] The Real Del Monte, Esmeralda, Antelope, Lady Jane, Winnemucca, Johnson, Pond, Young America, and Juaniata mines were also big producers.

Within three years Esmeralda's rich ore chambers were virtually gouged out, and the mines went into a rapid decline. Most of the mills were disassembled and shipped off to Bodie or Virginia City to be reerected. The batteries and amalgamating pans of these disassembled mills, which nobody had bothered to clean off during the boom days, were found to contain gold and silver worth thousands of dollars.[14] The average recovery of bullion had been about 80 percent, and no tailings had been saved. One miner estimated that "several millions of dollars floated off down the creek toward the East Walker river."[15] Despite this reckless extravagance, Esmeralda's total bullion production has been estimated at $16 million.[16] In 1864 alone, nearly $8 million in bullion was shipped out of the Wells, Fargo & Company's office in Aurora.[17] Among the mining towns of the Great Basin, only Virginia City and Bodie produced more bullion than Aurora.

Most miners did not strike it rich in Aurora, but the few who did, did so in a big way. The three discoverers arrived with almost nothing and left as rich men. Alec Gamble, a former college dean from Maine, was one of the original owners of the Wide West mine. He sold his stock for $275,000 and reinvested in the Real Del Monte mine. The Del Monte stock promptly increased several fold in value, and Gamble became a millionaire.[18]

Mark Twain, or Sam Clemens, as he was known in those days, almost had the same luck. He and his brother Orion had come west late in 1861, Orion to accept a job as Nevada's territorial secretary and Sam to escape the Civil War. Sam Clemens soon found himself in Aurora, occasionally prospecting for gold and silver and now and then writing a piece for one of the town's dailies, the *Esmeralda Star*. He spent most of his time telling stories in one or another of Aurora's many saloons or in a little cabin on

11.   Wasson, p. 45; Angel, p. 416.

12.   J. Ross Browne, *Report of J. Ross Browne on the Mineral Resources of the States and Territories West of the Rocky Mountains*, p. 336; Samuel L. Clemens, *Roughing It*, p. 164; *Sacramento Daily Union*, 19 March 1863.

13.   Wasson, *Account of Revival*, p. 45.

14.   Wasson, p. 46; Chalfant, *Outposts*, p. 56.

15.   Wasson, p. 46.

16.   U.S. Department of the Treasury, *Report on the Internal Commerce of the United States for the Year 1890*, Part II of Commerce and Navigation, 51st Cong., 2nd Sess., HR Executive Document 6 (Washington, 1891), p. 670; Angel, *History of Nevada*, p. 416.

17.   Wasson, p. 47.

18.   R. K. Colcord, "Reminiscences of Life in Territorial Nevada," pp. 116–17.

2. *The cabin of Sam Clemens and Cal Higbie on upper Pine Street (circa 1900). Clemens's cabin and the brick cabin next door were typical of dwellings in Aurora. (Credit: Nevada Historical Society)*

upper Pine Street which he shared with his hard-working partner Cal Higbie. When Clemens ran out of money and found he lacked the security to borrow any, he actually went to work at a local quartz mill. He lasted one day.

Then Higbie, Clemens's trusty partner, had some real luck. He discovered a fantastically rich "blind lead" that cut diagonally through the Wide West vein and had gone unnoticed by the West's people.[19] The lead was, therefore, public property. Higbie and Clemens immediately staked a claim, gave A. D. Allen, the foreman of the Wide West, a one-third share, and registered the claim with the recorder. The three men were on the verge of becoming millionaires. Clemens and Higbie sat up all night in their one-room cabin, discussing the grand houses they would build for themselves in San Francisco and the trip they would take to Europe.

Fate now interceded. The laws of the Esmeralda district required the locators of a claim to do a reasonable amount of work on their property within ten days, or it would revert to public domain. By virtue of a series of misunderstandings and unusual circumstances, neither Higbie, Clemens, nor Allen did the required work. All three believed that one of the others was doing it. At midnight of the tenth day a crowd of men, "duly armed and ready to back their proceedings," restaked the claim and recorded it as the Johnson.[20]

19. Clemens, *Roughing It*, pp. 186–87.

20. Clemens, p. 193.

Higbie had been out of town prospecting for the legendary Lost Cement mines with Gid Whiteman and returned just five or ten minutes too late. Clemens had been on a mission of mercy visiting a dangerously ill comrade and arrived in Aurora about the same time as Higbie—too late. Ironically, as Clemens rode into town he noticed the crowd of men on the hill, who had gathered to relocate his claim, and fancied that a new strike had been made. Only Allen returned in time to confront the new locators. With a cocked revolver in his hand, he insisted that his name must be added to the new ownership list or he would "thin out the Johnson company some."[21] Since Allen was known as to be as good as his word, he was given a share. Much to the chagrin of Higbie and Clemens, the Johnson became a real bonanza, producing millions of dollars worth of gold and silver. Higbie continued prospecting with never more than limited success, and Clemens left for Virginia City to become a reporter for the *Territorial Enterprise*.

The average prospector never had the success of an Alec Gamble or even the near-success of a Sam Clemens. Conditions in Aurora, noted Roswell K. Colcord, a prospector and later governor of Nevada, "were practically the same as at all other mining camps. A few men became rich quickly and were ruined later through speculation in stocks and dissipation."[22] The ordinary miner located a claim and sank a shaft, hoping to hit pay dirt. Meanwhile, in order to pay for the necessities of life, he probably had a second job at a quartz mill or another mine, earning four or five dollars a day.[23] These were good wages at a time when eastern workingmen earned only a dollar a day. Moreover, the cost of living in Aurora was not significantly higher than elsewhere. The mines were developing so fast in 1862 and 1863 that there was more work than there were workers; wages were therefore high. The *Esmeralda Star* noted in March of 1863 that at least three hundred jobs in the mills and mines were going begging.[24]

The miner lived in a small cabin made of stone and wood and cooked for himself. He was usually bewhiskered and wore a slouch hat, a woolen shirt, and trousers stuffed into high-topped boots. Slung or tucked into his belt was a revolver, and not infrequently he carried a derringer in an easily reached pocket. "We pack six shooters and derringers for fear of the knave," wrote George A. Whitney, an Esmeralda miner and hay rancher, to his brother in Iowa.[25] Sam Clemens noted that he had never had occasion to kill anybody with the Colt Navy revolver he carried, but he had "worn the thing in deference to popular sentiment, and in order that I might not, by its absence, be offensively conspicuous, and a subject of remark."[26]

The first settlement in the Esmeralda district was at the head of Esmeralda Gulch, where Hicks, Corey, and Braly had made their original camp. Within a few months, however, settlement had moved farther to the north. There, where Esmeralda and Willow gulches joined, grew the town of Aurora, named for the Roman goddess of dawn. At an elevation of 7,500 feet, Aurora was nestled among mountains—three of which were named after the discoverers—that rose another two or three thousand feet

21. Clemens, p. 194.

22. Colcord, "Reminiscences," p. 116.

23. *Sacramento Daily Union*, 21 March 1863.

24. *Esmeralda Star*, 14 March 1863, as reprinted in the *Sacramento Daily Union*, 19 March 1863.

25. George A. Whitney to William T. Whitney, 7 July 1863, Whitney Letters and Correspondence, 1862–1887.

26. Clemens, *Roughing It*, p. 197.

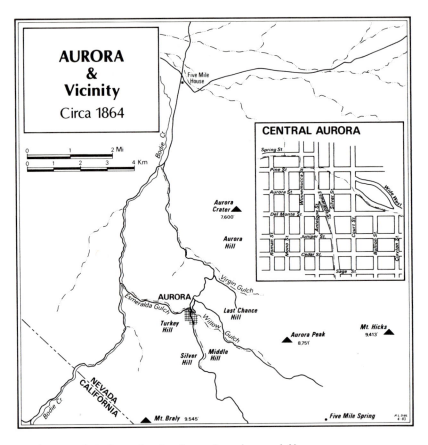

3.   *Aurora was located at an elevation of 7,500 feet and surrounded by mountains that rose still higher. Its grid pattern of streets was laid out early in 1861. (Cartography by Noel Diaz)*

higher. Two miles to the southwest lay Mount Braly (known now as Brawley Peaks), which reaches an elevation of 9,545 feet; a mile to the southeast was 8,751-foot Aurora Peak; four miles to the east was 9,413-foot Mount Hicks; and a dozen miles to the northeast was 10,520-foot Corey Peak.[27] On those mountains and on the hillsides immediately surrounding town, Aurorans found some piñon and juniper, but mostly sagebrush. A few small groves of stunted birch and aspen and patches of meadow grass grew along the creeks and around the springs.[28]

Aurorans quickly learned that the climate was harsh and the weather totally unpredictable.[29] At any time of the year it could be hot or freezing, raining, snowing, or clear, and windy or calm. Precipitation was not something to count on. The first two years of Aurora's existence were very wet, whereas the next two were desert dry. Al-

27.   U.S. Department of the Interior Geological Survey, *Aurora Quadrangle*, 1956.

28.   D. I. Axelrod, "MioPliocene Floras from West-Central Nevada," pp. 22–23.

29.   Samuel Youngs's Journal. Youngs maintained a daily record of Aurora's weather from November 1860 to December 1866.

though precipitation in that country averages twelve inches a year, most years are either well above or well below that average figure. Aurorans also found that seasonal temperature variations were great. Winter lows of fifteen to twenty degrees below zero were not uncommon, and summer highs in the eighties were normal. The diurnal temperature range could be dramatic: a forty-degree increase between sunrise and noon was common. If, as some writers contend, the rugged terrain and harsh climate of the West hardened the people and made violence less abhorrent to them, then Aurora could not have been located in a more violence-encouraging environment.

Prospectors are not the types to be deterred by rugged terrain or harsh climate. During the winter of 1860–1861, they trudged by the hundreds through snow that covered the ground to a depth of two feet, enduring near-zero-degree temperatures to reach Aurora. By February 1861 the town contained some 150 places of residence or business built along streets laid out in a grid pattern.[30] Spring, Pine, Aurora, and Del Monte streets, running east–west, intersected north–south Winnemucca, Antelope, Silver, and Court streets. Pine Street would become the principal thoroughfare. Town lots, covering an area nearly as large as Sacramento was then, were in the process of being surveyed and staked.[31] Although some of these town lots were already selling for $500 apiece, ground was set aside for a school, a courthouse, and other public buildings.[32]

At this early date most of Aurora's structures, which included two general stores, six warehouses, two meat markets, four blacksmith shops, one saddlery, two bakeries, and two carpenter shops, were simple wooden frames covered by tightly stretched canvas. Meals could be had for just twenty-five cents a serving at any of several restaurants, and room and board ran only $10 a week. These prices compared favorably with those in Sacramento and San Francisco. Aurora's two livery stables, however, charged $3 a day to feed a horse hay, $5 if grain were included. Already there were "six small drinking places and four large establishments with billiards and card tables, where much gambling was done." The population of Aurora in February 1861 was approaching eight hundred people, only a dozen of whom were women.

By April the number of businesses in town had reached twenty, and residences were estimated at four hundred.[33] A miner set the population at about twelve hundred people. "Two hundred," noted the same miner, "are on the hills prospecting, two hundred are building houses . . . , two hundred more are exhibiting rich specimens of silver ore—to their particular friends, of course; fifty are using their influence to get an old and well known ledge recorded under a new name. Claims are claimed on claims. The balance of the good citizens of Esmeralda District are taking or making cocktails, or observations, or discussing the relative merits and advantages of California State laws with Territorial laws." "Making cocktails" was right. Since the town was not yet officially organized, no licenses were required to sell liquor. Consequently, nearly every store in Aurora sold "red-eye" whiskey "to the thirsty prospector and traveler in quantities to suit spirits depressed or buoyant hopes."

Trains of immigrants were arriving daily—almost hourly—throughout the

30. *Sacramento Daily Union*, 9 March 1861.

31. Visalia *Delta*, 27 April 1861.

32. *Sacramento Daily Union*, 9 March 1861, described Aurora's buildings and their uses at this date.

33. Visalia *Delta*, 27 April and 11 May 1861, described the people of Aurora and their habits.

4.   *Downtown Aurora (circa 1865). View is east on Pine Street. Large, two-story, balconied building in the background is the county courthouse. When Aurora declined and lost the county seat, the courthouse was converted into the Esmeralda Hotel. Only one other photograph of Aurora during its boom years exists (see p. 67). (Credit: Nevada Historical Society)*

spring. A prospector noted that in one day on the Esmeralda road he passed forty-five wagons on their way to Aurora.[34] The first stagecoach to reach Aurora arrived in town at midnight on 15 April 1861 after a nineteen-hour drive from Carson City.[35] A capacity load of passengers was aboard, and each of the riders had paid a $20 fare for the trip to the new promised land. By July there were nearly two thousand people in Aurora.[36] Most of these residents were living in stone- or adobe-walled and canvas-roofed huts. Wood was scarce and prohibitively expensive at $150 per thousand board feet.[37] Four brickyards were soon answering the need for construction materials. One of the first buildings erected from brick was Patrick Hickey's general store. The new brick edifice replaced Hickey's original store, reputed to be the first in Aurora, which was made of canvas, wood, mud, and stone.[38]

Aurora thus became unique among western mining towns: most of its major buildings were made of brick. As a result, dozens of these structures would remain standing, and in good condition, well into the twentieth century. However, when used brick became fashionable for the fireplaces and patios of expensive homes, Aurora was doomed. Its brick buildings were sold to construction firms from southern California,

34.   Visalia *Delta*, 30 May 1861.

35.   Samuel Youngs's Journal, 15 April 1861.

36.   Kelly, *First Directory*, p. v.

37.   Visalia *Delta*, 30 May 1861.

38.   Chalfant, *Outposts*, p. 55.

and almost nothing of the town remains today. Yet, in a manner of speaking, Aurora lives on in the homes of Beverly Hills, Pacific Palisades, and Malibu.[39]

The summer of 1861 was made spectacular by the passing of a great comet with an "immense tail stretching nearly across the Heavens" and a bright display of the aurora borealis.[40] It was also made spectacular by phenomenal real estate appreciation. Town lots that had sold for a few hundred dollars apiece in early spring were now selling for $1,500 each.[41] Supplies and provisions did not keep pace with real estate. Although most goods had to be freighted into Aurora from Visalia or Sacramento, the majority of items sold for only slightly more than they did on the western side of the Sierra. One item, clothing, actually sold for less.[42] Room and board was still only $10 a week. If the Auroran cooked for himself, he could buy a hundred-pound sack of flour for $21, a dozen extra-large speckled gull eggs from Mono Lake for seventy-five cents, and fresh beef from Big Meadows or the Owens Valley at twenty cents a pound.[43]

Aurora continued to boom throughout 1862 and 1863. In April 1863 a miner reported, "Our town grows—rapidly in every respect—over 50 men per day have come in for the last two weeks, and people say they have hardly started in yet—still wages keep up."[44] In May the town of Aurora was incorporated through an election in which nearly 1,500 votes were cast.[45] During the summer of 1863 Aurora reached its zenith. The town boasted two daily newspapers, the *Esmeralda Star* (known as the *Union* after 1863) and the *Aurora Times*; two stage lines, the Pioneer Line and Wells, Fargo & Company; a telegraph, hundreds of businesses, nearly eight hundred houses or cabins, some three hundred commercial buildings, and a population estimated at five thousand people.[46] Women numbered between two hundred and three hundred, about five percent of the total population, and there were some eighty children. A small Chinese district existed, but no clue remains to the actual number of Chinese. Indians came into town to sell brook trout and gull eggs, and to stage dances for the entertainment of the whites, but for the most part the red men remained in the hinterland, hunting and gathering.

With some five thousand residents, Aurora was bursting at the seams. Every hotel, lodging house, and miner's cabin was jam-packed, and hundreds of people went without accommodations.[47] The streets were crowded with wagons that had carried freight over the Sierra on the new Sonora Pass trail. On both sides of Pine Street for its entire length new brick buildings, some three stories high, were being erected, and real estate prices continued an upward spiral until choice lots sold for $5,000 apiece or

39.　Don Ashbaugh, *Nevada's Turbulent Yesterday*, p. 123.

40.　Samuel Youngs's Journal, 30 June 1861; Visalia *Delta*, 25 July 1861. This was Tebbutt's comet. The earth passed through the comet's tail on 29 and 30 June 1861.

41.　Chalfant, *Outposts*, p. 55.

42.　Visalia *Delta*, 30 May 1861.

43.　Samuel Youngs's Journal, 13 Jan. 1861, 30 May 1861.

44.　George A. Whitney to William T. Whitney, 7 April 1863, Whitney Letters.

45.　G. Whitney to W. Whitney, 15 May 1863.

46.　Francis P. Farquhar, ed., *Up and Down California in 1860–1864: The Journal of William H. Brewer*, p. 420; Colcord, "Reminiscences," p. 114; Chalfant, *Outposts*, p. 57; California, *Report of the Superintendent of Public Instruction for 1864–65*, pp. 180–84.

47.　Farquhar, *Journal of William H. Brewer*, p. 420.

5.   By 1889 Aurora was only a skeleton of its former self. Hundreds of
wooden structures had been consumed for fuel, and dozens of brick buildings had been leveled and their bricks carted off. During the 1930s and
1940s, used brick became fashionable for residential use, and the last of
Aurora's many fine brick structures were demolished. View is southeast,
with the Real Del Monte hoisting works in the background on Last
Chance Hill. (Credit: Nevada Historical Society)

more.[48] The boom was not to last much longer, however. During the fall of 1864 Aurora
began a rapid decline.[49] Real estate prices fell faster than they had risen. On 8 February
1865 the now semiweekly rather than daily *Esmeralda Union* lamented that a "fine brick
house" sold for only $12 at a tax auction, and a two-story brick building, "which could
not have been purchased 18 months ago for $5000," was now offered for $500. Town
lots dropped in value by 95 percent. Just a year and a half after its peak, Aurora was
experiencing the beginning of the end.

Although the number of children in Aurora probably never exceeded eighty,
their education was given high priority. During Aurora's first year of existence, a twenty-
by-forty-foot brick schoolhouse was erected.[50] Twenty-seven children attended the
school in 1862, and fifty-one in 1863. Evidently the teacher was paid per pupil, for she
earned $216 in 1862 and $400 in 1863.[51]

Of far less importance to Aurorans than education was organized religious worship. The first church service was not held until October 1863, more than three years
after the town's founding.[52] It was four more months before the first church, the Meth-

48.   George A. Whitney to William T. Whitney, 7 June and 7 July 1863, Whitney Letters.

49.   *Esmeralda Union*, 30 Dec. 1864.

50.   Chalfant, *Outposts*, p. 55.

51.   *Report of the Superintendent of Public Instruction for 1864–65*, pp. 180–84.

52.   Samuel Youngs's Journal, 4 Oct. 1863.

odist Episcopal church, was built.[53] In November 1864 construction was begun on a Catholic church.[54] However, because of the rapid depopulation of Aurora during 1865 the church was never completed.[55] Despite the lack of churches, religious services were held in rented halls during 1864 for Catholics, Presbyterians, and Baptists. The establishment of these services coincided ironically with the decline of Aurora.

If Aurorans were less than zealous about religious service, they certainly were enthusiastic when it came to being served. Some twenty-five saloons—more than one for every two hundred Aurora men—kept the "boys" well watered.[56] P. J. McMahan's Del Monte Exchange featured fine French brandies and old whiskeys such as Virginia Mountain Dew. Frank Schoonmaker's Bank Exchange saloon carried the usual assortment of liquors, wines, bitters, and cigars and it also had a billiard room. There was always action at the Wide West saloon, but the finest Havana cigars and Old Tom Holland gin were available at Porter and Barber's.

After recording a claim a miner only had to cross Silver Street to imbibe Old Government and Old Virginia whiskey at Runyon and Harkness. Old London Dock brandy was available at the Sazerac saloon, and imported wines at the Merchant's Exchange. If a prospector's taste ran to beer, there was the Esmeralda Brewery, which claimed to have the finest lager beer on the West Coast. The proprietor, F. Staehler, maintained that he used only the best barley for malt and the purest mountain spring water from the Sierra Nevada. No one ever went thirsty in Aurora for lack of watering holes.

Almost as numerous as saloons were gambling houses and brothels. Roswell K. Colcord, then an Esmeralda prospector and later governor of Nevada, called Aurora "the wickedest town of its size in America."[57] The miner's favorite way to lose his gold or silver—the medium of exchange in Aurora—was at the card table playing faro, monte, or blackjack. Roulette was also popular. If the miner had any dust left after visiting the bar and gaming table, the prostitute was almost certain to relieve him of it. Nevertheless, few were upset with the night life of Aurora, although at one point the grand jury urged the authorities to take action against "the numerous disgusting Chinese brothels that exist on most of our public streets, to the great detriment of public morals and danger of property."[58] Nothing was ever done, however, beyond fining a couple of Chinese prostitutes $20 each.[59]

Perhaps the best description of Aurora night life was that of William H. Brewer, who visited the town during July 1863:

> Aurora of a Sunday night—how shall I describe it? It is so unlike anything East that I can compare it with nothing you have ever seen. One sees a hundred men to one woman and child. Saloons—saloons—saloons—liquor—everywhere. And here the men

53. *Virginia Daily Union*, 8 Jan. 1864.

54. *Esmeralda Union*, 23 Nov. 1864.

55. Angel, *History of Nevada*, p. 205.

56. *Esmeralda Star*, 20 Sept. 1862, 18 Nov. 1863; *Aurora Times*, 11 June and 7 Oct. 1864; *Esmeralda Union*, 23 March 1864–11 March 1865.

57. Colcord, "Reminiscences," p. 119.

58. *Esmeralda Union*, 31 March 1864.

59. *Esmeralda Union*, 6 May 1864.

are—where else *can* they be? At home in their cheerless, lonesome hovels or huts? No, in the saloons, where lights are bright, amid the hum of many voices and the excitement of gambling. Here men come to make money—make it *quick*—not by slow, honest industry, but by quick strokes—no matter *how*, so long as the law doesn't call it *robbery*. Here, where twenty quartz mills are stamping the rock and kneading its powder into bullion—here, where one never sees a bank bill, nor "rag money," but where hard silver and shining gold are the currency—where men are congregated and living uncomfortably, where there are no home ties or social checks, no churches, no religions—here one sees gambling and vice in all its horrible realities.

Here are tables, with gold and silver piled upon them by hundreds (or even thousands), with men (or women) behind, who deal *faro*, or *monte*, or *vingt-et-un* or *rouge-et-noir*, or who turn *roulette*—in short, any way in which they may win and you may lose. Here, too, are women—for nowhere else does one see prostitutes as he sees them in a new mining town. All combine to excite and ruin. No wonder that one sees sad faces and haggard countenances and wretched looks, that we are so often told that "many are dying off"—surely, no wonder![60]

If the Auroran enjoyed indoor dissipation, he also found time for several outdoor recreational activities and amusements. Bodie Creek and the East Walker River supplied the fisherman with trout, and the hunter learned that the local hills were full of sage hens.[61] Extended trips, especially during winter, were made to Mono Lake to hunt migrating and wintering waterfowl. Irish-born J. Ross Browne, a prolific and widely read author who traveled extensively in the West while serving as a U.S. commissioner of mining statistics during the 1860s, noted that "during the winter months the waters of the lake are literally covered with swans, geese, brant, ducks, and smaller aquatic fowl. It is incredible the number of these birds that appear after the first rains. Sportsmen find it a laborious job to carry home their game. A regular gunning expedition in this region results in nothing short of wholesale slaughter. Twenty or thirty teal duck at a single shot is nothing unusual."[62]

Dog fights or dog and badger fights were staged from time to time in Aurora. One miner thought the dogs provided "classic amusement" and estimated that "there must be at least two canine specimens to every man, woman and child in the community."[63] A dog and badger fight usually drew a sizable crowd and heavy betting. Because of his superior quickness, the badger invariably bested several dogs before he finally succumbed.[64] Aurorans never failed to admire the "pluck" of the ornery little fighter.

Perhaps the recreational activity one would least expect to find in a mid-nineteenth-century western mining town is skiing. Nevertheless, Aurorans took to the slopes by the dozens. "The citizens amused themselves," wrote prospector and territorial delegate Samuel Youngs, "in going up the mountains on snow shoes about 8 to 10 feet long, 4 inches wide, turned up in front like a sled runner. They use a pole like pushing a boat

60.   Farquhar, *Journal of William H. Brewer*, pp. 420–21.

61.   Samuel Youngs's Journal, 16 June 1861, 4 and 20 March and 27 June 1862, 5 June 1865.

62.   J. Ross Browne, *Adventures in the Apache Country: A Tour through Arizona and Sonora, with Notes on the Silver Regions of Nevada*, p. 422. For a biographical sketch of Browne see *The National Cyclopaedia of American Biography*, vol. 8, pp. 117–18.

63.   Chalfant, *Outposts*, p. 57.

64.   *Esmeralda Union*, 5 Sept. 1864; Browne, *Adventures in Apache Country*, pp. 421–25.

6.   *Cabins and mills and juniper and piñon dotted the hills that surrounded Aurora. After good snowfalls skiers could also be found on the
hills.* (Credit: California Historical Society)

and come down rapidly more than a mile a minute."[65] After each good snowfall the
mountains around Aurora would be covered with numerous telltale tracks. "There are
several gentlemen here," noted the *Esmeralda Union* on 4 February 1865, "who have
acquired wonderful proficiency in the use of these shoes, and it is pleasant to see them
ride down a moderately steep hill at railroad speed."

Skiing gave rise to many a tall tale in Aurora. One newspaper told of a prospector who left the summit of Mount Braly one morning, intending to ski to Esmeralda
Gulch. The prospector's speed grew greater and greater until, according to the reporter,
it could not have been less than a hundred miles an hour. Near the Esmeralda tunnel a
stump loomed up, and the luckless miner plowed straight into it. His legs and arms
wound around the stump so fast that his body was cut in twain but his skis kept going. The newspaper claimed to have received a dispatch from Wellington, some forty
miles away, that a lone ski had passed by there early in the afternoon. "Which way the
other shoe [ski] went," concluded the newspaper, "we don't know, but think it is still
running."[66]

Aurora's institutions of law enforcement and justice were not unlike those of
other western communities.[67] Law enforcement in and around Aurora was left to the
county sheriff and the township constable. The sheriff was the general law-enforcement

65.   Samuel Youngs's Journal, 7 Jan. 1862.

66.   *Esmeralda Union*, 4 Feb. 1865.

67.   See Frank R. Prassel, *The Western Peace Officer.*

officer of the county as well as the ex officio tax collector.[68] His duties included conserving the public peace, making arrests, preventing and suppressing affrays, attending courts of record having criminal jurisdiction within the county, and executing warrants and other processes. He was also required to summon jurors and run the county jail.[69] The sheriff was an elected officer, but he appointed his own deputies.

N. F. Scott, G. W. Bailey, and D. G. Francis served as sheriff during Aurora's heyday.[70] Scott was killed fighting Indians; Bailey and Francis, who served four terms each, retired unscathed. Because Aurora was the county seat for Mono (then Esmeralda) County, the sheriff's office and the county jail were in Aurora.

The county jail was evidently a sight to behold. In September 1862 the grand jury noted that although the jail was kept clean and the prisoners were well treated, the building was unsafe. Said the jury:

> The walls are badly sprung and cracked, owing probably to the insecure foundation in front. The ties which are supposed to hold the front to its place, they do not consider any security or benefit, and it would not surprise them any day to hear of its falling and especially when the snow begins to melt in the spring; neither do they consider it a secure place to keep a prisoner without a guard.[71]

The grand jury recommended that two or three "substantial" cells be built to confine persons convicted of criminal acts and keep them separate from other prisoners. Nothing was done, however, to improve the facility, and the grand jury of October 1863 found the jail totally unfit to secure the inmates. A half year later the grand jury again found the county jail "inefficient and insecure, and totally unfit for the lodgment and safe-keeping of prisoners therein."[72] No improvements were made, and at the end of 1864 the grand jury was noting once more that the county jail was "unfit for confining prisoners" and recommending that a safer building be procured.[73]

Surprisingly, there is record of only one escape from the county jail. Late in March 1864 three prisoners who were awaiting trial for grand larceny cut a hole through the jail wall and crawled to freedom.[74] A fourth prisoner, who was not associated with the first three, also crawled through the hole, walked leisurely down to the Sazerac saloon, had a drink, and then sauntered over to the courthouse to report the escape to Sheriff D. G. Francis. Although a large posse attempted to overtake the fugitives, it failed to turn up any trace of the men.

In addition to the county sheriff and the county jail, Aurora maintained a township constable, known in Aurora as the city marshal, and a city jail. The constable's jurisdiction did not extend beyond the township, unless the constable was deputized by

68. *California Statutes, 1861*, p. 235.

69. *California Statutes, 1850*, p. 258; *1851*, pp. 190–97; *1852*, p. 108.

70. Angel, *History of Nevada*, pp. 401–2, 405.

71. *Esmeralda Star*, 20 Sept. 1862.

72. *Esmeralda Union*, 31 March 1864.

73. *Esmeralda Union*, 23 Dec. 1864.

74. *Esmeralda Union*, 26 March 1864; George A. Whitney to William T. Whitney, 27 March 1864, Whitney Letters.

the sheriff. It was the duty of the constable to maintain order, attend the court of the justice of the peace, execute all orders issued by the justice, assist the district attorney, and run the city jail.[75]

The town constable was elected by a vote of the people, but he appointed his own officers, or policemen, as they were known.[76] Daniel H. Pine, M. Center, Robert M. Howland, and John A. Palmer held the office of constable or city marshal of Aurora during the town's boom years.[77] A small frame building containing a one-room office and two cells constituted the marshal's office and the city jail. Although the less than formidable structure appeared to invite escape, no jailbreaks ever occurred.[78]

Aurora boasted two militia companies, the Esmeralda Rangers (also referred to as the Rifles) and the Hooker Light Infantry (known as the Aurora City Guard after March 1864).[79] The Rangers, a company of cavalry, were officially organized on 2 April 1862 under the laws of California and were included in the Third Brigade, California Militia. H. J. Teel served as Captain and A. D. Allen as First Lieutenant of the fifty-five-man outfit. The weaponry of the Rangers included cavalry sabers and Starr's army pistols. Ranger uniforms were elegant: coats of fine, black broadcloth with stripes of gold lace on the collars and arms, and dark blue cloth pants with a broad stripe of gold running down each pant leg.[80] The Hooker Light Infantry, led by Captain Jacob Hess (then by Captain John A. Palmer) and First Lieutenant George H. Donnell, was not organized until 18 May 1863. Its sixty-three members carried rifled muskets with bayonets. Headquarters and armory for the militia companies were in the Wingate Building at the corner of Aurora and Silver streets. In 1864 both companies were dropped from the roster of the Third Brigade, California Militia, because the newly established boundary had left Aurora in Nevada.[81] Nevertheless, they continued to function until the end of the Civil War.

The success of the militia companies in attracting members and drilling regularly evidently inspired Joseph W. Calder to form a cavalry company from Aurora to fight in the Civil War. During August 1863 he began a correspondence with Nevada's territorial governor, James Nye, and on 4 December 1863 was commissioned captain and empowered to raise a cavalry company to be known as Company F, Nevada Volunteers.[82] By the spring of 1864 Captain Calder had recruited eighty-eight men, many of whom had been members of one of Aurora's militia companies.[83] Although the men had been promised active service in the Civil War, they did nothing more than a tour of duty at Fort Churchill, Nevada.

75. *California Statutes, 1850,* p. 263.

76. *California Statutes, 1861,* p. 238.

77. *Esmeralda Union,* 1 April, 2 May, 28 and 29 July 1864; Colcord, "Reminiscences," p. 117; Kelly, *First Directory,* p. 246.

78. *Esmeralda Union,* 31 March 1864.

79. *Report of the Adjutant-General of the State of California for the Year 1863,* pp. 181–82; *Esmeralda Union,* 16 April 1864; Samuel Youngs's Journal, 4 July and 27 Nov. 1864, 15 April 1865.

80. *Esmeralda Union,* 7 May 1864.

81. *Report of the Adjutant-General of the State of California from May 1, 1864, to November 30, 1865,* p. 15.

82. Joseph W. Calder to Governor James W. Nye, 14, 16, and 21 August 1863, in Unsorted Territorial Correspondence, Nevada Division of Archives.

83. *Virginia Daily Union,* 9 Jan. 1864; Angel, *History of Nevada,* pp. 267–68.

Aurora's court system consisted of a justice court and a county, or district (after September 1863), court.[84] F. K. Bechtel, J. W. Tyler, and John T. Moore served as justices of the peace during Aurora's boom years.[85] The first county court judge was J. A. Moutrie. He was followed by Alexander Baldwin and George Turner.[86]

Representing the people of the state as criminal prosecutor was the district attorney.[87] Between 1861 and 1866 five different men, R. E. Phelps, William M. Dixon, R. S. Mesick, George S. Palmer, and S. H. Chase, filled this post.[88] Another important county officer was the coroner. It was his duty, when informed that a person had been killed, committed suicide, or died suddenly under suspicious circumstances, to summon a jury and hold an inquest to determine the probable cause of death, and to render a verdict as to those responsible for that death. If the party determined responsible was still at large, the coroner was commanded by law to issue a warrant for his arrest.[89] The coroner could also bind over witnesses to testify at the subsequent trial.

Rounding out the institutions of justice in Aurora was the grand jury. It was the duty of the grand jury to inquire into public offenses committed within the county and, if warranted, hand down indictments.[90] The jury also audited the records and accounts of all the officers of the county. Members of the jury were chosen by lot from the list of registered voters.

Aurora, then, was one of the West's largest and most spectacular mining towns during the early 1860s. Hundreds of miles from any major city and isolated by rugged mountainous terrain, dominated by a harsh climate with violent and unpredictable weather, Aurora would have had no reason to exist were it not for the fabulous quantities of silver and gold that were mined from the surrounding hills. Although its life was brief, Aurora nevertheless developed all the governmental forms of a mature town. Its institutions of law enforcement and justice were highly structured and fairly sophisticated and not unlike those of other mid-nineteenth-century American towns. Aurora's population peaked at something over five thousand people, nearly all of whom were white and male. Of the small number of women in town, perhaps half were prostitutes. Family life was almost nonexistent. Aurorans paid little attention to organized religion, drank heavily, gambled incessantly, and carried revolvers and derringers. Only a few became wealthy, but wages were high and hopes were higher.

84.   Angel, *History of Nevada*, pp. 401, 403.

85.   Kelly, *First Directory*, pp. 245–52; *Esmeralda Union*, 30 March and 23 Nov. 1864.

86.   Angel, *History of Nevada*, pp. 401–3.

87.   *California Statutes, 1850*, p. 112; *1861*, p. 235.

88.   Angel, *History of Nevada*, pp. 401–2, 405.

89.   *California Statutes, 1850*, pp. 264, 265.

90.   *California Statutes, 1850*, p. 288.

2

NO
GOODEE
COW MAN

The Esmeralda strike and the spectacular growth of Aurora generated a tremendous demand for supplies. Merchants from Sacramento and San Francisco responded quickly. So did cattlemen from the southern San Joaquin Valley and the Tejon country of the Tehachapi Mountains. Early in the spring of 1861, they launched the first cattle drives to Aurora. The steers were driven through Walker Pass in the southern Sierra and then up the Owens Valley, finally reaching Aurora by way of Adobe Meadows. The drive was long—some three hundred miles—and rugged, and it took a toll both of men and of animals. Cattlemen soon began to look for ways to take advantage of the Aurora market and yet avoid the long drive. They had not failed to notice that the northern half of the Owens Valley was well suited for grazing cattle and only a short distance from Aurora. During the summer and fall nearly a dozen of them, including Samuel Bishop, Henry Vansickle, the McGee brothers, Allen Van Fleet, and Charles Putnam, established ranches in the valley.[1]

White settlement in the Owens Valley, however, meant encroachment on lands already occupied by Indians. Various bands of "Mono" and "Owens Valley" Paiute made the southern trans-Sierra country their home.[2] Their territory extended from the western reaches of Nevada to the crest of the Sierra, and from Owens Lake to just south of Lake Tahoe. The Washo were neighbors to the north, and the Panamint Shoshone, or Koso, lived to the south. Close linguistic relatives, the Monache, or Western Mono,

1.   San Francisco *Daily Evening Post*, 22 Nov. 1879; *Inyo Register*, 11 Feb. 1904, 15 Jan. 1914. Especially useful for the conflict between the Indians and the whites in the Owens Valley are the accounts of J. W. A. Wright, published in the *Daily Evening Post* on 22 and 29 November 1879, and those of W. A. Chalfant, which began appearing in the *Inyo Register* shortly after the turn of the century and were later included in his minor classic, *The Story of Inyo*. The accounts of both men are slightly flawed by occasional errors and omissions but are generally accurate and, most important, make use of several manuscript collections that have since been destroyed or lost.

2.   For territorial boundaries and linguistic areas, see Robert F. Heizer and Albert B. Elsasser, *The Natural World of the California Indians*, esp. pp. 5, 12, 19, and 29; and A. L. Kroeber, *Handbook of the Indians of California*, esp. pp. 574–92. Kroeber refers to the Paiute of the Mono Lake area and the Owens Valley as the Eastern Mono. For an in-depth look at the Paiute, including identification of the various bands of Owens Valley Paiute, see Julian H. Steward and Erminie Wheeler-Voegelin, *The Northern Paiute Indians*, esp. pp. 103–23.

lived across the divide of the Sierra on the upper reaches of the San Joaquin, Kings, and Kaweah rivers.

Before the arrival of the whites and the introduction of the steer, the Paiute of the southern trans-Sierra lived primarily by gathering pine nuts, seeds, berries, and fly larvae, and by digging roots.[3] This latter activity earned them, as it did many other Indian groups in California and the Great Basin, the opprobrious epithet "diggers." Several bands of Owens Valley Paiute dug more than roots; they also dug irrigation ditches and flooded low-lying valley land to increase the growth of seed- and tuber-producing plants which grew there naturally.[4]

Irrigation occurred at ten different sites from Pine Creek on the north to Independence Creek on the south. The most extensive irrigation system was at Bishop Creek where some six square miles of land, known as *pitana patü* to the Paiute, was watered.[5] Paiute women harvested the seeds and bulbs of the wild plants each fall. Since the Paiute only irrigated and harvested—they did not prepare the soil, sow the seed, or cultivate the plants—what they did has been called "irrigation without agriculture."[6] While Paiute women gathered nuts and seeds and dug roots, Paiute men hunted for antelope, deer, bighorn sheep, and jackrabbits and fished for trout. This way of life, in the arid and rocky trans-Sierra country, required a vast territory to support a small number of Paiute. The encroachment of whites, particularly ranchers, would certainly have an almost immediate effect on the ability of the Paiute to hunt and to gather food.

Violent conflict first erupted on range land just southeast of present-day Bishop.[7] Al Thompson, a cowboy working for Henry Vansickle, spied a Paiute herding a lone steer off into the brush. Giving no warning, Thompson grabbed his rifle and fired. The Indian fell to the ground dead. A few days later the Paiute evened the score. "Yank" Crossen, an Auroran who had only recently come into the valley to ride herd for Allen Van Fleet, was captured and killed. All that any whites ever saw of him again was his scalp, found at Big Pine.

During the next several weeks Indian conflict with the cowboys and ranchers continued. Prospectors, meanwhile, were safe from attack. The Paiute carefully differentiated between the miners, who seemed to pose little threat and had attacked no Indians, and the cattlemen, who had already killed a Paiute and were drastically altering the Indian way of life by stocking the range lands. "No goodee cow man" became a common expression among the Paiute.[8]

In an attempt to avoid further warfare, a peace conference was held at Samuel Bishop's San Francis Ranch on 31 January 1862.[9] Bishop and ten other ranchers repre-

---

3. For a description of the eating habits and cooking methods of the Owens Valley and Mono Paiute, see Steward and Wheeler-Voegelin, *Northern Paiute Indians*, pp. 115–18; C. Hart Merriam, *Studies of the California Indians*, pp. 117–22; Kroeber, *Handbook of Indians of California*, pp. 591–92; and Harry W. Lawton et al., "Agriculture among the Paiute of Owens Valley."

4. Lawton, "Agriculture among the Paiute of Owens Valley," pp. 13–50.

5. The irrigation system at *pitana patü* consisted of a dam on Bishop Creek and two main irrigation ditches. One ditch, some two miles long, led to wild-plant-producing land on the northern side of the creek, and the other, more than three miles in length, led to similar ground on the creek's south side.

6. See Julian H. Steward, "Irrigation Without Agriculture." Lawton and others argue that the work the Paiute did—irrigating and harvesting—was enough to say that they "practiced agriculture."

7. San Francisco *Daily Evening Post*, 22 Nov. 1879; *Inyo Register*, 18 Feb. 1904.

8. *Daily Evening Post*, 22 Nov. 1879.

9. *Daily Evening Post*, 22 Nov. 1879; *Inyo Register*, 18 Feb. 1904, 15 Jan. 1914.

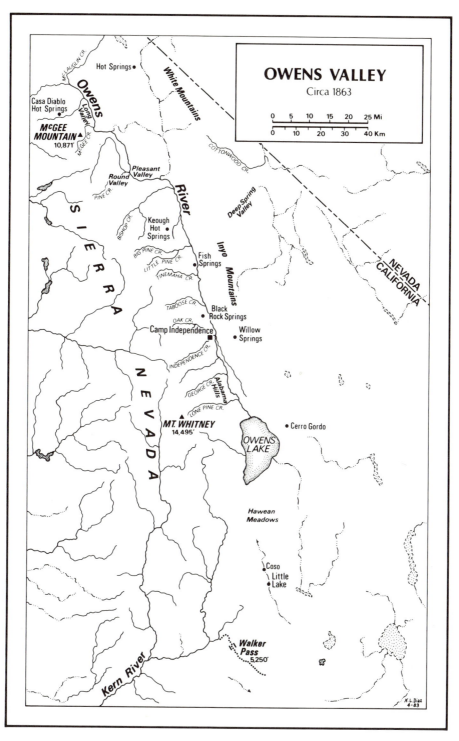

OWENS VALLEY
Circa 1863

0 5 10 15 20 25 Mi
0 10 20 30 40 Km

McLAUGLIN CR.

Hot Springs •

White Mountains

Owens

Casa Diablo
Hot Springs •

Long Valley

McGEE
MOUNTAIN ▲
10,871'

MCGEE CR.

COTTONWOOD CR.

Pleasant
Valley

Round
Valley

PINE CR.

River

Deep Spring
Valley

S I E R R A

BISHOP CR.

Keough
Hot
Springs

NEVADA
CALIFORNIA

BIG PINE CR.

LITTLE PINE CR.

Fish
• Springs

Inyo Mountains

TINEMAHA CR.

TABOOSE CR.

OAK CR.

Black
• Rock Springs

N E V A D A

Camp Independence ■

Willow
• Springs

INDEPENDENCE CR.

GEORGE CR.

Alabama Hills

LONE PINE CR.

MT. WHITNEY
14,495'

• Cerro Gordo

OWENS
LAKE

Hawean
Meadows

• Coso
Little
• Lake

Kern River

Walker
Pass
5,250'

N.L. Diaz
4-83

7.   *The Owens Valley contained little more than Camp Independence,
cattle ranches, and Paiute in 1863. Its grazing lands were used to raise
cattle for the Aurora beef market. (Cartography by Noel Diaz)*

sented the whites, while "Captain George" and "Captain Dick" spoke for several bands of Paiute. Captain George indicated, by drawing two lines on the ground, that the score was even: one Indian—the man shot by Al Thompson—and one white—Yank Crossen—had been killed. There was no reason for more bloodshed. With both the Paiute and the whites in a conciliatory mood, an informal peace treaty was quickly hammered out. The treaty recognized the right of the Indians to continue "their daily avocations" unmolested and the right of the whites to graze their cattle in the valley. Both parties would "live in peace and strive to promote amicably the general interests of both whites and Indians."[10] The treaty was signed by the three Paiute leaders with their marks and by the eleven white representatives with their signatures.

This treaty, like so many others—both official and unofficial—drawn up by whites and presented to Indians, had no chance to succeed. The treaty failed to recognize that the white and Indian ways of life were wholly incompatible, and made peaceful coexistence impossible. For the Paiute to continue "their daily avocations" unmolested, they would need to hunt and gather over every foot of the Owens Valley. To the whites, who did not comprehend that the Paiute were already making maximum use of the valley, the area appeared to be underutilized. Cattle grazing in the valley meant less forage for the indigenous animals, whose numbers would have to decline as the numbers of steers increased, and the destruction of native plants, whose seeds and roots were the staple of the Paiute diet. It would be only a very short time before the Paiute, who had always suffered from a precarious food supply, would begin to feel the effects of white encroachment. The Paiute would then have to prey on cattle and become beef eaters or starve.

This inevitable end was hastened by the severe winter of 1861–1862. Although there was a light snowfall in November, mild weather prevailed until Christmas Eve. Then, as Samuel Youngs of Aurora recorded in his diary, it "commenced snowing fast."[11] Day after day it snowed until the trans-Sierra country was cut off from the rest of the world. Temperatures dropped below zero. Although fires were kept blazing inside Aurora cabins, prospectors wore several layers of clothes when they slept. Upon awakening, they found that the buckets of water and loaves of bread that they had stored inside their cabins had frozen solid. During the second week of January the weather warmed slightly, and the snow became rain. The rain came down in torrents. Adobe cabins turned to mud and collapsed. Esmeralda and Willow gulches overflowed their banks and inundated Aurora. Water stood several inches deep in most buildings. "We have slept each night in our cabin," noted Youngs, "but wet, cold and very bad. Water leaked on my head each night." After a week the rain stopped and snow began to fall again. Within a few days the trans-Sierra was covered with a blanket of snow deeper than before the rain. On 23 January Youngs reported, "We have had but six days since December 24 that it has not stormed more or less—that is 26 days out of 30." A week later he recorded a temperature of fourteen degrees below zero outside his cabin's front door. The stage got through to Aurora only twice during January.

February and March saw a continuation of the Arctic winter with only occasional breaks. March did not go out like a lamb; on the last day of the month a storm left more than a half foot of new snow on the ground. "The coldest April morning I ever knew," wrote Youngs, a native of New York, the next morning. There were some twen-

10.   *Inyo Register*, 18 Feb. 1904, 15 Jan. 1914.

11.   Samuel Youngs's Journal, 25 Dec. 1862.

ty days of snow between the first of April and the twentieth of May when he reported
that his cabin was "about dry for the first time since January." The last snow of the season fell on 14 June, and snow was still ten feet deep on north-facing mountain slopes
two weeks later.

Aurorans suffered considerable hardship during the winter. They often ran out
of supplies of flour and other foodstuffs. Cattle driven in from the Owens Valley saved
them from going hungry more than once. The steers also saved the Paiute, not just from
hunger, but from starvation. They stole steers throughout the winter, before and after
signing the peace treaty with the Owens Valley ranchers. The Paiute must have understood that their thefts would be considered a violation of the treaty, but the severe winter
gave them little choice. Either they stole cattle or they starved.

Also playing a role in hastening the outbreak of war was the presence of "Joaquin Jim" in the Owens Valley. A small, compactly built, and agile Western Mono who
spoke English and Spanish fluently, Joaquin Jim would make life miserable for the
whites.[12] He had killed at least two white men before coming into the trans-Sierra
country, and was greatly feared, if not respected, by whites. The Visalia *Delta* grudgingly
admitted that he was "brave as a lion—his one redeeming quality."[13] His expressive,
glittering dark eyes—the "eyes of a basilisk," said one rancher—and high forehead perhaps betrayed another quality that whites were forced to admit that Joaquin Jim had in
abundance—intelligence.

For a time Joaquin Jim was an outcast among the Owens Valley Paiute, who
called him a "shah," or coyote, but he quickly rose to a position of leadership when
violent conflict erupted. He had long despised the white man and now spared no effort
in rallying the Paiute for war. Predictably, he did not attend the peace conference at the
San Francis Ranch, nor did any of the Paiute who followed him.

During February 1862 Jesse Summers purchased a small herd of cattle for the
Aurora beef market and contracted Barton and Alney McGee to drive the steers to
Aurora. When the McGee brothers made camp at Big Pine Creek, they were visited by
Joaquin Jim and several of his men.[14] According to the McGees, the Indians were surly
and demanded food. "Bart" offered Joaquin Jim a cup of coffee, but the Indian knocked
it into the campfire. Without hesitating a second, Bart leaped for the Indians' guns,
which were stacked to one side. After discharging the weapons, he returned them to the
Indians and ordered them out of camp.

The next day the McGees moved the cattle to the San Francis Ranch, and Bart
left for Charley Putnam's stone cabin on Independence Creek to recruit drovers. Although alert to the increasing Paiute hostility, Bart never suspected that he was beginning the ride of his life. At Fish Springs, about five miles south of Big Pine Creek, a
band of Paiute opened fire on him. Bart, riding one of the fastest horses in the valley,
spurred the animal into a gallop and escaped without a scratch.

Despite his harrowing ride, Bart was able to recruit fifteen drovers at Putnam's
and return with them without incident to the San Francis Ranch. Then, just as everyone
was settling down for the night, a party of Paiute, waving burning pitch-pine torches set

12.   San Francisco *Daily Evening Post*, 22 Nov. 1879; Visalia *Delta*, 16 April 1863; *Inyo Register*, 20 Sept.
1906.

13.   Visalia *Delta*, 16 April 1863.

14.   San Francisco *Daily Evening Post*, 22 Nov. 1879; *Inyo Register*, 18 Feb. 1904, 22 Jan. 1914. Jesse Summers is called James Summers by the *Aurora Times* and the Visalia *Delta*.

atop long poles, surrounded the ranch buildings. Dancing around the buildings, the Paiute proclaimed that they could spit out any bullets that might enter their bodies.[15] The whites, although absorbed in the pyrotechnic spectacle, remained calm, and no violence occurred.

Early the next morning, after an exciting if sleepless night, the cowboys began the cattle drive. Reaching Keough Hot Springs by dusk, the drovers bedded down the herd. Although pickets were posted, Paiute drove off nearly two hundred steers during the night. Three men followed the trail of the stolen beeves until they were stopped by some fifty Paiute. The Indians convinced the cowboys that they had done enough tracking for one day and had best return to the main herd.

The herd was driven on down to Putnam's, although its flanks were continually harassed by Paiute. The next three days passed quietly. Then a small group of Indians were spotted approaching the herd. Bart McGee and several other men, including Allen Van Fleet, ventured out to investigate. They found themselves face-to-face with "Chief" Shoandow and three other Paiute. Shoandow, described by an Auroran as "a large, finely built specimen of the American Indian—independent, proud, generous and high spirited—a primitive Alexander in disguise," was the leader of a peaceful band of Paiute.[16] It was said that he was honored nearly to the point of worship by his people.

Shoandow told the white men that he and his braves had come to recover three horses which had been stolen from them by whites. Shoandow himself had lost a black mare and a colt, and the tribal shaman, or "medicine man," had lost a small roan. Van Fleet told Shoandow that he might continue the search for the horses if he and his braves would lay their arms aside. The Indians refused. What happened next is debated. One report claimed that the whites fired first and the Indians "without showing any hostile intent . . . were shot down like dogs."[17] Bart McGee and Allen Van Fleet alleged that the fight began when an Indian unleashed an arrow.[18] The results of the fight would seem to indicate that the whites fired first. All four Indians and no whites were killed. Only one white, Van Fleet, was wounded.[19] He was struck in the side by an arrow and carried its obsidian head lodged underneath his ribs for the rest of his life.

Although the whites had suffered only one casualty, this fight would prove very costly for them in the long run. The death of Shoandow so enraged his people that they

15.   *Inyo Register,* 22 Jan. 1914. It is no accident that there are similarities here with the Indian Ghost Dance and Ghost Shirt beliefs of the late 1880s. Wovoka, the leader of the Ghost Dance during the late 1880s, was himself a Mono Paiute from the Walker River country. His father, Tavibo, was a shaman and a follower of Wodziwob, the tribal shaman of the Mono Paiute during the 1850s and 1860s. Wodziwob may have been responsible for the Paiute demonstration at the San Francis Ranch. His beliefs certainly influenced Tavibo and Wovoka. Wodziwob told his people that they could bring the dead back by performing a ritualistic dance— later called the Ghost Dance—and he prophesied a frightening upheaval in which God would appear on earth and transform it into a paradise. See Edward C. Johnson, *Walker River Paiutes: A Tribal History,* pp. 41–57; and James Mooney, *The Ghost-Dance Religion and the Sioux Outbreak of 1890.* Mooney's classic work was originally published as Part 2 of the *Fourteenth Annual Report of the Bureau of Ethnology to the Secretary of the Smithsonian Institution, 1892–93* (Washington, 1896).

16.   San Francisco *Daily Evening Post,* 22 Nov. 1879.

17.   *Daily Evening Post,* 22 Nov. 1879; see also Department of War, *The War of the Rebellion: A Compilation of the Official Records of the Union and Confederate Armies,* vol. 50, part I, pp. 966–67.

18.   *Inyo Register,* 18 Feb. 1904, 22 Jan. 1914.

19.   W. A. Chalfant says that Tom Hubbard was also wounded, but it is obvious that Chalfant confused this fight with a fight in the Alabama Hills in which Hubbard was in fact wounded. Compare the San Francisco *Daily Evening Post,* 22 Nov. 1879, the *Inyo Register,* 18 and 25 Feb. 1904, and W. A. Chalfant, *The Story of Inyo,* pp. 152–53.

immediately elected the redoubtable and truculent white-hater Joaquin Jim as their new leader. If Shoandow had lived, as an Auroran later noted, "such a crafty desperado as Joaquin Jim could never have become chief of his tribe."[20]

Whites now began to gather at Charley Putnam's ranch on Independence Creek. Around his stone house they erected a barricade of rocks, old wagons, and logs.[21] Volunteers from Aurora, including Sheriff N. F. Scott who carried a warrant for the arrest of Joaquin Jim, swelled the number of whites to forty-two. Charles Anderson, who had only recently arrived in the valley from Aurora, was elected captain of the defenders, who were armed with rifles, shotguns, and revolvers.

The whites decided that to sit and wait for the Paiute to attack invited disaster. Soon after dusk on 21 March 1862, half of the whites stole out of the fort and headed for the Indian encampment in the nearby Alabama Hills. As the first rays of sunlight reached the valley the next morning, the whites, positioned around the Indian camp, opened fire on the breakfasting Paiute. Although several Paiute were killed by the first volley, most managed to disappear into the clefts and caves of the rocky Alabama Hills.

For several hours the whites poured fire on the Indian position, but they were unwilling to risk an assault, and at one o'clock in the afternoon they broke off the engagement. Battlefield reports indicate that eleven Paiute were killed and a considerably greater number wounded.[22] No whites were killed, and only two were wounded, including Tom Hubbard. He may have been a special target, for he had been with Bart McGee and Allen Van Fleet when Chief Shoandow was gunned down.

Another band of Paiute was having better luck. The Indians found E. S. Taylor, one of the discoverers of Bodie's gold, alone in his cabin at Hot Springs (present-day Benton).[23] When they attacked the cabin, Taylor, half-Indian himself, fought back fiercely and, according to Indian reports, killed several Paiute before he died. His decapitated, arrow-riddled body and his head were later found by a group of passing whites. The head was passed around Aurora and Bodie for years afterward as a grisly souvenir of the Indian attack.

Fighting was now on in earnest. The Owens Valley Paiute called upon their relatives to the north, the Mono Paiute, to come to their aid. They also sent pleas for help to the Western Mono and to various Paiute bands in Nevada. Nevada Paiute had only recently suffered from clashes with whites themselves and were not anxious to support the Owens Valley Paiute. Numaga, a prominent Nevada Paiute leader, counseled his people against war. He spoke English fluently, had traveled in California, and fully appreciated the strength of the whites. Only the year before, he had urged an assembly of Paiute warriors not to attack the whites:

> You would make war upon the whites. I ask you to pause and reflect. The white men are like the stars over your heads. You have wrongs, great wrongs, that rise up like those mountains before you; but can you from the mountain tops reach and blot out those stars? Your enemies are like the sands in the bed of your rivers; when taken

20.   San Francisco *Daily Evening Post*, 22 Nov. 1879.

21.   *Daily Evening Post*, 22 Nov. 1879; *Inyo Register*, 22 Jan. 1914.

22.   *Daily Evening Post*, 22 Nov. 1879; *Inyo Register*, 25 Feb. 1904.

23.   *Daily Evening Post*, 22 Nov. 1879; *Inyo Register*, 18 Feb. 1904, 22 Jan. 1914; Joseph Wasson, *Account of the Important Revival of Mining Interests in the Bodie and Esmeralda Districts*, p. 6.

away they only give place for more to come and settle there. Could you defeat the whites in Nevada, from over the mountains in California would come to help them an army of white men that would cover your country like a blanket. What hope is there for the Pah-Ute? From where is to come your guns, your powder, your lead, your dried meats to live upon, and hay to feed your ponies with while you carry on this war? Your enemies have all these things, more than they can use. They will come like the sand in a whirl-wind and drive you from your homes. You will be forced among the barren rocks of the north, where your ponies will die; where you will see the women and old men starve, and listen to the cries of your children for food. I love my people; let them live; and when their spirits shall be called to the Great Camp in the southern sky, let their bones rest where their fathers were buried.[24]

Despite Numaga's sobering influence, some Nevada Paiute did join the fight. When several bands of Mono Paiute and one or two of Western Mono arrived in the Owens Valley, total Indian strength reached fifteen hundred to two thousand warriors.[25] Al-though most of the Indians were armed only with bows and arrows, at least a hundred of them had guns. The Aurora merchant firm of Wingate and Cohn was accused of supplying them with some of their guns and much of their ammunition.[26]

Nevertheless, Aurorans generally supported the beleaguered ranchers. When Al Thompson, the cowboy who had been the first to kill an Owens Valley Paiute, arrived in town with an urgent plea for assistance, a party of eighteen men, led by John J. Kellogg, a former army captain, was quickly organized.[27] Nearly as soon as the Aurorans reached the valley, they sighted a band of mounted Indians west of the Owens River. The Aurorans prepared themselves for battle and closed in on the Indians. The "Indi-ans" turned out to be a detachment of some thirty whites, led by "Colonel" Mayfield, coming up the valley from Putnam's.

When the two forces united, Mayfield's men related another tale of tragedy. At Big Pine they had come across the bodies of R. Hanson and J. Tallman, who had been killed by Indians.[28] Their corpses had been partially devoured by coyotes. Hanson could only be identified by his teeth. His brother, A. C. Hanson, was one of those riding with Mayfield.

The united parties spent a sleepless night. Paiute, hidden in the rocky hills nearby, howled continually until dawn. At the break of day on 6 April 1862, the citizen militia struck out for Bishop Creek where several bands of Paiute had been sighted. As the whites rode up the valley, they could see Paiute scouts watching their movements. One of the scouts, less cautious than the rest, ventured within rifle range of the white column and was shot dead by Tex Berry. Demonstrating that whites could also mutilate the bodies of their enemies, Dr. E. F. Mitchell of Aurora, the president of the Esmeralda mining district, scalped the dead Paiute and hung the gruesome trophy on his saddle.[29] The incident did not damage Mitchell's career: he later became the president of the

24.   Myron Angel, ed., *History of Nevada*, p. 151.

25.   San Francisco *Daily Evening Post*, 22 Nov. 1879; *Inyo Register*, 18 Feb. 1904, 22 Jan. 1914.

26.   *Inyo Register*, 25 Feb. 1904, 22 Jan. 1914.

27.   *Inyo Register*, 25 Feb. 1904, 22 Jan. 1914; Angel, *History of Nevada*, p. 166.

28.   See n. 27; *Daily Evening Post*, 22 Nov. 1879; *War of the Rebellion*, vol. 50, part I, p. 46.

29.   *Inyo Register*, 22 Jan. 1914.

Antelope and Real Del Monte mining companies, and in the fall of 1863 Aurorans elected him to the California Assembly.

Near noon the whites reached a large Paiute irrigation ditch just south of Bishop Creek and, appreciating the protection the ditch offered, made camp.[30] A short distance to the north, on the other side of Bishop Creek, were some five hundred Indians led by Joaquin Jim.[31] Not realizing that they were outnumbered (although not out-gunned) ten to one, the whites divided their force in two and sallied forth. Kellogg moved his men up along Bishop Creek, and Mayfield flanked him from the south. May-field got into trouble first. The Indians opened fire on the head of Mayfield's column, mortally wounding Harrison Morrison. From his vantage point, Kellogg could see that Mayfield was about to be enveloped, and he ordered Alney McGee to deliver the message to retreat. McGee arrived safely, but his horse dropped dead from bullet wounds.

The whites, advancing on the Indians only minutes before, were now in full retreat. Bart McGee, doubling up, carried the dying Morrison on his horse. Alney McGee protected the slowed riders from the rear, and Cage Pleasant protected them from the front. The McGee brothers happened to be looking at Pleasant, a volunteer from Aurora, when a bullet hole appeared in his coat. Without saying a word, Pleasant stood up in his stirrups and fell dead to the ground. For the moment, his body was left where it lay. A number of men, including A. C. Hanson, ascended a small hill and concentrated enough fire on the Indians for the McGees and the wounded Morrison to reach the ditch. During the action, Hanson avenged his brother's death by killing an Indian who was attempting to stampede the pack animals.

The whites retreated to the ditch and formed a defensive line. Their rifle fire killed two Paiute and held the rest at bay for the remainder of the afternoon. Shortly after dusk, firing from the Indians almost ceased. The whites, for the first time since the beginning of the battle, began to relax. Sheriff Scott of Aurora, still carrying the warrant for the arrest of Joaquin Jim, took time to smoke his pipe. As he lighted it, he carelessly raised his head above the rim of the ditch. A bullet struck him in the forehead, and he rolled to the bottom of the ditch, dead. The sheriff was the last casualty of the "Battle of the Ditch."

When the moon went down, the whites decamped and retreated to Big Pine Creek. Scott and Pleasant had been killed, and Morrison died from his wounds shortly after reaching the Big Pine. The whites also lost some eighteen horses and mules. Indian casualties were estimated at anywhere from five to fifteen dead. If the Paiute had been willing to suffer greater casualties, they no doubt would have been able to overrun the small contingent of beleaguered whites.

Meanwhile, the Indian troubles in the southern trans-Sierra had not gone un-noticed by government officials. On 18 March 1862, Samuel Youngs, who represented Aurora as a member of the Nevada territorial legislature, sent a report on the conflict to Nevada's governor, James Nye.[32] Nye was away in San Francisco, but Warren Wasson, the Indian agent for Nevada, received the report and then telegraphed the governor:

---

30.   This was the southern irrigation ditch at *pitana patü*.

31.   Estimates of Indian strength varied from as low as 400 or 500 to as high as 1,500. See the San Francisco *Daily Evening Post*, 22 Nov. 1879; *Inyo Register*, 25 Feb. 1904; Angel, *History of Nevada*, p. 166; *War of the Rebellion*, vol. 50, part I, p. 47.

32.   Samuel Youngs's Journal, 18 March 1862.

Indian difficulties on Owens River confirmed. Hostiles advancing this way. I desire to go and if possible prevent the war from reaching this territory. If a few men poorly armed go against those Indians defeat will follow and a long and bloody war will ensue. If the whites on Owens River had prompt and adequate assistance it could be checked there. I have just returned from Walker River. Piutes alarmed. I await your reply.[33]

Governor Nye conferred with the commander of the Department of the Pacific, General George Wright, and wired Wasson that the general would order fifty men from Fort Churchill, Nevada, to the scene of action. As was promised, Captain Edwin A. Rowe, commandant of the fort, ordered Lieutenant Herman Noble and a detachment of fifty men from Company A, Second Cavalry, California Volunteers, to "Aurora and vicinity."[34] "Upon all occasions," Rowe's orders to Noble continued, "it is desirable that you should consult the Indian Agent, Mr. W. Wasson, who accompanies the expedition for the purpose of restraining the Indians from hostilities. Upon no consideration will you allow your men to engage the Indians without his sanction."

Wasson and his Indian interpreter proceeded from Fort Churchill in advance of the troops.[35] At the Walker River Reservation, Wasson learned that the Paiute feared the outbreak of a general war with the whites. He therefore dispatched Indian messengers to carry a call for peace to all the different bands of Paiute.

On the bitterly cold morning of 1 April 1862, Wasson and the troops arrived in Aurora.[36] The next morning Wasson left, again in advance of the troops, and parleyed with a band of Mono Paiute on the shores of Mono Lake.[37] Although Wasson found the Indians highly excited, he succeeded in quieting them. Taking along a Mono Paiute to act as interpreter with the Owens Valley Paiute, Wasson joined the troops at Adobe Meadows on 4 April. Two days later Wasson and the troops reached the forks of the Owens River. Little did they know that only forty miles to the south at Bishop Creek, the Kellogg-Mayfield men were fighting for their lives.

While Wasson and the troops were working their way into the Owens Valley from the north, another force was pushing its way into the valley from the south. General James H. Carleton, commander of the Southern District of California, ordered Lieutenant Colonel George S. Evans of the Second Cavalry, California Volunteers, to the Owens Valley.[38] Leaving Camp Latham (located near present-day West Los Angeles) on 19 March 1862, Colonel Evans and some forty hand-picked men from Companies B, D, E, G, and I crossed the Tehachapi Mountains at Tejon Pass, dropped into the San Joaquin Valley, and then reached the trans-Sierra country by way of the Kern River and Walker

33.   Official Report of Indian Agent Warren Wasson to Governor James W. Nye, 20 April 1862, as quoted in Angel, *History of Nevada*, p. 166.

34.   Angel, p. 166. The Second Cavalry, California Volunteers, was organized and mustered into service at Camp Alert, San Francisco, on 30 October 1861. The regiment served throughout the Far West during the Civil War and was mustered out of service at Camp Union, Sacramento, in April 1866.

35.   Angel, p. 166.

36.   Samuel Youngs's Journal, 1 April 1862.

37.   Wasson's Report in Angel, *History of Nevada*, p. 166.

38.   For the initial excursion of Evans and the Second Cavalry into the Owens Valley see the *War of the Rebellion*, vol. 50, part I, pp. 46–49, 934–36, 939, 966–67, 972, 1025–26; and the San Francisco *Daily Evening Post*, 22 Nov. 1879.

Pass. They arrived at Owens Lake, at the southern end of Owens Valley, on 2 April, after a journey of more than three hundred miles.

Although his men and animals were fatigued, Evans pushed on up the valley and reached Putnam's makeshift fort on 4 April. He posted an officer and seven troopers at the "fort" to help protect the score of civilians gathered there, and the next day he continued north. At Big Pine Creek he met the retreating Mayfield-Kellogg party. Most of the party joined Evans, and the civilians and troopers headed for Bishop Creek.

On 7 April, as the Evans command approached the site of the Battle of the Ditch, they spotted a small force of Indians. A scouting party identified the "Indians" as agent Wasson, Lieutenant Noble, and the troopers from Fort Churchill. As ranking officer, Colonel Evans assumed command of the now formidable force and encamped on the spot of the previous day's battle. Cage Pleasant's body, or what remained of it— the Indians had stripped off the clothing and multilated the corpse—was retrieved, wrapped in a blanket, and buried.[39]

Wasson and Colonel Evans, a battle-hardened veteran of the Mexican War, discussed the growing Indian conflict at length. Wasson argued for a truce, but, as he himself noted, he "found little or no encouragement to make peace with the Indians, their [Colonel Evans and the civilians'] desire being only to exterminate them."[40] With this end in mind, Colonel Evans sent out scouting parties of a half-dozen men each in all directions. About noon on 8 April one of the parties reported that a large number of Indians had gathered in Round Valley.

Two hours later the whites rode into the valley and found themselves sur-rounded, not by Indians but by blowing snow. Nevertheless, Colonel Evans ordered an advance into the mountains that rimmed the valley. Less than an hour later, Evans, recognizing the futility of a chase in a snowstorm, recalled his men.

Early the next morning, Evans renewed the search for the Paiute. This time the quarry stalked the hunter. While ascending a narrow canyon on the northwest side of Round Valley, an advance party of troopers rode directly into a Paiute ambush. The first volley of bullets killed Sergeant Christopher Gillespie and seriously wounded Corporal John Harris, both of Company A.[41] The main body of men, three hundred yards below at the mouth of the canyon, rushed into action. Lieutenant Noble and his troopers, together with "Colonel" Mayfield and four other civilians, hurried to occupy the southern rim of the canyon, while Colonel Evans and his troopers climbed the north rim. The civilians, except for those who had followed Lieutenant Noble, remained poised at the canyon mouth.

Noble reached his objective, though he probably wished he had not. Indian fire was concentrated on his command from two directions. Mayfield was wounded, and the others were pinned down. The Paiute held the high ground, had a number of excellent rifles, and kept up a severe fire. "Nothing but mountain howitzers," commented one white, "could possibly dislodge the enemy in their mountain fastness."[42]

---

39.   Pleasant Valley, a few miles northwest of present-day Bishop, was named in his honor.

40.   Wasson's Report in Angel, *History of Nevada*, p. 167.

41.   Angel, p. 167; San Francisco *Daily Evening Post*, 22 Nov. 1879; California, *Records of California Men in the War of the Rebellion, 1861 to 1867*, pp. 202, 205, 874. Harris's wounds proved so serious that he was discharged for disability on 16 Sept. 1862.

42.   San Francisco *Daily Evening Post*, 22 Nov. 1879.

To remain in position would have been fatal. Lieutenant Noble ordered a retreat. Although the maneuver was well executed, one man was lost, the already wounded Mayfield. While riding a stretcher down the hill, Mayfield was killed by a second bullet. The round had passed between the legs of one of those carrying the stretcher before it struck Mayfield. One man's luck proved to be another's misfortune. Luckier still was John Hubinger, a bugler from Company E, who got cut off and surrounded by Indians. He fought his way out and had nothing more to show for it than a bullet-grazed ear.[43]

Meanwhile, Colonel Evans had found the north rim too steep to climb, and he, like Noble, was forced to retreat down the canyon. The disheartened whites camped that night on Bishop Creek. For the time being, they had to admit defeat. Moreover, Evans had exhausted his supplies, except for beef obtained from ranchers in the valley, and was forced to retreat down the valley to Putnam's "fort" on Independence Creek and prepare for a return to Camp Latham in Los Angeles. On 13 April, after a two-day layover at Putnam's, Evans and his command broke camp and headed south; Lieutenant Noble and Company A remained behind at the "fort" for a day before heading north for Aurora. Accompanying Evans were dozens of civilians who had decided to quit the Owens Valley. The civilians took some 4,000 steers and 2,500 sheep with them.[44] Although the Paiute were presumably pleased to see the exodus of the whites, they must have regretted the loss of the livestock which they were beginning to depend on for food.

When Evans reached Indian Wells, just to the east of Walker Pass, he parted company with the civilians and their livestock. The civilians turned west and took the established trail through the pass to the Kern River, while Evans continued south in an effort to find a new route to Los Angeles. With relative ease he pioneered a trail through the Antelope Valley, which shortened the distance to Los Angeles by more than seventy miles and saved several days' time. On 28 April he arrived at Camp Latham.[45]

The Owens Valley—in fact most of the southern trans-Sierra—belonged to the Indians in late April, May, and June of 1862. During those months several more violent confrontations between Indians and whites occurred.[46] One pioneer, traveling through the area with his family, livestock, and all his earthly possessions, lost everything but his wife and children to Indians. In another incident, a group of miners en route to Aurora from Visalia were fired upon by a band of Indians, but escaped unhurt. Nor was property safe. Anything left behind by the whites was destroyed. Even a quartz mill in the White Mountains was razed by Indians.

The white residents of the southern trans-Sierra country responded to the Indian attacks by besieging military authorities with letters and petitions that requested the return of the army to the Owens Valley.[47] As a consequence, Colonel Evans had only a brief rest before he was again ordered into the trans-Sierra. Leaving Fort Latham on 11 June with some two hundred men from Companies D, G, and I of the Second Cavalry, he reached the Owens Valley on 24 June.[48] The same day Evans and his troopers

43. *Records of California Men*, p. 235; *Inyo Register*, 3 March 1904, 29 Jan. 1914.

44. Wasson's Report in Angel, *History of Nevada*, p. 167.

45. *War of the Rebellion*, vol. 50, part I, pp. 48–49.

46. Visalia *Delta*, 17 July 1862.

47. *War of the Rebellion*, vol. 50, part I, 1025–26, 1047.

48. *War of the Rebellion*, vol. 50, part I, pp. 145–46.

surprised a small band of Paiute who were gathering fly larvae on the shores of Owens Lake. Two Paiute were killed, and eleven others, including seven women and two children, were captured and held as hostages. The troopers also captured large quantities of Indian foodstuffs—fly larvae, nuts, seeds, and grasses—and destroyed them. Late the following day Evans and his troopers hurried on to Putnam's. Arriving there on the morning of 26 June they found the citizens' makeshift fort in ruins. Even the stone walls of the cabin had been knocked down. The Indians, said to be in the area and reportedly a thousand strong, were nowhere in sight.

Evans spent the next week scouting the valley, destroying Indian food caches, and attempting to bring the Indians to battle. On 1 July he wrote to army headquarters in San Francisco saying, "The Indians claim the valley as belonging to them, and still insist upon it that no white man shall settle, or, as they term it, sit down in the valley. They say that whites may pass through to and from Aurora if they want to, or they may locate in the hills and work the mines, but must not sit down on the grass patches."[49] Evans said further, however, that if the mines were to be fully developed, the valley, regardless of the Indian right to it, would have to be settled by whites and brought into agricultural production to supply the miners with food. This would mean subduing the Indians, he noted, a task that could not be accomplished quickly: the valley was vast and almost treeless and the Indians could observe the movement of troops "for twenty or thirty miles ahead, and upon their approach they can and will scatter into the hills, where it is impossible to follow them." Evans, arguing that it would be necessary to starve the Indians into submission, concluded:

> These Indians subsist at this season of the year entirely upon the grass seeds and nuts gathered in the valley from the lake up, and the worms gathered at the lake. They gather this food in large quantities during the summer and prepare it for winter use, which together with the piñon nuts gathered in the mountains in the fall of the year, is their only subsistence. Without this food gathered and laid up they cannot possibly subsist through the winter. From the facts set forth above, the nature of these Indians and the surrounding country, it does seem to me that the only way in which they can be chastised and brought to terms is to establish a temporary post, say for one winter, at some point near the center of the valley, from which point send and keep scouts continually ranging through the valley, keep the Indians out of the valley and in the hills, so that they can have no opportunity of gathering and preserving their necessary winter supplies, and they will be compelled to sue for peace before spring and grass come again.

On the Fourth of July of 1862, Evans selected the site for the post that he had mentioned in his letter.[50] On Oak Creek, two miles north of Putnam's, Evans had a perimeter one mile square marked off and a fifty-foot flagpole erected. Troopers raised the Stars and Stripes and fired a salute, and Evans christened the post, in honor of the day, Camp Independence.

The same day a man named Cox, while on his way to the camp, was suddenly surrounded by a small group of Paiute.[51] They assured Cox that they had no intention

49.   *War of the Rebellion*, vol. 50, part I, p. 146.

50.   *War of the Rebellion*, vol. 50, part I, p. 147; San Francisco *Daily Evening Post*, 22 Nov. 1879.

51.   Visalia *Delta*, 17 July 1862.

of harming him and only wanted to know what Colonel Evans planned to do with the Paiute prisoners. Cox replied that if the Indians harmed no whites, the prisoners would be safe. The Paiute then asked Cox to tell Evans that they wanted peace and were ready to sign a treaty. Only the Indians upriver wanted to fight, they said. The next day several bands of Paiute, led by "Captain George" bearing a flag of truce, headed for the camp.

Meanwhile, there was another force approaching Camp Independence. On 11 May Captain Edwin A. Rowe and Company A, Second Cavalry, left Fort Churchill with orders to establish a camp at Aurora and to open negotiations with the Indians.[52] Three days later Captain Rowe arrived in Aurora and established a camp just outside of town. From there he proceeded with the bulk of his force to Adobe Meadows, where he had a friendly talk with Mannawahe and his band of Mono Paiute. Mannawahe unconvincingly disclaimed any participation in the recent fighting and promised to spread the word to the Owens Valley Paiute that the whites wanted peace. Captain Rowe continued south and made camp just across the Owens River from Camp Independence on 7 July. Evans rode out to meet him but was forced to abandon his horse and swim the Owens River, then at flood stage, to reach Rowe's camp. When Evans arrived at the camp he found that Captain George and some forty other Paiute men were already there.

Both the Indians and the whites quickly agreed to a cessation of hostilities. Captain George said that he was tired of fighting and wanted to be friends with the white man, and that if the whites would not bother him he would not bother them. He further stated that he would send word to all the Indians of the Owens Valley that he had made friends with the whites and that if any Indian stole from the whites he would send him to Colonel Evans for punishment. Captain George returned with Evans to Camp Independence and two days later Evans wrote to army headquarters: "Everything will be quiet hereafter, in my opinion, unless the whites first commit outrages upon the Indians. They are very badly frightened and, I think, are in earnest about wanting peace."[53]

In mid-July Major John M. O'Neill took command of Camp Independence and Companies D, G, and I of the Second Cavalry, when Colonel Evans was called out of the valley on an administrative task. Army headquarters in San Francisco ordered O'Neill to negotiate a peace treaty with the Indians. The treaty must require, said headquarters, that the Indians restore all property taken from whites and that four or five influential Indians and their families surrender themselves and be held hostage at Camp Independence as a guarantee of good faith. Before July was out O'Neill succeeded in negotiating such a treaty with Captain George and Tinemaha, another "great chief." Captain George, Tinemaha, and three other Paiute leaders agreed to serve as hostages.[54]

A few weeks later two Paiute leaders from the northern end of the Owens Valley, Tocobaca and Toyahnook, arrived at Camp Independence and surrendered themselves as hostages. They said that they accepted the peace treaty and claimed that they had only gone to war after white men stole their property, outraged their women, and killed four of their people, including "the old chief of the Monaches." Major O'Neill now held seven Paiute leaders and their families as hostages. Also in his custody were a

52.   *War of the Rebellion*, vol. 50, part I, pp. 148–49; San Francisco *Daily Evening Post*, 22 Nov. 1879.

53.   *War of the Rebellion*, vol. 50, part I, p. 149.

54.   *War of the Rebellion*, vol. 50, part II, p. 75. George and Tinemaha creeks in the Owens Valley were named after the Paiute leaders. Captain George's Paiute name was Tosahoidobah. See *War of the Rebellion*, vol. 50, part I, p. 213.

horse, a Colt revolver, a musket, a Sharps carbine, two double-barreled shotguns, and nine rifles that various Indians had delivered to the camp since the signing of the treaty.[55]

Although several bands of Paiute were still said to be "surly," the rest of the summer passed quietly. Ranchers and miners began a cautious return to the valley. "The Indian troubles have finally ceased to scare the timid or retard our progress, from the fact that a military post has been established on Owens' River," wrote a white resident of the valley. "So those wishing to pay us a visit need have no fears of leaving their scalps."[56]

The principal trouble facing the army during August and September of 1862 was not Indians but lack of supplies. Provisions ordered from Los Angeles never arrived on time, and when they did reach camp they were in insufficient quantities. By September the situation was becoming critical. Some men were barefoot, others were clothed in rags, and all were hungry. Morale was deteriorating badly. On the Saturday night of 13 September a storm hit the area that left the mountains covered in snow and dropped temperatures to freezing in the valley. With his men at the breaking point, O'Neill decided to move his entire command southward, hoping to meet a supply train coming from Los Angeles. He struck camp on Monday morning and headed south. The next day, as he approached Owens Lake, he spotted a supply train of sorts; it was Colonel Evans leading some troopers and a lone freight wagon north. Although not entirely what O'Neill had hoped for, the single wagon was full of provisions. When the two parties met, camp was made on the spot and the men were fed. By the following day the entire force, again under the command of Colonel Evans, was back at Camp Independence.[57]

Colonel Evans now issued a call made by John P. H. Wentworth, Superintendent of Indian Affairs for the Southern District of California, for all the Indian leaders of the Owens Valley to come to Camp Independence.[58] Wentworth, saying he represented the "Great Father at Washington," promised to meet with the "chiefs" on 20 September 1862 and to give them presents and provisions. About a hundred Paiute leaders arrived at the camp at the appointed time, but Wentworth failed to show. After waiting for the agent for ten days, the Paiute became highly indignant and reportedly said, "Whites mucho big lie. No give nothing." Evans, in an attempt to appease the Indians, had his quartermaster begin to give them daily rations of fresh beef.

Superintendent Wentworth finally arrived at Camp Independence in early October and immediately dispatched runners to the different Paiute bands.[59] Wentworth was soon distributing gifts and rations to some four hundred Paiute. He told them of "the folly of endeavoring to oppose the government that was desirous of aiding them" and assured them that whereas "any indication of rebellion would be met with prompt and severe punishment, good behavior would secure its [the government's] fostering care." The Indians, reported Wentworth, were willing to live in peace if the government would protect them and provide a means of support.

---

55.   *War of the Rebellion*, vol. 50, part II, pp. 91–92.

56.   Visalia *Delta*, 25 Sept. 1862.

57.   *War of the Rebellion*, vol. 50, part I, pp. 149–50; part II, p. 122.

58.   *War of the Rebellion*, vol. 50, part I, pp. 151–52.

59.   The following account is drawn from Department of the Interior, *Report of the Commissioner of Indian Affairs for the Year 1863*, pp. 105–7.

On 6 October 1862 a truce was signed, and the Indians celebrated the event with a great dance. Loaded down with gifts and apparently greatly contented, they then dispersed. Captain George remained behind as a hostage to ensure that they would remain peaceful. Wentworth now wrote to William P. Dole, the Commissioner of Indian Affairs, pleading for the official establishment of an Indian reservation in the Owens Valley. Said Wentworth:

> I laid off a reservation of about six townships, bounded by the Big Pine creek on the north, George's creek on the south, Owen's river on the east, and the Sierra on the west. The amount of land [nearly 140,000 acres] will seem large for the number of Indians, (about 2,000,) but it must be remembered that it is only in small spots that it is susceptible of cultivation, the balance being scarcely fit for grazing purposes, and none of it attractive to settlers. Placed on a reservation where the agent's authority is respected by the emigrants, and where they know they are secure from interference and are treated with kindness, experience has demonstrated there is no difficulty in managing the Indian. The troubles in the State have always arisen outside of the reserves.
>
> Should the Department agree with me, as I trust it will for I see no other way of keeping these Indians quiet, I hope it will recommend to Congress the immediate appropriation of $30,000 for the purpose of enabling me to establish this reservation. That sum, judiciously expended in the purchase of seed, stock cattle, mules, wagons, ploughs, etc., would place these wretched people beyond the necessity of stealing for a livelihood, and would relieve the Government from any further expense for their support, as well as dispense with the necessity of maintaining an expensive military post in a country where everything has to be hauled a distance of 300 miles over a sandy road, with water only at long intervals, and every obstacle to surmount which is objectionable for a military depot. Already the Government has expended many thousands of dollars in sending and keeping troops there to suppress difficulties that would never have occurred had Congress appropriated, a year ago, for this reservation.

Wentworth further noted that the discovery of gold and silver at Aurora and other spots in the area had quickly transformed a formerly unknown region into a great thoroughfare and precipitated conflict with the Indians. But an Indian war must be avoided, he stressed. The gold and silver that the region produced was sorely needed by the Union, burdened with the Civil War, and an Indian uprising would close mines. "The importance of prompt action by Congress in this matter," concluded Wentworth, "cannot be presented more strongly than in the fact that it can, by a small appropriation, if made at once, secure permanent peace with a people who have shown themselves formidable in war, and save the Government the enormous expense attendant upon an interminable Indian difficulty which will inevitably occur."

Commissioner Dole was not impressed by Wentworth's arguments. Since the proposed Owens Valley reservation could not hold more than two thousand Indians, reasoned Dole, another location should be sought: a location "ample for the wants of all the Indians" of the southern district of California. Secretary of the Interior J. P. Usher agreed with Dole, and Wentworth's recommendations were disapproved.

Meanwhile, with the Indians quieted, Colonel Evans moved Companies D and I from Camp Independence to Visalia, a hotbed of "Jeff Davis traitorism," and a mile north of the town established Camp Babbitt.[60] Company G, about a hundred strong and

---

60.   *War of the Rebellion*, vol. 50, part I, pp. 152–153; part II, p. 139; Visalia *Delta*, 27 November 1862.

commanded by Captain Theodore H. Goodman, was left behind to garrison Camp Independence. Goodman spent much of his time supervising the construction of adobe barracks, officers' quarters, stables, a guardhouse, and other camp buildings. He resigned his commission on 31 January 1863 and was replaced by Captain James M. Ropes.[61]

Although there were several isolated incidents of conflict between Indians and whites during the fall and winter, it was not until early spring that a major outbreak of violence occurred.[62] On 1 March 1863, Captain George, after receiving his supply of rations, disappeared from Camp Independence. The next day the Paiute renewed the war with a surprise attack on four prospectors, the brothers Hiram, Albert, and William Ayres, and James McDonald, who were camped along Big Pine Creek. The attack came at dusk while Hiram Ayres was away from camp, chopping wood in the nearby hills. McDonald managed to yell a warning before he was felled by a volley of arrows. William Ayres ran for his life, but was hit by an arrow before he could get out of range. With the arrow stuck in his back, he crawled into a clump of thick underbrush and hid. The Paiute tracked him into the brush and even poked his body with sharpened sticks without discovering him. Albert Ayres escaped unscathed. He had at first attempted to aid McDonald, but McDonald insisted that Ayres run for his life and warn the other settlers and prospectors. McDonald, although punctured by four arrows, was still alive when the Paiute reached him. They refused to kill him quickly, choosing instead to stone him to death.

A band of Paiute led by "Captain Jack" then looted and ransacked the cabin of Henry G. Hanks and his partners of the San Carlos Mining and Exploration Company, based in San Francisco. Everything in the cabin, except for some laboratory equipment, was either destroyed or stolen. Among the missing items were several guns and a store of ammunition. After this attack Hanks, who would later become California's state mineralogist, wrote to his associates in San Francisco:

> I am beginning to change my mind about Indians. I used to think they were a much-abused race and that the whites were generally to blame in troubles like this, but now I know to the contrary. Those very Indians who had been entertained at our house were the ones to attack it, and would have murdered us had we been at home. . . .
>
> I want you to use all your influence to have the Indian reservation done away with, and to prevent a treaty until the Indians are punished severely. The citizens of this valley are exasperated to that extent that they will not respect any treaty until the Indians are completely conquered and punished. The Indians are a cruel, cowardly, treacherous race. The whites have treated them well, paid them faithfully for all services performed by them, and have used the reservation only after gaining the consent of Captain George, their chief. After living on the charity of whites all winter, having gambled away the blankets and beads given them by the Government, they now, without giving us the slightest warning, pounce down like vultures, rob those who have treated them best, and murdered where they could without danger to themselves. They rush upon their prey in great numbers, like a pack of wolves, and not satisfied with filling the bodies of their victims with glass-pointed arrows, beat them into a pumice with stones. Can we be expected to give such inhuman wretches a chance at us again? We call upon you, the people of California, State and Federal authorities, to have this

---

61. *Report of the Adjutant-General of the State of California, from May 1st, 1864, to November 30th, 1865,* p. 500.

62. Visalia *Delta,* 12 March 1863; *Inyo Register,* 10 March 1904.

reservation and this set of wild savages removed to some other point. This valley is the natural thoroughfare through the mountains, and destined by nature to be the seat of a large population.[63]

Several other cabins were subsequently ransacked, and then another prospector was killed.[64] The Indians, evidently needing lead for bullets, ripped out sections of a pipe that supplied water to Ida, a small mining camp near present-day Manzanar. With the pipe destroyed, miners Curtis Bellows and Milton Lambert found it necessary to carry water from a nearby spring to Ida. On 3 March 1863, Bellows and Lambert were returning from the spring when a band of Paiute ambushed them. Bellows pulled out the first arrow that struck him, then a second one killed him. Lambert raced back to Ida and frightened off the Paiute by shouting orders to several imaginary companions.

While these incidents were occurring, Captain Ropes sent out a seven-man scouting party commanded by Lieutenant James C. Doughty to recapture Captain George.[65] Near Black Rock Springs on 3 March 1863, the same day that Bellows was killed, the troopers rode into an ambush. Privates Jabez F. Lovejoy, John Armstrong, George W. Hazen, and George Sowerwine, and Lieutenant Doughty were all hit. Private Sowerwine's horse was shot out from under him, but he doubled up with Lovejoy, and the bloodied scouting party rode furiously back to Camp Independence. That evening Private Lovejoy died of his wounds.

Three days later, Captain Ropes led nearly thirty troopers and several civilian volunteers to Black Rock Springs. When the white force approached the springs, the Paiute, well concealed in craggy lava beds, opened fire. Captain Ropes, knowing that it would be impossible to dislodge them from their natural stronghold, retreated slowly, hoping to draw them out of the lava beds. The Paiute were not fooled by the ruse. They remained in position and derided the whites by "throwing sand in the air and yelling like fiends."[66] Captain Ropes could do nothing but lead an ignominious retreat back to Camp Independence. He realized that the number of men in his command was too small to carry on an effective campaign against the Paiute and requested reinforcements. Consequently, on 11 March 1863, Lieutenant Stephen R. Davis and forty-five men from Company E left Camp Babbitt to aid Captain Ropes.[67]

Meanwhile, early in March, Jesse Summers and his wife and daughter, Alney McGee and his mother, and the McGees' "faithful negro" Charley Tyler, left Aurora, bound for Visalia.[68] Unaware that hostilities had been renewed, they traveled leisurely and made camp on the night of 6 March 1863 at the "upper crossing" of the Owens River. The next day they forded the river and traveled on to Big Pine Creek, where circling buzzards attracted them to the stripped, arrow-riddled, and battered corpse of

63.   Henry G. Hanks manuscript collection (destroyed in the San Francisco fire of 1906) as quoted in the *Inyo Register*, 10 March 1904.

64.   Visalia *Delta*, 12 March 1863; San Francisco *Daily Evening Post*, 22 Nov. 1879; *Inyo Register*, 12 Feb. 1914.

65.   See n.64; *Records of California Men*, pp. 255, 877; *Report of the Adjutant-General of the State of California, from May 1st, 1864, to November 30th, 1865*, p. 547.

66.   *Inyo Register*, 10 March 1904.

67.   *War of the Rebellion*, vol. 50, part II, pp. 346–47; Visalia *Delta*, 12 March 1863.

68.   *Aurora Times* (date unknown) as reprinted in the Visalia *Delta*, 16 April 1863; *Inyo Register*, 10 March 1904, 12 Feb. 1914; San Francisco *Daily Evening Post*, 22 Nov. 1879.

8. "Chief John," a Paiute shaman, survived the war with the whites and lived into the twentieth century. He was reputed to be 105 years old when this photograph was taken in 1906. (Credit: Los Angeles County Museum of Natural History)

James McDonald. Now alerted in a most gruesome manner to the uprising, they hurried south toward Camp Independence, all the while watching smoke signals rise ominously from the hills below Fish Springs.

Suddenly a band of more than a hundred Paiute swept out of the hills. The whites turned their horses and wagon and headed for the Owens River. At a full gallop the party plunged into the river, only to have the wagon become mired at midstream. With no time to lose, the horses were cut loose and mounted by the women, and they galloped across the river and south toward Camp Independence. By now the Paiute had reached the river and sent a volley of bullets and arrows into the party. Summers and McGee caught horses from the remuda they had been driving and raced for the camp.

The Paiute pursued and shot at the fleeing settlers, but everyone except Charley Tyler reached Camp Independence safely. Mrs. McGee was so stiff that she had to be lifted from her horse and was then unable to stand. Seventeen horses and a wagon—its contents included $600 in cash—had been lost, and Tyler was missing. When Summers and McGee last saw him, he was trying to catch one of the horses of the remuda with his lariat. They hoped he had succeeded and had ridden to Aurora.

Tyler had not escaped. He was captured by the Paiute, who considered him a special prize, for he was known to have killed several Indians. Tyler had been a member of the McGee–Van Fleet party that gunned down Chief Shoandow and three other Paiute, and he had also participated in the Alabama Hills fight and the Battle of the Ditch. The Paiute now made him suffer for his actions. For three days he was tortured, then bound with withes and roasted to death.[69]

To prevent other travelers from being caught unaware, Captain Ropes sent Lieutenant Doughty and a dozen troopers to the upper crossing of the Owens River to warn travelers and post notices of the Paiute uprising. Privates James R. Johnston and William K. Potter of Company G were sent on to alert Aurora. The privates alerted Aurora without incident, but on their return trip they ran into a band of some three hundred Paiute led by Captain George. The Paiute leader, who had known the two cavalrymen at Camp Independence, signaled for them to join the Paiute in a feast. Johnston and Potter, reckoning that they themselves would be the main course, respectfully declined. Spurring their horses, the cavalrymen raced for Camp Independence. The Paiute gave chase and opened fire. A bullet hit Johnston in the hand and another creased his horse's neck, but he and Potter outdistanced the Paiute and reached the camp without further incident.[70]

By now most whites had fortified their cabins and mining camps and were ready for the Indians. Except for some minor incidents, all was quiet during mid-March. Then on the night of 18 March 1863, several ranchers spied a band of Paiute warriors feasting on a stolen steer in a camp on George Creek.[71] The next morning the ranchers counted thirty-seven Paiute as the Indians left camp in single file and headed south. The ranchers, believing that the Paiute intended to intercept the Aurora–Visalia mail carrier, hurried off to Camp Independence.

69.   Visalia *Delta*, 25 Jan. 1865; San Francisco *Daily Evening Post*, 22 Nov. 1879. Charley's Butte, not far from the intake for the Los Angeles Aqueduct, was named in his honor.

70.   *Inyo Register*, 20 March 1904, 19 Feb. 1914; *Report of the Adjutant-General of the State of California, from May 1st, 1864, to November 30th, 1865*, p. 547.

71.   Visalia *Delta*, 2 April 1863; San Francisco *Daily Evening Post*, 22 Nov. 1879; *Inyo Register*, 19 Feb. 1914.

On hearing the ranchers' report, Captain Ropes dispatched Lieutenant Doughty and twenty troopers, who were joined by a nearly equal number of civilian volunteers, to George Creek. There the white force picked up the Indian trail and followed it south along the western side of the Alabama Hills to a ravine just above Cottonwood Creek. With no warning, a bullet ripped through the hat of one of the whites, leaving a clean hole in the hat but not touching the man's head. The Paiute were well concealed in the rocky ravine and laid down a brisk fire. Lieutenant Doughty deployed his main force as skirmishers and sent Sergeant Ward Huntington and a squad of men charging into the ravine. The charge killed several of the Indians and forced the others to retreat down the ravine toward Owens Lake. The Paiute retreated from position to position until they found themselves backed up against the western shore of the lake. By now sixteen of their number had been killed, and their guns were so dirty that they had to pound the ramrods with stones to force bullets down the gun barrels. It was no longer a contest, and the surviving Paiute sought refuge in the lake. Swimming against a strong headwind, they made little progress. The whites lined up on the shore of the lake and, by the light of a full moon, methodically shot the swimmers to death one by one.

Except for one Paiute who escaped to the west during the fight, all the warriors—thirty-six by count—were slain. The lone survivor was last seen climbing into the Sierra, stopping only to make "derisive signs" to the whites. Corporal Michael McKenna, who was later decorated for bravery for his actions in the fighting, was the only white casualty. He was wounded in the chest when struck by an arrow. Charley Tyler's pistol was found on one of the dead Paiute, and booty taken from the McGee-Summers party, on others.

In response to the continuing warfare, more reinforcements were sent into the Owens Valley. Captain Herman Noble, commanding Company E, Second Cavalry, arrived at Camp Independence on 4 April 1863.[72] Captain Noble was not new to the Owens Valley or to Indian fighting. Only the previous year he had accompanied Indian agent Warren Wasson into the valley, and was second in command to Colonel Evans in the fighting that had occurred in Round Valley.

With the confidence that fresh troops usually bring, Captain Ropes now led 120 troopers of Companies E and G and 35 civilian volunteers in pursuit of a large body of Paiute reported to be some thirty miles north of the camp.[73] On the afternoon of 10 April 1863, the whites made contact with an estimated two hundred Paiute in the Sierra foothills just north of Big Pine Creek. The fighting lasted until nightfall, when, under the cover of darkness, the Paiute were able to withdraw into the mountains. The Paiute suffered several killed and wounded; no whites were killed, and only two were wounded, privates Thomas Spratt of Company G and John Burton of Company E.

The wounded troopers were placed in the bed of a wagon, and an eight-man detail was ordered to take them back to Camp Independence. Near Fish Springs the soldiers were ambushed by Captain George and a hundred Paiute. A running battle ensued. One trooper dashed ahead to the camp for reinforcements while the others tried to keep the pursuing Paiute at bay. Arriving just in time to save the detail, the rescue party scattered the Paiute "like a flock of quail."

72. *Records of California Men*, p. 181.

73. *Records of California Men*, p. 181; San Francisco *Daily Evening Post*, 22 Nov. 1879; *Inyo Register*, 10 March 1904, 19 Feb. 1914.

In the meantime, still more reinforcements were moving toward Camp Independence. On 9 April 1863, the same day that Captain Ropes left for Big Pine Creek, Captain Albert Brown and seventy-one men of Company L, Second Cavalry, passed through Aurora on their way to the Owens Valley.[74] The troopers carried with them a mountain howitzer and an ample supply of shell and canister shot. They also carried fifty Minié-ball muskets for distribution to civilians. Captain Brown told the citizens of Aurora that his orders were to march directly to Camp Independence and not to attack any Indians en route. Nevertheless, if he were attacked, said Captain Brown, he would send for civilian reinforcements from Aurora.

While Captain Brown and Company L were moving toward the valley from Aurora, Captain Moses A. McLaughlin and Company D, Second Cavalry, were moving in from Visalia.[75] Captain McLaughlin left Camp Babbitt on 12 April 1863 and followed the Kern River to Keyesville. There he learned that a large party of Indians was camped near Whiskey Flat (modern Kernville) and that the Indians had killed a white man in Kelsey Canyon and had stolen more than a hundred head of cattle. According to Jose Chico, a local Indian leader who had a farm on the Kern River, the offending Indians were mostly renegades from the Owens Valley. They had come into the Kern River country, he said, to gather recruits and to incite the local Indians to war against the white man.

Taking Chico along as a guide and interpreter, McLaughlin set out for the Indian camp. He reached the camp at dawn on 19 April and took the Indians by surprise. Allowing the old men and boys and those Indians that Chico could vouch for to remain behind, McLaughlin marched the others, thirty-five by count, out of the camp. The marching Indians evidently soon realized the fate that awaited them and tried to make a fight of it. Having no weapons but the knives that some of them had concealed on their persons and the sticks and stones which others grabbed from the ground, the Indians could offer little resistance and were quickly slaughtered. Most were shot to death; a few were run through with sabers. "This extreme punishment, though I regret it, was necessary," said McLaughlin, "and I feel certain that a few such examples will soon crush the Indians and finish the war in this and adjacent valleys. It is now a well-established fact that no treaty can be entered into with these Indians. They care nothing for pledges given, and have imagined that they could live better by war than peace."

Whites generally agreed with Captain McLaughlin and accepted the slaughter as a wartime necessity. "This act," commented a correspondent for the Visalia *Delta*, "the harshness of which at first view appeared astounding, is generally approved of by the friends of the Union who are gradually waking up to the necessity of energy in war, whether it be against the secesh or Indians."[76]

Captain McLaughlin arrived at Camp Independence on 24 April 1863 and, as senior officer, assumed command. The day after his arrival at the camp, McLaughlin led a three-day reconnaissance in force. This was an indication of things to come. Under Captain McLaughlin's aggressive and resourceful command, the troopers would see plenty of action during the next month. McLaughlin also used a novel strategy. Colonel Evans had operated only in the daytime and had his men chase the Indians from the

74. *Esmeralda Star*, 11 April 1863, as reprinted in the Visalia *Delta*, 23 April 1863.

75. Visalia *Delta*, 23 April 1863; *Records of California Men*, p. 181; *War of the Rebellion*, vol. 50, part I, pp. 208–10.

76. Visalia *Delta*, 23 April 1863.

valley, up the canyons, and into the mountains. McLaughlin reversed the action. He had his men ascend the mountains at night and secrete themselves until daylight. Then they moved down the canyons, surprising the Indians and flushing them into the valley. The strategy was an enormous success.

On 3 May Lieutenant Francis McKenna and thirty men of Company G routed a group of Paiute in the Inyo Mountains, killing several and driving the rest into troopers under the command of Lieutenant George D. French stationed in the valley below.[77] French's men killed another of the Paiute and mortally wounded three. Captain Noble led Company E on a patrol that resulted in the capture of thirty Indians at Big Pine Creek on 11 May. A few days later Captain McLaughlin and another patrol destroyed the camp of Joaquin Jim, but Jim and his men escaped into the mountains. Company L, under the command of Captain Brown, was in the field for the entire month of May and destroyed some three hundred bushels of pine nuts and seeds that the Indians had cached near Bishop Creek. Sergeant Henry C. Church and four men of Company L surprised a band of fourteen Paiute near the headwaters of the Owens River and killed four of them. Even civilian parties were now besting the Indians. Alney McGee and H. Hurley, leading a group to Aurora, killed three Indians in a fight in mid-May.[78]

With over a hundred men killed and many others wounded or taken prisoner, and with hundreds of bushels of seed destroyed, the Paiute were, for the time being, well-beaten. Sergeant Daniel McLaughlin of Company D met with Captain George and led him into Camp Independence on 22 May 1863.[79] When Captain George had left the fort in March his face was plump and round; now it was sunken and hollow. "The Indians," as the Visalia *Delta* aptly put it, "are hard up for food."[80] No food meant no war, and day after day Indians came to Camp Independence and surrendered. Captain George's band was followed by those of "Captain Dick" and Tinemaha.[81] By June there were some five hundred Indians in camp and by July the number had swelled to nearly a thousand.

Not all whites, however, were ready to accept peace. Two Indian messengers who were sent to bring in the Paiute of the White Mountains were fired on by some miners. The messengers never returned and probably became renegades who preyed on prospectors.[82] In another incident a small band of Paiute on their way to Camp Independence to surrender was attacked by a group of miners. Three of the Indians, including a young girl, were killed and scalped. One of the miners, Frank Whetson, was arrested by Lieutenant French and placed in irons. Whetson spent the next few months imprisoned at Camp Independence and Fort Tejon. Said Captain Ropes:

> Of the Indians who escaped from this attack most of them made their way to the mountains, where they now are and where they will remain for all that anyone can

77. The following military actions were reported in *Records of California Men*, pp. 181–82, and *War of the Rebellion*, vol. 50, part I, pp. 210–12; part II, pp. 414, 423.

78. *Inyo Register*, 26 Feb. 1914.

79. *Records of California Men*, p. 181; *War of the Rebellion*, vol. 50, part I, pp. 209–10; Visalia *Delta*, 4 June 1863.

80. Visalia *Delta*, 28 May 1863.

81. Visalia *Delta*, 25 June 1863.

82. *Esmeralda Star*, 30 July 1863, as reprinted in *Report of the Commissioner of Indian Affairs for the Year 1863*, p. 100.

do to drive them out. Never again can any of them be induced to place any faith in the promises of white men, and if another outbreak occurs it will be far the most desperate we have ever seen. I should have mentioned that the last party of Indians mentioned also bore a white flag, traveled openly in the road in daylight, and that their purpose was known to everyone. But for such ruffians as those who fired upon them, unarmed as they were, there would not today be a hostile Indian in the entire country; and those who may hereafter suffer will have Mr. Whetson and others of like ilk to thank for it.[83]

There were those who believed that Whetson and his fellow prospectors were justified. Milo Page, a prospector who participated in the war, noted that the band of Paiute that Whetson fired on was the same one that killed four of Whetson's partners—Hall, Turner, Shepherd, and White—a few months earlier. Recovered from the dead Indians were Hall's rifle and Turner's coat.[84] The Visalia *Delta*, although noting that "the Indians had on articles of dress known to belong to Whites who had been murdered," deplored the killing of the Indians and urged restraint: "We know that it must be very trying to the self-control of any one to let an Indian pass under such circumstances, but yet it ought to be done, as a different course endangers the lives of the entire community."[85]

Just like some whites who were not ready to call it quits, there were those Indians who refused to surrender. Joaquin Jim's band of Paiute remained at large and continued to prey on the unsuspecting traveler or prospector. About the middle of June one of the most prominent citizens of Visalia, Thomas M. Heston, was killed by Paiute somewhere between Adobe Meadows and Aurora.[86] Similar attacks, usually attributed to Joaquin Jim, continued to plague the valley. In late June, Captain McLaughlin with ninety soldiers and twenty-six Indians, including Captain George, trailed Joaquin Jim and his band of warriors through Round Valley and over 12,400 foot high Italy Pass into the western Sierra.[87] The chase continued for another week before Joaquin Jim's trail turned cold.

On 11 July 1863, Captains McLaughlin, Noble, and Ropes with a detachment of seventy cavalrymen from Companies D, E, and G and twenty-two foot soldiers from the Fourth Infantry, California Volunteers, left Camp Independence with some 900 Indians, bound for the San Sebastian Reservation near Fort Tejon.[88] Travel was slow, and it was not until 22 July that the Indians, about 50 of whom slipped away en route, were delivered to agent John Wentworth. Wentworth was angry because Congress had not approved his request of the previous year for an Owens River reservation and $30,000 in relief funds. At that time the Commissioner of Indian Affairs, William P. Dole, had disapproved of the Owens Valley as a location for an Indian reservation, and Representative Aaron A. Sargent had stated to Congress that the amount of money requested was excessive and that there were not 500 Indians in the entire valley. Wentworth now reported to the Bureau of Indian Affairs that the 850 Indians

83.   Commissioner's *Report*, p. 100.

84.   *Inyo Register*, 20 Sept. 1906; Visalia *Delta*, 23 July 1863.

85.   Visalia *Delta*, 23 July 1863.

86.   Visalia *Delta*, 2 July 1863.

87.   Visalia *Delta*, 25 June 1863; San Francisco *Daily Evening Post*, 22 Nov. 1879.

88.   *War of the Rebellion*, vol. 50, part II, pp. 535–36; *Records of California Men*, p. 182; *Report of the Commissioner of Indian Affairs for the Year 1863*, pp. 99–100; Visalia *Delta*, 23 July 1863.

delivered to the reservation probably represented only about one-third of the total. He further contended that

> the government has expended nearly ten times the amount asked for in that report in trying to suppress the present Indian War. Had Congress promptly made that appropriation, no Indian War would have been waged, and the country would have been saved more than two hundred and fifty thousand dollars to its treasury, the lives of many of its valuable citizens, and many of the poor, ignorant, misguided Indians, to whom the government have promised protection would to-day, instead of being dead, be living and tilling the soil of their native valley and through their own willing hands, obtaining an honest and well earned livelihood.
>
> These Indians, like all others of their race, are very exacting, and a promise to them unfulfilled they look upon as a just cause for war. Therefore it is of the utmost importance that Congress awaken to the necessity of giving, in future, heed and consideration to the reports of its agents upon the condition and wants of the Indians under their respective charges.[89]

Agent Wentworth now concluded his report by asserting that, because of mining activity in the region, the Owens Valley was "entirely impracticable" for an Indian reservation and that "the Indian and white race can never live peacefully in close proximity to each other."

Wentworth apparently failed to see the contradiction in his own report. If his conclusions were true, then little good would have come from the establishment of a reservation in the valley during the winter of 1862–1863 unless whites could have been kept out of the area. Prospectors and ranchers were already there, however, and more were coming. The United States government had never fought with much vigor against encroachment by whites on lands reserved to Indians, and it is unlikely that the Owens Valley would have been an exception. Wherever whites had demanded Indian land, sooner or later the Indians were forced to cede their holdings.[90]

Wentworth also failed to note that the Paiute uprising came after they had received gifts and rations throughout the winter. Captain George's band of Paiute, for example, who had left Camp Independence loaded down with blankets and food, became one of the most active warrior bands in the spring. Wentworth apparently forgot that it was the Indians, not the whites, who renewed hostilities as soon as spring arrived. Moreover, there is no evidence that the Paiute conceived of themselves as potential yeoman farmers who would soon be "tilling the soil of their native valley."

The Paiute of the trans-Sierra country were primarily hunters and gatherers. Although there were bands of Paiute in the Owens Valley who irrigated wild plants, even those bands cannot be considered agricultural. Furthermore, it was the job of the women, not the men, to gather nuts and seeds and to dig roots. That the Paiute men would have voluntarily abandoned their manner of living and become farmers is unlikely. They were certainly proud of what they were and, as events proved, were willing to fight to protect their way of life.

89. *Report of the Commissioner of Indian Affairs for the Year 1863*, p. 99.

90. For a survey of Indian treaties and the inevitable Indian loss of their lands, see, e.g., Helen Hunt Jackson, *A Century of Dishonor*; Charles C. Royce, *Indian Land Cessions in the United States*; Edward H. Spicer, *A Short History of the Indians of the United States*.

Finally, Wentworth neglected to mention that the most aggressive, or perhaps the most freedom-loving, band of Paiute, the one led by Joaquin Jim, did not attend the peace conference of October 1862 at Camp Independence and was party to no agreements. Considering all of these circumstances, it is unlikely, even if Wentworth's recommendations had been followed, that an Indian war could have been avoided—unless, of course, the United States government would have been willing to keep whites out of the Owens Valley.

On 17 July 1863, Captain McLaughlin received orders to abandon Camp Independence and to reoccupy Fort Tejon.[91] Two weeks later he led Companies D and G out of the Owens Valley (Company L had left at the end of May, and Company E at the end of June).[92] Sporadic Indian attacks continued during the summer of 1863. Many of these were attributed to Joaquin Jim who, with the abandonment of Camp Independence, now considered himself overlord of the southern trans-Sierra. He even marked his principal territory, Round Valley, with a war banner of scarlet, trimmed with raven feathers. A few other bands of Paiute were also active, and it was still dangerous for whites to travel alone.

In August, Stephen Orjada was ambushed by Indians as he rode from Keyesville to Walker's Basin.[93] One round carried away two fingers of his left hand, and several others barely missed him. Orjada spurred his mule, but the stubborn beast, "with the perversity for which that animal is fabled," refused to move. He dismounted and outran the Indians to safety. At about the same time, nine prospectors in Little Round Valley held off an attack by a large band of Paiute, two of whom were killed.[94] A few weeks later two prospectors from Aurora, Mark Cornish and W. L. Moore, killed two Paiute while repulsing an attack on the southeast edge of Adobe Meadows.[95] The prospectors were chased back to Aurora, but arrived safely. Still another two Paiute, reputed to be members of Joaquin Jim's band, were killed by miners in the White Mountains.[96] Even without having to contend with the Second Cavalry, the Indians were faring badly. Their luck was about to change.

In early September four horse-mounted prospectors found themselves in Round Valley—Joaquin Jim's territory—as they followed Pine Creek into the Sierra in search of timber.[97] The prospectors, members of a church group from San Francisco, had crossed into the trans-Sierra, in the belief that goodwill and generosity would win the friendship of the Indians. Now, despite having been warned by other whites of Indian

---

91. *Report of the Commissioner of Indian Affairs for the Year 1863*, p. 100; *War of the Rebellion*, vol. 50, part II, pp. 515–16, 535. Chalfant says that Captain McLaughlin without authorization sold Camp Independence to Warren Mathews and was later courtmartialed and dismissed from the service for the action. McLaughlin was courtmartialed and dismissed from the service early in 1864, but the cause of the dismissal was the misuse of government goods at Fort Tejon. McLaughlin was later cleared of any wrongdoing and his military privileges were fully restored. See the service record of Captain Moses A. McLaughlin, Company D, Second Cavalry, California Volunteers; *Records of California Men*, p. 225; *War of the Rebellion*, vol. 50, part II, p. 544; Visalia *Delta*, 17 Dec. 1863, 4 Feb. 1864; *Inyo Register*, 17 March 1904, 26 Feb. 1914.

92. *Records of California Men*, pp. 190, 191, 194.

93. Visalia *Delta*, 27 August 1863.

94. *Inyo Register*, 5 March 1914.

95. *Inyo Register*, 5 March 1914; San Francisco *Daily Evening Post*, 22 Nov. 1879.

96. *Inyo Register*, 5 March 1914.

97. Visalia *Delta*, 24 Sept. 1863; San Francisco *Daily Evening Post*, 22 Nov. 1879; Ezra D. Merriam's personal account in the Henry G. Hanks manuscript collection as quoted in the *Inyo Register*, 5 March 1914.

hostility and despite signs of Indians, they began working their way up a steep trail toward a timber-covered ridge. When they were only twenty-five yards from their destination, the quiet of the eastern Sierra was shattered by the roar of a dozen rifles. "My God, I'm shot!" cried Silas Parker as he fell from his saddle. Two bullets had ripped through his chest.

Edward Ericson, Edmund Long, and Ezra Merriam grabbed their rifles and jumped to the ground. With bullets kicking up the dirt around them, they ran to cover behind outcroppings of rock that bordered the trail. The Paiute had laid a neat ambush: they were in front and on both flanks of the prospectors. Although the Paiute rifle fire was intense, Ericson tried to assist the wounded Parker, who lay helpless in the middle of the trail. As soon as Ericson exposed himself, a round tore into his thigh. Merriam could see the blood streaming out of Ericson's leg and tried to move to another position to better cover his partner. Merriam did not get far. He missed his step and tumbled down a steep hillside to the edge of Pine Creek.

Working his way through the riparian undergrowth, Merriam finally hid in a dense clump of chaparral. He could hear rifle fire from above, but for two hours he saw no Paiute. Just when he thought he might be safe, seven Paiute appeared on the opposite bank of the creek. They motioned to others on his side of the creek and pointed to where he was concealed. Merriam sprang to his feet and raced pell-mell down the canyon. The Paiute whooped and gave chase.

For a time Merriam was able to outrun his pursuers, but gradually they began to gain on him. In desperation, he plunged into the creek. The current swept him downstream faster than the Paiute could run, but after a half mile he was carried over a waterfall and was slammed into the creek bottom. He found himself caught between two rocks, and struggle though he might, he could not free himself. With his lungs screaming for air, Merriam gave one final push. He broke free and popped to the surface. Pausing only to gulp in some air, he resubmerged and swam to shore. He discovered a small ledge of rock that jutted out from the shore just above the surface of the water. Merriam sank under the ledge until he was well hidden, leaving only his nose above the surface.

The Paiute were now swarming over both banks of the creek. They scanned Merriam's hiding spot from the opposite bank. They stood on the rock ledge under which he lay. They found his hat, which had washed ashore. Never once did they enter the stream themselves. For three hours the Paiute sat and waited and watched, and for three hours Merriam lay still and silent under the ledge. By now he had a new enemy: chilled to the bone, he was beginning to freeze to death. To move meant certain and possibly cruel death at the hands of the Paiute. Not to move meant certain death from exposure.

Suddenly the Paiute stood up and headed back upstream. Merriam relaxed but still remained hidden for another half hour before he let the current carry him downstream. He floated quietly along until he caught hold of a protruding branch. With great difficulty, he pulled himself ashore and slowly and painfully regained full use of his limbs. He hid in a canebrake until nightfall and then cautiously made his way down into the Owens Valley.

Once Merriam reached the valley, word of the attack spread rapidly. George K. Phillips, a veteran prospector from Aurora, organized a force of thirty men and established a base camp in Round Valley. Merriam guided the force to the scene of the ambush, where the stripped and bullet-riddled bodies of Edward Ericson and Edmund Long were found. Signs indicated that the two prospectors had been dragged along the trail by ropes tied around their necks. The body of Silas Parker was never found. The whites conjectured that Parker was still alive when captured and was taken to another location for torture.

The bodies of Ericson and Long were placed in shallow graves and covered with pine branches, soil, and rocks. A member of the force eloquently described what happened next:

> One man said: "Come, boys, let's go; we can do no more for the poor fellows." Then in a lower and tremulous voice he added: "God give his soul a better show than this." I have listened to long prayers in grand cathedrals, where the sunlight poured in through stained glass windows and fell on pews of carved oak, but I never heard so fervent, so touching a prayer as this, far away in this mountain land, among the pines, under the shadow of the giant Sierras, where the river, deep in the wild and rocky canyon below, murmured the requiem of the dead; where the blue sky, widespread, extends from mountain range to mountain range, over mile upon mile of valley land and wooded hills. We left them, sadly and silently, and went up to our comrades on the hill.[98]

The whites examined the scene of the ambush and then followed tracks to a Paiute camp, where they found dozens of baskets of piñon nuts, but no Paiute. They also found the bridle to Merriam's horse, and Ericson's boots and hat. A blood-splattered bullet hole in the hat told the story of Ericson's end. Each man packed as many piñon nuts as he could carry, and the rest were burned. The whites concluded that further pursuit of the Paiute would be futile and returned to the valley.

In October some five hundred Paiute, nearly half of whom were warriors, assembled at a point twenty-five miles southeast of Aurora for a great fall feast and "pine nut dances."[99] The Paiute, led by Joaquin Jim and "Captain Tom," had unknowingly camped directly in the path of a twenty-man survey team running California's eastern boundary. The surveyors made presents to the Paiute leaders, distributed food, and explained, through an interpreter, their intentions. The Paiute in reply demanded that the whites leave their arms in camp when they went out to survey. This less than subtle stratagem caused the surveyors to pack up their equipment and what was left of their provisions and head back to Aurora posthaste.

During the winter of 1863–1864 the Paiute, as in the previous winter, were relatively quiet. Nothing more than minor incidents were reported. Captain McLaughlin with a detachment of fifteen men arrived at Camp Independence in early December, but spent only a week in the valley before returning to Camp Babbitt.[100] The Paiute, in contrast to their actions in 1862 and 1863, mounted no spring offensive in 1864. But during the summer they were seen moving their women and children into the mountains, and the whites reasoned that they were contemplating a new campaign. Toward the end of July, James G. Anderson, a prospector from Aurora, was shot to death

98.   Henry G. Hanks manuscript collection as quoted in the *Inyo Register*, 5 March 1914.

99.   *Appendix to Journals of Senate and Assembly of the Fifteenth Session of the Legislature of the State of California*, "Annual Report of the Surveyor-General for the Year 1863," p. 40.

100.   *War of the Rebellion*, vol. 50, part II, p. 699; Visalia *Delta*, 17 Dec. 1863.

by Indians in his cabin along the Walker River.[101] Then another white was wounded, and a horse trader was killed and his livestock stolen.[102]

Reacting to these events, the whites formed two companies of militia after their pleas for military assistance went unheeded.[103] The militia companies visited the various Paiute camps and let it be known that if the Paiute continued killing and stealing, they would be punished without mercy. The warnings apparently had an effect; no more incidents occurred until late in the fall.

Early in November 1864, a Paiute man and woman wandered into the mining camp of A. W. Crow, Byrnes, and Mathews, three prospectors from Aurora.[104] The miners had been working their Deep Springs Valley claim, the Cinderella, since summer. They had been on friendly terms with the local Paiute and had no reason to view these two arrivals with suspicion. Mathews was cooking dinner at the time, Crow was operating the windlass to their shaft, and Byrnes was seventy feet below ground digging at the shaft bottom.

The woman asked Mathews for something to eat, and as he turned to fetch the food, the Paiute man shot him in the head. The pistol ball entered Mathews's temple and exited through his lower jaw. The Paiute left him for dead. At the same time, other Paiute opened fire on Crow, killing him instantly. Byrnes, at the bottom of the shaft, was wounded in both arms but not killed. The Paiute, not yet satisfied, hurled several hundred pounds of rock into the shaft. Byrnes somehow managed to protect himself with his shovel and then wisely played dead. Convinced that Byrnes was dead, the Paiute ransacked the camp and left.

Mathews, although horribly wounded, began to stir. Struggling to his feet, he crept over to the mine shaft, where he saw the dead form of Crow and listened for movement below. Byrnes was playing dead and trying not to make a sound, and Mathews's wound prevented him from calling to Byrnes. Moreover, the Paiute had stolen the windlass rope. Mathews, reckoning that Byrnes must have been killed, set out for the Owens Valley.

For two days Mathews, a man in his late fifties who had come to California in 1831 aboard a hide-and-tallow ship, pushed himself through the White Mountains, suffering terribly from his wound and lack of water. On the third day of his ordeal and nearing death from dehydration, he reached the Owens River and was greeted by cold, limpid water from the Sierra Nevada. Mathews could not drink a drop. His throat was so clotted with blood that swallowing was impossible. With great anguish, he decided that he might as well try to ford the Owens and push on to the settlements. He stepped into the river and promptly slipped on a rock and fell into the water. It was a lucky fall. The clot in his throat was broken loose, and he painfully drank his fill. A cowboy later spotted Mathews and carried him to a ranch near Big Pine. There Mathews slowly regained his health, if not his voice, with regular feedings administered through a cow's horn. A party of men was dispatched to the Cinderella mine, and Byrnes, who had almost given up hope after five days of suffering at the bottom of the shaft, was rescued.

101.   *Esmeralda Union*, 5 August 1864.

102.   San Francisco *Daily Evening Post*, 22 Nov. 1879; *Inyo Register*, 31 March 1904.

103.   See n. 102 and *War of the Rebellion*, vol. 50, part II, pp. 989–90, 1017.

104.   *Esmeralda Union*, 21 Nov. 1864; Visalia *Delta*, 30 Nov. 1864; *Inyo Register*, 31 March 1904.

Meanwhile, the band of Paiute responsible for the attack at the Cinderella mine raided another mine some ten miles away.[105] The miners there held the Indians at bay long enough to saddle horses and gallop madly out of camp. The Indians gave chase, but after a running fight of forty miles the whites escaped. Joaquin Jim was said to have been the leader of the Indians.

Despite these attacks the whites took no organized action against the Paiute. All was again quiet until the very end of the year. About an hour before sunrise on 31 December 1864, Mary McGuire and her six-year-old son, Johnny, and two workmen, were awakened by the noise and the light of the fire that was burning the roof of the McGuires' cabin.[106] The cabin had been built by Mary's husband, John McGuire, at Hawean Meadows (now covered by Haiwee Reservoir) as a way station on the road from Visalia to Aurora. McGuire was now away on business in Bend City, but Thomas Flanigan and Daniel Newman, two men he had hired to build an irrigation ditch, were at the cabin. They ran outside to extinguish the fire, supposing that it had occurred by accident. To their surprise, they were greeted by a hail of arrows and were driven back into the cabin.

Mary McGuire, her son, and the men now began to knock off the roof shingles from inside the cabin and to douse the flames with brine from barrels of corned beef. They had almost succeeded in controlling the fire when the Indians threw new brands onto the roof. The heat now became so intense that it was impossible for them to remain inside. The men urged Mary McGuire to take the only choice left and attempt with them to dash past the Indians. "It is of no use," she is said to have replied, "nothing can save us." Unable to persuade Mary McGuire to join them, the men dashed out of the cabin and ran for their lives. Flanigan's hat was shot off his head, and Newman was struck in the forehead by an arrow, but both men managed to reach Little Lake, some eighteen miles to the south. They were both exhausted, and Newman was near collapse from loss of blood.

In the meantime, two riders traveling from Aurora to Visalia spotted the smoke rising from the McGuire way station. They raced to the station and found Mary McGuire riddled by fourteen arrows and near death. Beside her lay her dead son, Johnny. He had been hit by six arrows, his arm had been broken, and his forehead had been bashed in by a club. The boy also had had his teeth pounded out to prevent him, as the Paiute believed, from returning after death as a wild animal who might attack an unsuspecting Indian. Mary McGuire, wounded though she was, had somehow managed to pull every one of the arrows out of her son. The two of them had evidently put up a stout defense; an ax was found alongside her body, and the boy had a stone tightly clenched in his fist, indicating that, as one settler termed it, "he died grit."

Express riders soon carried the news to the Owens Valley, Visalia, and Aurora. The whites of these areas were enraged by the killing of Mary McGuire and her son. The McGuire way station had become a landmark, and the family was liked by all. H. T. Reed, a pioneer of the southern trans-Sierra and an occasional correspondent for the Visalia *Delta*, wrote:

---

105. *Esmeralda Union*, 21 Nov. 1864.

106. Sources for the following account are the Visalia *Delta*, 11, 18, and 25 Jan. 1865, and the *Esmeralda Union*, 7 Jan. 1865.

Both Mr. and Mrs. McGuire had done more for the "Poor Indian" than they were able, often denied themselves to feed them. Her loss is deeply felt by all, and no one who has ever stopped there will fail to remember the hearty welcome and the happy face of bright, intelligent little Johnny and his noble mother. They have erected a monument in the hearts of all who knew them by their many acts of disinterested kindness, sympathy and love; and a tear is to-day coursing its way down the cheek of many a Pioneer in sympathy for the husband and father who is so cruelly bereft of all; and in memory of the loved ones so cruelly murdered.[107]

The militia companies, known as the Home Guard, now swung into action. Their cry was for extermination. A member of the Guard from Lone Pine wrote to Colonel L. W. Ransom at Camp Babbitt:

For some time past we have been compelled to let the Indians do as they please. If a white man kills an Indian he must leave the country or be imprisoned. I think things have reached the point, that either the white people must leave this Valley or the Indians killed off, or in some other way got rid of. We have fed them all Summer, and it is a pretty hard thing now, because we are unable to do it any longer on account of County Taxes, high price of living, and altogether are unable to do it any longer to have our throats cut and butchered. Only last week an Indian drew his knife on my wife because she would not let him take possession of the kitchen and give him sugar in his coffee. The bodies of the killed [Mary McGuire and her son] were brought to this place (Lone Pine) and buried. "Poor Indian" is played out with this settler.[108]

The militia followed the trail of the Indians from the smoldering ruins of the McGuire cabin to a camp on the eastern shore of Owens Lake. At daybreak on 5 January 1865 the whites attacked. The Indians were taken by complete surprise—they had as usual not posted sentries—and some thirty-five of them, including women and children, were killed.[109] John McGuire himself got some measure of revenge by killing two Paiute men.[110] Only two girls and a boy were spared.

Soon after this slaughter, seventeen Paiute were killed near Taboose ranch in the foothills of the eastern Sierra.[111] In several other scattered incidents Paiute were killed, including two who had evidently taken part in the Cinderella mine attack. These latter two were first captured—one of them with A. W. Crow's gun on him (Crow was the prospector killed at the Cinderella mine)—and put under guard at Lone Pine. A local settler wrote the night of the capture that the Indians "will hardly see the sun rise to-morrow."[112] He was right.

107. Visalia *Delta*, 18 Jan. 1865.
108. Visalia *Delta*, 11 Jan. 1865.
109. *Esmeralda Union*, 18 Jan. 1865.
110. *Inyo Register*, 26 March 1914.
111. San Francisco *Daily Evening Post*, 22 Nov. 1879.
112. Visalia *Delta*, 11 Jan. 1865.

9. During the 1860s and 1870s, way stations sprang up throughout the trans-Sierra country. These "truck stops" of the nineteenth century provided meals and lodging for teamsters and hay for their horses—or, as in this photograph, for their twenty-mule teams. Indians burned John McGuire's station at Haween Meadows to the ground. (Credit: Los Angeles County Museum of Natural History)

Ironically, now that the Indians of the southern trans-Sierra had been dealt these blows, the army returned. On 13 January 1865, Captain John G. Kelly, a former Pony Express rider who had won his army commission in a poker game with Nevada governor James Nye, arrived at Bishop Creek with Company C, First Nevada Infantry, and on 1 April began the reoccupation of Camp Independence.[113] Violent conflict between Indians and whites was nearly over. There would only be a few more incidents during 1865.

On 28 February 1865, J. N. Rogers, an Owens Valley rancher who had participated in the slaughter of the Indians at Owens Lake in January, was attacked by a band of Indians as he drove his wagon loaded with hay by Hell's Gate, four miles north of McGuire's way station.[114] Rogers took off on foot, reasoning that the Indians were more interested in his horses and hay than in him. Several of the Indians rushed for his wagon, but most of them followed him. He managed to hold the Indians at bay by pausing now and then to shoot at them with his revolver. Wounded a half-dozen times by arrows and nearly exhausted from loss of blood, Rogers reached Little Lake six hours later.

The very next day two prospectors from Aurora, Robert Rabe and Isaac Stewart, were killed by Paiute near Walker Lake.[115] According to the report of a friendly Indian, the men were taken by complete surprise. Rabe was lighting a campfire when he was shot in the back and killed, and Stewart was scouting the route the prospectors would take the next morning, when the Paiute swept down on him. The four horses the prospectors had with them were probably the cause of the attack, although the *Esmeralda Union* noted that Stewart had flogged an Indian some time earlier, and this may have inspired the Indians to seek revenge.

During the summer of 1865 Indians burned the Willow Springs, Lotta, and Union mills and wounded one miner.[116] This was the last gasp of Paiute resistance. Sometime during the winter of 1865–1866, Joaquin Jim died near the Casa Diablo geysers in Long Valley. His death was evidently a natural one, although one report had him killed the previous winter by other Indians.[117] Without the forceful leadership of the redoubtable firebrand, the Paiute had little hope of ever again launching a major or even a minor offensive against the whites. Disturbances generally ceased in the trans-Sierra country, although isolated incidents were reported in remote mountain areas for another two years.

John Shipe, a prospector and trapper who had perhaps gone a little mad, continued to hunt down and kill Paiute who had fled to the mountains.[118] Shipe had been one of those with Frank Whetson when the white men killed and scalped three Paiute who were on their way to Camp Independence to surrender in July 1863. The white men had claimed at that time that the killings were retribution for four of their partners who had been killed by Paiute. Shipe continued the apparent vendetta against the Paiute until his death in 1867. Squads of soldiers were frequently sent to arrest him, but they were never successful.

113. San Francisco *Daily Evening Post*, 22 Nov. 1879.

114. Visalia *Delta*, 15 March 1865.

115. *Esmeralda Union*, 11 March 1865; Angel, *History of Nevada*, pp. 169–70.

116. San Francisco *Daily Evening Post*, 22 Nov. 1879.

117. *Daily Evening Post*, 22 Nov. 1879; *Esmeralda Union*, 7 Jan. 1865.

118. *Daily Evening Post*, 22 Nov. 1879; *Inyo Register*, 20 Sept. 1906.

Camp Independence was occupied until the summer of 1877, when it was abandoned for good. Captain Noble and Company E, Second Cavalry, California Volunteers replaced Captain Kelly and Company C, First Nevada Infantry, during November 1865.[119] Captain Noble and his outfit remained there until May 1866, when they were replaced by regulars who had served under General Philip Sheridan. These hardened veterans of the Civil War had the last two known clashes with the Indians. In August 1866 they killed several warriors on the eastern side of Owens Lake and took many prisoners, and in March 1867 they routed a band of Indians who had attacked miners at Coso.

Conflict between Indians and whites in the southern trans-Sierra cost the lives of no less than two hundred Indians and thirty whites; perhaps another hundred Indians and whites were wounded. Nearly a thousand Indians were removed to reservations. The conflict paralleled the rise and decline of Aurora. The first killings occurred in 1861, full-scale warfare in 1862 and 1863, a rapid tapering off of conflict in 1864, and a final few sparks in 1865 and 1866.

The cattle drives to Aurora first aroused Paiute curiosity, and then the stocking of the range land of the Owens Valley ignited the war. The Paiute initially attacked only the cattlemen, but soon turned on prospectors as well. Aurora was the outfitting center and point of departure for these prospectors who, after the Esmeralda strike, were roaming the southern trans-Sierra in ever greater numbers. The whites' activities of cattle grazing and mining were not compatible with the Paiute way of life. Conflict could have been avoided only if whites had been kept out of the region or if the Indians would have voluntarily abandoned their customary way of life and become a reservation-settled agricultural people.

Indian agents Warren Wasson and John P. H. Wentworth thought that the Paiute should and could become farmers. The Paiute, however, were a hunting and gathering people, and food gathering was the job of the women, not the men. That men from Joaquin Jim's band, or any other band for that matter, would have voluntarily become farmers toiling behind plows was a less than realistic assumption; that they *should* have done so was nothing more than ethnocentricism and paternalism on the part of Wasson and Wentworth. For their part, the Paiute, though they did not accept the philosophy of the Indian agents, did accept the agents' gifts and rations as tribute and must have thought that the white man was either cowed, terribly gullible, or stupid.

The warfare that occurred in the trans-Sierra country was not unlike that which occurred elsewhere in California and the American West.[120] The Paiute fought as individual bands with only an occasional coordinated effort. They had little sense of strategy and no logistical support to sustain a protracted fight against the white invaders. The Paiute could possibly have held back the white advance for years if they could have developed an overall plan of defense, unity of command, and a system of supply. Expecting the Paiute to have made such developments, however, is as unrealistic as expecting them to have voluntarily become farmers. The various bands of Paiute were fiercely independent and only rarely came together for a common purpose. The intelli-

119. *Records of California Men*, p. 191.

120. See, e.g., Keith A. Murray, *The Modocs and Their War*; Lafayette H. Bunnell, *Discovery of the Yosemite and the Indian War of 1851*; C. Gregory Crampton, ed., *The Mariposa Indian War, 1850–1851*; Paul I. Wellman, *The Indian Wars of the West*; Carl C. Rister, *Border Command: General Phil Sheridan in the West*; George A. Custer, *My Life on the Plains*; John G. Bourke, *On the Border with Crook*; Robert M. Utley and Wilcomb E. Washburn, *The Indian Wars*; Don Russell, "How Many Indians Were Killed."

10. *White ranchers quickly replaced the Paiute in the Owens Valley. This family squatted on land near Independence. (Credit: Southwest Museum)*

11. *Many Paiute were still living in their traditional huts—albeit with some modern modifications—into the twentieth century. This family of Owens Valley Paiute is being visited by the local schoolmarm. (Credit: Los Angeles County Museum of Natural History)*

gent and resourceful Joaquin Jim came as close as anyone to being a commanding general, but even his influence seldom extended beyond his own band.

The Paiute were superb at laying ambushes and hit-and-run raiding, but they attacked only when they had a significant advantage and little chance of losses. Individual whites or small groups of whites were prized targets. Citizen militia and the United States Army were generally to be avoided. The Paiute evidently did not believe that it was courageous or glorious to die in battle. Their purpose was to kill their enemy, but only if they could do so without harm to themselves. The Battle of the Ditch was just one of several examples in which the Paiute could have overrun and annihilated the whites if they had been willing to suffer a substantial number of casualties.

The Paiute were nearly always outgunned. They did have some guns, but not nearly enough to arm more than a small number of their men. Moreover, the guns were mostly old, smooth-bore muzzle loaders.[121] One trooper who served in the Owens Valley war with the Second Cavalry noted that arrows fired by the Indians often had more force than the lead balls of the muzzle loaders.[122] This was probably caused by improper charging. The Paiute did not have an adequate supply of gunpowder. Nor did they have enough lead to make bullets, as evidenced by the theft of lead pipe from the mining camp of Ida. Moreover, the Paiute did not regularly clean their firearms. In one battle their guns became so fouled that they had to force bullets down the gun barrels by pounding the ramrods with stones.

Perhaps more important for the Paiute than lack of unity, strategy, and weaponry was lack of food. Since their food supply depended on hunting and gathering in the less than bountiful trans-Sierra country, the Paiute could not cache enough food to wage a long war against the white invaders. The whites, especially the United States Army, quickly learned that destroying Paiute food caches was tantamount to destroying the Paiute themselves, proving once again that it is easier to starve a fierce enemy into submission than to fight him. This led to the so-called surrender of Captain George and others after spring and summer raids. The Paiute would then live off the white man's rations during the fall and winter, only to renew warfare with the coming of spring. When they had exhausted their food supplies, they would return to Camp Independence and again make "peace." Many whites found it impossible to accept this cyclical status of the Indians, and some, such as Frank Whetson and his partners, shot down Paiute who were under a flag of truce.

Although the Paiute never intentionally took prisoners, a white captured alive was a great prize because he could then be tortured. Ironically, the most famous torture victim was not a white but a black, Charley Tyler, who was tortured for three days and then roasted to death. Almost all white corpses were found stripped of clothing and mutilated. Scalps were taken, and in a few instances whites reciprocated in kind. Torture was not something the Indians reserved for the whites. Long before any whites set foot in California, Paiute and other Indians had practiced torture.[123]

The war saw possibly the first manifestation of the Ghost Dance. The group of Paiute that danced around the cabins and sheds of the San Francis Ranch and proclaimed

---

121. *Inyo Register*, 20 Sept. 1906.

122. *Inyo Register*, 22 Feb. 1900.

123. Kroeber, *Handbook of the Indians of California*, esp. pp. 400, 468–69, 633, 843–44. Torture did not play the important role among California Indians that it played among Indians in other regions of North America. See, e.g., Anthony F. C. Wallace, *The Death and Rebirth of the Seneca*, esp. pp. 103–7, and Richard Irving Dodge, *The Hunting Grounds of the Great West*, esp. p. 422.

that they could spit out any bullets that might enter their bodies were performing a ritual that would eventually spread to the Sioux on the northern Plains. Wodziwob, the tribal shaman of the Mono Lake Paiute, was probably responsible for the demonstration at the San Francis Ranch. It is no accident that one of his followers, Tavibo, was the father of Wovoka—the Indian messiah and leader of the Ghost Dance during the late 1880s and early 1890s.[124]

The Second Cavalry, California Volunteers, bore the brunt of the fighting for the United States Army. The outfit consisted entirely of volunteers from California and Nevada and, like other Civil War units, had a large number of Irish immigrants and first-generation Irish-Americans. These men were encouraged to enlist by promises of active service in the East. Instead, they served their country chasing Indians in the southern trans-Sierra. Although they considered it less than glorious duty and were paid only seven dollars a month, desertions were surprisingly few.

Just as surprising, the officers proved highly capable. Captain Moses A. McLaughlin was an able and aggressive commander who quickly turned the tide against the Indians. His ruthless slaughter of the Indian prisoners at Whiskey Flat was characteristic of the man who crossed into the trans-Sierra with only one purpose in mind: eliminate the Indian menace. Within a couple of months he had nearly accomplished that goal. Indian raids were only sporadic affairs after McLaughlin's stay at Camp Independence, and the war for the Owens Valley was over.

Citizen militia also played a significant role in the fighting. The first volunteer company was raised in Aurora and included Sheriff N. F. Scott, who died in the Battle of the Ditch. In nearly every fight civilians aided the military, and in the final major confrontation it was two Owens Valley civilian militia companies that routed the Paiute. The civilians, many of whom had had friends or loved ones killed or wounded in Indian attacks, proved more ruthless than the military. Whereas the army often took Indian prisoners and, with only one exception, treated the captives humanely, the civilians rarely did so. On several occasions civilians shot down Paiute women and children, although the army restricted its targets to men.

Since the whites were trespassers in Paiute territory, ultimate responsibility for the conflict lay with the whites. The whites were, in effect, invading foreign territory. From the perspective of the whites, however, there appeared to be ample room for settlement. There were no Paiute farms, no ranches, no mines, no industry, no roads or bridges, no permanent settlements. Paiute were only occasionally sighted and then only in small groups. The land generally appeared to the whites as if it were uninhabited or only very sparsely settled. The whites did not comprehend that the Paiute were already, as required by their way of life, utilizing the land to its fullest capacity. Nor did the whites comprehend that stocking the range lands with cattle would force the Paiute to either abandon their way of life or fight against white encroachment. Most Paiute chose to fight.

---

124. In 1885 Wovoka, Jack Wilson to the white ranchers of the Walker River country, began having visions of a cataclysm that would cover the earth with a new layer of soil, sweet grass, and great herds of buffalo. Whites would be buried under the new soil; Indians who performed the Ghost Dance would be lifted into the sky and suspended there until the cataclysm was over; dead Indian warriors would be brought back to life. By 1890 Wovoka had become, for the Indians, the Messiah, and the Ghost Dance and the wearing of Ghost Shirts, to repel bullets, had spread to the Sioux on the northern Plains. The United States Army thought the Ghost Dance a threat to security and made moves to suppress it, which eventually led to the Wounded Knee massacre. See note 15 of this chapter.

3

POLITICS, THE
CIVIL WAR, AND
THE BOUNDARY

Politics, the Civil War, and the location of California's eastern boundary were sources of lawlessness and violence in Aurora. An assassination attempt, a duel, numerous beatings and stabbings, several cases of voting fraud, and a legal battle between Mono and Esmeralda counties were directly related to the white-hot political disputes of the Civil War and to the question whether Aurora was located in California or in Nevada. Aurora was nearly three years old before its exact location was finally determined, and its boom years, 1861–1865, coincided with the Civil War.

As early as 1860 enough miners were prospecting in the southern trans-Sierra country to petition the California legislature to create a new county in the state.[1] During the winter of 1861 the growing town of Aurora had joined in the drive for a new county. Since Nevada Territory had not yet been created, the Aurorans applied to the California legislature. They had no intention of becoming part of Mormon Utah. "The people of the district," one Auroran contended, "have decided on applying to the California Legislature for a new county, to be called Mono, saving a large portion of the citizens from being victims of anarchy, or still worse, of being subjected to the hated and oppressive laws of Utah."[2]

Early in 1861 bills were introduced into both the California senate and assembly to create a new county in the trans-Sierra.[3] Inasmuch as Aurora was booming and the population was swelling, there was no opposition to the bills. The only conflict came over the name of the proposed county. The senate preferred "Esmeralda," and the assembly favored "Mono." After a short debate, the Indian name Mono was chosen, and on 24 March 1861 the bill became law.[4] This same law designated Aurora the coun-

1. *California Senate Journal, 1860*, p. 317.

2. W. A. Chalfant, *Outposts of Civilization*, pp. 54–55.

3. *California Senate Journal, 1861*, p. 312; *California Assembly Journal, 1861*, pp. 243–70.

4. *California Senate Journal, 1861*, pp. 312, 343, 546; *California Assembly Journal, 1861*, pp. 319, 348, 606, 615; *California Statutes, 1861*, p. 235. The meaning of the Indian name Mono is not positively known. A few have claimed that it is nothing more than the Spanish word *mono*, meaning monkey. Others argue that it derives from *monai* or *monoyi*, Yokut words meaning fly or flies. The most likely explanation for this

ty seat and provided for an election to be held for county officials (with the exception of the county judge, who was to be appointed by the governor) on 1 June 1861. For purposes of representation in the state legislature the new county was attached to Tuolumne County.

The Mono County bill defined the western boundary of the county as the "summit of the Sierra Nevada Mountains" and the eastern boundary as the "eastern boundary of the State."[5] Aurora, naturally, was considered to lie west of the state line. California legislators had relied on Clayton's map of the Esmeralda mining district, which indicated that the diggings and the nascent town of Aurora were in California.[6] Clayton's map, however, was not the product of an official survey of California's eastern boundary. The boundary, although it had been established in California's state constitutional convention in 1849 and was well defined on paper, had not yet been formally surveyed and marked with monuments. To remedy this situation the California legislature on 26 March 1861—just two days after Mono County had been created—appointed a commissioner to cooperate with the U.S. surveyor in locating the boundary line and appropriated $10,000 for expenses.[7]

Meanwhile, on 2 March 1861, President James Buchanan, in one of his last official acts, signed into law a bill creating the Territory of Nevada. The bill defined Nevada's western boundary as "the dividing ridge separating the waters of Carson Valley from those that flow into the Pacific."[8] Because the crest of the Sierra and not California's eastern boundary was made the western boundary of Nevada, a proviso was added to the bill that California would have to "assent" to the loss of her trans-Sierra lands before they could officially become part of Nevada. The trans-Sierra would be a bone of contention between California and Nevada for the next three years.

Aurorans responded to the organization of Nevada Territory immediately. In early April 1861 a petition asking the California legislature "to cut this piece of her territory off and let it become part of Nevada" was circulated in Aurora.[9] Within one day, however, another petition was circulated, which pled for "a speedy county organization in California." The supporters of this second petition asserted that they had the greater number of signatures. Several fights broke out over the issue as it became obvious that the allegiance of Aurorans was deeply divided between California and Nevada.

For the time being, California was clearly the leader in the race to organize the Esmeralda mining district. The election for Mono County officers was set for the first of June, and the newly appointed governor of Nevada, James W. Nye, was not expected in the territory until July. By early May political activity was causing a good deal of excite-

---

derivation was the Mono practice of eating fly larvae, which they found in abundance at Mono and Owens lakes. Another possibility is that the Yokut, who lived in the San Joaquin Valley and the foothills of the Sierra Nevada, thought the Mono could scale the granite cliffs of the Sierra as the fly walks up the wall of a house. The Mono called themselves Numu, meaning simply "persons." See A. L. Kroeber, *Handbook of the Indians of California*, p. 584.

5. *California Statutes, 1861*, p. 235.

6. Visalia *Delta*, 2 Feb. 1861.

7. *California Statutes, 1861*, pp. 235–38; Myron Angel, ed., *History of Nevada*, p. 402.

8. *United States Statutes at Large*, XII, pp. 209–10.

9. Visalia *Delta*, 11 May 1861. The source for the following quoted matter is the *Delta* of 11 and 28 May and 6 June 1861.

ment in Aurora. Politicians, noted one miner, "are floating around with great alacrity at present, in anticipation of the coming election." Two weeks later the same miner noted that "numerous candidates soliciting the suffrages of the people hourly appear in their peculiar winning capacities, to captivate the votes of the dear people—7 for Sheriff—5 for Clerk, and a myriad for the smaller offices, at present constitute the number of individuals that are in this age of self-sacrifice willing to immolate themselves upon the altar for their country's good."

The town was also stirring with news of the secession of the southern states. In response, a number of Aurorans erected a flagpole and unfurled the Stars and Stripes. "Not a voice was raised," asserted one of the participants in the flag raising, "in opposition to this insignia of our people's continuous love and fidelity to the Union and the laws. Such is the strength of the Union sentiment here, that all candidates who avow a sympathy for the Jeff Davis traitorism, will receive not hardly a single vote." Considered in light of subsequent events, this statement was a bold exaggeration.

On 1 June 1861, N. F. Scott was elected Mono County sheriff, Richard M. Wilson, clerk, R. E. Phelps, district attorney, J. H. Smith, assessor, William Feast, treasurer, and L. Tuttle, surveyor. Charles R. Worland, Edmund Green, and J. S. Schultz were chosen county supervisors, and the governor of California appointed J. A. Moutrie county judge.[10] Most Aurorans celebrated the election by getting drunk. "We have just organized our county," commented a wry Auroran, "and think we have a pretty fair set of officers—they can all drink plenty of whiskey—but whether they can steal or not remains to be seen, and that is a qualification for a California officer."[11]

Not everybody in Aurora was happy with the election results, however. Since several of the newly elected officers were Democrats, Aurora Republicans were disgruntled and now generally fell into the pro-Nevada camp. Although the distinction was sometimes blurred, Democrats usually favored allegiance to California, which had been strongly Democratic throughout the 1850s, while Republicans favored Nevada. The leading Republican and advocate of Nevada annexation in town was Samuel Youngs, a veteran of the California gold rush, former member of the New York state assembly, and an erstwhile colonel in the New York state militia. Youngs had arrived in Aurora in late November 1860, making him one of the town's pioneers.

When the Civil War erupted, Youngs, an ardent Unionist, sent a request to a friend in the East to mail him the Stars and Stripes. He received the flag on 3 June 1861 and at daybreak of the following morning hoisted it over his cabin. Three weeks later he posted notices around town calling for a gathering of Unionists, and in an evening meeting on 29 June 1861 the "Esmeralda Union Club" was formed. Not surprisingly, Youngs chaired the meeting and wrote the club's constitution. The meeting, according to Youngs, was well attended by enthusiastic Unionists, who concluded the evening's business with patriotic songs. A week later, at the next meeting of the Union Club, Youngs was elected the club president.[12] Despite hard work by Youngs, the Democrats of Aurora completed their organization ahead of the Republicans. On 18 June 1861, the Democrats had formed the "Aurora Club," which included among its members the dis-

10. Angel, *History of Nevada*, p. 401; California, Historical Records Survey Project, *Inventory of the County Archives of California, No. 27, Mono County*, p. 7.

11. Visalia *Delta*, 4 July 1861.

12. Samuel Youngs's Journal, 25 Nov. 1860, 29 June and 6 July 1861.

trict attorney, R. E. Phelps, and the justice of the peace, Timothy Machin.[13] Their meetings were also said to be well attended.

When Governor James W. Nye arrived in Carson City in July 1861, Youngs met personally with him.[14] At that meeting and in a subsequent letter, Youngs urged the governor to lay claim to Aurora. Youngs contended that Aurorans were "very earnestly in favor of getting clear of our present county officers, who before the Election declared themselves good Union men and since have shown the 'Old Leaven' or 'Cloven Foot,' talking and acting very badly. All that we now require is to give them their deserts—*it is all important* to have the line run between this [Aurora] and California. . . . When you order the election for a Legislature if you give us the opportunity we will elect and send a *good Union* Representative."[15]

On 24 July 1861, Governor Nye proclaimed that a general election for members of the territorial legislature was to be held on 31 August 1861.[16] Nye also divided Nevada into election districts and, disregarding California's claim to Aurora, made Aurora part of District One. The district was entitled to one councilman and two representatives. In the August election, Dr. John W. Pugh easily won the seat for the Nevada territorial council, and Samuel Youngs and William E. Teall were elected by large margins to the Nevada house of representatives.[17] All three were staunch Republicans and residents of Aurora, which was, of course, the county seat of Mono County, California.

Meanwhile, on 26 August 1861 the voters of California, which included Aurorans, went to the polls. Mono County, together with Tuolumne County, elected Leander Quint, a Union Democrat, to the state senate, and B. K. Davis, a Breckinridge Democrat, to the assembly.[18] Republicans were outraged. Youngs called Tuolumne and Mono counties "Sodom" and urged Governor Nye to have the boundary surveyed so that Sodom would be "struck from the territory."[19] The defeated Republican candidates for the assembly and the senate, Nelson M. Orr and Joseph M. Cavis, protested the election when they discovered that the Mono County supervisors had created an imaginary election district in the White Mountains and then stuffed the ballot box with false returns.[20] The first of many voting frauds had occurred.

The Nevada territorial legislature first met on 1 October 1861.[21] In November the legislature created Esmeralda County and made Aurora the county seat.[22] California, however, had no intention of relinquishing her claim to Aurora, and the town now

---

13. Visalia *Delta*, 4 July 1861.

14. Samuel Youngs's Journal, 18 July 1861.

15. Samuel Youngs to James W. Nye, 24 July 1861, Unsorted Territorial Correspondence, Nevada Division of Archives.

16. Angel, *History of Nevada*, p. 78.

17. Angel, pp. 78–79; Samuel Youngs to James W. Nye, 19 Sept. 1861, Unsorted Territorial Correspondence.

18. *Inventory of the County Archives of California, No. 27, Mono County*, p. 8.

19. Samuel Youngs to James W. Nye, 19 Sept. 1861, Unsorted Territorial Correspondence.

20. *California Senate Journal, 1861*, pp. 325–38, 346–55; "Report of Testimony Taken before the Senate Committee on Elections in the Contested Election Case. Joseph M. Cavis, Contestant, against Leander Quint, Respondent," *Appendix to Journals of Senate and Assembly, 1861*.

21. *Laws of Nevada Territory, 1861*, p. 168; *Nevada Council Journal, 1861*, p. 1.

22. *Laws of Nevada Territory, 1861*, p. 269; Angel, *History of Nevada*, p. 402.

became the county seat for two different counties in two different states. To avoid conflict with California, the Nevada territorial legislature exempted Esmeralda County from an act that required election of county officers throughout the territory on 14 January 1862 and empowered Governor Nye to appoint officers and organize the county whenever he deemed it appropriate to do so. The legislature also appropriated $1,000 for the survey of the California-Nevada boundary from Lake Bigler (Tahoe) to Aurora.[23]

Governor Nye now announced before the territorial legislature that he would lobby in California for approval of a Sierra crest boundary. Governor Nye's message implied that a tactful approach, emphasizing the "natural frontier" of the Sierra, would result in California's yielding the trans-Sierra portion of her "vast domain."[24] Two commissioners, Isaac Roop, former governor of the provisional Nevada territory and now a territorial councilman from Susanville, and R. M. Ford, a territorial representative from Silver City, were chosen to accompany Nye. Meanwhile, the San Francisco press began to protest the proposed transfer of territory.[25] Its concern was focused on the Esmeralda mines, which were thought by some to be richer than those of the Comstock Lode.

To prepare the way for Governor Nye and commissioners Roop and Ford, the Nevada legislature forwarded a memorial to the California legislature. "The people of Nevada," the memorial said in part, "beseech their generous and powerful neighbor to grant the prayers of a weaker commonwealth."[26] On the evening of 21 March 1862, a special joint session of the California legislature heard the Nevada memorial read by Ford, a detailed discussion of the boundary question, and presentation of annexation petitions (i.e., trans-Sierra settlers wishing to be annexed to Nevada) by Roop, and an eloquent plea by Nye. Nye noted the continual conflicts over jurisdiction, the excessive cost of an accurate survey, and the haven for desperadoes which the trans-Sierra border zone provided. California's arbitrary, straight-line boundary, Nye contended, was to blame; a natural boundary following the crest of the Sierra would solve these problems. Nye closed his plea by contrasting "California's glistening seacoast" with "Nevada's frowning desert from which was extracted the wealth that flowed into the lap of a prosperous San Francisco! Why shouldn't a magnanimous neighbor surrender a narrow strip of land in exchange for the silver of the Nevada mines?"[27]

The appeal of the Nevada delegation was not without effect. A bill to cede to Nevada all lands east of the Sierra crest was introduced in the California legislature. The legislature was reluctant, however, to part with the revenue from the mines (primarily in the Esmeralda district), taxable farmland (mostly in the Honey Lake Valley), and the yellow-pine forests (found on the eastern Sierra slopes) of the trans-Sierra region. Also, the construction of a projected trans-Sierra railroad would be complicated by the boundary change. Furthermore, the legislature maintained that because the boundary of California was defined by the state constitution, an amendment would be needed to change it, a process which would take three years. In a futile last-ditch stand,

23. *Laws*, p. 269; Angel, p. 402.

24. *Nevada Council Journal, 1861*, pp. 97, 113, 115; San Francisco *Daily Evening Bulletin*, 31 Oct. 1861.

25. *Daily Evening Bulletin*, 1 and 14 Nov. 1861, 21 March 1862; *Daily Alta California*, 22 and 25 March 1862.

26. *California Senate Journal, 1862*, p. 387.

27. *Daily Alta California*, 22 March 1862.

Nye argued that the federal government took precedence over the California constitution, and that since Congress had already defined the boundary in the organic act which created Nevada territory, all that remained was for California to "assent to the same."

California withheld her assent, and in late March 1862 the commissioners returned to Nevada. Nevada then failed in an attempt to have the boundary of the organic act legalized in Congress without California's assent.[28] For the moment, Nevada was defeated. Mono County officers continued to govern Esmeralda, and the California legislature continued to grant toll and water franchises for the area.[29] When the Esmeralda Rangers, Aurora's first of two Civil War militia companies, was organized on 2 April 1862, it was incorporated under California law and included in the Third Brigade, California Militia.[30]

Some Aurorans still held out hope that California might cede its trans-Sierra lands, but most realized that the issue would be resolved only when the boundary was surveyed. Those who favored California sovereignty, usually Democrats, contended that the boundary line ran northeast of Aurora through the "Five Mile House," while the pro-Nevada faction, normally Republicans, asserted that the line ran southwest of Aurora through Bodie.

The Civil War intensified the division over the boundary. Republicans were strongly pro-Union, of course, whereas many Democrats in Aurora sympathized with the plight of the South, and some were what onetime Aurora miner and later Nevada governor Roswell K. Colcord called "rank Secessionists."[31] This latter group included L. B. Hopkins, the superintendent of the Real Del Monte mine, R. B. Sanchez, mayor of Aurora and president of the town's principal bank, and several prominent mining figures.

During the spring of 1862, the Confederate sympathizers of Aurora began to hold meetings and rallies as the town became a regional center for pro-secessionists. Word of their actions reached Colonel (later General) Patrick Edward Connor, commander of the military district of Utah. On 6 August 1862, Connor issued "Order No. 1" from Fort Churchill, Nevada. It read:

> Being credibly informed that there are in this district persons who, while claiming and receiving protection to life and property, are endeavoring to destroy and defame the principles and institutions of our Government. . . . It is therefore most rigidly enjoined upon all commanders of posts, camps and detachments, to cause to be promptly arrested and closely confined until they have taken the oath of allegiance to the Government of the United States, all persons who from this date, shall be guilty of uttering sentiments against the Government, and upon the repetition of the offense, to be again arrested and confined until the fact shall be communicated to these headquarters. Traitors shall not utter treasonable sentiments in this district with impunity, but must seek some more congenial soil, or receive the punishment they so richly merit.[32]

28. *House Journal, 1861–1862,* 37th Cong., 2nd Sess., p. 616; *Congressional Globe,* 37th Cong., 2nd Sess., p. 1847.

29. *Inventory of the County Archives of California, No. 27, Mono County,* p. 9.

30. *Report of the Adjutant-General of the State of California from May 1, 1864 to November 30, 1865,* p. 15.

31. R. K. Colcord, "Reminiscences of Life in Territorial Nevada," p. 118.

32. Angel, *History of Nevada,* p. 266.

Aurora's secessionists decided to put Colonel Connor's order to the test. The *Esmeralda Star* reported that on Saturday night, 16 August 1862, "a band of rebels made a complete pandemonium of our town, and continued their hideous orgies until late on Sunday morning, cheering for Jeff Davis, Stonewall Jackson and the Southern Confederacy."[33] The "rebels" took particular delight in hooting and cheering for the Confederacy in the presence of Lieutenant Herman Noble of Company A, Second Cavalry, California Volunteers, who was in Aurora to regain his health after fighting Paiute in the Owens Valley. Because Lieutenant Noble's company was camped some twenty-five miles south of town at Adobe Meadows, Noble called upon the Esmeralda Rangers to help him arrest the troublemakers. The most outspoken of the Confederate sympathizers, Augustus Quinton, was arrested and after a brief fight was dragged off to the county jail.

Sheriff G. W. Bailey, however, would not allow Quinton to remain in jail without a warrant for his arrest or a written order from Fort Churchill. Consequently, Quinton was removed to the Rangers' armory in the Wingate Building. In the meantime, Aurora secessionists were gathering arms, buying ammunition, and molding bullets. The word was out that they planned to rescue Quinton. In response, Minié-ball muskets were distributed to all the members of the Rangers as well as to volunteer Union men, the guard over the prisoner was doubled, and the town was put on alert. These preparations evidently dissuaded the Confederate sympathizers from any violence, and except for a few barroom fights, the night passed quietly.

On Monday morning, the entire company of Rangers with colors flying marched Quinton out onto Pine Street and formed a hollow square around him. Lieutenant Noble administered the loyalty oath to Quinton and then told the assembled townspeople that the prisoner was but a tool in the hands of others, who had incited him to cheer for traitors on a test of Colonel Connor's order. The next violators of the order, warned Lieutenant Noble, would not get off so easily.

The *Esmeralda Star*, edited by Edwin A. Sherman, a vehement Unionist who had served in the Mexican War as a major in the army, hoped that Quinton's arrest would "prove a salutary lesson to those who would insult our flag or defy the authority of the Government." Without mentioning any names, the paper contended that there were traitors in Aurora who had given the rebels aid and comfort, but that the traitors were now exposed and would be closely watched. "Traitors have come in here from other quarters," concluded the *Star*, "but they will find this to be too hot a Union community for any of their kind, and the sooner they get out of it the better it will be for them, and if they remain we expect to enjoy the explicit pleasure in a few days of administering to them the oath of allegiance."

The *Star*'s editorial on top of the public humiliation was evidently too much for "Gus" Quinton. After stewing for a month, he attacked Sherman while the latter was walking past Haskell's saloon on the evening of 18 September 1862.[34] Quinton stepped out of the saloon, knocked the *Star*'s editor to the ground with a cane, then drew his revolver and took aim. When Sherman heard the clicking of the gun as it was cocked, he leaped to the side. Quinton fired and the round hit Sherman in the leg. Not

33.   The following account is drawn from the *Esmeralda Star*, 23 August 1862, as reprinted in the Visalia *Delta*, 2 Sept. 1862; and Angel, *History of Nevada*, pp. 266–67.

34.   *Esmeralda Star*, 20 Sept. 1862; Visalia *Delta*, 2 Oct. 1862; *Sacramento Daily Union*, 23 Sept. 1862.

pausing to fire a second shot, Quinton ran to his horse, sprang into the saddle, and galloped out of town.

The attack did not silence Sherman. Two days later he wrote that the *Star* would continue "to express our sentiments for the Union and against rebels and traitors."[35] Although Sherman believed that Quinton was merely the hired tool of powerful and covert secessionists in Aurora, he argued that Quinton had broken his oath, that death would be his military penalty if he were captured, and that no writ of habeas corpus could save his neck. Tempers were now flaring in Aurora, and fights were frequent. In one scuffle a "secessionist" slashed a "Union man" rather badly with a knife.[36]

Territorial elections were held throughout Nevada in September. However, Governor Nye had not yet organized Esmeralda County, so no election of county officers was held there, and Mono County officers continued unopposed. There was, nevertheless, an election in Esmeralda County for four seats to the territorial house of representatives. Arthur M. McKeel, Joseph W. Calder, John S. Ross, and A. D. Allen emerged victorious.[37] Allen resigned before he took his seat, and Esmeralda had but three representatives during the second session of the territorial legislature. The representatives were all "good Union men," although the ballot box in the White Mountain precinct had been stuffed in an attempt to elect Confederate sympathizers.[38] The *Esmeralda Star* of 20 September 1862, alluding to the election fraud of 1861, wryly commented that the precinct was noted for "rolling up vast invisible majorities . . . through the agency of secesh mediums." In reality, a group of well-armed Aurorans carrying poll-lists had ridden to the precinct and enrolled every Indian they could find. The Indians, who included Joaquin Jim, were bribed with "mucha hogady" (much food) and led to the polls to vote a "secesh" ticket.

During the fall of 1862, Aurorans who favored Nevada sovereignty exerted ever greater pressure on Governor Nye to organize Esmeralda County. On 2 December 1862 Nevada's territorial legislature passed a joint resolution that requested Nye to organize the county.[39] His only response was the appointment of William M. Dixon as district attorney of Esmeralda County.[40]

Governor Nye's reluctance to organize Esmeralda County was caused by border problems which had arisen in the Honey Lake Valley. There, Nevada had gone ahead and organized Roop County out of territory claimed and governed by Plumas County, California. This conflict of jurisdiction led to the "Sagebrush war" in which several men were wounded and relations between Nevada and California were severely strained.[41]

35. *Esmeralda Star*, 20 Sept. 1862.

36. *Sacramento Daily Union*, 23 Sept. 1862.

37. Angel, *History of Nevada*, p. 402.

38. *Esmeralda Star*, 20 Sept. 1862.

39. *Laws of Nevada Territory, 1862*, Resolution No. 1, p. 193.

40. Angel, *History of Nevada*, p. 402.

41. For a complete account of the "Sagebrush war," see "Report of Sheriff of Plumas County," and "Report of Joint Committee at Susanville," in the *California Senate Journal, 1863*, App. 34, pp. 4–8; William H. Naileigh to Orion Clemens, 23 Feb. 1863, Box 1 (S), Nevada State Archives, Carson City; the minutes of the "Peace Meeting," Frank Drake and H. U. Jennings, 16 Feb. 1863, Box 1 (S), Nevada State Archives, Carson City; *Territorial Enterprise*, 17 Feb. 1863, and Marysville *Appeal* of 20 Feb. 1863, as reprinted in the San Francisco *Daily Evening Bulletin*, 23 Feb. 1863; San Francisco *Daily Evening Bulletin*, 25 Feb. 1863; Plumas *Union*, 18 Feb. 1863, and *Territorial Enterprise*, 3 March 1863, as reprinted in the San Francisco *Daily Evening Bulletin*, 5 March 1863.

In the peace negotiations that followed the conflict, it was decided that the location of the California-Nevada border must be definitely determined.

During April 1863 the California legislature enacted into law a bill "to survey and to establish the eastern boundary of the state of California and to request the governor of Nevada to join the survey."[42] The surveyor-general of California, J. F. Houghton, appointed surveyor John F. Kidder to represent California on the joint boundary commission.[43] Orion Clemens, secretary of Nevada Territory and acting-governor in Nye's absence, contracted surveyor Butler Ives to represent Nevada.[44] Clemens was eager to have the boundary run, believing that it would leave Aurora in Nevada. He wanted Esmeralda County organized immediately and the Democratic officers of Mono County replaced with "honest and capable Union men."[45] However, the *Esmeralda Star*, although staunchly "Union," published an editorial that favored remaining in California. "The young suckling, Mono County, which has drawn its milk from the full breasts of its parent state of California," said the editorial, "will hardly like to turn to the dry nurse of Nevada Territory which has not yet been admitted into the family of married states, and brought to her milk."[46]

By June 1863 the Kidder-Ives survey team was in the field, or more properly, in the waters of Lake Tahoe. When the surveyors established that the beginning point of the oblique portion of the California-Nevada boundary lay in the southeast corner of the lake, Governor Nye became convinced that Aurora was in Nevada. He therefore appointed a full contingent of Esmeralda County officers and sent Judge George Turner to Aurora to preside over Nevada's second district court.[47] On arriving in Aurora, Turner found Judge Alexander Baldwin (who had replaced J. A. Moutrie) of Mono County holding court. With the recent "Sagebrush war" as an example of what not to do, it was decided that both Turner and Baldwin would hold court. By careful management no conflict of authority resulted from the concurrent court sessions. Actions were brought before either court depending on the preference of the litigants. A large majority of these actions went before Judge Baldwin because the Esmeralda mining district had been incorporated under the laws of California.

The Nevada territorial elections were slated for 2 September 1863, and this time Esmeralda County would fully participate. Both the Republicans and the Democrats began to organize their forces during July and August. Nye was bombarded with letters from Aurora Republicans seeking appointments to county offices and naming the "Copperheads" in town.[48] Joseph W. Calder, who would recruit Company F, Nevada Cavalry Volunteers, during the winter of 1864 in Aurora, wrote to Nye claiming that Aurora was a haven for "renegade Copperheads" from California. "We are," warned Calder, "by no means certain of election of our ticket. Let the Copperheads elect their

42. *Statutes of California*, 1863, pp. 617–19.

43. C. H. Sinclair, "The Oblique Boundary Line between California and Nevada," p. 268.

44. Angel, *History of Nevada*, p. 101.

45. Orion Clemens to Samuel Youngs, 9 April 1863, Unsorted Territorial Correspondence.

46. *Esmeralda Star*, [?] April 1863, as quoted in the *Sacramento Daily Union*, 24 April 1863.

47. Angel, *History of Nevada*, p. 403.

48. John N. Dudleston to James W. Nye, 3 August 1863; George S. Palmer to James W. Nye, 11 August 1863; J. W. Calder to James W. Nye, 14, 16, and 21 August 1863; Cyril Hawkins to James W. Nye, 2 Sept. 1863; all in Unsorted Territorial Correspondence.

Mono County officers; they will have control over very few." Two days later, Calder wrote to the governor asking permission to form a militia company under the laws of Nevada (the Esmeralda Rangers and Hooker Light Infantry were formed under the laws of California) because the safety of Aurorans demanded it.[49] The political situation in Aurora was volatile, and violence seemed imminent.

As the election drew near, it became obvious that the boundary survey team would not reach Aurora in time. To avoid exacerbating an already explosive situation, Mono County and Esmeralda County agreed to an unusual voting procedure. The citizens of Aurora would cast their ballots for two different slates of candidates: one for Mono County, California, and one for Esmeralda County, Nevada. This unique procedure reduced tensions considerably in Aurora. On election day, polls for Esmeralda County were opened in the militia armory; those for Mono County were opened in the city jail. During the election "considerable hilarity was exhibited and good feeling prevailed, people voting at one place and then passing down the street to vote at the other, thus making sure to hit it on one side if they missed it on the other."[50] Republicans emerged victorious in both counties, with over 2,300 votes cast.[51] The exact margin of victory is not known, but it seems to have been substantial. As one jubilant Republican put it, "We just went in and wiped out all the rebs all to the devil."[52] An all-night victory party was held, featuring a torchlight procession through the streets of Aurora, patriotic speeches, and the firing of a cannon.[53]

The Democrats did not take the loss lightly. Their only hope now, however, was for the Kidder-Ives survey team to locate Aurora in California. By late September, some three weeks after Aurora's dual election, Aurora was found to be in Nevada by the narrow margin of "some three and one-third miles."[54] The survey team was supposed to continue running the line to the Colorado River, but twenty-five miles below Aurora Joaquin Jim and several hundred hostile Paiute forced the team to quit the field.[55] Although the survey was incomplete—it had not been run to the Colorado River and then adjusted back to Lake Tahoe for errors—both California and Nevada accepted it.[56]

In Aurora, however, there were a few zealous supporters of California sovereignty who claimed that the surveyors bent the boundary line around Aurora to make the town part of Nevada. One of these outspoken California adherents was Robert E. Draper, owner and editor of the *Aurora Times*.[57] Draper had begun publishing the *Times* in Aurora during April 1863, and the paper had always favored California sovereignty. Moreover, the *Times* was strongly Democratic; the *Esmeralda Star* called it

49. J. W. Calder to James W. Nye, 14 and 16 August 1863, Unsorted Territorial Correspondence.

50. Angel, *History of Nevada*, p. 403.

51. Angel, p. 403; Colcord, "Reminiscences," p. 117.

52. George A. Whitney to William T. Whitney, 4 Sept. 1863, Whitney Letters and Correspondence.

53. G. Whitney to W. Whitney, 4 Sept. 1863; Frederick K. Bechtel to James W. Nye, 5 Sept. 1863, Unsorted Territorial Correspondence.

54. "Annual Report of the Surveyor-General for the Year 1863," *Appendix to Journals of Senate and Assembly of the Fifteenth Session of the Legislature of the State of California*, vol. 1 (Sacramento, 1864), p. 68.

55. "Annual Report" (above), p. 40.

56. *California Assembly Journal, 1863–1864*, p. 763; *Statutes of Nevada, 1864–1865*, pp. 133–34, 347.

57. Angel, *History of Nevada*, p. 297.

12.   As this stock certificate indicates, Aurora and the Esmeralda mining district were originally thought to be in California. (Credit: Nevada
Historical Society)

Copperhead.[58] Draper's views on the Civil War and on the recent boundary survey
were evidently too much for Dr. William Eichelroth to stomach. Eichelroth, a survivor of the Paiute massacre of the Ormsby expeditionary force at Pyramid Lake in 1860,
challenged Draper to a duel. On 5 October 1863 they met at Bodie Ranch, six miles
west of Aurora.[59]

The two antagonists presented a striking contrast. The Republican, Eichelroth, was of medium height and weighed 220 pounds; the Democrat, Draper, was over
six feet tall and thin as a rail. With Esmeralda County deputy sheriff H. J. Teel standing
by as a spectator, Eichelroth and Draper fired at each other from forty paces. Their first
rounds missed, but on the second fire Draper was hit in the shin. This was evidently
enough to satisfy the honor of each, for they called it quits and shook hands. Eichelroth
was hailed as a marksman, and Draper was left with a game leg. If Eichelroth's intention
had been to silence Draper or to intimidate him into compromising the strongly Democratic stance of the *Aurora Times*, Eichelroth failed. Draper and the *Times* remained,
as the *Star* noted, Copperhead.

The location of the boundary left Mono County, California, without a county
seat and with its records deposited in a Nevada town. Colorful tales have been told of
how Mono ranchers who were "armed to the teeth" rode into Aurora and seized the
county records.[60] These tales are pure fiction. The removal of the records was peaceful
and quiet. Mono County clerk Richard M. Wilson and treasurer William Feast simply
loaded the county records into a wagon and carried them across the state line to Bodie.[61]

58.   *Esmeralda Union*, 5 May 1864.

59.   Angel, *History of Nevada*, pp. 153, 297; Colcord, "Reminiscences," p. 117; Joseph Wasson, *Account
of the Important Revival of Mining Interests in the Bodie and Esmeralda Districts*, p. 49; *Virginia Daily Union*,
9 Jan. 1864.

60.   Chalfant, *Outposts*, p. 79.

61.   Angel, *History of Nevada*, p. 403.

In the spring of 1864, Bridgeport was voted the new county seat of Mono, and the records were transferred there.[62]

Aurorans soon realized that they had made a mistake by not impounding the records immediately. When Esmeralda County asked for copies of the records, Mono County demanded $10,000 for the transcription. The Nevada legislature approved the proposed transcription on 9 February 1864, but then had to repeal the act when Aurorans refused to pay the amount asked by Mono County.[63]

Mono County did leave Aurora with something—some $30,000 in outstanding warrants.[64] Mono contended that the expenses were incurred in and for the benefit of Aurora, and that, therefore, Esmeralda County should be held responsible for the payment of the warrants. Esmeralda responded by suing Mono, but failed to win the case. Finally, on 2 March 1867, the Nevada legislature approved an act to pay off the warrant holders.[65]

With the boundary finally determined, Mono County judge Alexander Baldwin declined to hear any more cases and transferred the operations of his court to Bridgeport. Most of the other Mono County officers, however, remained in Aurora, and the governor of California was forced to appoint replacements.[66] William Feast continued to act as treasurer of Mono County, although he resided in Aurora. The sheriff of Mono County, H. J. Teel, resigned and became the deputy sheriff of Esmeralda County under Sheriff D. G. Francis. Teel and Francis had agreed that whichever one of them was forced to move from Aurora when the boundary was determined would be spared this misfortune by being appointed deputy to the sheriff who remained.

Judge George Turner of the Second District of Nevada began to hold court in Aurora on 8 October 1863.[67] The first question that arose was one of jurisdiction; Turner, naturally, ruled in favor of Nevada. Several major court battles would be fought in Turner's court during the next few months. The most important of these—the conflicting claims of the Real Del Monte and Pond mining companies—involved a vein that produced silver and gold worth millions of dollars.

Although the boundary question was now settled, political issues related to the Civil War still aroused Aurorans to lawlessness and violence. On cool and windy 7 September 1864, Esmeralda County held an election for county officials. Candidates generally represented the "Union party" (mostly Republicans) or the "People's party" (mostly Democrats). The election was fairly close, with the Union party emerging victorious.[68] Edwin Sherman, in an article entitled "A Glorious Victory," gloated over the win of the Union party and joyfully announced the demise of the People's party. "The People's ticket," asserted Sherman, "was supported by every ruffian and Jeff Davis brawler

62. *Statutes of California*, 1865, p. 144.

63. *Laws of Nevada Territory*, 1864, p. 93; *Statutes of Nevada*, 1865, p. 94; A. S. Peck to James W. Nye, 10 April 1864, Unsorted Territorial Correspondence; *Esmeralda Union*, 30 August and 30 Dec. 1864, 4 Jan. 1865.

64. *Esmeralda Union*, 4 Jan. and 11 Feb. 1865.

65. *Esmeralda Union*, 21 Dec. 1867.

66. Angel, *History of Nevada*, p. 403.

67. *Sacramento Daily Union*, 21 Oct. 1863.

68. The following accounts are from the *Esmeralda Union*, 10 Sept. 1864.

13. *Aurora's boom coincided with the Civil War. Politics aroused strong passions, and political rallies and speechmaking were major events. This photograph was probably taken during the presidential election campaign of 1864. The balconied brick building is the county courthouse. View is west on Pine Street. (Credit: Nevada Historical Society)*

in town." Sherman named Bill Pendergast and Tom Carberry as examples of the ruffians and "notorious characters" who supported the People's party.

Sherman, who had been shot and beaten for his editorial remarks after the arrest of Gus Quinton, was about to get it again. At seven o'clock on the evening of 9 September 1864 as Sherman rounded the corner at Pine and Antelope streets, he ran into Pendergast, Carberry, and several others who "were standing by with their pistols and knives ready." Pendergast collared Sherman and asked him if he had authored the article in the *Union* (formerly the *Star*). When Sherman said that he had, Pendergast let go with a blow that bloodied Sherman's nose. Sherman swung back with a newspaper file-stick. Before the fight could go any further, the crowd that had gathered about the two men pulled them apart. Pendergast, much the larger and stronger of the two and a known brawler, would have thrashed Sherman thoroughly.

In the presidential election on 8 November 1864, Aurorans cast 613 votes for the Republican candidate, Abraham Lincoln, and 418 for the Democrat, George McClellan. There were several cases of illegal voting by Democratic "ruffians," but the grand jury declined to indict "the guilty parties," because of the "delicate nature of the election law."[69] What this evidently meant was that it would have been difficult to win

69. *Esmeralda Union,* 23 Dec. 1864.

a conviction. Moreover, since Lincoln had won, the largely Republican grand jury was apparently not overly concerned about any election irregularities.

The last incident of violence or lawlessness related to politics occurred on 15 April 1865.[70] When the telegraph brought word of the assassination of Abraham Lincoln, most Aurorans went into mourning. A. G. Judy, however, was delighted. He called Lincoln a tyrant and said that the late president ought to have been dead long ago. Captain John G. Kelly of Company C, First Nevada Infantry, happened to be in town searching for a deserter. When Captain Kelly heard of Judy's statements, he summoned the Esmeralda Rangers to arrest the "secessionist." Once in custody, Judy refused to take the oath of allegiance. He relented the next day when he was told that he would be sent to Fort Churchill to pack a fifty-pound sack of sand on his back until he changed his mind.

Politics, the Civil War, and the California-Nevada boundary, then, were responsible for several acts of lawlessness and violence in Aurora. The most violent of these acts did not involve the town marshal or the militia; nor did they involve any political figure. These acts of greatest violence were directed at Aurora's outspoken newspaper editors. Edwin Sherman of the *Esmeralda Star* was shot once, beaten twice, and threatened many times. R. E. Draper of the *Aurora Times* was shot in a duel and was threatened on numerous occasions. Neither editor bothered with diplomacy when stating his position, and both paid dearly for this lack of tact.

Attacks on newspaper editors and newspaper offices were not unusual during the Civil War. In California alone, mobs destroyed the offices of five newspapers, and troopers of the Second Cavalry, California Volunteers, wrecked the office of a sixth.[71] Those attacks, however, were all directed against Copperhead newspapers and were perpetrated by large groups of men. In Aurora, both the Copperhead Draper and the Unionist Sherman were attacked. These editors were confronted not by mobs of anonymous men but by individual citizens. The fights that resulted pitted one man against another, and one of the fights was a formal *affaire d'honneur*.

Aurora was a border town both literally and figuratively. It literally sat on the boundary between California and Nevada and figuratively sat on the boundary between the North and the South. Just as Aurora was a little closer to Nevada than to California, it was also a little closer to the North than to the South. Politics during these Civil War years were superheated, and political divisions ran deep. Aurorans actively participated both as candidates and as voters in every election. Democracy was very much in evidence in Aurora. Yet efforts to subvert the democratic process, such as voting fraud and other irregularities, were also a feature of nearly every election in Aurora. Whether this would have been true without the deep political divisions engendered by the Civil War is hard to say.

Fistfights and, occasionally, fights with knives, over political disputes were not uncommon. Shootings, however, were reserved for newspaper editors. The so-called secessionists threatened a mass attack once, but with that exception Aurorans settled their political disputes individually. Undoubtedly, the presence of two militia companies

70.   Samuel Youngs's Journal, 15 and 16 April 1865; Chalfant, *Outposts*, pp. 63–64.

71.   On the night of 5 March 1863 some thirty troopers from Camp Babbitt, located a mile north of Visalia, broke into the office of the Visalia *Equal Rights Expositor*, a Copperhead, if not secessionist, newspaper, and destroyed the press and nearly demolished the office. See Department of War, *The War of the Rebellion*, vol. 50, part II, pp. 341–42.

in Aurora and the occasional appearance of the Second Cavalry and the First Infantry on their way to fight the Paiute in the Owens Valley inhibited organized overt Confederate activity.

Finally, although the boundary controversy caused a small-scale war to erupt between Plumas County and Roop County in Honey Lake Valley, Mono County and Esmeralda County were able to settle their disputes peaceably, if not amicably. There were extended legal battles over county records and debt, but there was no bloodshed.

4

ROBBERY, ROWDYISM, AND COMBAT

Aurora was home to highwaymen, rowdies, and killers. During the town's heyday, no fewer than five stages were robbed, fistfights and drunk and disorderly conduct were daily occurrences, and at least seventeen men were beaten, knifed, or shot to death.[1] Aurorans drank heavily, were well armed, and did not passively accept threats or insults. The "appalling frequency" of shootings and gunfights, lamented the *Esmeralda Union*, "has given our city such an unenviable reputation for lawlessness wherever it is known abroad."[2]

The Aurora stage, even with armed guards aboard, and freight wagons were stopped and robbed with greater frequency than were individual citizens of Aurora. During 1863 and 1864, the stage and freight wagons suffered seven holdups; during the same period there is record of only four robberies of individuals. The stage was the most prized target of highwaymen because it frequently carried gold and silver bullion worth thousands of dollars. "The Aurora bullion," reminisced an Aurora stage driver, "was just the kind the road agents liked. It was run in small bars and so rich in gold that it had the yellow color, not like the heavy white bricks that you see on the Comstock now."[3]

To protect this bullion, armed guards, known as shotgun messengers, often rode with the stage driver. Whether or not messengers were aboard, road agents had several advantages: they could take the stage by surprise; they could carefully sight their guns without having to control a team of horses or to contend with a rocking stage; and they could effect a speedy escape on fresh horses hidden near the holdup scene. Surprise was probably the key element. The same Aurora stage driver commented:

---

1. Since the newspaper record for 1862 and 1863 in Aurora is incomplete, it is impossible to compile a definitive record of all acts of robbery and rowdyism during those two years. Those acts, unless they led to a court trial or were highly dramatic, were not generally mentioned in sources other than newspapers. Such is not the case for killings. Several different kinds of source material—court records, letters, diaries, early histories, and newspapers in other Western towns—recorded killings. Nevertheless, there were killings in Aurora that cannot be fully documented by the extant historical sources. See n.21.

2. *Esmeralda Union*, 12 Dec. 1864.

3. *Bodie Standard*, 20 July 1881.

14.   *The stage en route from Carson City to Aurora (circa 1863).*
Concord coaches and six-horse teams were standard. (Credit: California
Historical Society)

Until you have been suddenly called upon to look down the opening of a double-barreled shotgun, which has a road agent with his hand on the trigger at the other end you can have no idea how surprised you are capable of being. I have had a six-shooter pulled on me across a faro table; I have proved that the hilt of a dirk can't go between two of my ribs; I have seen four aces beaten by a royal flush; but I was never really surprised until I looked down the muzzle of a double-barreled shotgun in the hands of a road agent. Why, my friend, the mouth of the Sutro tunnel is like a nailhole in the Palace Hotel compared to a shotgun.[4]

Surprise was occasionally on the driver's side. In 1863 a plucky little Aurora stage-driver called "Dutch Jake" outsmarted a couple of highwaymen with a novel trick.[5] Dutch Jake had been robbed several times before—normally a driver would be fired once he had been robbed twice, but Dutch Jake was known to be a "dead square man"—and he was anxious to get even. When he was told that a consignment of bullion would be aboard his stage on its next run, he begged that no shotgun messengers be allowed to accompany him. From past experience he felt that most messengers were "cowardly blowhards" and would only get in the way. After the stage manager agreed that no messengers would ride up top with him, he hitched up a special team of ornery mules and rigged a shotgun next to him in the driver's seat. Vowing to demonstrate that his mules were smarter than any guards, he whipped the team out of town.

Sure enough, a couple of hours outside of Aurora, two road agents sprang out of the roadside chaparral. One grabbed the bits of the lead mules, while the other, with

4.   *Bodie Standard,* 20 July 1881.
5.   *Bodie Standard,* 20 July 1881.

his gun leveled at Dutch Jake, walked alongside the mules back to the coach. Just as the second robber passed the hind legs of the lead team, Jake's rigged shotgun roared. The mules kicked and bolted; one highwayman was kicked into the chaparral and the other was trampled. It was several miles before Jake regained control of the spooked beasts, but the bullion was safe. Other than the highwaymen, only the mules suffered any damage: each of the lead mules had had their inside ears shot off.

Road agents were normally interested only in the treasure box and not in the passengers on board the stage. In a robbery of the Aurora stage en route to Genoa in late October 1864, two road agents politely informed the passengers that they had come only for the express company's treasure box.[6] They emphasized that they wanted nothing belonging to the passengers. Nobody was prepared to argue with the highwaymen in any case; the road agents were armed with double-barreled shotguns and revolvers.

Freight wagons were not safe from highwaymen either. In December 1864, two teamsters freighting goods from Aurora to Latrobe were stopped by a couple of masked "greasers" in two different incidents.[7] One teamster was relieved of $40 in an early morning holdup; the other lost $70 to the robbers in the afternoon.

Occasionally, individual travelers would be accosted. In July 1864, Antone Shanworth was beaten and robbed of $1,000 by what the authorities thought to be an organized band of robbers who operated in the vicinity of Indian Wells.[8] Aurora's city marshal, John A. Palmer, arrested two men, George W. Davis and William H. Jackson, for the attack on Shanworth. Both men had stolen articles on their persons, and Davis had been arrested the year before in the mining town of La Paz on the Colorado River, for horse stealing. At that time the American miners in La Paz voted to hang him, but the Mexican miners there were opposed to hanging for horse stealing and thought he should be jailed instead. The Americans decided "Judge Lynch" would solve the problem, but before they could act a Mexican let Davis escape. The *Esmeralda Union* demonstrated an anti-Mormon bias when it noted that Davis was "an apostle of Brigham Young, from whom, perhaps, he learned his trade."[9]

In August 1864, three Aurorans on their way to Washoe were stopped and robbed by four mounted highwaymen near the East Carson River.[10] The robbers took $75 in cash, a fancy six-shooter valued at $125, and two derringers, and then rode off toward the Sierra. Three months later three celebrating Chinese who were returning to Aurora from Dogtown were held up just below the Fogus quartz mill.[11] Three masked men pistol-whipped the Chinese (two of them were seriously injured) and then relieved them of some $300 in gold dust. William Carder, a belligerent town rough and a feared gunfighter, and two of his friends, Hack Mead and Frank Williams, were arrested for the crime, but were soon released for lack of evidence.

Some highwaymen had a conscience. In late November 1864, an old prospector, T. Cook, was stopped by two masked men one evening about two miles north of

6.   *Esmeralda Union*, 27 and 28 Oct. 1864.

7.   *Esmeralda Union*, 9 Dec. 1864.

8.   *Esmeralda Union*, 28 and 29 July 1864.

9.   *Esmeralda Union*, 29 July 1864. Neither Davis's nor Jackson's name appears again in any newspaper or court record, indicating that the two men were probably released for lack of evidence.

10.   *Esmeralda Union*, 16 August 1864.

11.   *Esmeralda Union*, 10 Nov. 1864.

15. *Hank Monk drove stagecoaches throughout the trans-Sierra country, including runs to Aurora and Bodie. He became famous when he gave Horace Greeley a hair-raising ride across the Sierra. (Credit: California Historical Society)*

town.[12] The robbers pressed their revolvers against Cook's head and demanded his money. Just then one of the men recognized Cook and told his partner that Cook was poor. Without hesitating, they allowed the old man to go on his way. The *Esmeralda Union* expressed the belief that the robbers must have been residents of Aurora. "There is a number of men in this city," observed the newspaper, "who have no visible means of support, but who always dress well, and are seldom without money. Such men should be watched. Although some of them are honest, we believe that a few of them would not only rob a man, but murder him were it necessary to do so in order to get his money and escape detection."

Burglary and petty theft were evidently not much of a problem in Aurora. During 1864 and 1865 only two incidents were reported.[13] In August 1864, two engineers employed at the Durand mill carried off and hid several critical engine parts, forcing a halt to milling. When arrested and brought before the justice of the peace, the engineers asserted that the mill owed them nearly $1,000 in back wages and that they were determined to force the mill to pay up. The matter was settled when the mill agreed to pay them their wages in return for the missing engine parts. Surprisingly, the judge fined the engineers, not the mill, the court costs. In February 1865 a thief stole a number of chickens from a woman's backyard. He left his pipe behind as a calling card, and it was soon being passed around town in an attempt to identify its owner. The *Esmeralda Union*, obviously not treating the theft very seriously, contended that "he that would steal chickens from a lady, would be hog enough to eat 'em without calling in a friend."[14]

Various forms of rowdyism, including drunk and disorderly conduct, target practice in the city streets, and fistfights, were common in Aurora. Drunks not infrequently passed out on Aurora streets and usually wound up spending the night in the city jail.[15] If it were a first offense and no disturbance had been made, the drunk was simply released the next morning. However, if the drunk had created a disturbance or was a habitual offender, he could expect an appearance before the justice of the peace and a fine of $15 or $20. Occasionally the arresting officer would encounter more serious trouble. In August 1864, when Deputy Sheriff H. J. Teel arrested Charles Gillespie for disturbing the peace, a half-dozen drunken men interfered, and a brawl erupted. The police eventually subdued the drunks and packed them into the overflowing city jail. The *Esmeralda Union* wryly noted that the justice of the peace, John T. Moore, "will do a thriving business during the next two or three days."

Some twenty-five saloons kept the "boys" well watered, so it is no wonder that "drunk and disorderly conduct" was a common charge. Aurorans loved to drink and were suspicious of anyone who did not. Thomas R. Chapin, the superintendent of an Aurora Sunday school, was called "Miss Chapin" by the miners because he was a non-drinker.[16] Aurora drinkers imbibed such enormous quantities of alcohol that they more

12.   *Esmeralda Union*, 28 Nov. 1864.

13.   The newspaper record for 1864 and 1865 is fairly complete. Although not all burglaries and petty thefts would necessarily have been reported, the fact that only two were reported indicates that those crimes must have been infrequent and of no great significance.

14.   *Esmeralda Union*, 15 August 1864, 22 Feb. 1865.

15.   The sources for this paragraph are the *Aurora Times*, 11 June 1864, and the *Esmeralda Union*, 30 March, 1 April, 2 May, 15 and 25 July, 1 and 2 August, 1864.

16.   Ella Sterling Mighels, *Life and Letters of a Forty-Niner's Daughter*, p. 242.

than doubled the price of eggs when eggnog was in season.[17] Fortified with a few drinks, Aurorans would stagger out of the saloons and engage in pistol practice at any available target. "The boys," noted one Auroran, "have a reprehensible practice of shooting at targets across the main street, a diversion not eminently calculated to soothe the nerves of one having occasion to cross the line of their fire. The terror thus inspired, however, is supposed to considerably enhance the fascination of the sport."[18]

As one might suspect, fistfights were common in Aurora and the police took notice of only the more serious encounters. One fistfight proved fatal. At the Bamboo mine on Last Chance Hill in March 1864 a fight erupted between two miners, Connor and Montgomery. Conner pummeled Montgomery so severely that he died two weeks later of head injuries he had received in the fight. Connor was held to answer, but since he had acted in self-defense, the case against him was dismissed. Several months after Montgomery's death, two feuding miners met in a fight billed as "rough-and-tumble," meaning that no holds were barred. A spot outside the city limits was selected, and by fight time a large crowd had gathered. The combatants appeared dangerously mismatched: one was a much larger man than the other. Nevertheless, they squared off. Suddenly the smaller man unleashed a blow that knocked his larger opponent to the ground and into unconsciousness. The crowd stood in stunned disbelief and then watched as the smaller man dropped a stone he had concealed in his fist. When a few spectators protested what they thought was an unfair advantage, a bystander remarked, "That's perfectly fair, boys; hitting 'em wid the stone is the rough part, and knocking him down is the tumble part."[19]

Most fistfights in Aurora did not have serious, let alone tragic, consequences. Some were even comical affairs. During a celebration and a demonstration of fire fighting held by Aurora's volunteer fire fighters, a spectator, Thomas Griffith, jumped on the fire engine and refused to get off.[20] The "First Assistant" of the fire fighters, John Vernon, knocked Griffith off the engine with a well-aimed swing of a trumpet. Police rushed in and arrested both Griffith and Vernon. The volunteer fire fighters, enraged at Vernon's arrest, now attacked the police. Order was eventually restored, but the fire fighters then canceled the celebration and pulled their engine back into the firehouse. There they sulked and demanded Vernon's release, while crowds of spectators tried to coax them out. The strike continued until the police released Vernon, who then triumphantly led his men, fire engine in tow, back into the street.

At least one fistfight had an international flavor, involving, as the *Esmeralda Union* noted on 15 August 1864, "two men, one from Cork and the other from Paris." The fight grew out of a dispute over a load of potatoes the Irishman had brought into Aurora for sale to the Frenchman. When the Frenchman reneged on the price he had agreed to pay for the potatoes, the Irishman dumped the entire load into the street. The Frenchman now assumed "a pugilistic attitude." At this the Irishman became so enraged that "the pinfeathers on his brawny arms rose like the hair of a toothbrush after rubbing the finger heavily across" and he hit the Frenchman with several powerful blows that

17. *Aurora Times*, 2 Jan. 1864, as quoted in the *Virginia Daily Union*, 9 Jan. 1864.

18. As quoted in W. A. Chalfant, *Outposts of Civilization*, p. 54.

19. *Esmeralda Union*, 30 March and 5 Sept. 1864.

20. *Aurora Times*, 22 Feb. 1864, as quoted in the *Virginia Daily Union*, 26 Feb. 1864.

"ought to have satisfied any reasonable man." The crowd of spectators then stopped the fight before any more damage was done.

For serious fighting, Aurorans preferred guns and knives. Most men were armed with either a revolver or a derringer, and everyone carried a knife, which was used more often as a tool than a weapon. The Colt Navy, a .36 caliber, octagon-barrel, six-shot revolver, noted for its perfect balance and accuracy, was the most popular side arm. The heavier, .45 caliber, six-shot Colt Dragoon also saw considerable use. Guns were normally carried in a coat pocket or stuck in the waistband or belt. Only rarely were they holstered. During Aurora's boom years, at least thirteen men fell victim to the gun and no fewer than three to the knife.[21] There were also several instances where shots were fired but nobody was killed, and where gunplay was only threatened. A few of these armed encounters resulted from disputes over women, some over property, but most over who was the better man, affronts to personal honor, careless insults, challenges to pecking order in the saloon, and loyalty to friends.

Women were scarce in Aurora, and it might be assumed that the few women in town were often fought over. Such was not the case. Only three armed confrontations over women are known to have occurred. In April 1861, one Auroran shot at another, who had been making amorous overtures to his wife.[22] In July 1863, George Whitney's roommate was told by an angry husband that he would be killed.[23] The roommate was accused by the husband of being too "intimate" with his young and pretty wife. Whitney mediated the dispute and succeeded in calming the angry husband by giving him $100, a watch, and ten shares of mining stock. Whitney's roommate thought that the price was quite a bargain, indicating that he was, perhaps, guilty.

The most unusual and deadly love triangle in Aurora's history began to unfold during the spring of 1864.[24] Fifty-five-year-old, Kentucky-born and Mississippi-bred Charles E. H. Wheaton fell in love with the young and beautiful wife of William B. Lake. Although she in no way returned Wheaton's love and was true to her husband, Wheaton persisted in writing her love letters and stopping by her house whenever her husband was out. "Billy" Lake, a bookkeeper originally from Bangor, Maine, asked Wheaton to direct his amorous intentions elsewhere, but Wheaton insisted that "spirits" had willed Mrs. Lake to him body and soul.

Month after month, Wheaton continued to write his letters and to proposition Mrs. Lake, all to no avail. Wheaton finally came to believe that the spirits were directing him to kill Billy Lake and take Mrs. Lake for his own. Lake received word of Wheaton's latest delusion, and was prepared when Wheaton came gunning for him on the night of 27 September 1864. As Wheaton walked up Pine Street with his right hand holding a cocked revolver in his coat pocket, Lake came down the street with a double-barreled shotgun. Lake spotted Wheaton first, and the shotgun roared. The first discharge hit

---

21.   The Esmeralda Grand Jury of March 1864 asserted that "within the last three years some twenty-seven of our citizens have come to their deaths by the hand of violence" (*Esmeralda Union*, 31 March 1864). Four more men died violent deaths in Aurora after March 1864. Therefore, if the grand jury's total is correct, there were thirty-one homicides in Aurora during its boom years. Only seventeen homicides can be documented by the extant historical sources.

22.   Visalia *Delta*, 30 May 1861.

23.   George A. Whitney to William T. Whitney, 7 July 1863, Whitney Letters and Correspondence.

24.   G. Whitney to W. Whitney, 1 Oct. 1864; *Esmeralda Union*, 28, 29, and 30 Sept. 1864.

Wheaton in the chest and side, shattering his right arm, and the second struck him in the face and neck. Wheaton slumped to the ground in front of the Wide West saloon and died fifteen minutes later. A bystander was hit in the leg by some stray pellets, but the wound was not serious.

Lake was arrested by Sheriff D. G. Francis and placed in the county jail. The next day the coroner's jury met and rendered a unanimous verdict of justifiable homicide. The decision, said the *Esmeralda Union* on 30 September, "was the verdict of the citizens generally before the Jury was ever impanneled." Lake, a longtime resident of Aurora, was known to be a peaceable man who was not easily provoked.

Disputes over property—city lots, mining claims, and ranch lands—were not uncommon, but were rarely resolved violently. When violence did occur, however, death nearly always resulted. David Webber was the first to die under these circumstances.[25] On 17 March 1861 in a dispute over an Aurora city lot, he was shot to death by a man named Wilson. A little more than a year later, a miner named Gebhart, while trying to defend a claim on Last Chance Hill, was shot by a man named Gossland.[26] Gebhart lingered on for a while, then died.

A few days after Gebhart was shot, three men armed with revolvers entered the Monitor, a mine that Sam Clemens and his partners had been working, and laid claim to it. Clemens and company hurried to the Monitor and demanded possession. The claim jumpers refused, saying that "they were in the hole, armed, and meant to die for it, if necessary." Clemens and his partners chose not to try to evict them, and Clemens bitterly wrote his brother, "Now you understand the shooting scrape in which Gebhart was killed the other day."[27] No so easily intimidated as Sam Clemens, Edward McGrath killed Thomas McLaughlin in a similar dispute over a mining claim in February 1863.[28] In the only instance of armed conflict over ranchland, Sid Huntoon, whose name is seen today in the place names Huntoon Springs and Huntoon Valley, shot James Buckland when the latter attempted to jump a portion of Huntoon's ranch in April 1864.[29] Buckland was hit in the ribs, but he survived the wound.

Most armed conflict in Aurora was not the result of love triangles or property disputes. Arguments or personal feuds, for a variety of reasons unrelated to women or real estate, caused the majority of armed encounters and resulted in the deaths of twelve men. Some of these encounters never got beyond the confrontation stage, and others saw guns misfire or shots fired without effect.

On a Wednesday night in October 1863, John Gorman and John E. Campbell fell into an argument in an Aurora saloon. Gorman, with a revolver in one hand, slapped Campbell on the face with the other. Campbell took no immediate action, but a short while later sent Gorman a formal request for a duel. The formality surprised at least one Auroran. "The said parties are of a class," claimed an Aurora correspondent for the *Sacramento Daily Union*, "which heretofore settled their disputes summarily, by ear-

---

25. *Aurora Times*, 2 April 1864, as quoted in the *Virginia Daily Union*, 6 April 1864.

26. *Samuel Youngs's Journal*, 17 March 1861; Samuel Clemens to Orion Clemens, 13 April 1862, in Albert B. Paine, ed., *Mark Twain's Letters*, vol. 1, p. 67.

27. Samuel Clemens to Orion Clemens, [?] April 1862, Unsorted Territorial Correspondence, Nevada Division of Archives, Office of the Secretary of State.

28. Myron Angel, ed., *History of Nevada*, p. 344.

29. George A. Whitney to William T. Whitney, 15 April 1864, Whitney Letters and Correspondence.

croppings, or with pistols and knives on the spot, to the great danger of innocent people near them."[30]

Gorman and Campbell agreed to meet the next day at Clayton's ranch, just outside of Aurora, and to duel with a revolver in one hand and a bowie knife in the other. They were to begin firing at a distance of thirteen paces, and if neither fell at the first fire, they were to advance two paces and fire again. They could then close at will.

The combatants and a large crowd of "admirers of such scenes" were assembled at Clayton's ranch at the appointed time, but just as the duel was about to begin, Sheriff D. G. Francis arrived and halted the exhibition. Everybody returned to Aurora, cursing the sheriff for having spoiled the fun. A few hours and hundreds of drinks later, the duelists and the spectators left again, this time crossing the state line into California. Nothing could halt the duel now, it seemed. The crowd fell silent as Campbell and Gorman began stepping off the prescribed distance. Just then, Gorman's wife rode onto the field of battle. She pulled her horse up between the men and forbade them to fight. "Her presence produced a healing balm," said the *Daily Union*'s correspondent, and Gorman and Campbell called it quits. This time everyone, including the spectators, was "apparently satisfied."

There were other nonfatal armed encounters. One evening in March 1864 an Aurora businessman was walking home from work when a rough-looking character grabbed him by the throat and put a revolver to his head. Just before the assailant pulled the trigger, he discovered he had the wrong man. He holstered his gun and remarked, "It's a good thing for you that you were not H——; if you had been I would have sent you home on short notice."[31]

An even more breathtaking incident occurred a half year later when a man named Turner began quarreling with "an old gentleman" named Hoops. Turner drew his revolver, pressed it against Hoops's head, and pulled the trigger. The gun misfired. Hoops then grabbed a piece of cord wood and broke it on Turner's head. Turner was knocked to the ground and his skull was fractured. The next day he was brought before the justice of the peace and fined forty dollars. The *Esmeralda Union* said that the fine and the cracked skull "served him right."[32]

Not only guns misfired; so did shooters. Occasionally shots would be fired, and at close range, without the intended victim's being touched. "Doc" Garvin, the superintendent of the high-producing Antelope mine on Silver Hill, had his life threatened by an unidentified man. When the man showed up at the Antelope, Garvin came out of the company office with his revolver blazing. The man was untouched, but he was persuaded to leave.[33]

Aurora was not without its comic relief. Two rowdies, one of whom the *Esmeralda Union* described as "a rough of the first water, a flourisher of the revolver, and bowie knife of awful length, breadth, weight and keenness," got into a dispute while drinking in a saloon. After a long exchange of obscenities, which attracted a large crowd, the "rough of the first water" drew his revolver. The other rough ran for his life, pursued

30. *Sacramento Daily Union,* 21 Oct. 1863.

31. *Esmeralda Union,* 1 April 1864.

32. *Esmeralda Union,* 23 Nov. 1864.

33. *Esmeralda Union,* 27 Sept. 1864.

by the gun-wielding rough, who was in turn pursued, at a safe distance, by the crowd. The fleeing rough was too drunk to run far, and he soon collapsed. The armed rough was quickly upon him and readied the gun for the coup de grace. The gun did not fire. It could not fire. It was a toy. "Side-splitting laughter" seized the many spectators when they realized they were the butt of a practical joke.[34]

Most armed conflict culminated, not in practical jokes, near misses, misfires, or aborted duels, but in death. Knives could be as effective as guns. In April 1863 an unidentified Chinese stabbed a miner named McKinty at Winters Mill.[35] A week later McKinty died of the wound. What became of the Chinese is not known. A short time later, Johnny Donovan fatally stabbed Richard McGuire when the two old enemies met in the billiard room of the Pony saloon.[36] Donovan and McGuire were members of rival gangs and were considered less than desirable citizens. A justice of the peace quickly ruled McGuire's death justifiable homicide. The Merchant's Exchange saloon saw a long-standing feud between James Downey and Martin Doran erupt into a brawl late one Christmas night. Downey got the advantage and plunged a knife into Doran. Doran died on the spot.[37] The coroner's jury rendered a verdict of justifiable homicide, and Downey was not prosecuted.

Despite the knife's obvious effectiveness, the gun remained the weapon for settling personal disputes resulting from affronts, insults, challenges, feuds, or gang loyalty. Lee Vining may have been the first Auroran shot to death in a personal dispute. Vining, a scion of an Indiana Quaker family, erected a sawmill on the creek that now bears his name and began supplying Aurora with lumber in 1861.[38] One night in the Exchange saloon some trouble started. The report of a gun was heard. Everyone dived for cover or ran for the street. When the commotion subsided, Vining was found lying dead on the wooden sidewalk in front of the saloon. He had been shot in the groin— the round evidently severed an artery—and had quickly bled to death. An examination indicated that a gun in his pocket had inflicted the fatal wound. Whether Vining had accidently fired the gun prematurely while pulling it out of his pocket to shoot someone else, or whether the gun had discharged during a struggle, remains a mystery.

The death by shooting of Dr. F. Chorpenning, an Aurora physician and the acting assistant surgeon for Company A, Second Cavalry, California Volunteers, was far less mysterious.[39] On 28 July 1862, Chorpenning was shot in a fight with William Pooler. Although the damage done by Pooler's Colt Dragoon revolver was considerable, Chorpenning struggled on for two weeks before he died. His funeral was attended by a large number of Aurorans, including one of Sam Clemens's mining partners, Dan Twing. For the funeral, Twing wore the best clothes he possessed: a badly yellowed white shirt and an old greasy and wrinkled black coat. "In this gorgeous costume," wrote Sam Clem-

---

34. *Esmeralda Union*, 1 Sept. 1864.

35. Angel, *History of Nevada*, p. 344.

36. *Aurora Times*, 2 April 1864, as quoted in the *Virginia Daily Union*, 6 April 1864; Chalfant, *Outposts*, p. 65.

37. Samuel Youngs's Journal, 31 Dec. 1866; Angel, *History of Nevada*, p. 347.

38. Francis P. Farquhar, "Lee Vining," p. 84.

39. *Esmeralda Star*, 20 Sept. 1862; Records, A, District Court, Mono County, pp. 37, 39, 57, 62; Samuel Clemens to Mrs. Moffett, 15 August 1862, *Mark Twain's Letters*, p. 81; Angel, *History of Nevada*, p. 344.

16.   *The hearse in Aurora was well used and carried many a gunshot victim to the grave. (Credit: Huntington Library)*

ens, "he attended the funeral. And when he returned, his own dog drove him away from the cabin not recognizing him."[40]

The day before the funeral took place, Pooler quietly left town. A warrant was issued for his arrest, and City Marshal Dan Pine set out on his trail. Marshal Pine tracked Pooler to Big Meadows (present-day Bridgeport) and there, on the night of 13 August 1862, took him into custody. During the night, Pooler escaped. Early the next morning, sheriff deputies George McQuade, James Honness, and F. B. Taylor, also armed with a warrant for Pooler's arrest, arrived at Big Meadows and learned of the escape. The deputies, representing the Mono County sheriff, G. W. Bailey, found Marshal Pine less than helpful. He seemed to have no idea what direction Pooler might have taken and was not anxious to pursue him. The deputies began to suspect that Marshal Pine might have allowed Pooler to escape.

Deputy McQuade thought that a cabin near Roberts lumber mill on the East Walker River just might be the hiding place of the fugitive. Persuading a reluctant Marshal Pine to join them, McQuade and the other deputies struck out for the cabin. They had not gone far when they discovered Pooler's footprints, and sure enough, they led in the right direction. The lawmen quickened their pace and soon caught sight of the cabin on the opposite side of the East Walker. A man suddenly emerged from the dwelling and hurried upriver toward the Sierra. He looked like Pooler to the deputies, but Marshal Pine said they were mistaken. Disregarding the marshal, Deputy Honness readied his rifle. "It is him but don't shoot," cried Marshal Pine.

With some difficulty, the lawmen forded the East Walker and tracked Pooler a quarter-mile upriver to a copse of willow. Deputy McQuade yelled to the hidden fugitive, urging him to surrender. When there was no reply, McQuade fired into the thicket. Still

40.   Samuel Clemens to Mrs. Moffett, 15 August 1862, *Mark Twain's Letters,* p. 81.

there was no answer. The lawmen now began a cautious advance into the thicket. McQuade, catching sight of a shining object, opened fire. Pooler was hit in the arm and dropped his Colt Dragoon revolver, the shining object that had revealed his position. With the shotguns of deputies McQuade and Taylor now leveled at him, Pooler surrendered.

Although it was still early in the morning, Marshal Pine wanted to wait until five o'clock in the afternoon before escorting Pooler into Aurora. Deputy McQuade, suspecting that Marshal Pine had some subterfuge in mind, wanted to leave immediately. McQuade knew that there would be trouble as soon as Pooler's friends learned that he had been wounded and captured. McQuade prevailed over Pine. By noon, the marshal, deputies, and prisoner were on their way to Aurora. They reached town without further incident before nightfall. Just why Marshal Pine seemed so reluctant to arrest Pooler is not clear. Pine was not alone in his reluctance. Several men had attempted, the day before, to dissuade Deputy McQuade from pursuing Pooler. They had urged the deputy to abandon the chase because Pooler had "gone over the Sierras" and he was "well armed and would not be taken alive."[41] Pooler evidently had a number of good friends, and Marshal Pine seems to have been one of them.

On 6 September 1862, Pooler was arraigned in the Mono County district court in Aurora and charged with murder.[42] He pleaded not guilty. The trial was delayed five times as Pooler's attorney succeeded in having dozens of jurors disqualified. After three weeks the trial finally commenced. The long-awaited trial was over in one day, and Pooler was found not guilty.

It was a common remark in Aurora that Irish-born John E. Campbell was as "brave as a lion."[43] He was well known for his barroom brawls and for his near-duel with John Gorman. The *Aurora Times* described Campbell as an honest and industrious miner who was "warm hearted, generous, outspoken and manly; but, unfortunately, like so many of his countrymen, high-tempered and impulsive to rashness." By virtue of hard work, Campbell had acquired some property and had interests in several mines. His hard work during the day was occasionally followed by a spree at night. On such occasions he was a terror.

Near midnight on the Monday evening of 6 June 1864 Campbell strode into the Del Monte Exchange saloon. Within minutes he found himself in an argument with H. T. Parlin, a large and powerful miner. Both men reached for their guns. Campbell's quicker draw enabled him to fire first. A split second later Parlin fired. Both of their shots missed. Before Campbell could fire again Parlin grabbed him and, using a six-shooter as a club, split his scalp open with several terrific blows. But Campbell "never flinched in the least" and, fighting back, refused to be knocked down. He desperately tried to fire his gun, but the revolver's cylinder had jammed after the first shot. The struggle continued until Parlin backed Campbell over a barrel. With his gun hand now free, Parlin fired twice. The first shot hit Campbell in the side and the second in the stomach.

Bystanders now intervened. Despite a lacerated scalp, a possible fractured skull, and two gunshot wounds, Campbell got to his feet and asked to renew the fight. But the fight was over for Campbell. Less than four hours later he died as a result of the injuries

41. *Esmeralda Star*, 20 Sept. 1862.

42. Records, A, District Court, Mono County, pp. 37, 39, 57, 62.

43. *Aurora Times*, 11 June 1864.

he had received. He was coherent and brave to the very end and said before his death that he regretted only not having killed Parlin. "Few men," said the *Aurora Times* in referring to Campbell, "possessed a higher degree of physical courage."

Parlin surrendered himself to the authorities and on Tuesday afternoon a coroner's inquest was held. The coroner's jury, reasoning that Parlin had acted in self-defense, rendered a verdict of justifiable homicide and Parlin was released from custody.

William Carder, a native of Tennessee who had arrived in the California goldfields during the 1850s, was one of Aurora's most feared gunmen. Roswell Colcord claimed that Carder "could push his hat off the back of his head, draw, and put a bullet through it before it reached the ground."[44] "Carder's only method of fighting," noted the *Esmeralda Union*, "was with deadly weapons, in the use of which he was probably more expert than any other man on the Pacific Coast. . . . His quickness and proficiency in the use of deadly weapons were almost beyond belief, and his remarkable coolness and bravery rendered him the terror of the community."[45]

The *Esmeralda Union* should have said the terror of the community since the elimination of the Daly gang. Before that had occurred, Carder, as brave and expert a gunfighter as he was, certainly did not terrorize everyone in town, especially not John Daly or his boys, including John "Three-Fingered Jack" McDowell. McDowell, a native of Ireland, had immigrated to New York during the 1840s, fought in the Mexican War, and come to California in the gold rush.[46] He had made his mark as a gunfighter in the mining camps of Tuolumne County and later in Virginia City, before joining the Daly gang in Aurora. The early morning hours of Tuesday, 2 February 1864, found him and Carder and several others playing poker in Porter's saloon on Antelope Street.[47] An argument erupted over the money at stake. Carder put his hand on his revolver and remarked that anyone who contradicted him was a "damned liar." McDowell sprang to his feet. "Fight, you son of a bitch, fight," he exclaimed. Carder backed down.

Although Carder was married and had an eight-year-old stepson, he spent most of his time gambling and drinking in Aurora's saloons. Unless he was lucky at cards, it is not clear how he supported himself and his family. Highway robbery may have been one way. He was arrested once for relieving a Chinese miner of several hundred dollars in gold dust, but there was not enough evidence to prosecute him.[48] Nevertheless, Carder, like many other gunmen, operated on both sides of the law. While he was living in the California Mother Lode town of Columbia, the city marshal, John Leary, was murdered. Carder was made second in command of the posse that was assembled to track down the murderer, and it was Carder who eventually captured the culprit.

During the late fall of 1864, Carder left Aurora with Moses Brockman to visit the Montgomery mining district on some undisclosed business. They returned separately to Aurora, Carder arriving first. Brockman came into town a while later, but without a horse that Carder had wanted him to bring in from Adobe Meadows. Carder exploded with rage and threatened to "whip" Brockman.

44. R. K. Colcord, "Reminiscences of Life in Territorial Nevada," p. 116.

45. *Esmeralda Union*, 12 Dec. 1864.

46. *Aurora Times*, 10 Feb. 1864, as quoted in the *Virginia Daily Union*, 14 Feb. 1864.

47. *Sacramento Daily Union*, 13 Feb. 1864.

48. *Esmeralda Union*, 10 Nov. 1864.

Brockman carefully watched Carder's movements for the next few days. Then on Saturday, 10 December 1864, Carder went on a tear and, according to the *Esmeralda Union*, tried "to provoke quarrels with several of our most peaceable citizens, whom he abused most outrageously by slapping them in the face, kicking them, pulling their ears and twisting their noses."[49] Carder was also said to have threatened to kill Brockman. Brockman decided that he would be a dead man if he waited for Carder to come after him. Learning that Carder was in the Exchange saloon, Brockman secreted himself in an unused doorway near the entrance to the saloon and readied his buckshot-loaded double-barreled shotgun. About half-past eleven o'clock Carder casually strolled out of the Exchange. From point-blank range Brockman let go with both barrels. The buckshot hit Carder in the neck, "tearing a most shocking hole" and killing him instantly. Brockman then laid down his gun and surrendered to the city marshal, John Palmer.

The next day the coroner held an inquest on Carder's body. The testimony was decidedly in Brockman's favor. Brockman was termed a sober, industrious miner who normally conducted himself in a quiet, peaceable, and orderly manner. Carder was called an expert gunfighter who was feared by even the bravest fighters of the day. After listening to all the testimony, the coroner's jury promptly returned a verdict of justifiable homicide. The jury evidently felt that Brockman had had no other choice: if he had waited for Carder to come gunning for him, he would have been a dead man. Moreover, Carder had threatened Brockman's life and was an expert gunfighter. Therefore the killing of Carder, in the eyes of the jury and evidently of Aurorans in general, was justified. Roswell Colcord went further. He thought "the killing of Bill Carder was a necessity."[50] Carder's wife, Annie, thought differently. She termed the killing an assassination, said the Lord would avenge her husband's death, and had a marble tombstone made for Carder and engraved with her sentiments.

Other fatal shootings in Aurora included John Daly's killing of George Lloyd in a gunfight and murder of William Johnson, Badgely's death at the hands of Tyrrell in a gunfight, and the mysterious "slime pond murder."[51] In this latter killing an unidentified man was shot to death near the Wide West mill and his body was dumped into the mill's slime pond. A man had allegedly witnessed the crime, and two suspects were arrested. When it came time to testify before the coroner's jury, however, the witness had no recollection of the shooting, and the suspects were set free. It seems probable that the killing was gang related.

Robbery, rowdyism, and personal combat were a fact of life in Aurora. Fights, with and without weapons, occurred with regularity, while burglary and petty theft were virtually nonexistent. Highway robbery of the stage was usually restricted to the treasure box. Passengers were normally not robbed. A few travelers on the road were robbed, but even there we find the example of the highwaymen releasing the poor prospector with his belongings intact. Lawmen did not have much luck apprehending the highwaymen. Lawmen spent most of their time in Aurora policing the various forms of rowdyism. Here they were most efficient in arresting drunks. There is no record of any lawman actually being involved in a gunfight. The county sheriff or the city marshal invariably came

49.　*Esmeralda Union*, 12 Dec. 1864.

50.　Colcord, "Reminiscences," p. 116.

51.　Angel, *History of Nevada*, pp. 344–45; *Aurora Times*, 2 April 1864, as quoted in the *Virginia Daily Union*, 6 April 1864; Chalfant, *Outposts*, p. 66.

17.   *Bill Carder was one of the fastest guns in Aurora. His marble tombstone was cracked and damaged but still recognizable when this photograph was taken in 1928. (Credit: Huntington Library)*

upon the scene after the violence had occurred. The showdown between the lawman and the badman, such a common feature of Westerns, never occurred in Aurora.

Deadly confrontations between individual civilian citizens of Aurora did occur. No fewer than sixteen Aurorans died from gunshot or knife wounds, and a seventeenth died from a beating. There were also a number of near-miss armed encounters, which could have pushed the number killed up considerably. This type of encounter has been largely ignored in Western literature, where only killings are usually noted.[52] The amount of violence, therefore, has often been underrepresented. Certainly, confrontations in which shooting is only threatened, or a gun misfires, or shots are fired and no one is hit are still violent and say perhaps as much about the character of a town as do confrontations that result in death.

52.   See, e.g., Robert R. Dykstra, *The Cattle Towns*. Dykstra bases his conclusions on violence in the Kansas cattle towns solely on the total number of men killed.

Killings in Aurora were almost routinely judged justifiable homicide by the coroner's jury. In the one case that did go to court, the defendant was judged not guilty. This evidently did not trouble most Aurorans, who lived their lives in relative safety. They were unconcerned when a badman killed another badman, or when the fight seemed to be fair, or when a man was forced to protect his own life. We will see, however, that Aurorans reacted differently when an innocent citizen was gunned down in cold blood.

5

THE DALY GANG

The cold and snowy month of April 1863 found James Sears walking along the Esmeralda Road en route to Aurora.[1] At Johnson's Station on the banks of the West Walker River, he came upon an unattended, saddled horse standing in front of the way station. Without hesitating, he sprang into the saddle and galloped away. The owner of the stolen horse, German immigrant Louis Wedertz, came running out of the station and raced down the road after Sears. But Wedertz quickly realized the folly of his pedestrian pursuit and returned to ask the station-keeper, William R. Johnson, for help.

Johnson ordered hired-hand John A. Rogers into action. Rogers saddled the best horse at the station, armed himself with a Colt Navy revolver, and set out upon Sears's trail. After some twenty-five miles of hard riding, he finally caught sight of the horse thief in the Sweetwater Valley. A short gallop brought Rogers to within shouting distance, and he ordered Sears to dismount. When Sears failed to respond, Rogers drew his Colt Navy and took a well-aimed shot. Sears was blown out of the saddle and hit the ground dead.

Rogers secured Sears's body to the stolen horse and returned to the station. Wedertz, elated over the return of his horse, commended Johnson and Rogers for their prompt and effective action. The following day, Rogers rode to Carson City and delivered the body to the authorities. The coroner's jury accepted Rogers's version of the shooting and found him innocent of any wrongdoing.

Rogers now thought he might enjoy the big-city life for a day or two before returning to the way station. It was not to be. He was advised to leave town immediately; rumor had it that a notorious gunfighting friend of Sears was in town and wanted to even the score. Rogers slipped quietly out of town and returned to work. Not too much time passed before the friend of Sears, John Daly, arrived at the way station. Rogers was away at the moment, and Johnson, the station-keeper, refused to reveal his whereabouts. Daly left in a rage, determined that Johnson, as well as Rogers, must die.

John Daly, only twenty-five years old, was already one of the West's most feared

---

1. *Virginia Daily Union*, 11 Feb. 1864, as quoted in the *Sacramento Daily Union*, 13 Feb. 1864; Myron Angel, ed., *History of Nevada*, p. 422; R. K. Colcord, "Reminiscences of Life in Territorial Nevada," p. 115.

gunmen. Born in New York of Irish parents, Daly came west at an early age and earned his reputation as a deadly gunfighter in Sacramento, the Fraser River country of British Columbia, and Virginia City.[2] He had already killed at least four men and possibly as many as ten.[3] The *Aurora Times* thought him "rather fine looking" and commented that "nature had done enough for him to have entitled him a position of respectability."[4]

Daly and several of his friends and followers—soon to be known as the "Daly gang"—had arrived in Aurora early in 1863. They had quickly found employment as gunmen for the Pond mining company.[5] The Pond and the Real Del Monte were waging a legal battle over conflicting claims on Last Chance Hill.[6] They would spend several months and hundreds of thousands of dollars on two trials, one in Aurora and one in Carson City. Outside of court the Pond and the Del Monte would spend thousands more on hired guns. Daly and his "boys" were hired primarily to oppose the hired guns of the Del Monte and to intimidate the company's executives and any witnesses who might testify on behalf of the Del Monte.[7]

Daly's small house, located on an Aurora hillside, served as headquarters for the gang. Several gang members lived there, and a number of others stayed there occasionally. Some, like Three-Fingered Jack McDowell, lived with their favorite prostitute. McDowell, one of the wildest of the Daly boys, stayed with Ellen "Nellie" Sears. Nellie, a relative of James Sears, occupied a room in Eliza "Lizzie" Woodriff's house on Aurora Street. Eliza Dennison lived in another room in the same house. In a nearby house were gang favorites Mary Smith, Adelaide "Kit" Carson, Anna Haskill, and Elizabeth Williams. These women generally confined their professional work to their own rooms. They did not often frequent saloons, nor did any other woman, prostitute or not. The saloon was mostly an all-male preserve.

Pond money enabled the Daly boys to live well. They wore freshly laundered shirts and tailored suits and ate at Aurora's best restaurants. They usually awoke at about noon or one o'clock—Daly himself often luxuriated in bed smoking a pipe until the early afternoon—and did not hit their stride until midnight. By then they could most often be found in a saloon, seated at a card table, playing poker—some of the Daly boys listed their occupation as gambler—and drinking whiskey. Although more than a few of the boys often imbibed prodigious quantities of whiskey and ended the evening drunk, Daly drank cautiously and nearly always remained sober. Gambling and drinking frequently continued until three or four o'clock in the morning, when it was time to bed down with a chosen "girl" or return to Daly's house or other lodgings. Woe to the man who woke up any of the boys before the sun was high.

---

2. *Aurora Times*, 10 Feb. 1864, as quoted in the *Virginia Daily Union*, 14 Feb. 1864; Angel, *History of Nevada*, p. 422.

3. *Aurora Times*, 10 Feb. 1864, as quoted in the *Virginia Daily Union*, 14 Feb. 1864; Ella Sterling Mighels, *Life and Letters of a Forty-Niner's Daughter*, p. 39.

4. *Aurora Times*, 10 Feb. 1864, as quoted in the *Virginia Daily Union*, 14 Feb. 1864.

5. *Esmeralda Star*, 17 Feb. 1864, as quoted in the *Virginia Daily Union*, 21 and 24 Feb. 1864; Stockton *Independent*, date unknown, as quoted in Hubert H. Bancroft, *Popular Tribunals*, vol. 1, p. 610.

6. Carson *Daily Independent*, 26 Nov. and 1, 9, and 16–19 Dec. 1863; 10 Jan. 1864, as quoted in Angel, *History of Nevada*, p. 340; *Aurora Times*, 24 Feb. 1864, as quoted in the *Virginia Daily Union*, 28 Feb. 1864; Joseph Wasson, *Account of the Important Revival of Mining Interests in the Bodie and Esmeralda Districts*, p. 48.

7. *Esmeralda Star*, 17 Feb. 1864, as quoted in the *Virginia Daily Union*, 21 and 24 Feb. 1864.

Daly did not let this lifestyle interfere with the gang's obligations to the Pond.[8] H. T. Parlin, who had mining interests on Last Chance Hill, was scheduled to testify on behalf of the Del Monte. Daly assigned one of his men to kill Parlin. When word was intentionally leaked to Parlin that he was a "marked man," he sold out his mining interests and left for the East Coast. Another man targeted for death was Dr. E. F. Mitchell, president of the Real Del Monte. Mitchell, like Parlin before him, learned of the plot. Although he refused to run, he moved to a more secure house and hired a bodyguard. He avoided sitting or standing in front of windows or doorways, and he never ventured out at night. Still another man allegedly marked for death was William Van Voorhees, an attorney for the Del Monte. He too was guarded and maintained the utmost vigilance.

The Daly gang exerted its influence through legal channels as well. In the 1863 election for city marshal, Daly executed a masterstroke. Seeing that the field of candidates was crowded, with no one candidate standing out, Daly had one of his men run for the office. With the vote of the more respectable citizens of Aurora distributed among many candidates, Daly's man emerged with a plurality. "No sooner had the Marshal been sworn in," asserted the *Esmeralda Star*, "than the worst villains that ever infested a civilized community were appointed policemen, and with but few exceptions they were composed of as hard a set of criminals as ever went unhung."[9] John Daly himself served as a deputy marshal.[10]

Policemen now began collecting license fees and pocketing the money. Gambling, prostitution, drunkenness, and fighting increased, and punishment decreased. Nevertheless, Aurorans were not outraged. The average citizen was still relatively safe. The "ruffians" fought mostly among themselves. "So long as they did not molest peaceable citizens," noted the *Esmeralda Star*, "their shooting and killing one another was borne with by the people with utter indifference."[11] John Daly seemed to understand. The first man he killed in Aurora was one of his own gang members, George Lloyd.

Lloyd was as rough a character as could be found in the West. He and his two brothers had operated the Mountaineer saloon in Sacramento during 1861 and 1862.[12] There he had gotten into several fights, including a bloody rough-and-tumble fight with John Daly, which was the talk of the town. Shortly afterward, Lloyd was involved in a deadly shootout. For some time there had been trouble between his brother, Edward Lloyd, and Thomas Coleman. On a wharf at the foot of K Street, Coleman confronted Ed Lloyd. Both men drew pistols and fired simultaneously. Joe McGee and F. N. Smith, revolver-armed friends of Coleman, joined in. George Lloyd, the Lloyds' cousin Patsey Callahan, and a friend named McAlpine, who were there with Ed Lloyd, could not do much to even the odds. Except for a knife one of them carried, they were unarmed. In the uneven exchange, Smith shot Ed Lloyd through the back of the head, killing him instantly, and McGee drilled George Lloyd in the shoulder and McAlpine in the wrist.

Smith was arrested for the killing of Ed Lloyd and spent the next six months in the county jail before the charges against him were dropped. Less than fifteen minutes

8.   *Esmeralda Star*, 17 Feb. 1864, as quoted in the *Virginia Daily Union*, 21 and 24 Feb. 1864.

9.   *Esmeralda Star*, 17 Feb. 1864, as quoted in the *Virginia Daily Union*, 24 Feb. 1864.

10. *Aurora Times*, 10 Feb. 1864, as quoted in the *Virginia Daily Union*, 14 Feb. 1864.

11. *Esmeralda Star*, 17 Feb. 1864, as quoted in the *Virginia Daily Union*, 24 Feb. 1864.

12. Stockton *Independent*, date unknown, as quoted in Bancroft, *Popular Tribunals*, vol. 1, p. 609.

18 and 19.   *Real Del Monte hoisting works on Last Chance Hill
(above) and the Del Monte mill in Bodie Gulch (below). The mill contained a battery of thirty steam-powered stamps and cost $250,000 to
build in 1863. (Credit: Nevada Historical Society)*

after Smith was released from jail, George Lloyd found him and opened fire. Four bullets hit their mark, and Smith died on the spot. Lloyd was arrested and tried for the killing, but after several trials he was acquitted. Deciding that the time was now propitious for a change of scenery, Lloyd joined Daly and his men in a move to Aurora. Callahan was not among them. He stayed in Sacramento and, the next year, was stabbed to death in the Bank Exchange saloon.

In Aurora, George Lloyd, like the other members of the Daly gang, found work as a hired gun for the Pond mining company. Lloyd was the gang member who had frightened H. T. Parlin into selling out his mining interest and leaving town. Although Lloyd was evidently loyal to Daly, their rough-and-tumble fight in Sacramento demonstrated that the men had not always seen eye to eye and that Lloyd was brave enough to challenge Daly. The Saturday night of 24 October 1863 found the two arguing in P. J. McMahan's Del Monte Exchange saloon. They went for their guns. Several shots were fired, and Lloyd slumped to the floor dead. Daly had killed, by some counts, his eleventh man.[13]

In November the Pond and Real Del Monte trial opened in the district court in Aurora.[14] The court's session ended in Aurora with the trial still in progress. Consequently, in early December the trial was moved to Carson City, and a new jury was impaneled. Daly and a couple of his men, Jack McDowell and S. B. Vance, arrived there ahead of the trial and ran into Joe McGee, an old enemy of theirs. McGee had killed several men, including Jack Williams and Tom Reeder, both friends of Daly. Daly, McDowell, and Vance now rolled dice to determine who should kill McGee. Daly won. On the Wednesday night of 9 December 1863—one year after the death of Jack Williams—Daly found McGee in the St. Nicholas saloon. Using the same gun that McGee had used to kill Williams, Daly shot McGee dead.[15]

On 10 January 1864, after having spent enormous sums for attorneys and hired guns—the Real Del Monte alone spent more than a half-million dollars—the Pond and the Del Monte settled their dispute out of court when the second trial ended in a hung jury.[16] His services no longer required by the Pond, Daly returned to Aurora and learned that during his absence a new marshal, Daniel H. Pine, had been elected.[17] Pine had reorganized the police force and fired Daly-gang policemen. Daly's power bases—the Pond and the marshal's office—were now gone, but he was in no hurry to leave Aurora. He had one last score to settle.

On the Monday afternoon of 1 February 1864, William Johnson arrived in Aurora to sell a few bushels of potatoes that he had grown at his way station.[18] The thirty-seven-year-old Johnson had been operating the way station since 1861 and was

13.   *Esmeralda Star*, 17 Feb. 1864, as quoted in the *Virginia Daily Union*, 21 Feb. 1864; Stockton *Independent*, date unknown, as quoted in Bancroft, *Popular Tribunals*, vol. 1, p. 610; Angel, *History of Nevada*, p. 345; *Aurora Times*, 10 Feb. 1864, as quoted in the *Virginia Daily Union*, 14 Feb. 1864.

14.   Carson *Daily Independent*, 26 Nov. and 1, 9, and 16–19 Dec. 1863; 10 Jan. 1864, as quoted in Angel, *History of Nevada*, p. 340.

15.   Angel, *History of Nevada*, pp. 344–45; *Bodie Standard*, 5 and 19 April 1882.

16.   Carson *Daily Independent*, 19 Dec. 1863, 10 Jan. 1864, as quoted in Angel, *History of Nevada*, p. 340; Wasson, *Account of Revival*, p. 48.

17.   *Esmeralda Star*, 17 Feb. 1864, as quoted in the *Virginia Daily Union*, 24 Feb. 1864.

18.   *Virginia Daily Union*, 11 Feb. 1864, as quoted in the *Sacramento Daily Union*, 13 Feb. 1864.

well known to those who traveled the Esmeralda Road.[19] He had first crossed into the trans-Sierra country during the summer of 1859 after having operated stores in Sacramento and Kelsey's Diggings. He had tried to develop a milling operation and had freighted goods over the Sierra before settling down with his wife at the way station. Life at the way station had been uneventful until Johnson's hired hand, John Rogers, gunned down James Sears.

Johnson sold his potatoes and ambled over to the Merchant's Exchange saloon at the corner of Pine and Winnemucca streets to enjoy some of the proceeds of his sale.[20] There he spent the next several hours drinking, playing billiards, and gambling. One of Daly's men affected a friendship for him, and when the Merchant's Exchange closed at about two o'clock in the morning, they strode arm in arm over to Porter's saloon on Antelope Street. Most of the Daly gang, including Daly himself, were there waiting. Johnson was too drunk to understand the gravity of the situation and allowed himself to be treated to several more drinks by members of the gang.

Finally, at about half-past four o'clock, Johnson staggered out of the saloon and headed for his lodgings. Daly, Three-Fingered Jack, William Buckley, and James "Massey" Masterson were waiting for him. Just as Johnson passed the post office on his way up Antelope Street, they sprang out from behind a woodpile. Buckley felled Johnson with a blow from a pistol, and Daly shot him through the head. Evidently to make sure that Johnson would not somehow survive the shooting, Buckley then severed the victim's jugular vein with a bowie knife. It was unnecessary; Johnson was already dead. James Sears had been revenged.

By mid-morning on Tuesday, most Aurorans had learned of the murder, which, noted the *Aurora Times*, "caused great feeling and excitement in town today."[21] Gunmen killing gunmen was one thing, but this time an innocent man had been murdered. By noon, coroner John T. Moore was holding an inquest over the body. A large crowd assembled outside his office and anxiously followed the proceedings. Into this milling and angry crowd came S. B. Vance, who had been subpoenaed to appear before the coroner's jury.[22] While Vance waited to be called into the coroner's office, a rumor spread through the crowd that he was one of the murderers. This was evidently proof enough for W. F. Watkins, a miner and longtime resident of Aurora, who took a shot at Vance with a derringer. Vance was hit in the groin and seriously wounded. Nevertheless, he drew a revolver and got off three shots of his own, which all missed Watkins.

Daly and Buckley were sitting across the street in the Del Monte Exchange saloon when the shooting occurred.[23] They rushed to the scene and, with their hands on their revolvers, called for the man who had shot Vance. For a few moments it looked as if a bloody shootout would erupt, but Marshal Dan Pine arrived and arrested Watkins. Vance was taken to his own house and placed under armed guard. His wound was treated, and it was said that he "suffered great pain with remarkable fortitude."

19. *Sacramento Daily Union*, 11 Feb. 1864; *Virginia Daily Union*, 3 and 5 Feb. 1864.

20. *Aurora Times*, 9 Feb. 1864, as quoted in the *Sacramento Daily Union*, 13 Feb. 1864.

21. *Aurora Times*, 2 Feb. 1864, as quoted in the *Virginia Daily Union*, 5 Feb. 1864.

22. *Aurora Times*, 2 Feb. and 31 March 1864, as quoted in the *Virginia Daily Union*, 5 Feb. and 3 April 1864.

23. *Aurora Times*, 31 March 1864, as quoted in the *Virginia Daily Union*, 3 April 1864.

This near free-for-all following the murder of Johnson unnerved much of the population of Aurora. On Tuesday afternoon, some four hundred Aurorans met in Armory Hall in the Wingate Building and formed the "Citizens' Safety Committee."[24] A twelve-man executive council was elected, and John A. Palmer was chosen "First Officer." Palmer, the commander of the Aurora City Guard, one of the town's two militia companies, had led vigilantes during 1858 in the Mother Lode town of Columbia. The Citizens' Safety Committee was divided into four companies, each with its own officer. The men carried not only their own personal arms but also forty rifles belonging to the militia. With its organization completed, the committee resolved:

> That while we recognize the right of self-defense to exist in communities, as well as in individuals, we also recognize the supremacy of the law; and so long as a hope remains that the parties guilty of the horrible crimes which have been committed in our midst may be brought to justice by legally constituted authorities, the members of this association will confine themselves to aiding the officers of the law in the efficient discharge of their duties.
>
> Resolved, that we intend to see that the laws are enforced and the guilty brought to justice.[25]

Ostensibly, then, the committee was pledged to assisting the sheriff and the marshal, not to the usurpation of their duties.

Meanwhile, the coroner's inquest continued. Testimony revealed that Gaitano Bacigalupi, better known as "Italian Jim," had been in Porter's saloon the previous night and had been with William Johnson when the station manager began his ill-fated walk up Antelope Street.[26] Coroner Moore, who was also a justice of the peace, issued a subpoena for Italian Jim and ordered Marshal Pine to bring him before the jury. But Italian Jim was not in town. He had left on the morning stage for Carson City. After fifty miles of hard riding, Pine overtook the stage at Wellington and lightened its load by one passenger.

The next day Italian Jim appeared before the coroner's jury. He was asked to state his occupation. "Gamble when I have money, mine when broke," said the veteran of the Calaveras County diggings. With great reluctance, he then began to testify. At first, he said nothing that would incriminate the Daly gang, but eventually revealed all he knew. He described how Daly, Buckley, Three-Fingered Jack, and Massey had lain in wait for Johnson and had killed him. Italian Jim further testified that he had left town on the morning stage at Buckley's insistence. During the next several days, a number of witnesses gave testimony that strongly supported him. These witnesses, like Italian Jim, had at first been afraid to reveal anything that might incriminate Daly and his men. A couple of them claimed that Buckley had threatened their lives, but that the presence of the Safety Committee had given them the courage to speak up. The names of three of the witnesses were kept secret in order "to better serve public policy."[27]

24.   *Virginia Daily Union,* 5 Feb. 1864; *Sacramento Daily Union,* 10 Feb. 1864; *Esmeralda Union,* 31 March 1864; Samuel Youngs's Journal, 2 Feb. 1864.

25.   *Sacramento Daily Union,* 10 Feb. 1864.

26.   *Aurora Times,* 9 Feb. 1864, as quoted in the *Sacramento Daily Union,* 13 Feb. 1864; *Virginia Daily Union,* 11 Feb. 1864, as quoted in the *Sacramento Daily Union,* 13 Feb. 1864.

27.   See n. 26; *Sacramento Daily Union,* 10 Feb. 1864.

While the coroner's jury continued to take testimony and examine evidence, arrest warrants were issued for John Daly and all members of his gang suspected of having been involved in Johnson's murder. The police, assisted by members of the Safety Committee, did their duty with unusual vigor. "Never have we known officers," commented the *Aurora Times*, "to labor more zealously to ferret out and to apprehend the perpetrators of a crime."[28] Daly, Three-Fingered Jack, Massey, Thomas "Irish Tom" Carberry, and Pliney Gardiner were all arrested in Aurora. S. B. Vance was already in custody. A posse, led by Sheriff D. G. Francis, was sent to Adobe Meadows, where more gang members, including William Buckley, were believed to be hiding. In the meantime, Mrs. Johnson arrived in town for her husband's funeral. Johnson's coffin was followed to the Aurora graveyard, said a newspaper correspondent for the *Sacramento Daily Union*, by "the largest funeral procession ever seen in this town."[29]

On the Friday evening of 5 February 1864, Sheriff Francis returned from Adobe Meadows with gang members Mike Fagan, John Gillman, and Wash Parker, but without Buckley. A search for Buckley was begun in the tunnels and shafts on Last Chance Hill when rumor spread that he was hiding there. Then a reliable report reached Aurora that a man answering Buckley's description had been seen passing Mackay's ranch, some twelve miles south of town. The man was said to be on foot and headed toward Mono Lake. Early Saturday morning two posses, one led by Sheriff Francis and the other by Deputy Sheriff H. J. Teel, set out in pursuit.[30]

Teel's posse headed directly for Mono Lake, while Francis's men took a circuitous route via Adobe Meadows. For several days the posses searched in vain, suffering greatly in subfreezing weather. Teel's party rounded Mono Lake no less than three times without finding a trace of Buckley. Finally, a few of Teel's men stopped at Lee Vining's old cabin on Rush Creek, which flows into Mono Lake from the southwest. Two men were staying in the cabin. When asked if they had seen anything of Buckley, one of them replied ambiguously, "He is not here."

Their dog, who was barking at something in the sagebrush, indicated otherwise. The searchers shouldered their guns and moved toward the object of the dog's attention. Out of an old sagebrush-covered prospect hole sprang Buckley. "Boys, you have got me this time," he exclaimed. A few minutes later Teel and the rest of the posse arrived. With Buckley in custody, they left immediately for Aurora.

For four days and nights Buckley had eluded the trackers. During his flight he had observed Sheriff Francis at Adobe Meadows, and Deputy Teel's camp had been so near to him that he could listen to the posse's campfire conversation. At another point, one of the searchers had ridden so close to Buckley that his horse almost stepped on the fugitive as he lay concealed in the sagebush. If it had not been for the dog at Vining's Rush Creek cabin, Buckley might have slipped away and had still another narrow escape to talk about.

During his flight, Buckley had displayed remarkable stamina and fortitude. He had run and walked from Aurora to Mono Lake, then entirely around the lake and on

28. *Aurora Times*, 10 Feb. 1864, as quoted in the *Virginia Daily Union*, 14 Feb. 1864.

29. *Sacramento Daily Union*, 10 Feb. 1864.

30. *Esmeralda Star*, [?] Feb. 1864, as quoted in Bancroft, *Popular Tribunals*, vol. 1, p. 606.

to Adobe Meadows, and then back to Mono Lake and halfway around it to Rush Creek. In four days he had covered over a hundred miles of the roughest terrain imaginable. He had been without food, and his clothing had done little to protect him from nighttime temperatures, which dropped well below freezing. He did not light a fire for fear of exposing his position. Buckley was later said to have declared that he would rather be hanged than suffer again from such cold and hunger.

While the posses had been searching for Buckley, the Safety Committee, now some six hundred men strong, had opted for a vigilante solution and had taken nearly full control of Aurora. All roads leading to Aurora were guarded, as were all the city streets. A heavily armed guard surrounded the coroner's office, another one, the jail, and a third one paraded up and down the streets.[31] On the Sunday afternoon of 7 February 1864, after being in session for nearly a week and hearing the testimony of dozens of witnesses, the coroner's jury rendered its verdict: John Daly, William Buckley, John McDowell, and James Masterson had murdered William Johnson, and S. B. Vance was an accessory to the crime.[32]

The vigilantes, although they believed that Daly and his accomplices were guilty beyond a shadow of a doubt, thought that if the killers were allowed to go to trial, they might escape punishment through a change of venue to Carson City, delaying tactics, and intimidation of witnesses.[33] On Monday, the day after the coroner's jury announced its verdict, a squad of vigilantes rushed into the Aurora jail, overpowered Deputy Sheriff D. S. Demming and Marshal Pine, and took possession of the jail and the prisoners.[34] At five o'clock the next morning, Deputy Sheriff Teel arrived in Aurora with the captured Buckley. The vigilantes took possession of the prisoner and kept Teel under armed guard in his own house. A few hours later, the Safety Committee sentenced Daly, Buckley, McDowell, and Masterson to death and declared martial law in Aurora. The mines, mills, and all businesses were closed, and a gallows, large enough to hang four men, was erected in front of Armory Hall on Silver Street. People for miles around began flocking to town. "I beheld the men of the quartz mills," recalled the daughter of a prominent Auroran, "running by our toll gate to be present crying hoarsely, 'Let me pull on the rope!' "[35] By mid-morning Tuesday no fewer than five thousand people were gathered around the gallows.

Governor James Nye, who had been receiving reports by both mail and the telegraph of the activities in Aurora, now became truly alarmed. He telegraphed Samuel Youngs, declaring that there must be no violence.[36] Youngs replied to the governor, "Everything peaceable and orderly. No opposition to officers. Four men will be hung at twelve o'clock."[37] Five minutes later, Deputy Sheriff Teel telegraphed the governor and

31.   *Sacramento Daily Union*, 10 Feb. 1864.

32.   *Aurora Times*, 9 Feb. 1864, as quoted in the *Sacramento Daily Union*, 13 Feb. 1864.

33.   *Esmeralda Star*, 17 Feb. 1864, as quoted in the *Virginia Daily Union*, 24 Feb. 1864.

34.   H. J. Teel to James Nye, 11:35 A.M., 9 Feb. 1864, California State Telegraph Company, Unsorted Territorial Correspondence, Nevada Division of Archives; *Virginia Daily Union*, 10 Feb. 1864.

35.   Mighels, *Life and Letters of a Forty-Niner's Daughter*, p. 38.

36.   Samuel Youngs's Journal, 9 Feb. 1864.

37.   There are several versions of Youngs's message, with no significant differences. See Samuel Youngs to James Nye, 11:30 A.M., 9 Feb. 1864, California State Telegraph Company, Unsorted Territorial Correspondence; *Virginia Daily Union*, 10 Feb. 1864; Samuel Youngs's Journal, 9 Feb. 1864.

contradicted Youngs on one important point. Teel reported that the officers of the law had lost control of the situation as of Monday afternoon and that now "everything is in the hands of the citizens."[38] Governor Nye ordered a hundred troops at Fort Churchill to hold themselves in readiness and, together with Provost Marshal Jacob Van Bokkelen and U.S. Marshal Warren Wasson, left immediately for Aurora.[39]

At noon a special guard of vigilantes marched the condemned men to the gallows. The guards, with fixed bayonets, formed a hollow square around the scaffold, and Daly and the others mounted the platform "with a firm step, and surveyed the immense crowd with apparent cool indifference."[40] John Daly took a proffered drink of brandy and then pointed at a member of the Safety Committee who was brandishing a revolver. "You son of a bitch," Daly defiantly exclaimed. "If I had a six-shooter I would make you get."[41] Daly then took several silver dollars out of his pocket and threw them to the crowd. He motioned for the crowd to move in closer and declared:

> There are two innocent men on this scaffold. You are going to hang two in-nocent men. Do you understand that? I am guilty. I killed Johnson; Buckley and I killed Johnson. Do you understand that: Johnson was a damn old Mormon thief. He was the means of killing my friend, and I lived to die for him. Had I lived I would have wiped out Johnson's whole generation.

Daly sat down on the scaffold, evidently spent from the effort and feeling the effects of the brandy. William Buckley, a native of New York who had come west with his family in the gold rush before joining Daly, now stepped forward and addressed the crowd:

> Gentlemen, I do not stand up before you to say I am innocent. Daly and I are guilty. There are two innocent men on this scaffold, McDowell and Masterson. I deserve to be punished, and I die a brave man.
>
> I want you [a friend named Daniel Toomy who was standing near the scaffold] to see to getting a coffin for me, and that any debts which you may contract on my account I have made arrangements to pay.
>
> Adieu, boys. I wish you all well. All of you boys must come up to my wake in John Daly's cabin tonight. Be sure of this. Good bye, God bless you all.

Buckley now stepped aside and dictated a letter to a friend, Patrick Gerety. In the letter, addressed to his brother Crist in San Francisco, Buckley said that he was ready to stand before the Maker and would die a brave man. He also noted that the county sheriff owed him $180 and the Pond mining company another $470. His message concluded:

38.   H. J. Teel to James Nye, 11:35 A.M., 9 Feb. 1864, California State Telegraph Company, Unsorted Territorial Correspondence.

39.   *Virginia Daily Union*, 10 and 16 Feb. 1864.

40.   *Aurora Times*, 10 Feb. 1864, as quoted in the *Virginia Daily Union*, 14 Feb. 1864.

41.   This and all subsequent quotations of the condemned men come from the *Aurora Times*, 10 Feb. 1864, as quoted in the *Virginia Daily Union*, 14 Feb. 1864.

> Give my first and last love to my dear, dear mother. God bless her. But don't let her know that my death was the ignominious death of the gallows. You will also let Father and Johnny know of my death, and keep from them too, if possible, the circumstances. Good bye. God bless you all. Pray for me, for I have yet hopes in a merciful God and Savior.

John McDowell, known to all as Three-Fingered Jack, now stepped forward to address the crowd. In a loud voice McDowell proclaimed:

> Gentlemen, I am as innocent of this as the child unborn. You are going to murder me. This is murder, gentlemen. I am as innocent as the man in the moon. Is there no show for me? Am I to be murdered? Yes, you are determined to murder me. I don't want my body to be buried with the balance of them. Where is Nellie? Where is Jim Litz?

Nellie Sears and some friends of Three-Fingered Jack then went to the scaffold and spoke to him. When they left he straightened up and said to the crowd, "Good bye, boys." With that McDowell pulled a derringer from his pocket, put it to his breast, and pulled the trigger. It failed to fire. He hurled it to the ground and exclaimed, "The son of a bitch of a pistol has fooled me!" McDowell then repeated his assertion of innocence and said that he would haunt the beds of the vigilantes. Realizing that further protestation was useless, he stepped back and declared, "I'll die like a tiger."

James "Massey" Masterson, a native of New York who had been in the mining camps of the West for several years, now took his turn. Appearing perfectly cool and unconcerned, Masterson simply stated, "Gentlemen, I am innocent." "Yes, Buckley and I did the deed," Daly added immediately.

McDowell and Masterson's protestations of innocence had no effect on the vigilantes. All four men now had their hands tied, their eyes bandaged, and nooses adjusted around their necks. The Reverend C. Yeager said a final prayer, and at half-past one o'clock a small cannon that stood beside the gallows was fired. This was the signal that five thousand spectators had waited for. The rope was cut, and Daly, Buckley, McDowell, and Masterson disappeared through the trapdoor and into eternity.[42] The bodies were left to dangle from the gallows until after dark, when friends of the executed men were allowed to cut them down.

On the snowy Wednesday evening of 10 February 1864, a little more than twenty-four hours too late to stop the hanging, Governor Nye, U.S. Marshal Wasson, and Provost Marshal Van Bokkelen arrived in Aurora.[43] The governor found everything quiet and orderly. But when he saw the gallows with the four ropes still dangling from the crossbeam, he ordered the sheriff to have the "devilish machine" removed at once. The sheriff, perhaps fearing the wrath of the Safety Committee, hesitated until the governor proposed that he himself would tear it down.

42. *Aurora Times*, 10 Feb. 1864, as quoted in the *Virginia Daily Union*, 14 Feb. 1864; *Virginia Daily Union*, 11 Feb. 1864; *Visalia Delta*, 18 Feb. 1864; Angel, *History of Nevada*, pp. 345, 423.

43. *Esmeralda Star*, 13 Feb. 1864, as quoted in the *Virginia Daily Union*, 17 Feb. 1864; *Virginia Daily Union*, 16 Feb. 1864.

The next morning Governor Nye met with the executive council of the Safety Committee. The council explained to Nye the reasons for their actions and emphasized that the coroner's jury had found conclusive proof of the men's guilt. The governor's response to the vigilantes was mild. He ordered the vigilantes to return the military arms they had used to the armory and, for the time being, the saloons to close at nine o'clock. But if any more vigilante action occurred, warned Nye, he would put the town under martial law. Provost Marshal Van Bokkelen was partly responsible for Nye's tempered response to the vigilantes. Van Bokkelen himself had been a vigilante. Thirteen years earlier he had served as chief of vigilante police for the San Francisco Committee of Vigilance of 1851.[44] Now he found himself empathizing with the Safety Committee, which closely resembled San Francisco's 1851 committee, and calming the governor. Nye, Van Bokkelen, and Wasson remained in Aurora through the weekend and, evidently satisfied that everything had returned to normal, left for Carson on Monday morning.

All had not returned to normal. The Safety Committee continued to operate and now had squads of men deliver orders of banishment to various town "roughs." The *Esmeralda Star* supported the Committee's action with the rallying cry "Hemp for assassins and for outlaws banishment."[45] The vigilantes carried out the work so zealously that there was "a general skedaddling of murderers, gamblers, and thieves."[46] What Aurora lost, Carson City and Virginia City gained. Residents of those two towns were soon complaining that the banished men were taking up residence there.[47]

In late February, James Masterson's brother arrived in Aurora to settle Massey's estate.[48] Friction quickly developed between the brother and the vigilantes and came to a climax when he allegedly threatened several vigilantes. The Safety Committee then ordered him to leave town. He refused. With that, the vigilantes fired the signal gun— a small cannon—and in less than twenty minutes four companies of vigilantes were assembled on Silver Street. Sheriff Francis offered Masterson's brother the protection of the jail and told him that it would be impossible to hold off the vigilantes unless he agreed to leave town. The brother saw that further resistance to the vigilantes was futile, and he was escorted out of Aurora.

Because of this incident and a number of other questionable arrests and orders of banishment, the vigilance committee began to meet organized resistance. On 3 March 1864, a group of more than fifty dissidents sent the following petition to Governor Nye:

> Your petitioners, residents and citizens of Aurora, Esmeralda County, Territory of Nevada would most respectfully represent: That there is now an armed organization in our midst, acting in open defiance of the law and constituted authorities; that this organization, without even the pretence of legal right, is continuing to arrest citi-

44. Bancroft, *Popular Tribunals*, vol. 1, p. 355.

45. *Esmeralda Star*, 17 Feb. 1864, as quoted in the *Virginia Daily Union*, 21 Feb. 1864.

46. San Andres *Register*, 27 Feb. 1864, as quoted in Bancroft, *Popular Tribunals*, vol. 1, p. 609.

47. *Virginia Daily Union*, 13 Feb. 1864.

48. Bancroft, *Popular Tribunals*, vol. 1, pp. 610–11; J. J. Coddington and George Whitney to James Nye, 9:25 P.M., 2 March 1864, California State Telegraph Company, Unsorted Territorial Correspondence; D. G. Francis to James Nye, 3 March 1864, California State Telegraph Company, Unsorted Territorial Correspondence.

zens and residents among us, and compelling them, by an overwhelming force, to leave and abandon a place where they have seen fit to come and live. These proceedings are being carried on by an armed multitude, overpowering the legally constituted officers, upon the pretext of charges that are preferred in secret against parties protesting their entire innocence, and who are denied the opportunity of defence, of confronting their accusers, or even of knowing who they are.

Within a very few hours one of these orders to leave has been issued and enforced by this organization at the imminent peril of the safety of our town, and the lives of the officers of the law and a large number of citizens called to their aid, but rendered powerless from the fact that all the public arms are in the hands of the organization referred to. . . .

We, therefore, your petitioners, earnestly urge upon your excellency to adopt some measures by which our society may be held and protected within the law, the imminent danger of a disastrous outbreak and bloodshed be avoided, and the rights of all be protected and secured.

The *Aurora Times* reacted to the petition immediately. The very next day the newspaper editorialized that the petition

shows that there is an opposition to the Citizens' Safety Committee in our midst, to which its protracted session is giving strength. We have no desire to see Aurora declared in a state of insurrection; no wish to have troops sent here. As set forth yesterday, the effect would be most injurious to the interests of the city. If the committee would get through with their business and disband at once, the opposition now manifesting itself would fall to the ground and amount to nothing. The danger of a bloody collision between the officers of the law and the committee, which threatens hourly to come about, is by no means a pleasant subject to contemplate.[49]

Before Governor Nye was forced to call out the troops at Fort Churchill, Sheriff Francis wired him that the vigilance committee was officially disbanding and that "no more disturbance is looked for."[50]

Meanwhile, S. B. Vance, charged with being accessory after the fact to the murder of William Johnson, was still in county jail recovering from his wound and awaiting trial. Vance had only narrowly missed being hanged. Since evidence presented before the coroner's jury indicated that he was not with Daly at the time of the murder, the vigilantes decided to let the district court decide his fate.

Vance believed his chances of acquittal were good, and he improved them considerably when he refused to participate in a jail break. On the Friday night of 25 March 1864, three prisoners managed to tunnel through the jail wall with nothing more than a knife, and to escape.[51] Vance crawled through the hole also, but then walked

49.   Petition and editorial, *Aurora Times*, 4 March 1864, as quoted in Bancroft, *Popular Tribunals*, vol. 1, p. 608.

50.   D. G. Francis to James Nye, 5 and 9 March 1864, California State Telegraph Company, Unsorted Territorial Correspondence.

51.   *Esmeralda Union*, 26 March 1864; George A. Whitney to William T. Whitney, 27 March 1864, Whitney Letters and Correspondence, 1862–1887.

leisurely down to the Sazerac saloon and had a drink before reporting the escape to Sheriff Francis.

On Monday, 28 March 1864, Vance's trial opened in the district court at Aurora.[52] Spectators crammed into the courtroom to witness the action, but nothing more was accomplished the first day than selecting a jury. Judge George S. Turner refused to excuse jurors because they were familiar with the case; everyone in Aurora had read, heard, and formed opinions about Johnson's murder. Jurors were excused only if they thought they could not give Vance a fair trial. Vance's attorneys requested a continuance, but the motion was denied, and testimony began on Tuesday. Final arguments were presented on Wednesday evening before a packed courtroom. The defense attorneys delivered, said the *Aurora Times* on 31 March, "ingenious, powerful and eloquent" speeches that were as fine a "display of legal ability and forensic eloquence" as could be seen in the West. The jury was out for only half an hour before it returned a verdict of not guilty. Vance was overjoyed. Judge Turner admonished him to lead a better life in the future and discharged him.

A week later Vance was on the Aurora stage bound for Virginia City. "I'm going back to Aurora when the people get cooled down a little, and I'll make it mighty hot for some of them," Vance allegedly remarked to another passenger.[53] Vance never returned to Aurora, but he did continue gunfighting. After stays in Virginia City and San Francisco, where he was arrested for assaulting a man, he moved on to the mining camps of Montana, establishing himself as a "badman" in that region also.[54] In August 1867 he returned to Nevada to visit the state's latest boom town, Austin. There he ran into Irish Tom Carberry, another former member of the Daly gang in Aurora. Irish Tom had been regarded as one of Aurora's most deadly gunmen, and now he was the premier shootist in Austin. Vance, not ready to accept an inferior status, immediately challenged Irish Tom to a duel. Carberry, who was unarmed at the time, was told to get himself "heeled" and come back shooting. Vance commenced firing as soon as Carberry reappeared on Austin's main street. Irish Tom held his fire. With bullets whizzing by him, he coolly walked toward Vance. When he came within close range, he rested his revolver across his arm, took careful aim, and shot Vance dead.[55] Irish Tom was now the only gunfighter of note left from the once powerful Daly gang.

Irish Tom was not through gunfighting. Early on the morning of 5 September 1868, Irish Tom and Charles Ridgely traded insults when an old grudge between the two erupted into an argument.[56] Irish Tom told Ridgely to go and arm himself and come back shooting. Moments later, Ridgely stepped out of the International Hotel onto Austin's main street. Irish Tom jumped into the street to meet him, and both men began firing simultaneously. Their first shots missed, as did Ridgely's second and third. Irish Tom's second and third shots drilled Ridgely in the chest, and within minutes he was dead.

52. *Aurora Times*, 28 and 31 March 1864, as quoted in the *Virginia Daily Union*, 1 and 3 April 1864; *Esmeralda Union*, 1 April 1864.

53. *Esmeralda Union*, 16 April 1864.

54. *Aurora Times*, 11 June 1864; Angel, *History of Nevada*, p. 348.

55. Angel, p. 348; *Esmeralda Union*, 12 Sept. 1868.

56. *Esmeralda Union*, 12 Sept. 1868.

Irish Tom was the last of the Daly gang to make news. The gang had produced enough deadly gunmen to rival any of the more familiar gangs of the Old West. Certainly, neither the Plummer gang nor the James brothers, the Doolins, the Daltons, the Wild Bunch, or the Hole-in-the-Wall gang ever produced a shootist any cooler or more accurate than Irish Tom. Nor were any of those gangs led by a gunfighter more deadly than John Daly.

Daly reportedly returned to Aurora on the first anniversary of his hanging—as a ghost. W. Hazen claimed that Daly, dressed in a long white coat and high boots, came into his bedroom on three successive nights and spoke to him. Daly, according to Hazen, said that he was the keeper of a prison filled with "murderers and Mormons" in the spirit land. Showing his scarred legs and chest to Hazen, Daly said that he was tortured periodically for the murder of William Johnson. "Friend," warned Daly, "commit no evil deeds. Look at my torn flesh and take warning! If you have a heart, weep!"[57] The Daly ghost made an appearance at Armory Hall a couple of weeks later. He laughed loudly and shrilly and seemed impervious to the bullets fired at him. The *Esmeralda Union* noted that "had the gentlemen who fired at the 'ghost' hit their mark, some practical joker still in the flesh would have received an unwelcome reward for his foolhardiness."[58] Still other reports had Daly appearing at the site of the execution at midnight on the ninth day of any month.

Although Aurora's vigilantes failed to rid the town of ghosts, they certainly succeeded in destroying the powerful Daly gang and banishing several redoubtable gunmen. Six months after Aurora's outburst of vigilantism the *Esmeralda Union* reported that most local gunmen had left town. "Many of them," said the newspaper on 10 August 1864, "have gone to Virginia City, some to Idaho Territory and not a few to Mexico, while a considerable number of them have met with violent deaths and gone where ordinary fuel is generally supposed to be a superfluity. A few of the villainous gang still remain, but they have been taught to respect the majesty of the law and no longer dare cut and shoot with impunity." Other factors, of course, were also responsible for the general exodus of badmen from Aurora: the Pond–Del Monte dispute had been settled, Aurora was beginning a general decline, and new gold and silver strikes were being made in other locales. Nevertheless, the quadruple hanging and the banishments were probably the most powerful incentives for the badmen to seek other fields of operation.

Aurora's vigilantes were never held to answer for their extralegal actions. The district court did order the Esmeralda grand jury to investigate the Citizens' Safety Committee, but the jury's report was nothing more than a justification of the committee's action. The report contended that the committee was "composed of over six hundred of our best, most substantial and law-abiding citizens." These citizens took the law into their own hands, said the jury, only because institutions of law enforcement and justice in Aurora had failed to punish "many notorious villains" during the last three years. Postponement of trials, the great difficulty and expense of procuring witnesses, the cost of prosecution, legal technicalities, general inefficiency, and "the indifference of those sworn guardians and ministers of the law" were all cited as reasons for this failure. The grand jury, while deploring the need for a vigilance committee, believed that the community had the right "to assert the right of self-preservation and the supremacy of natural

---

57.   *Esmeralda Union*, 25 Feb. 1865.

58.   *Esmeralda Union*, 11 March 1865.

law over defective statutory forms and tedious tribunals, when, thereby, the substantial ends of justice can be best or alone attained, and society relieved of the horrors of unchecked and triumphant villainy."[59]

Although the grand jury was not without bias—members of the jury had also been members of the Safety Committee—it nevertheless accurately assessed the mood of the town. Aurorans generally thought that if the law had been allowed to take its normal course, Johnson's murderers would have gone unpunished. Thus the only effective course of action was outside the law. The vigilantes, while acknowledging that they had not lived up to the letter of the law, believed that they had certainly been true to its spirit.

Aurora's Safety Committee fits one scholar's model of a "socially constructive" committee of vigilance.[60] The committee was supported by an overwhelming majority of Aurorans, including the town's leading citizens; it was well regulated; it dealt quickly and effectively with a criminal problem; it left the town in a more stable and orderly condition; and when opposition to it did develop, it disbanded. Moreover, the committee made no attempt to supersede Aurora's regular institutions of law enforcement and justice in matters that did not pertain to the Daly gang. Unlike San Francisco's Committee of Vigilance of 1856, Aurora's Safety Committee had no political motives.

The vigilantes of Aurora represented a well-established tradition in the West. By 1864 California had seen more than thirty vigilante movements, and Nevada, Washington, Colorado, and Montana, another fifteen.[61] Several members of the Safety Committee, including first officer John A. Palmer, were veterans of these earlier movements. Nor were Aurora's vigilantes alone in their actions during the winter of 1864; while they were hanging John Daly and the others, Montana vigilantes were stringing up Henry Plummer and several members of his gang.[62] For most Aurorans, Daly's hanging was the last they would see of vigilantism. A few Aurorans, however, found themselves in Bodie years later and there became members of another vigilance committee, the Bodie 601.

59.   *Esmeralda Union*, 31 March 1864.

60.   Richard Maxwell Brown, *Strain of Violence: Historical Studies of American Violence and Vigilantism*, p. 118.

61.   Brown, pp. 305–19.

62.   See Thomas J. Dimsdale, *The Vigilantes of Montana*. During 1863 Henry Plummer, sheriff of Beaverhead County in Montana Territory, led a gang of highway robbers known as the Innocents. His illegal activities came to light early in 1864, and on 10 January he was hanged.

6

THE LAST OF
THE OLD-TIME
MINING CAMPS

Eight miles southwest of Aurora lay Bodie. Although gold was discovered there in 1859, a year before the Esmeralda strike, little excitement was generated until a real bonanza was struck in 1877. Then, during the next six years, Bodie produced nearly $15 million worth of gold and silver bullion. Total production eventually surpassed $20 million. Among the mining towns of the Great Basin, only Virginia City produced more bullion. Ironically, the discoverers of Bodie's wealth never shared in it.

During the summer of 1859 reports of rich strikes in the trans-Sierra country began to reach California. The fabulous Ophir vein of the Comstock Lode was discovered in June by Peter O'Riley and Patrick McLaughlin, and in July new strikes were reported around Dogtown and Monoville.[1] Prospectors were soon trekking eastward across the Sierra to these new El Dorados. Among the dozens of prospectors who followed the Sonora Pass trail that summer into the trans-Sierra were Terrence Brodigan and W. S. Bodey.[2] Their backgrounds were radically dissimilar, yet their quest was the same.

As a young man Brodigan had emigrated from his native Ireland to Australia, where instead of prospecting for gold he raised sheep. The gold rush brought him to California, and he eventually settled in Sonora. There he became the proprietor of a hotel and a livery stable, while continuing to prospect now and then. New York-born Bodey, an occasional resident of Brodigan's hotel, was making his living as a tinsmith in Poughkeepsie when he caught the gold fever in 1848. Leaving behind a wife and six children, he booked passage on the *Matthew Vassar* and sailed around the Horn to California. He spent the next ten years working the placer deposits of the Mother Lode. Although he never had more than modest success, he was able to send money home

1. For the Comstock Lode, see Dan de Quille, *The Big Bonanza: An Authentic Account of the Discovery, History, and Working of the World-Renowned Comstock Lode of Nevada,* and Grant H. Smith, *The History of the Comstock Lode, 1850–1920.* For Dogtown and Monoville, see San Francisco *Daily Evening Post,* 15 Nov. 1879; Carl P. Russell, "Early Mining Excitements East of Yosemite"; W. A. Chalfant, *The Story of Inyo,* p. 126; William M. Maule, *A Contribution to the Geographic and Economic History of the Carson, Walker and Mono Basins in Nevada and California,* pp. 25–26.

2. *Bodie Standard,* 27 Oct. and 7 Nov. 1879; *Bodie Chronicle,* 3 Nov. 1879; Joseph Wasson, *Account of the Important Revival of Mining Interests in the Bodie and Esmeralda Districts,* p. 5.

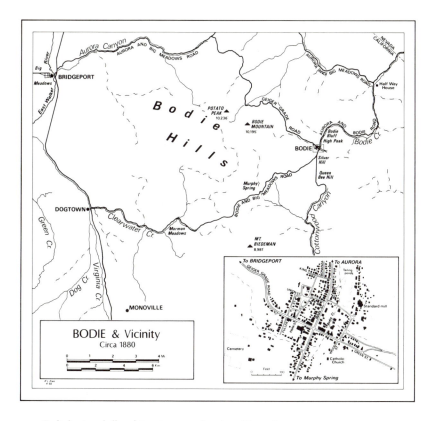

20. *Bodie lay in a shallow depression at an elevation of 8,400 feet, sur-rounded by mostly barren mountains. Development in the town was con-centrated along Main Street, which trended north–south and paralleled Bodie Creek. (Cartography by Noel Diaz)*

regularly to support his wife and children. He persevered because he knew he would strike it big somewhere up the next gulch.

Brodigan and Bodey crossed into the trans-Sierra separately, but joined forces at Monoville. Together with Patrick Garrity, William Doyle, and E. S. Taylor, they left the Mono diggings and, under Brodigan's leadership, worked their way north and north-east, leaving the ground behind them pockmarked with prospect holes. At Esmeralda Gulch a threatening band of Paiute forced them to turn back to the south. Brodigan led the prospectors over a high, sagebrush-covered ridgeline and into a shallow valley. Lik-ing the appearance of the land, they brought their burros to a halt. Bodey picked a likely spot and began to dig yet another prospect hole. He turned over a shovelful of dirt, then another, and another. Suddenly he straightened up and exclaimed, "This looks like pay dirt at last, and if it is, you know and I know we came a hell of a ways to find it."[3]

All hands now fell to work, and well into the evening the prospectors feverishly dug and washed the pay dirt. Yellow bits of metal kept turning up. Finally, Doyle shouted, "Come on, boys, we can't do any less than drink the last part of the bottle. We'll take our chances on a snake bite to drink a toast to Bodey, and the best showing we've seen

3. *Bodie Chronicle*, 3 Nov. 1879.

on the Eastern slope of these Sierra Nevada Mountains."[4] Winter was fast approaching, however, and the prospectors realized that serious working of the claim would have to wait until spring. They built a small cabin at the discovery site and returned to Monoville for supplies. There it was decided that Bodey and Taylor would return to the cabin, and that Brodigan, Garrity, and Doyle would cross the Sierra to Sonora for the winter.

Brodigan gave Bodey his parting blessing, and the two parties headed off in opposite directions. Although neither party knew it, a blizzard had hit the Sierra and was moving east with frightening speed. Brodigan, Garrity, and Doyle were beginning the climb up to Sonora Pass when the storm roared down on them. Fighting blinding snow and howling winds, they retraced their steps out of the mountains and eventually reached Sonora by way of the Carson Valley and the Placerville Road.

Bodey and Taylor were more than halfway up Cottonwood Canyon, less than four miles from the cabin, when the blizzard caught up with them. If they were to live, they would have to reach the cabin. Snow, driven by howling winds, quickly piled up in great drifts. Each step the prospectors took became a struggle. To lighten their loads, they abandoned pack after pack of supplies until they carried only the barest essentials. Bodey's strength finally failed him, and he fell exhausted into the snow. Taylor, a part-Cherokee veteran miner who was less than five feet tall, lifted Bodey onto his back and staggered forward another hundred yards before he, too, fell from exhaustion.

Leaving Bodey wrapped in a blanket, Taylor again pushed onward. The blizzard was now so intense that he could see no more than a few feet ahead. A half mile of struggling brought him to a rocky, black bluff which he recognized as the bluff that rose behind the cabin. Heading in what he thought must be the direction of the cabin, he stumbled into the crude structure. There he warmed himself by a fire and gulped down several cups of hot coffee before setting out to rescue Bodey. He returned to what he thought must be the spot where he left Bodey, but could find no trace of his partner. In the face of the blizzard, he searched for several more hours without any luck.

The storm continued unabated for the next two days. When the skies finally cleared, Taylor again ventured out to search for Bodey. Snow lay several feet deep on the ground and was piled into great drifts in areas exposed to the wind. In those conditions, Taylor's efforts were doomed to failure. Conditions did not improve. Storm after storm hit the trans-Sierra country that winter. Mining operations were shut down for several months, and travel was nearly impossible. During one period all communication between Gold Hill and Virginia City was interrupted, although the two towns were but a mile apart.

Taylor, alone in the cabin, was haunted by thoughts of Bodey throughout the winter. There were nights when he swore that he could hear his partner calling for help. Time passed slowly. When the snows finally melted in the spring, Taylor discovered Bodey's body, less than a mile from the cabin. Coyotes had gotten there first. Only naked bones, a bowie knife, a revolver, and the blanket that Taylor had originally wrapped Bodey in remained. Taylor now wrapped the bones in the blanket and buried them on the spot. Bodey was gone, but his name would remain.

During the summer of 1860 the Bodey mining district was organized.[5] To avoid mispronunciation, the name was soon being spelled Bodie. Edmund Green was elected

4. *Bodie Chronicle*, 3 Nov. 1879.

5. Wasson, *Account of Revival*, p. 6.

president of the new district, A. D. Allen, secretary, and Jeremiah Tucker, recorder. Some twenty claims, all located on Bodie Bluff and a lower ridge that extended southward from it, were officially recorded by the end of July.[6] Bodie Bluff reached an elevation of nine thousand feet. Six hundred feet lower, at the base of the bluff, the town of Bodie developed. The climate, terrain, and vegetation were nearly identical to what miners found at Aurora, only a two-hour ride to the northeast. However, since Bodie was almost a thousand feet higher than Aurora, winters at Bodie were even more severe. Sam Clemens claimed there were only two seasons in the area: the breaking up of one winter and the beginning of the next. "So uncertain is the climate in Summer," said Clemens, "that a lady who goes out visiting cannot hope to be prepared for all emergencies unless she takes her fan under one arm and her snowshoes under the other. When they have a Fourth of July procession it generally snows on them, and they do say as a general thing when a man calls for a brandy toddy there, the barkeeper chops it off with a hatchet and wraps it up in paper, like maple sugar. And it is further reported that the old soakers haven't any teeth—wore them out eating gin cocktails and brandy punches."[7]

The mines at Bodie developed slowly because of the far more spectacular strikes at Aurora and Virginia City. Bodie's ore, at least that which had already been discovered, paled in comparison. Most of the original locators at Bodie drifted off to other towns: Terrence Brodigan to Virginia City; Patrick Garrity, Edmund Green, and A. D. Allen to Aurora; and E. S. Taylor, after a stay in Aurora, to Hot Springs (present-day Benton). Taylor never got over Bodey's death and spent much of his time prospecting alone. Early in 1862 a band of Paiute found him alone in his cabin at Hot Springs.[8] As soon as the sun set, the Paiute attacked. The half-Cherokee Taylor fought back fiercely and killed several Paiute before he was finally overpowered and killed. His bullet-riddled body and his severed head were later found by a group of Aurorans on their way to fight the Paiute in the Owens Valley. Taylor's head was saved and was later passed around Aurora and Bodie as a grisly souvenir of the Indian war. Of the discoverers of the ore, only Brodigan would one day return to Bodie. During the town's heyday, he bottled spring water and delivered it to hotels and restaurants. One of his sons served as a deputy constable in Bodie and another became the secretary of state of Nevada.[9]

The development of the mines at Bodie was retarded, not only by prospectors rushing off to more promising strikes at Aurora and Virginia City, but also by the lack of investment capital; it, like the miners, had gone to those other strikes. In an attempt to attract investment capital, several mines merged early in 1863 to form the Bodie Bluff Consolidated Mining Company.[10] No less a figure than Leland Stanford, the governor of California, was made president of the company. The Bodie Bluff proffered over 11,000 shares of stock and set its worth at more than a million dollars. Stock certificates featured a rendering of the bluff, a score of mines, and the Isabella tunnel. This work of art did little to impress potential investors, however, and the next year another consolidation

6.   Wasson, p. 6; Grant H. Smith, "Bodie: The Last of the Old-Time Mining Camps," p. 75.

7.   Samuel L. Clemens, *Roughing It*, p. 204.

8.   San Francisco *Daily Evening Post*, 22 Nov. 1879; *Inyo Register*, 25 Feb. 1904; Wasson, *Account of Revival*, p. 6.

9.   R. K. Colcord, "Reminiscences of Life in Territorial Nevada," p. 113.

10.   Wasson, *Account of Revival*, p. 7.

occurred. The new company, the Empire Company of New York, controlled over 38,000 shares of stock, several mill sites, tunnel rights, and numerous buildings.[11] The Empire set its worth at $10 million and, to entice investors, prohibited assessments. (It was common practice in those days to "assess" stockholders for the cost of mining operations until the mine could pay for itself.)

By 1864 Bodie contained a boarding house and some twenty wood and adobe houses.[12] The town was laid out along Bodie Creek in the shadow of Bodie Bluff. Only sagebrush and bunchgrass decorated the bluff and the other mountains that surrounded the town, "presenting even to the eye of a traveler who had just been surfeited with the deserts of Arizona a wonderfully refreshing picture of desolation."[13] Nevertheless, there were precious metals in those hills, and with the formation of the Empire Company the town was on the upswing. Streets were being surveyed and marked with stakes, and real estate speculation was vigorous. Real estate promoters spoke of the brilliant future of Bodie and offered "choice" lots for sale. The promoters failed to mention that the lots had not been surveyed or staked. The population of the entire district probably did not exceed fifty. Two miners had their wives with them, but the rest were without women. One visitor to Bodie thought this a blessing:

> These jolly miners were the happiest set of bachelors imaginable; had neither chick nor child, that I knew of, to trouble them; cooked their own food; did their own washing; mended their own clothes, made their own beds, and on Sundays cut their own hair, greased their own boots, and brushed their own coats; thus proving by the most direct positive evidence that woman is an unnecessary and expensive institution which ought to be abolished by law. . . . True, I must admit that the honest miners of Bodie spent a great deal of their leisure time in reading yellow-covered novels and writing love-letters; but that was probably only a clever device to fortify themselves against the insidious approaches of the enemy.[14]

Over the next four years, the Empire Company poured several hundreds of thousands of dollars into its mines on Bodie Bluff.[15] The company also bought the Fogus quartz mill at Aurora, moved it to Bodie, and increased the number of its stamps from twelve to sixteen. Despite these heavy capital expenditures, the Empire Company never struck ore worth much more than the cost of processing. The venture was a bust. In 1874 the Fogus stamp mill, which the company had purchased for $45,000 a decade earlier, was sold for delinquent taxes for $450. Independent mines suffered much the same fate as the Empire Company. Although they all struck ore, none of the ore was rich enough to make their operations profitable. Many of them were abandoned, then relocated, then abandoned again.

11. Wasson, p. 7.

12. J. Ross Browne, *Adventures in the Apache Country*, p. 418.

13. Browne, p. 398.

14. Browne, pp. 398–99.

15. Wasson, *Account of Revival*, p. 7.

In 1875 the Bunker Hill mine, which was first located in 1861 and was subsequently sold and relocated three or four times, struck a rich vein.[16] The vein was exposed by a cave-in just when the two new locators of the Bunker Hill were about to abandon the mine. Over the next year or two they mined and milled gold and silver ore that netted them $35,000, and then they sold out for twice that much to a mining syndicate based in San Francisco. The mine was renamed the Standard, and 50,000 shares of stock went on the trading block. New shafts were sunk, and several drifts and crosscuts were run. Each new tunnel exposed rich veins of quartz bearing both gold and silver, some of the ore assaying as high as $6,000 per ton. Bodie's bonanza had finally been struck.

San Francisco money now began to pour into Bodie. During 1877 no fewer than a dozen mining companies were incorporated, including the Standard, the Bulwer, and the Bodie.[17] These three mines, together with the Noonday, which was incorporated early in 1878, yielded the bulk of Bodie's gold and silver. In 1877 nearly $1 million worth of bullion was shipped out of Bodie, over $2 million in 1878, $2½ million in 1879, and over $3 million in both 1880 and 1881. Then bullion shipments dropped to slightly more than $2 million in 1882 and less than $1 million in 1883.[18]

By 1883 the majority of Bodie's mines had ceased operations. Although the district had by then produced some $14 million worth of bullion, only the Standard and the Bodie had consistently operated at a profit. The Standard continued to mine gold profitably well into the twentieth century. Bodie's total bullion production has been estimated at some $21 million.[19] The Standard accounted for about $14 million of this, the Bodie for $4 million, the Noonday for $1 million, and the Bulwer for a half million.

During the late 1870s and early 1880s, there were over thirty Bodie mining properties on the San Francisco Stock Exchange. Stock quotations were telegraphed to Bodie daily, and nearly everyone speculated in the market. One resident asserted that the most popular expression in Bodie after "Let's take a drink" was "How are the stocks today?"[20] The price of a share of any particular stock fluctuated daily, and oftentimes the fluctuation was extreme. During the summer of 1878 a share of Bodie rose in value from $0.50 to over $50.00. The same share sold for $5.50 in March 1879 and then for $48.00 in May.[21] Other stocks experienced fluctuations only slightly less radical. Fortunes—on paper—were made and lost and made and lost again with surprising regularity. A speculator who had lost his entire savings in a stock venture commented, "Nearly everybody in Bodie, at one time or another, had a good deal of money, but almost everybody left the camp broke when the bottom dropped-out."[22]

Because of the fabulously rich strikes of the Standard and the Bodie, however, it seemed that investment in mining stock was a good gamble. It was only a matter of time, thought many a Bodieite, before the other mines hit the rich ore also. The Mono

16.   *Bodie Standard*, 9 April 1880.

17.   Wasson, *Account of Revival*, pp. 25–26.

18.   Bodie *Daily Free Press*, 3 Nov. 1880, 5 Jan. 1881, 4 Jan. 1883; *Bodie Standard*, 2 August 1882.

19.   Smith, "Bodie," p. 75; H. W. Fairbanks, "The Mineral Deposits of Eastern California," p. 148; California State Mining Bureau, *Eighth Annual Report of the State Mineralogist*, pp. 396–97.

20.   Smith, "Bodie," p. 77.

21.   *Bodie Standard*, 24 August 1881.

22.   Smith, "Bodie," p. 77.

mine, for one, had operated at a loss during 1879 and 1880. Yet, since it was adjacent to the Bodie, there was hope that the Bodie vein would one day be found to extend into the Mono. By 1881 over a half million dollars had been poured into the Mono by its stockholders, and still no Bodie vein. From a high of $14.50 a share in 1879, Mono stock dropped to a low of $0.30 in early 1881.[23]

The principal stockholders of the Mono, mostly wealthy San Francisco speculators, now hatched a plot, not only to save their original investments but also to reap large profits. They began to buy Mono stock and subtly spread the rumor that the Mono had struck the Bodie vein. "Hundreds of people," recalled a former Bodieite, "who thought they alone had received this 'inside information' eagerly bought the stock. My mother heard the rumor, eagerly invested her savings account of $1,500, and advised me to do likewise with the $600 that I had saved for my education. As soon as 'the insiders' had unloaded all the stock they could on the public, the shares began to fall rapidly in price; they dropped from $12 to practically nothing in a short time."[24]

By 1882 most people in Bodie had come to the realization that none of the mines in the district, except the Standard and the Bodie, had made any real profits. Moreover, it had also become apparent to Bodieites that for the most part, their speculation in stocks was enriching only the wealthy stock manipulators in San Francisco. Consequently, the value of most stocks plummeted to near nothing during 1882, and all but four or five mines were shut down. Bodie's mining boom, much of which consisted of paper profits and hope, was over.

The town of Bodie itself boomed and declined in step with the mines. During the summer of 1877 Bodie began to expand rapidly. By fall, Frank Kenyon, one of the West's pioneer newspapermen, began to publish the *Bodie Standard*. The newspaper, which would be printed in Aurora until its presses were moved to Bodie in May 1878, announced in its sixth edition:

> But a few short months ago, Bodie was an insignificant little place. Now, she is rapidly growing in size and importance; and the people are crowding in upon her from far and near, and Why? Because of rich discoveries in GOLD, yellow glittering precious Gold. The baseness of man, and yet his antidote, his blessing and his curse. His happiness and his misery. His solace and his affliction. The forger of change, and manumitter. The pastor and the prison, and the releaser. The richman's strength. The poorman's weakness.[25]

People flocked to Bodie from everywhere in the West: from Virginia City and Grass Valley, from Sacramento and San Francisco. The first stagecoach arrived in Bodie in late December 1877 loaded with passengers. By February 1878 the town had a population of about fifteen hundred, over a third of whom had no employment.[26] Nevertheless, new arrivals were averaging ten a day. There were only four lodging houses and some two

23. *Bodie Standard,* 24 August 1881.
24. Smith, "Bodie," p. 78.
25. *Bodie Standard,* 14 Nov. 1877.
26. *Reno Gazette,* 26 Feb. 1878.

hundred cabins and houses to shelter all these people. The real necessities of life, however, had been provided for: Bodie was already home to seventeen saloons and fifteen
brothels. The town also boasted six restaurants, five general stores, a Wells, Fargo &
Company express office, and two stage lines. Lumber was expensive at ten cents a board
foot, and lots were selling for a hundred to a thousand dollars apiece. Building was
progressing at a frantic pace, despite howling winds, drifting snow, and temperatures
that rarely rose above freezing.[27]

During May 1878 a telegraph line was completed to Bodie, and the citizens
sent their first dispatch: "Bodie sends greetings and proclaims to the mining world that
her gold mines are the most wonderful yet discovered."[28] The frantic pace of construction increased with the coming of spring, and new mining claims were being recorded
daily. In July the United States Land Office was moved from Independence in the Owens
Valley to Bodie to meet the demand for its services. So many men came into Bodie
during the summer and fall of 1878 that most of them went without accommodations
and were forced to sleep on billiard tables and saloon floors.

Traffic on Bodie's streets was regularly congested with wagons of all varieties.
There were large freight wagons drawn by twenty-mule teams, ore wagons hauling rock
to be crushed in the mills, wood wagons bringing in firewood, hay wagons headed for
livery stables, and lumber wagons on their way to construction sites. Materials and
supplies were stacked alongside Main Street, Bodie's principal thoroughfare, for its entire length. Through this traffic came men on foot and men on horseback, and six-horse
stagecoaches "filled with passengers from deck to keel. Sixteen is an average load; but,
as a stagecoach or streetcar is like a can of sardines, there is always room for just one
more."[29] By the end of 1878 Bodie's population had swelled to about four thousand, and
new arrivals were said to be coming into town at the rate of thirty a day.[30] The number
of saloons now surpassed forty and there were some eight hundred structures of all types,
all built of wood. Early in 1879 O'Day and Fraser opened a brickyard, and soon a number
of brick buildings were under construction.

Bodie's boom continued throughout 1879 and peaked in 1880. The federal
census of 1880 counted 5,373 persons in Bodie.[31] Nearly half were foreign born: approximately 850 Bodieites had been born in Ireland, 750 in Canada, 550 in England
and Wales, 350 in China, 250 in Germany, 120 in Scotland, 100 in Mexico, 80 in
France, and 60 in Sweden and Norway.[32] Of the native-born Americans, about 900 had
been born in California and 550 in New York. With the exception of 350 or so Chinese,
a few dozen Indians, and 19 "colored," Bodie was all white.[33] Women, many of whom

27.   *Bodie Standard*, 30 Jan. 1878.

28.   Wasson, *Account of Revival*, p. 23.

29.   *Bodie Standard*, 18 Sept. 1878.

30.   *Bodie Standard*, 25 Dec. 1878.

31.   Department of the Interior, Census Office, *Statistics of the Population of the United States at the Tenth
Census* (Washington, 1883), p. 108; *Bodie Standard*, 27 July 1881. Population estimates of 6,000 or more
were regularly voiced by the town's newspapers. Since the U.S. Census traditionally undercounts, the newspapers may have been accurate in their higher estimates. See, e.g., the *Bodie Morning News*, 21 May 1879,
and the *Bodie Standard*, 22 Dec. 1879.

32.   *Tenth Census*, pp. 428, 498.

33.   *Tenth Census*, p. 382.

21.   *Bodie in 1880 was home to more than 5,000 people. The Standard mill is in the left foreground with Main Street running left to right across the photograph. The brothels of Bonanza Street can be seen behind Main Street at the extreme right, and to their left on King Street are the commercial buildings and residences of Chinatown. (Credit: California State Library)*

were prostitutes, accounted for only about 10 percent of the population, and there were probably no more than 150 children.[34]

A goodly number of Bodie's residents were what was known as "mining-camp men."[35] These were men who had come to California during the gold rush, or shortly thereafter, and had been rushing to each new excitement ever since. By Bodie's time they were a dying breed, who made Bodie the "last of the old-time mining camps." They were not only prospectors but also professional men, gamblers, businessmen, and badmen. "These men," commented one Bodieite, "were virile, enthusiastic, and free livers; bound by few of the rules of conventional society, though with an admirable code of their own: liberal-minded, generous to a fault, square-dealing, and devoid of pretense and hypocrisy. While the mining camps were not entirely composed of men of this type, it was they who gave the camps their distinctive flavor."[36]

With a population of well over five thousand, Bodie had become a sprawling metropolis. Main Street, which ran generally north and south and paralleled Bodie Creek, was the principal thoroughfare. It was intersected by King, Union, and Green streets and paralleled by Fuller, Prospect, Bonanza, and Wood streets. Several smaller streets connected these major arteries. The intersection of Main and King was "downtown" Bodie. No less than 450 businesses lined the streets of Bodie, and seven quartz

34.   *Bodie Standard*, 30 Jan. 1878, 22 Feb. 1879.

35.   Smith, "Bodie," p. 65.

36.   Smith, "Bodie," p. 66.

mills were perched on the hillsides.[37] There were two banks, the Mono County Bank and the Bank of Bodie, a postoffice, a telegraph office, a United States Land Office, four livery stables, a dozen hotels, six general stores, and numerous restaurants, markets, barbershops, and other small businesses. Two stage lines made daily runs to Carson City and Virginia City, and three daily newspapers and one weekly kept Bodieites abreast of local, national, and world affairs.

Linking Bodie to the outside world were several privately owned toll roads. These roads were built under county franchises, and their toll rates were regulated by the county. The most traveled toll road was the Big Meadows and Bodie Road, operated by J. C. Murphy.[38] The road ran west from Bodie through Murphy Springs, Mormon Meadows, and Dogtown, and then north to Big Meadows (present-day Bridgeport). There the road connected with the Sonora and Mono Road, a county highway which crossed the Sierra by way of Sonora Pass.[39] Over this route came the finest goods that San Francisco had to offer, including the latest inventions. One day the first shower stall, complete with overhead sprinkler, arrived in Bodie and was placed on display at Gillson and Barber's general store. The new contraption, commented the *Bodie Standard* on 25 September 1878, "consists of a closet and looks like a 'sweat-box' formerly used as a means of torture." Delicacies also came to Bodie through Sonora Pass. George Callahan's Can Can restaurant, reputed to be Bodie's finest, featured oysters from San Francisco Bay as well as fresh duck from Mono Lake and fresh trout from the Sierra.

Bodie, like Aurora, was home to an extraordinary number of saloons. Much of Main Street was lined with saloons, nearly fifty in all, or about one for every hundred Bodie men. The *Bodie Standard*, on 19 October 1879, said it believed that the street "has more saloons in a given length than any thorofare in the world." Their names indicated that Bodie was, indeed, an old-time mining camp: American Flag, Argonaut, Assessment, Aurora, Bank Exchange, Bonanza, Caledonian, Carson, Comstock, Delta, Dividend, Empire, Gold Brick, Headquarters, Oasis, Occidental, Oriental, Parlor, Parole, Pioneer, Reno, and Shamrock.

The better Bodie saloons, such as Patrick Gallagher's Shamrock or Dick McAlpin's Parlor, occupied a room some thirty feet wide and seventy-five or a hundred feet deep. A bar abutted one wall, and a "chop stand," specializing in fried chops, steaks, and ribs, ran along the other. At the rear of the saloon or in an adjoining room were located the gambling tables. Faro, twenty-one, red and black, draw poker, and roulette were the favorite games.[40] A billiard table or two could also be found in many saloons.

The saloon was the most important social institution in Bodie. Bodie's saloons were crowded with men—women, including prostitutes, almost never ventured into the saloons—every night of the week. One Bodieite recalled that "nearly everybody drank, nearly everybody gambled."[41] Besides serving imported "whiskies from Cork City, Ire-

---

37. *Bodie Standard*, 26 March 1880.

38. A toll of $1 was charged for a loaded (half-price unloaded) freight wagon, 50¢ for a buggy, and 25¢ for a horseman; hogs and sheep were 3¢ apiece, and steers were 5¢ a head. See the *Bodie Chronicle*, 12 June 1880.

39. Late in 1863, when Aurora was booming, the Mono and Tuolumne county supervisors authorized the construction of a wagon road from Sonora through Sonora Pass to Big Meadows. Named the Sonora and Mono Road, work on it was begun in 1864 and completed in 1868. See *Bodie Standard*, 8 March 1879, and Carl Russell, "Early Mining Excitements East of Yosemite," p. 52.

40. *Bodie Standard*, 25 Dec. 1878; Bodie *Daily Free Press*, 11 Dec. 1879.

41. Smith, "Bodie," p. 70.

22.   Main Street was decorated with flags, banners, and cut trees each
Fourth of July. Nearly fifty saloons lined Main Street and kept the cele-
brators well lubricated. Sign on the right reads "Boots Polished or Oiled.
Done by White Labor." (Credit: California Department of Parks and
Recreation)

land," as did Patrick Fahey's Mono Brewery, the saloons also served Bodie's own powerful home brew: a whiskey said to be made "from old boots, scraps of iron, snow-slides and climate, and it only takes a couple of 'snorts' to craze a man of ordinary brainpower."[42]

The fame of Bodie's whiskey soon spread to San Francisco, where the newspapers printed tongue-in-cheek reports of the fluid. When a visiting Bodieite asked for a drink at a Market Street saloon, a local paper reported that the barkeeper served him a mixture of alcohol, turpentine, Perry Davis pain-killer, Jamaica ginger, and pepper sauce. The Bodieite downed the concoction without batting an eye and exclaimed, "Young man, that's whiskey. I ain't tasted nothin' like it since I left Bodie two weeks ago today. That's real genuine licker, kinder a cross 'tween a circular saw and a wildcat, that takes holt quick, en hols on long. Jus' you go to Bodie and open a saloon. And with that whiskey you might charge 4 bits a glass for it and the boys 'ud never kick."[43]

Bodie's drinking stories are legion. There was the old alcoholic named Midson, who one winter night was thrown out of a saloon into the street.[44] He toppled over into a snowbank and passed out. There he lay until some passerby discovered him the next morning. By then he was frozen solid and showed absolutely no signs of life. Some friends placed his rigid figure next to a fire and literally thawed him out. Miraculously, Midson revived and with his first breath asked for a drink. Doctors commented that any ordinary

42.   *Daily Free Press*, 15 Dec. 1880.

43.   *Bodie Standard*, 27 Feb. 1879.

44.   *Daily Free Press*, 29 Dec. 1879.

man would have died from exposure. Midson did not even catch pneumonia. John Peters was as lucky as Midson. After a night of hard drinking, Peters was groping his way home in the dark. Thoroughly drunk, he wandered off the trail and fell a hundred feet down a mine shaft. When discovered the next day, he was perfectly well except for a few bruises.[45]

Just as puzzling to local physicians was the remarkable case of a Bodieite who became drunk without drinking.[46] The man in question woke up perfectly sober the morning after a drunken night in the saloons. By midday, however, he felt himself growing gradually more intoxicated until by late afternoon he was roaring drunk again. Witnesses swore that he had not touched a drop of liquor that day. A story that stretches credulity even further tells of an "old stiff," renowned for his erudition in drinking matters, who was challenged to identify every drink put to his lips while he was blindfolded. Different types of whiskey, brandy, gin, rum, and wine were all given to him. He identified every one. Then he was given a glass of water. He tasted it, smacked his lips, swirled it around in his mouth, and swallowed it. He did this several more times. Finally, he gave up in despair and admitted that the boys had stumped him; he could not identify the drink.

Occasionally, quantity rather than quality was the criterion involved in the challenge. A big, strong woodchopper named Logart, reputed to be a "hard-drinker," was challenged to the feat of downing three gills (nearly a pint) of whiskey without stopping.[47] Bets were placed, and the contest began. Logart drank the whiskey down with apparent ease, but then was seized with convulsions and fell to the floor. He vomited and writhed in pain and "his face grew perfectly blue and white alternately." Medical aid was summoned, but the doctors were of little help. Logart lay insensible for another two hours before he finally recovered.

There were those in Bodie who frowned on the drinking exploits of the "boys." One fall evening in 1881 a temperance lecturer, Colonel C. M. Golding, delivered a stirring speech before a packed house at the Miners' Union Hall. Ironically, most of the men in attendance were hard drinkers who had come to the lecture to relieve the "monotony and dullness of the times." Golding excoriated Bodie's liquor dealers and saloonkeepers, many of whom were in the audience. The proprietor of the Bank Exchange saloon, Joe McDermott, thought that "the lecture is good, possessed of argument and no man in Bodie could pass a more pleasant and edifying hour than by listening to it, but if they think they can deliver more temperance lectures than I can sell whiskey, why just let them keep it up."[48] Nevertheless, the temperance people won a small victory when the Mono County supervisors enacted a law that prohibited saloons from opening on Sundays. Just one month later, the Mono County district attorney announced that he was discontinuing prosecution for violation of the Sunday-closing law.[49] Wholesale violation had made the law impossible to enforce.

By 1879 some fifteen Bodie saloons had gambling rooms, and dozens of professional gamblers had taken up residence in the town, an indication of Bodie's prosperity.[50]

45. *Bodie Standard*, 6 March 1878.
46. *Bodie Standard*, 8 March 1882.
47. *Daily Free Press*, 7 Feb. 1880.
48. *Daily Free Press*, 20 Oct. 1881.
49. *Daily Free Press*, 15 Jan. 1882.
50. *Bodie Standard*, 25 Dec. 1878.

Mining towns were judged successful only when they could claim large numbers of "sports" or "genteel loafers," as the professional gamblers were known. The sports spent most of their time in the saloons or brothels. "Their chief delights," said Bodie's *Daily Free Press*, "are wine, women and billiards; their occupation is faro, and occasionally a game of 'draw.' "[51]

The sport was cool and confident, usually "a man of education," a good judge of human character, and "in spite of his calling," said the *Bodie Standard*, "preserves a dignity, a strength of character recognized by all classes and is ever ready to defend his manhood against any encroachments."[52] He wore snow-white shirts, tailored suits, polished boots, and fine jewelry. This sartorial splendor was not all for show: if he ever went broke, he could use his expensive outfit as collateral for a stake. The sport's credit was invariably good because he always promptly paid his debts when he won. His greatest delight was to entice several hardworking miners into a game of cards just as payday dawned. "That he will win," commented the *Daily Free Press*, "is as sure as death and assessments, unless he is completely out of luck; and even then his superior sagacity is usually sufficient to pull him through."[53]

In a day when the average miner earned only about $25 for a sixty-hour work-week, some of the stakes were enormous. Jack Gunn won nearly $4,000 one night playing faro against the house in the Parole saloon. Another gambler came away from a seven-up game in the Temple saloon with $1,300. And a Mexican "played his wife off at a game of poker, and she went off perfectly satisfied with her new liege."[54]

A distant second to the saloon as a social institution in Bodie was the brothel. Brothels were concentrated along Bonanza Street, also known as Virgin Alley or Maiden Lane.[55] Bonanza ran from King Street northward to the edge of town, and was just west of and parallel to Main Street. Brothels and dance houses, which lined both sides of the street, were separated by a number of small cabins in which the "girls" lived. Several saloons that fronted on the west side of Main Street opened in the rear onto Bonanza Street. Prostitutes rarely ventured into the saloons, but they did spend many working hours in the dance houses. There they would waltz drunken miners dizzy, being certain that the miners stopped now and then to purchase more drinks at the bar.[56] If the men had any money left at the end of the evening, the prostitutes would lead them away to private rooms.

Bodieites also found time to participate, as contestants and spectators, in a variety of sports. Wrestling was by far the most popular sport, but foot racing and horse racing, animal fights, hunting, and target shooting also had their devotees. Wrestlers usually fought in one of three styles: collar-and-elbow, Cornish, or Greco-Roman. For a time Rod McInnis dominated the main event, then came James Pascoe, Harry and Frank Gallagher, Dan McMillan, and H. C. Bell.[57] These men fought for a predeter-

51. *Daily Free Press*, 11 Dec. 1879.

52. *Bodie Standard*, 22 Feb. 1879.

53. *Daily Free Press*, 11 Dec. 1879.

54. *Bodie Standard*, 18 March and 3 Dec. 1880.

55. See, e.g., the Bodie *Daily Free Press*, 20 Nov. and 9 Dec. 1879, 11 Sept. 1880; *Bodie Standard*, 28 Nov. 1879, 5 April 1880, 12 July 1882; Wasson, *Account of Revival*, p. 25; Smith, "Bodie," p. 71.

56. *Daily Free Press*, 7 March 1880; *Bodie Morning News*, 14 August 1879.

57. *Daily Free Press*, 21 May and 10 August 1880, 13 Jan., 2 Feb., and 27 April 1881; *Bodie Standard*, 4 May, 6 and 13 July, and 14 Dec. 1881.

mined purse—sometimes as much as $500—and a percentage of the gate. Although thousands of dollars were wagered on the matches, and spectators regularly numbered in the hundreds, only one serious disturbance ever occurred at the matches.

Before a packed house at the Miners' Union Hall in August 1880, Rod McInnis met Eugene Markey for the collar-and-elbow heavyweight title of Bodie.[58] McInnis, a miner at the Standard, was supported by the working men of Bodie; Markey, a former police officer who spent most of his time in saloons, was backed by the local sports. Both groups had bet heavily on their favorites, and the match was considered even money. As soon as the three-fall match began, however, it became obvious that McInnis was the better wrestler. Markey, knowing that he could not throw McInnis, fought defensively. For several minutes the two men struggled and then, with a quick movement, McInnis threw Markey to the canvas. The sports, with several thousands of dollars riding on Markey, were thoroughly shaken. Then McInnis threw Markey a second time, but referee Johnny Riordan disallowed the throw.

The sports now knew it was only a matter of time before Markey went down again. To save themselves, they had two of their men, special officers Dave Bannon and Robert Whitaker who were supposed to be responsible for preventing disturbances in the hall, stage a fight. Bannon and Whitaker drew their revolvers and began waving them wildly and exchanging epithets. "The immense crowd," reported the *Daily Free Press*, "made a rush for the sidewalk, carrying the doors along with it. Lights were put out, chairs thrown about, windows and lamps broken."[59]

During the stampede referee Riordan was carried into the street and told by several armed men not to return to the hall if he valued his life. Gradually, the spectators drifted back into the hall. Riordan was not among them and could not be found. McInnis's backers were furious. The next day Riordan surfaced and announced that the match would continue that evening. Markey failed to appear at the appointed time, and McInnis was announced the winner. Whether the sports paid off their debts is not known.

Numerous foot races, both walking and running, were also held in Bodie. Most of these were long-distance affairs; a few of them covered a hundred miles or more. In one grueling seventy-two-hour walking match conducted in the Miners' Union Hall, George Wilcox completed 230 miles to W. H. Scott's 229 miles.[60] Scott was a veteran professional from San Francisco, but he could never quite catch the young Bodieite Wilcox, who was thoroughly acclimated to the altitude of over eight thousand feet. Wilcox walked away with the winner's purse of $500. It was a walking match also that saw the only appearance of female athletes in Bodie. Daisy Livingstone and Kitty Franklin, two prostitutes, strode a ten-miler before a large audience in Bodie's gymnasium one winter evening.[61] Daisy won by over nineteen laps.

Shorter races were usually run only during Bodie's Fourth of July celebrations, but there were exceptions. One summer evening Harvey Boone and Ben Eggleston met in a seventy-five-yard race held on Main Street.[62] When Boone arrived at the starting line, attired only in a suit of long, red-flannel underwear and red socks, the more than

58. *Daily Free Press*, 10 and 12 August 1880; *Bodie Standard*, 9 August 1880.

59. *Daily Free Press*, 10 August 1880.

60. *Daily Free Press*, 9 Jan. 1881.

61. *Bodie Standard*, 15 Feb. 1881.

62. *Bodie Standard*, 19 July 1882.

five hundred spectators roared their approval. Moments later Eggleston jogged up to the line "in high-toned white lamb's wool undershirt and drawers, with stockings to match," and the crowd wildly applauded and roared again. Although Eggleston took an early lead in the race, Boone pulled even at the midway mark and went on to win by a yard.

Horses were occasionally raced at Booker Flat on the south edge of town.[63] Charles O'Malley's mare Nellie was generally considered the fastest horse in the county. Animal fights were also not uncommon.[64] Usually dogs were pitted against each other or other animals, including badgers, bobcats, and bears. There were also Bodieites who hunted animals. One expedition to the Mono Lake region brought back 3 deer, 1 black bear, 2 mountain lions, 300 ducks, 164 geese, and 91 rabbits.[65] It took a couple of ore wagons to haul the kill to town. For Bodieites who did not have the time to enjoy the hunt, there was the Bodie Rifle Club, which held shooting matches every Sunday near the Red Cloud mine and a turkey shoot each Thanksgiving. Pistol practice could be taken each afternoon at the town gymnasium, and there were always dozens of men on hand attempting to win the daily pool.[66]

Unlike Aurorans, Bodieites generally paid little attention to national politics and almost none to local politics. On the morning of 23 June 1878 when election judges Pat Kelley and J. McGrath opened the polls for the election of delegates to the state constitutional convention, there was no one there to vote.[67] Only a few voters straggled in during the next several hours, and there was a brief flurry of activity at lunchtime and again around dinnertime. Total ballots cast numbered only 176, out of a population of nearly 2,000. "This was the most important election which has been held for many years in California," commented the *Bodie Standard* on 26 June, "and it is to be deeply regretted that so little interest was manifested."

The presidential and congressional election year of 1880 saw considerably more political activity. Several Republican and Democratic rallies were held during September of 1880, in which hundreds participated.[68] Nevertheless, in the November election only 1,200 votes were cast for president (the Republican, James Garfield, won over the Democrat, Winfield Scott Hancock, 640 to 553)—and Bodie contained well over 5,000 residents. Even in this presidential election Bodie's political apathy was apparent. In Aurora the Civil War and the California-Nevada boundary dispute had caused bitter political divisions, large voter turnouts, election frauds, duels, and assassination attempts, but in Bodie barely 20 percent of the residents, most of whom were eligible to vote, bothered to cast ballots.

The only political issue that consistently aroused Bodieites, or at least Irish Bodieites, was England's continued occupation of Ireland and her oppression of the Irish. Bodie boasted a local chapter of the Land League of Ireland, which was devoted to placing the Irish tenant farmer back "in possession of the land which rightfully belongs to him."[69] The Land League had been founded during the fall of 1879 at Castlebar,

63.   *Bodie Standard*, 8 June, 6 and 13 July 1881.

64.   *Daily Free Press*, 12 May, 10 and 15 Sept. 1880; *Bodie Standard*, 9 Oct. 1880, 1 and 15 Feb. 1882.

65.   *Bodie Standard*, 23 Nov. 1881.

66.   *Daily Free Press*, 25 August, 23 and 26 Sept., 26 Oct., 2 and 23 Nov. 1880.

67.   *Bodie Standard*, 26 June 1878.

68.   *Bodie Standard*, 18 and 27 Sept. 1880.

69.   *Daily Free Press*, 25 Feb. 1881.

County Mayo, Ireland, after the failure of more than a dozen legislative attempts to amend oppressive English land law in Ireland.[70] The league aided the Irish tenants and organized protests against English landlords. The term "boycott" was coined during this period when Irish tenants refused to work lands overseen by Charles Boycott for an English landlord. The repressive measures—including the demolition of thousands of homes and, in one instance, the bayoneting of women and children—that the English took against Irish tenants throughout Ireland gave the movement its momentum.[71]

Newspapers and journals in the United States, such as Patrick Ford's *Irish World* and John Boyle O'Reilly's *Boston Pilot*, enlisted the support of Irish-Americans for the Land League. Charles Stewart Parnell, the president of the league, made a trip to the United States and addressed Congress. Within months, local chapters of the league sprang up across America, and money began to flow to Ireland to support families—some twenty thousand a year—evicted from their farms by English landlords.[72] Money also went to finance the defense of Land Leaguers, including all of the league's officers, who were arrested by the English.

The Bodie chapter of the Land League was established on the Wednesday evening of 22 December 1880. "For seven centuries," said Judge Thomas Ryan in the chapter's first meeting, "Ireland has been fighting for liberty. . . . Those who have gathered here to-night should not respond as Irishmen, merely, but as citizens of the leading republic of the earth and aid in liberating the oppressed people from English rule."[73] Weekly meetings of the chapter regularly filled the Miners' Union Hall to overflowing.[74] Speeches, music, songs, and fund raising highlighted the meetings. Featured speakers included chapter presidents Thomas Ryan and John F. McDonald and such prominent Bodieites as Judge John McQuaid, Patrick Reddy, J. C. McTarnahan, and Father John B. Cassin.

If Bodieites, with the special exception of the Land League, were less than enthusiastic about politics, they were downright apathetic about organized religion. Although John B. Cassin, a Catholic priest, and G. B. Hinkle, a Methodist Episcopal minister, both arrived in Bodie during 1878, neither of them had a church until late 1882. Before then the Miners' Union Hall was used for Sunday services; Catholics met at ten o'clock in the morning, followed by Methodists at two in the afternoon. Fund-raising events were held now and then by the women of Bodie for the building of churches for both denominations. One benefit during the summer of 1880 raised over a thousand dollars for Father Cassin.[75]

Nevertheless, not until July 1882 was construction begun on a Catholic church. Two months later the church was completed, and on 10 September Father

70. See Seumas MacManus, *The Story of the Irish Race*, pp. 625–58, for an account of the Land League of Ireland.

71. On 1 January 1880 at Carraroe, County Galway, a detachment of the Royal Irish Constabulary—the British police force for Ireland—mounted a bayonet charge into a group of Irish mothers and their children who were protesting eviction (MacManus, pp. 631–32).

72. Official British sources report that from 1849 to 1882 English landlords evicted 482,000 Irish families. Irish historians contend that even this enormous figure falls far short of the true total of families evicted. Since the average Irish farm family during the nineteenth century consisted of a father, mother, and six children, nearly four million Irish must have been forced off the land from 1849 to 1882 (MacManus, pp. 634–35).

73. *Daily Free Press*, 23 Dec. 1880.

74. *Bodie Standard*, 13 April 1881; *Daily Free Press*, 23 Dec. 1880, 25 Feb. and 1 Sept. 1881.

75. *Bodie Standard*, 9 July and 25 Dec. 1880.

Cassin dedicated it to Saint John the Baptist. A Methodist church had also been under construction during the summer of 1882, and its doors were opened only a week after those of the Catholic church. Now that Bodie finally had two churches, the need for them was rapidly diminishing. During 1882 the majority of Bodie's mines closed, and two-thirds of its population drifted away to other camps.

School was another institution of little significance in Bodie. In early January 1878 the first term of the first public school in Bodie commenced in the home of Annie Donnelly.[76] Although in 1878 there were some forty or more school-age children in Bodie, only fourteen showed up for classes. Donnelly appealed to the parents of Bodie to send their children to school. Enrollment increased gradually until Donnelly's house could no longer accommodate the students. The summer term was postponed because no school facility could be found.

Classroom space was eventually leased in the Cary Building on Main Street, and a special tax was levied to provide funds for the construction of a schoolhouse. By late February 1879 a schoolhouse, complete with cupola, had been erected on Green Street, and Mrs. Donnelly was expecting to greet some eighty students for the spring term. Truancy remained a problem in Bodie, especially among the town's older boys. The lessons they learned in the classroom paled in comparison with those they learned on the streets of the West's wildest mining town in 1879.

Institutions of law enforcement and justice in Bodie were similar to those in Aurora. Bodie, however, was not the county seat of Mono County as Aurora had been. Therefore, the county sheriff, county jail, district attorney, and superior court were located not in Bodie but in Bridgeport, some fifteen miles away, over a twisting mountain road. Law enforcement in Bodie was left to a town constable and his deputies, or police officers, as they were commonly known, and a justice of the peace held court.

Serving as constable for several terms during Bodie's boom years was John F. Kirgan.[77] Kirgan originally came to California in 1848 after serving in the Mexican War, where he won decorations for bravery at Monterrey and Buena Vista. He was sergeant at arms during California's first constitutional convention and again during the first meeting of the state legislature at Vallejo. Elected Bodie town constable in 1878, Kirgan served on and off until March 1881, when his sulky overturned on Main Street and he was fatally injured.[78] Kirgan was highly respected and well liked. Others serving as Bodie town constable included S. G. Stebbins and James S. Herrington.[79] Kirgan also served as jailer of the Bodie jail during the town's heyday. The jailer was appointed by the county sheriff and carried the title of deputy sheriff. Much of the time Kirgan held the jobs of constable and jailer simultaneously. The first Bodie jail was built late in 1877 and contained only two small, poorly ventilated cells.[80] Within a year or two it could no longer accommodate the steadily increasing number of prisoners, and Kirgan was forced to lodge some of the men in a cabin next door.

A new jail was finally built in August 1880 and "furnished with all the articles for comfort that can be found in any jail on the coast."[81] From a front office a hallway

76.   *Bodie Standard*, 9 Jan. and 29 May 1878, 22 Feb. 1879.

77.   *Daily Free Press*, 6 Feb. and 16 Sept. 1880, 13 Jan. 1881; *Bodie Standard*, 3 June 1880.

78.   *Daily Free Press*, 9 March and 2 April 1881.

79.   *Daily Free Press*, 6 Feb. 1880, 13 Jan. 1881.

80.   *Bodie Standard*, 28 Nov. 1877; *Daily Free Press*, 17 July and 3 Aug. 1880.

81.   *Daily Free Press*, 27 Aug. 1880.

23.   *Although today the Bodie jail appears a less than formidable structure, it suffered only one jailbreak during Bodie's boom years. (Credit: California Historical Society)*

led to four cells, two on each side, and through a heavy rear door to an exercise yard surrounded by a high planked fence. All doors were reinforced with iron, and each cell had an iron-grated front and "the latest improved locks." Ironically, just two months after the new jail was completed, Bodie's first and only jailbreak occurred. While Kirgan was away, two prisoners somehow managed to slip into the exercise yard and scale the fence to freedom. The *Daily Free Press* thought that the prisoners must have "had pressing business on the outside."[82]

Kirgan always kept the jail clean and orderly and personally supervised the preparation of all meals. The *Daily Free Press* called Kirgan's jailhouse food "wholesome and ample," and the *Bodie Standard* thought that "not a better quality of food is found on any table in the county."[83] Meals were served twice a day at a daily cost of less than a dollar per man. Kirgan put on a special affair each Thanksgiving. The prisoners were moved to write the *Bodie Standard*: "We, the boarders of the 'Hotel de Kirgan,' express our heartfelt and sincere thanks and gratitude to the proprietor of said institution for the courteous manner and bountiful feast of which we partook for Thanksgiving Dinner. The table was complete in every particular. . . . Hoping that Kirgan may live to enjoy the good of this world and Thanksgiving dinners for many years, we remain, Respectfully, 'The Boarders.' "[84] Very few western lawmen ever received such a tribute from their prisoners.

Although Bodieites petitioned the state legislature for the appointment of a superior court judge who would sit in Bodie, only justices of the peace ever held court

82.   *Daily Free Press*, 14 Nov. 1880; *Bodie Standard*, 13 Nov. 1880.

83.   *Daily Free Press*, 27 Aug. 1880; *Bodie Standard*, 9 Aug. 1880.

84.   *Bodie Standard*, 26 Nov. 1880.

in the town.[85] Participants in superior court cases were forced to travel to the Mono County courthouse in Bridgeport. Jurors were especially annoyed by this inconvenience. When a large number of jurors were summoned one July to hear a number of murder cases, the *Bodie Chronicle* commented, "We presume the road to Bridgeport will be perfectly blue from the 'cussing' that will be indulged in by those meandering towards the Capital of Mono."[86] Bodieites were exceptionally adept at inventing excuses to free themselves from jury duty. A deputy sheriff often spent several days attempting to round up the requisite number of jurors.[87]

Fortunately for Bodieites, most cases were handled by local justices of the peace. Justice court was held in a room above the Rosedale saloon on Main Street, and court was often adjourned so that the liquid refreshment served downstairs could be enjoyed. Justices paid themselves and the officers of the court out of the fines they levied. "This practice is demoralizing," said the *Daily Free Press* on 17 July 1880, "and an inducement to the imposition of heavy fines." A half year later, when a new justice of the peace was installed, the newspaper commented, "The new machine has been oiled up, Justice has had her eyes properly bandaged, and everything is ready for business."[88] Justices of the peace during Bodie's heyday included R. L. Peterson, Thomas Newman, A. M. Phlegar, and D. V. Goodson.

Bodie also boasted its own National Guard company. The guards met at the fire station, usually on Tuesday evenings, and held rifle practice on a range near the Queen Bee Hill on Sundays. The company could have passed for a unit of the Fenians, the nineteenth-century precursor of the Irish Republican Army. Nearly every member of the company carried an Irish name. The officers included Callahan, Kelly, and McPhee; the noncommissioned officers, Fahey, Kearney, Markey, and O'Brien; and the privates, Boyle, Carroll, Costello, Finnegan, Lyons, McGrath, Mullin, O'Donnell, O'Keeffe, Phelan, Shea, Thornton, Tobin, and Whelan.[89]

The legal profession was well represented in Bodie by attorneys Patrick Reddy, John McQuaid, Thomas P. Ryan, John Kittrell, Frank Owen, R. S. Minor, and more than a dozen others. Reddy, both literally and figuratively, stood head and shoulders above his colleagues.[90] He was, as one Bodieite recalled, "easily the most striking figure in town." Reddy was large, powerfully built, and handsome. He had a commanding personality and was a born fighter and leader of men. His origins were humble. He was born in Woonsocket, Rhode Island, in 1839, shortly after his impoverished parents

85.   *Daily Free Press*, 14 March 1880.

86.   *Bodie Chronicle*, 24 July 1880.

87.   *Bodie Standard*, 25 Dec. 1878.

88.   *Daily Free Press*, 20 Feb. 1881.

89.   *Bodie Morning News*, 21 August and 6 Sept. 1879.

90.   The following biographical sketch of Patrick Reddy was drawn from: *Bodie Standard*, 4 Sept. 1880; *Sacramento Daily Record-Union*, 1 Jan. 1883, 1 Jan. 1885, and 6 Jan. 1897; *San Francisco Call*, 28 Oct. 1896, 13 August 1897, 10 and 27 June, 6 July, 31 August, and 25 Dec. 1900, and 4 Nov. 1901; *San Francisco Chronicle*, 5 March 1885, 27 June 1900, and 9 June 1904; *San Francisco Bulletin*, 26 June 1900; *San Francisco Examiner*, 27 June 1900; Smith, "Bodie," p. 73; Colcord, "Reminiscences," p. 117; Oscar T. Shuck, ed., *History of the Bench and Bar of California*, pp. 538–39; *The Bay of San Francisco*, vol. 2, pp. 140–41; Daughters of the American Revolution, *California: Fifty Years of Progress*, p. 297, and *Records of the Families of California Pioneers*, vol. 25, p. 246; Reda Davis, *California Women: A Guide to Their Politics, 1885–1911*, p. 196.

arrived in the United States from County Carlow, Ireland. Like many other Irish-Americans of that era, although he was born in America he had been conceived in Ireland.

Reddy came to California in February 1861 and worked as a laborer in Contra Costa County and as a miner in Placer County, before he crossed into the trans-Sierra country in 1863. Virginia City, Aurora, Darwin, and Montgomery were some of the mining camps he lived in. His years in those camps were said to have been nothing less than wild and reckless: one contemporary went so far as to call him the "terror" of Aurora in 1863. The next year he was shot in the arm by an unknown assailant while walking down B Street in Virginia City. He lost the arm as a result of the wound, but he never lost his fighting spirit. Thirty-three years later, when he was nearly fifty-eight years old, he emerged from the state supreme court in Sacramento to see a number of people rushing out of the post office nearby. When one of those fleeing the building told Reddy that there was an armed man inside threatening to kill a woman, Reddy ran into the post office. He found the man, later identified as Peter Hulsman, standing over a woman and brandishing a revolver. One-armed Patrick Reddy lunged for the gun and grabbed it before Hulsman could fire. Another man then jumped on Hulsman's back. Hulsman, in a last desperate effort, tried to turn the gun on Reddy and fire. But Reddy jammed his thumb between the hammer and cylinder of the revolver as Hulsman cocked it and, when Hulsman pulled the trigger, the hammer fell on Reddy's thumb. Reddy and the other man then wrestled Hulsman to the floor. After the police arrived, Reddy had his thumb, which was bleeding profusely, bandaged and, as the *San Francisco Call* put it, "continued on down the street as if nothing unusual had happened."

Shortly after Reddy lost his arm—he would later call it a blessing in disguise—he married and began to study law. In 1867 he was admitted to the bar and began to practice law in Independence, a location that enabled him to attract business from the entire southern trans-Sierra region. Responding to the great boom at Bodie, he moved his practice there in April 1879 and by 1880 his law office occupied the entire top floor of the Molinelli Building on Main Street. The *Bodie Standard* called it "the most imposing law office outside of San Francisco." Although Reddy's dark auburn hair was beginning to turn white and he was gaining an ever more dignified appearance, he occasionally went on a spree. Then he would proceed from saloon to saloon, ordering drinks for everybody and challenging Bodie's strongest men to arm-wrestling matches.

Reddy dominated both the justice court at Bodie and the superior court at Bridgeport. He prepared his briefs carefully, had almost total recall, and captivated judge and jury with a commanding voice, beautiful diction, and a lilting Irish brogue. Years later in San Francisco, law students would crowd into the courtroom to watch him perform. In Bodie, Reddy won the reputation of supporting the underdog. He donated his services to dozens of Bodieites who could not afford to pay him, while his wealthy clients were charged reasonably high fees. He was known to occasionally slip $20 gold pieces into the hands of destitute miners and to treat them to elegant dinners. Reddy was also active in politics. He was a founding member of the Bodie chapter of the Land League of Ireland, a Mono and Inyo county delegate to the state constitutional convention in 1878–1879, and a state senator from 1883 to 1887. Although Reddy stopped prospecting and mining when he lost his arm, he never stopped dabbling in mining stock. He was a part-owner of several mines, including the Yellow Aster, which made Randsburg famous. The name of his favorite mine, the Defiance, symbolized his character.

In 1881 Reddy opened a law office in San Francisco, while maintaining his practice in Bodie for another two years. Within a few years and with the addition of

24. *Patrick Reddy dominated the courtroom in Bodie and Bridgeport. He is seen here in his latter years in San Francisco. (Credit: California Historical Society)*

junior partners William H. Metson—whom Reddy trained earlier in Bodie—and J. C. Campbell, Reddy had established one of San Francisco's most prominent law firms. His firm represented clients from throughout the Far West, including Alaska, and, as in Bodie, the clients were often underdogs. When the mine owners of the Coeur d'Alene district in Idaho, with the support of state and federal troops, tried to destroy the miners' union during the 1890s by hiring strikebreakers, shooting union leaders, and imprisoning hundreds of miners in bullpens, Reddy rushed to the scene to aid the miners. "He distinguished himself," noted the San Francisco *Bulletin*, "against the best legal talent of the Northwest in the numerous cases which grew out of those labor troubles." During the 1890s Reddy was also bold enough to publicly support women's suffrage.

Reddy died at his home on Pacific Avenue in San Francisco early on the morning of 26 June 1900, after a month-long battle with Bright's disease, complicated by pneumonia. Among those at his bedside were his wife of thirty-six years, Emma, and his younger brother, Edward "Ned" Reddy, who had come to California with him in 1861 and who had shared many of his experiences in the mining camps of the trans-Sierra. They said that the famed attorney died with a smile on his face. Later that morning, when lawyer James G. Maguire announced in the United States Circuit Court in San Francisco that Patrick Reddy had died, the judge ordered the court adjourned for the day as a tribute to Reddy.

Reddy left an estate valued at over a quarter-million dollars, a substantial sum in 1900, yet it was only a small portion of what he had made in his lifetime. Oliver Roberts, a lifelong friend of Reddy, said shortly after Reddy's death, "Senator Reddy earned more than a million dollars in his profession as a lawyer, and if he dies a comparatively poor man, it is because he had given most of it away. He knew everybody in the mining regions of California, and he seldom came back from a trip without bringing with him one or two of the old boys who were crippled by accident or disease, and as soon as they were able to get out of the hospital he would grub stake them and send them back to whatever camp they wanted to go. Many an old-timer will miss Pat Reddy. He was a big man, Pat was, and his heart was as big as his body."

Reddy's presence in Bodie, as a mature attorney of unusual ability, added something very special to the town. Bodie was otherwise a town much like other western mining towns, especially Aurora. Bodie, like Aurora, had a mostly white and male population of over five thousand, numerous saloons and brothels, conventional institutions of law enforcement and justice, a brief but spectacular boom period, and mines that produced millions in bullion. And, of course, Bodie was located just eight miles away from Aurora at approximately the same elevation; the two towns shared the same climate, terrain, and vegetation. Nevertheless, there were important differences. Whereas Aurora's politics had been superheated by the Civil War and the California-Nevada boundary dispute, Bodie's political life was uninspired and mundane. Also, the Owens Valley Indian War, occurring during Aurora's boom, was only a memory by the time of Bodie's strikes in 1877 and 1878. The war had ended organized Indian resistance to white encroachment, and Bodieites traveled the trans-Sierra country with no fear of Indian attack. Finally, Bodie did not enjoy full employment as did Aurora, where jobs often went begging. A good number of Bodieites spent much of their time unemployed.

7

VIOLENCE AND
THE MINORITIES

Although Bodie was populated primarily by English-speaking whites, there were sizable minorities of Chinese and Mexicans, a small number of Indians, and a handful of blacks. The total number of individuals from these groups probably reached six hundred, or about 10 percent of Bodie's population. Minority citizens, like those representing the majority group, were involved in violence and lawlessness.

Bodie was home to some 350 or more Chinese.[1] Chinese had been coming to California in large numbers ever since the gold rush. Most of these Chinese came from the Pearl River Delta region of southeastern China.[2] Chaotic political and economic conditions there compelled many a young Chinese man to emigrate overseas, first to Malaysia, then to the Philippines, and only after the great gold strike, to California. Their goal was not permanent residency in California. They intended to stay only until they had earned enough money to give them a respected and secure place in Chinese society back home. They were sojourners rather than immigrants and, as such, had no intention of becoming Americanized. Only a few learned English or adopted Western dress. For the most part, they stayed clustered in Chinatowns and, except through work, had little contact with the American society at large.

Bodie's Chinatown occupied the extreme northwestern portion of the town. Lining both sides of King Street, Chinatown's principal thoroughfare, were laundries, small stores, opium dens, and a joss house, complete with a bronze statue of Confucius. Religious ceremonies were conducted regularly in the joss house, and each February a great celebration was held to usher in the Chinese New Year. The celebration included a parade, led by a band of gongs, drums, cymbals, and "other instruments of ear torture," down a highly decorated King Street.[3] For the most part, the Chinese adhered to their own customs, wore their native dress, braided their hair in queues, and spoke only

1. U.S. Department of the Interior, Census Office, *Statistics of the Population of the United States at the Tenth Census* (Washington, 1883), pp. 382, 498. The Census reported 363 Chinese in Mono County in 1880. Almost all were residents of Bodie. Since the Census traditionally undercounts population, especially minority and transient population, it is likely that Bodie was home to at least 350 Chinese and probably considerably more.

2. See Gunther Barth, *Bitter Strength: A History of the Chinese in the United States, 1850–1870*, pp. 9–31.

3. *Bodie Standard*, 11 Feb. 1880.

Chinese. The residents of Chinatown were a distinctly alien element in Bodie, and Chinatown was generally left to govern itself.

Helping to provide some governmental structure for Chinatown were its two tongs, or companies, as they were called by white Bodieites.[4] Tongs developed from the secret Triad Society in China.[5] The Society was established late in the seventeenth century in southeastern China for the purpose of overthrowing the Ch'ing dynasty and restoring the Ming. During the eighteenth century the Society's many autonomous chapters acted as vehicles for the expression of popular grievances against government authority. Some chapters engaged in what E. J. Hobsbawm would call "social banditry," while others concentrated on fraternal and protective activities. When the Chinese began migrating overseas, chapters of the societies—tongs, as they became known—migrated with them. Tong membership was based solely on interest and need, unlike the Chinese clans, which required common kinship, or the *hui kuan* associations, which united those who hailed from the same homeland region or spoke the same dialect.

Tongs became especially important in the United States precisely because they offered some governmental structure for Chinatowns. Because Chinatowns contained no eligible voters (the Chinese were denied citizenship) they were, for the most part, left out of the political process, and regular municipal government was not extended to them. Besides helping to fill this void, the tongs were also involved in opium trafficking, gambling, and prostitution. It was from these activities that the tongs derived their financial support. The various tongs often came into conflict, sometimes violent, over the regulation of Chinatown's opium dens, gambling halls, and brothels. Bodie's principal tongs, the Sam Sing and the Yung Wah, were no exception. Although they continually battled for control of Chinatown, at the same time they constituted unofficial administrative bodies.

Most lawlessness and violence in Chinatown was associated with opium and the numerous King Street opium dens. Although Chinese immigrants were responsible for introducing opium smoking to California, it was the English who were primarily responsible for the opium trade. The great bulk of opium consumed in China came from opium poppies grown on the lands of the British East India Company in Bengal.[6] The East India Company began shipping opium to China in 1773 and by 1830 was making a profit of nearly four million pounds sterling a year from the trade. Although the importation and sale of opium was prohibited by Chinese imperial edicts, the British government did everything it could to promote the illicit trade. In the 1830s the trade furnished the British treasury with three and a half million pounds sterling a year and gave England a positive balance of trade with China.[7] When the Chinese made serious efforts to stop the trade in 1838 and 1839, the English waged the Opium War and through the Treaty of Nanking forced China to open more of her ports for trading and to cede Hong Kong to England.[8]

4. *Bodie Standard*, 24 July 1878. Whites in Bodie evidently confused the town's tongs with the famous Six Companies of San Francisco's Chinatown.

5. For a description of the Triad Society, Chinese clans, *hui kuan*, and tongs, see Barth, *Bitter Strength*, pp. 77–108; Stanford Lyman, *Chinese Americans*, pp. 8–53; Lyman, *The Asian in the West*, pp. 33–56.

6. Hsin-pao Chang, *Commissioner Lin and the Opium War*, p. 48.

7. Chang, p. 49.

8. See Chang, *Commissioner Lin and the Opium War*; Peter Ward Fay, *The Opium War 1840–1842*; Maurice Collis, *Foreign Mud*.

When it is smoked, opium at first stimulates the imagination and produces a sense of well-being.[9] This is followed by a drowsy, dream-filled state during which smokers retire to a cot or a bunk to enjoy the fantasies of the mind. Smoking opium helped the Chinese of Bodie cope with a sense of homelessness, a scarcity of Chinese women, and a daily routine of manual labor. In this way opium fulfilled much the same need for the Chinese that alcohol fulfilled for the whites. There were dangers inherent in opium. Its use could become habit-forming. Once addicted, the user needed the drug as much as he needed food or water. Also, if opium was consumed by eating or drinking, a deadly overdose could occur.

Not much notice was taken of Bodie's opium dens until February 1879, when a white man, William Brown, died from an opium overdose.[10] Brown, a forty-six-year-old opium addict, died suddenly after first smoking and then eating opium in Sing Ton's opium den. Considerable attention was now focused on the opium dens. The *Bodie Morning News*, on 23 May 1879, contending that "the practice of smoking this deadly poison is much more common among the higher class of people than is generally supposed" and the "vile passion is constantly gaining ground," called for the enactment of a state law prohibiting the sale and the use of opium. The newspaper noted that Nevada had already enacted such a law and that the law was being "enforced with vigor."

Bodie was not alone among California towns in its opposition to opium dens. Nevertheless, not until late in February 1880 was a bill that prohibited the operation of opium dens introduced into the state legislature.[11] Although the bill soon became law, Bodie's lawmen, evidently receiving protection money from drug traffickers, made no attempt to close the opium dens. Whites continued to patronize the dens, and not a few of them became opium addicts, or fiends, as they were called in Bodie. Opined the *Daily Free Press* on 7 March 1880,

> The opium fiend is the most pitiable object to be found. . . . Bearing a ghastly livid countenance, expressionless eyes and emaciated constitution; a mind impaired, morally and intellectually; totally unfit for work, and perfectly oblivious to anything that is respectable or wholesome. An opium fiend is a manhater; the vice makes him so, and he is uncomfortable when in the company of respectable people. They are a peculiar set; they possess "a wondrous kind" among themselves; loan money and "stand in" on all propositions that relate to their "little world."

Two months later, on 6 May, the *Daily Free Press* noted that the number of white persons who frequented Chinatown to indulge in the "villainous and destructive" habit of opium smoking was still increasing. Since the demand for bunks in opium dens sometimes exceeded the supply, new quarters were constantly being erected. And this was at a time when growth in the rest of Bodie had leveled off.

Disturbances in the opium dens were also on the increase. A lively little row between a Mexican and a Chinese one Tuesday night was followed by a white man, G. L. Osgood, pummeling "an ancient-looking Chinaman with a beard." A number of

---

9.   For a discussion of opium use by Chinese immigrants, see Lyman, *Chinese Americans*, pp. 99–105.

10.   *Bodie Standard*, 1 March 1879.

11.   Bodie *Daily Free Press*, 28 Feb. 1880.

Chinese testified that Osgood had precipitated the fight, while several of Osgood's friends swore the Chinese had been the aggressor. The justice court jury evidently favored the testimony of the Chinese witnesses over that of the whites, for it found Osgood guilty of battery.[12] The first opium den shootout occurred two days after Osgood's trial. On the Monday afternoon of 7 June 1880, a dispute arose between two white men, William Bart and James Flannery, and several Chinese.[13] Three or four shots were fired, and one of the Chinese was hit in the shoulder. His wound was not considered serious. Bart was arrested for the shooting and later pleaded guilty in justice court. He was fined $24.

By the summer of 1880 the number of "opium fiends" had grown to about fifty. The *Daily Free Press* asserted on 28 July that young men were constantly taking "the down-hill grade by way of Chinatown," and although there was a state law against opium smoking, "no officer attempts to break up the nefarious business." Chinatown was called the most corrupt place in Mono County. Opium addicts were now, however, becoming a nuisance outside of Chinatown and, although public officials continued to dally, private individuals took action. Early in August a number of saloonkeepers banned "opium fiends" from their establishments.[14] This was a serious blow to the addicts who depended on the faro tables and the generosity of drunken miners as a means of support.

Special officers were hired to keep the addicts out of the saloons. Trouble began almost immediately. On the Sunday night of 8 August 1880, the special officer at John Wagner's saloon, a lavish establishment on the northwest corner of Main and King streets, ordered several addicts to leave.[15] They refused. The officer drew his gun, and the addicts drew theirs. Patrons of the saloon ran into the street for safety, even though the faro game was having a good run. The addicts held their ground, contending that since gambling was also prohibited by state law, it was the height of hypocrisy for saloonkeepers to dare to ban anyone. The saloon was forced to close for the night.

Three weeks later the confrontations between officers and addicts turned deadly. At about ten o'clock on the Wednesday night of 1 September, George Watkins came into the Comstock saloon to check on the faro game.[16] The Comstock's special officer, Robert Whitaker, recognized Watkins as one of the banned opium addicts. Whitaker caught Watkins unaware and, using a revolver as a club, knocked him unconscious. Whitaker delivered several more blows, which broke off two of Watkins's teeth. Watkins was then dragged out of the saloon, and friends carried him to his room.

Shortly after midnight Watkins returned to the Comstock, this time armed with a double-barreled shotgun and accompanied by a friend, John Sloan. Sloan pushed open the saloon's front door, and Watkins stepped in and found Whitaker standing at the end of the bar. Whitaker tried to jump behind the bar but was too slow. Watkins's shotgun blast caught him in the stomach.

Watkins and Sloan ran from the scene, but were arrested a few hours later and lodged in the city jail. Doctors, meanwhile, were doing what they could for the seriously wounded Whitaker. The prognosis was not good. Nevertheless, when his wife visited

---

12. *Daily Free Press*, 19 Nov. 1879, 6 June 1880.

13. *Daily Free Press*, 8 June 1880.

14. *Daily Free Press*, 10, 11, and 12 August 1880.

15. *Daily Free Press*, 10 August 1880.

16. *Daily Free Press*, 2, 3, 4, and 5 Sept. 1880; *Bodie Standard*, 3, 4, and 11 Sept. 1880.

him he assured her that it was only "a trifling wound" and said he would be all right. Less than twenty-four hours later he was dead.

Rumors of vigilante action quickly spread throughout Bodie. To protect the prisoners, a large force of officers and friends of Watkins and Sloan guarded the jail on Thursday night. The Friday, 3 September, edition of the *Bodie Standard* exacerbated this already tense situation when it announced the death of Whitaker and commented:

> It was a cold blooded assassination, concerted and planned by a brutal murderer. The man was slaughtered like a dog and given no chance for his life. What officer or citizen's time may come next is a question now to be seriously asked. The town overrun with opium fiends, who have no visible means of support, dress fine and have some money, men robbed nightly, burglaries committed without hinderance, officers shot down in the discharge of their duty, is bringing matters to such a crisis that a "601" [a number popularly used to designate vigilance committees] will be compelled to clean out the mass of crime.

The *Daily Free Press* responded the same day with a contrary opinion. It argued that there was absolutely no necessity for vigilantism in Bodie, where "there is every form of official protection already in existence, the chief drawback consisting in lack of good or well-balanced juries. . . . If good citizens will but half do their duty as witnesses, jurors, etc., there are good courts and officers enough to soon bring about a better state of affairs." The last thing the town needed, emphasized the *Free Press*, was the dreadful experience and consequences of lynch law.

On Friday afternoon the coroner's jury charged Watkins with the murder of Whitaker and named Sloan as an accessory. Watkins hired Patrick Reddy to defend him, and Sloan retained Thomas Ryan. Bodieites anticipated the trial with relish, but there would be no trial. Watkins awoke very early Saturday morning, suffering terribly from the head and face wounds inflicted by Whitaker. The prisoner called for opium to relieve the pain. Sloan gave jailer John F. Kirgan a bottle of medicine, allegedly a mixture of sarsaparilla, port wine, and opium, to take to Watkins. Sloan recommended that Watkins take two spoonfuls. Kirgan gave Watkins the bottle and a short time later noticed that he had fallen asleep. At about ten o'clock that morning a deputy sheriff checked on Watkins, who appeared to be in a deep sleep, and found that he was dead.[17]

A postmortem examination was conducted on the body, but there was disagreement over the cause of death. The *Daily Free Press* reported that the doctors concluded that Watkins died of a cerebral hemorrhage as a result of his head injuries.[18] The *Bodie Standard* reported the same doctors as saying that Watkins died as a result of an overdose of chloral hydrate.[19] The bottle of medicine that Kirgan had taken to Watkins was nearly one-third full when it was given to him. The bottle was later found to be totally empty. The discrepancy between Sloan's description of the medicine as sarsaparilla, wine, and opium and the doctor's mention of chloral hydrate was left unresolved.

While Watkins's postmortem examination was being conducted, Whitaker's funeral took place. A number of his friends, his wife, and his infant son attended. The

17.   *Daily Free Press*, 4 and 5 Sept. 1880.

18.   *Daily Free Press*, 5 Sept. 1880.

19.   *Bodie Standard*, 11 Sept. 1880.

next day he was joined in the cemetery by Watkins, whose large funeral procession meandered through Bodie before arriving at the graveyard. The authorities evidently felt that justice had been done, for Sloan was not prosecuted.

Although opium addicts and saloonkeepers would have no more serious confrontations, opium dens continued to be plagued by sporadic outbursts of violence. On the Tuesday evening of 23 November 1880, Ah Fo was severely wounded in a knife fight with another Chinese in a King Street opium den.[20] Ah Fo had accused the other man of stealing two dollars. On a Saturday afternoon two weeks later, an opium addict and the Chinese proprietor of a den began arguing over the price of four pipes of opium. The Chinese drew a gun and was about to shoot the addict when another man wrested the gun away. The addict then struck the Chinese a severe blow on the head with a thick cane and ran for his life, "closely followed by half a dozen Chinamen who would have killed him if the opportunity had offered itself."[21] Hop Ki's den saw a fight erupt on the Saturday night of 26 February 1881 when an opium addict accused the den's waiter of shorting him on his purchase of opium.[22] The addict's scalp was split open and several Chinese were bruised. One shot was fired, but the only casualty was an oil lamp.

The opium dens were rather quiet during the spring months of 1881. Then at the beginning of summer a killing occurred in Ah Kip's den.[23] Sunrise on the Tuesday morning of 7 June 1881 found several men in Ah Kip's, smoking pipes of opium. Into the den walked David "Tex" Hitchell, a former police officer and "a rough of the roughest type," who was said to be in an ugly mood. He immediately began verbally abusing the other smokers. One of them, James Stockdale, asked Hitchell to quit trying to provoke a fight. When Hitchell persisted, Stockdale got up to leave, saying that he was not interested in fighting or quarreling. Hitchell jumped to his feet and exclaimed, "I don't give a damn if you do go, you damned son of a bitch." Using his gun as a bludgeon, Hitchell then struck Stockdale on the side of the head and knocked him to the ground.

Hitchell's anger was not yet sated. He stuck his cocked revolver into Stockdale's face and was about to pull the trigger when an onlooker yelled, "Tex, for God's sake don't murder the man." Stockdale quickly added, "Don't murder me, I haven't got any pistol." Hitchell continued to press his revolver into Stockdale's face for a few seconds, then pulled it back and said to Stockdale, "I won't murder you, you son of a bitch; go heel yourself and I'll kill you before night." Stockdale got up and replied, "You ought not to abuse me in this way; I am not an able-bodied man, and I have no gun to defend myself."

Everybody, except Hitchell, who was busy cursing and kicking the den's stove, then cleared out of Ah Kip's. Some five or ten minutes later three shots rang out from the den. A number of men raced to the scene and found Hitchell shot in the stomach and bleeding profusely. He was rushed to Bodie's only hospital, but the opium-smoking rough died shortly after arriving.

Suspicion for the murder rested upon Stockdale. After a Chinese, who lived above Ah Kip's den, testified that he had heard Stockdale's voice coming from the den below immediately before the shooting, Stockdale was charged with murder. Stockdale

---

20. *Daily Free Press*, 24 Nov. 1880.

21. *Daily Free Press*, 5 Dec. 1880.

22. *Daily Free Press*, 27 Feb. 1881.

23. *Bodie Standard*, 15 and 22 June 1881.

retained Patrick Reddy as his attorney and voluntarily surrendered himself to the authorities. In the examination of Stockdale in justice court, the district attorney was forced to move that the prisoner be discharged for lack of evidence. To the satisfaction of the large crowd of spectators, the motion was granted.

Although there was not enough evidence to prosecute Stockdale, the *Bodie Standard* noted that it "is generally believed that he shot the deceased, and it is doubtful if there is a man in Bodie at all conversant with the circumstances but what believes that justice has been done all round—both in the shooting and in the acquittal. A desperate, dangerous and worthless man has been slain and whether by the hand of Stockdale—a quiet, inoffensive man . . . or by the hand of some one else, no one cares." At least one person did care: Nora Pine, Hitchell's girlfriend, committed suicide by taking an overdose of opium.[24]

Chinatown's opium dens continued to operate until the early fall of 1881, when Deputy Sheriff Andy Showers announced that the hitherto disregarded state law against opium smoking and dealing would be enforced.[25] Anyone caught "hitting the pipe" would be subject to a $500 fine, and opium dealers would face a $1,000 penalty. Why law enforcement officials waited so long to enforce the ban on opium is not known. By the time they did act, opium smoking in Bodie had fallen off by half.[26] Although most opium dens closed shortly after the announcement by Deputy Showers, a few continued clandestine operations. Only one man was punished for violation of the opium law during the next year. In November 1882, Ah Fong was sentenced to twenty-five days in the city jail for selling opium to white people.[27]

Chinatown saw violence aplenty outside of the opium dens. On the warm Tuesday evening of 11 August 1879, gunfire erupted in Chinatown shortly after nine o'clock.[28] Several officers rushed to the scene of the shooting and found the town's rival tongs engaged in battle. The warfare continued for nearly an hour before the police were finally able to separate the combatants. At least one Chinese, known only as "China George," was killed, and several others were seriously wounded. Witnesses said that another three or four Chinese were killed and their bodies were carried away. Some thirty Chinese were arrested and packed into the city jail's four cells "like sardines in a box." Pistols, revolvers, and knives of all shapes and varieties were found in the "mysterious folds" of their clothes and confiscated.

Testimony before the coroner's jury indicated that the members of one tong had conspired to kill China George, a leading member of Chinatown's other tong. George had told Deputy Sheriff Patrick Phelan several hours before the battle that he, China George, had been marked for death. Eight Chinese were indicted for murder, but the charges against them were dropped, one by one, for lack of evidence. By the end of October the last of them, Ah Chouey Joe, had been released.[29]

Even before Ah Chouey Joe was released, another battle between the two rival tongs nearly erupted. Trouble had been brewing during the Tuesday evening of 21 Oc-

24. *Bodie Standard*, 17 August 1881.

25. Bodie *Daily Free Press*, 14 Oct. 1881; *Bodie Standard*, 19 Oct. 1881.

26. *Bodie Standard*, 19 Oct. 1881.

27. Jail Register: Bodie Branch Jail, p. 51.

28. *Bodie Morning News*, 12 August 1879; *Bodie Standard*, 12 August 1879.

29. *Bodie Morning News*, 31 Oct. 1879.

tober 1879, and at about one o'clock the next morning the two tongs squared off. Guns and knives were drawn, but the dispute was somehow ended without bloodshed. "These pagan quarrels," commented the *Bodie Morning News*, "will result in half a dozen dead heathens some fine day, a consummation not much to be regretted."[30] The coroner's jury which investigated the death of China George was only slightly less extreme in its pronouncements; it recommended that Chinatown be relocated outside Bodie's town limits because the Chinese were "a public nuisance; [it said] that their continual shooting affrays endangered the lives of citizens; that the filth, engendered in their hovels, threatens a pestilence."[31]

Most violent confrontations between Chinese were individual affairs. Tong affiliation may have been a factor that exacerbated disputes between individual Chinese, but nowhere is it mentioned as a primary cause. More often than not, the primary cause of these disputes was a woman. Chinese women were in very short supply in Bodie, as they were in every other overseas Chinese settlement during the nineteenth century.[32] With few exceptions, only Chinese men emigrated overseas. Although at least half of the men were married, they were not accompanied by their wives. Bringing a wife along on a California sojourn was something only a few affluent merchants could afford. Most wives were left behind to live, according to Chinese custom and family law, in the homes of the sojourners' parents.

During the 1870s and 1880s Chinese men outnumbered Chinese women in the United States by more than twenty to one.[33] The inevitable result of this imbalance was prostitution, which became a flourishing business in Chinatown. Prostitutes were slaves in all but name. They did not enter the trade willingly. In China young women were sold into indentured servitude by impoverished parents, kidnapped, captured by pirates or raiding bands, or won as the spoils of a feudal war. When they reached the United States these women were usually sold or contracted to Chinese brothel-keepers or merchants. Some women were sold and resold again and again. Few escaped. Enforcement for the system came from the secret societies. It is not surprising, considering these conditions, that conflict over Chinese women in Bodie was frequent and sometimes violent, and that occasionally the women were brutally abused.

Rival claims to a woman caused a Chinese to shoot and wound two other Chinese in what the *Bodie Morning News*, on 26 March 1879, called "a regular Melican man's shooting affray." The shooter disappeared from the scene, and Chinese witnesses, including those who were shot, refused to identify him. The elopement of Chun San and a woman "possessed" by Ye Park on Christmas Eve of 1881 resulted in a second shooting.[34] Ye Park went to Deputy Sheriff Andy Showers with his problem. Since California law did not recognize indentured servitude, Ye Park must have represented the elopement as a kidnapping. Within a short time, Showers, a second deputy, and Ye Park were atop a buckboard in pursuit of the fleeing couple.

At Deep Wells, a way station on the Aurora and Benton road, they caught up with the lovers, who had stopped to rest and feed their team of horses. The deputies

30. *Bodie Morning News*, 23 Oct. 1879.
31. *Bodie Standard*, 13 August 1879.
32. Lyman, *Chinese Americans*, pp. 86–96; Lyman, *Asian in the West*, pp. 27–31.
33. Lyman, *Asian in the West*, p. 28.
34. *Bodie Standard*, 28 Dec. 1881.

were about to make a peaceful arrest of Chun San, when Ye Park drew a gun and began shooting. Before Showers could subdue him, Ye Park fired two rounds, one of which hit Chun San in the side. Chun San was rushed off to Aurora for medical treatment, and Ye Park was arrested and charged with assault with intent to commit murder.[35]

On 17 February 1882, the superior court of Mono County found Ye Park guilty as charged and sentenced him to thirteen years in the state penitentiary at San Quentin.[36] A month later he was transferred from Bodie to San Quentin to begin serving his sentence. During June of 1882 his attorneys won a new trial for him, and he was transferred back to Bodie and then on to the county jail at Bridgeport.[37] Ye Park's new trial was set for early 1883, but on 18 December 1882 Ye Park escaped from custody and was never recaptured.[38]

A woman's preference for a Chinese known only as "Wild Sam" precipitated a knife fight between Wild Sam and Tro Chow one Tuesday evening on King Street.[39] Tro Chow and a bystander who attempted to separate the fighters suffered cuts before the fight was stopped. No arrests were made.

Occasionally, Chinese women were the victims of the violence. Late one night, James McVarish heard a woman's screams coming from a building that he rented to Chinese laundrymen. He rushed inside and found two Chinese endeavoring to help a horribly battered and gashed Chinese woman while several other Chinese "were sitting around contentedly enjoying an opium-smoke."[40] The woman's boyfriend had attacked her in a jealous rage and left her face, head, and neck looking like "raw meat." None of the Chinese present attempted to interfere, nor would they identify the culprit. "A rope," commented the *Bodie Standard*, "would be almost too good for this scoundrel."

As Wing Kent learned, Chinese men did not always attack Chinese women with impunity. Wing Kent was a prosperous, young laundryman "of prepossessing appearance" who fell in love with a Chinese prostitute.[41] In return for her promise to remain faithful to him only, he gave the woman $300. Before long the woman decided she loved another and plotted to leave town with the new man. Wing Kent learned of her plans and confronted the woman in a small house on King Street. He demanded the return of his money. When she refused, he exploded with rage and attacked her with a meat cleaver. By the time she escaped into the street she looked as if she "had been run over by a railroad train." Police officers soon arrived and took her off to the hospital and Wing Kent off to jail where he was charged with attempted murder.[42] A week later, superior court found him guilty of assault with intent to commit murder and sentenced him to thirteen years in the state penitentiary.[43] "The Chinaman," said the *Bodie Standard*, "took his dose of medicine with philosophical indifference."[44]

35.   Jail Register: Bodie Branch Jail, p. 30.

36.   Minute Book, Criminal, Dep't No. 2, Superior Court, Mono County, pp. 92, 95.

37.   Jail Register: Bodie Branch Jail, pp. 36 and 40.

38.   Minute Book, Criminal, Dep't No. 2, Superior Court, Mono County, p. 164.

39.   *Bodie Standard*, 19 April 1882.

40.   *Bodie Standard*, 12 June 1878.

41.   *Bodie Standard*, 2 Nov. 1881.

42.   Jail Register: Bodie Branch Jail, p. 30.

43.   *Bodie Standard*, 16 Nov. 1881; Minute Book, Criminal, Dep't No. 2, Superior Court, Mono County, pp. 74, 80, 82.

44.   *Bodie Standard*, 16 Nov. 1881.

Not all attacks on women had such serious consequences. During a Chinese New Year celebration, Ah Fouk forsook his normal pipe of opium for a bottle of Irish whiskey.[45] By the time he got to his girlfriend's King Street room, he was thoroughly drunk. He scattered the furniture about the room and then turned on his girlfriend and beat her with "a highly ornamented roast pig." Before Ah Fouk injured the woman seriously, a police officer arrived and arrested him. In justice court, Ah Fouk's attorney argued that the whiskey had simply caused Ah Fouk to act "like all drunken men do." Ah Fouk was fined $25 plus court costs and set free.

King Street boasted several gambling dens, and nearly every Chinese in Bodie gambled, yet gambling caused almost no violence in Bodie. Gambling was an integral part of Chinese life and as ancient as China itself.[46] The Chinese believed that their success in life was determined as often by fate as by hard work. Gambling, they believed, was nothing more than the working out of this fate. They accepted their losses stoically, but they also firmly believed that great wealth could come to them at any moment. One good night's gambling could give the lonely sojourner enough money to return to his wife and family in China and live in comfort, whereas it took years of laboring in mines, laundries, and restaurants to accomplish the same goal.

Gambling was also one of the few recreational activities readily available to the sojourners. Bodie's King Street gambling establishments were even busier than the opium dens or brothels. "The dreams of an opium smoker or the dissipations waiting in a house of prostitution," said a scholar of the sojourners, "ranked second in attraction to the fascination which a gambling table radiated. Here, desperate daring could change the course of a gambler's life with one single stroke of luck."[47] Fan-tan was the most popular game of chance. Meaning "repeated division" in Cantonese, fan-tan players attempted to guess the number of beans (or other counters) that would be left over when a pile of the beans was divided by four. It was a fan-tan game that caused King Street's only violent confrontation related directly to gambling.[48] A laundryman and a fan-tan operator got into a dispute over a bet and wound up pummeling each other and rolling about on the ground in a crowd of spectators.

Disputes over debts produced only two violent confrontations between Chinese.[49] One confrontation saw two Chinese slash each other with knives over a $10 debt; a second resulted in Ah Gin taking a couple of shots at Sam Jemsen. The first shot missed its mark and lodged in a chair in Thomas Kennedy's furniture store. The second shot was on target, but it hit a silver coin in Jemsen's pocket and was deflected without causing injury. When he was arrested, Ah Gin claimed that Jemsen owed him some money. The situation may have been exacerbated by tong affiliation: Ah Gin belonged to the Sam Sing, and Sam Jemsen was a member of the rival Yung Wah. Justice court charged Ah Gin with assault with intent to commit murder and bound him over to await the action of the grand jury. In the meantime, Ah Gin remained free on a $2,000 bond. Two months later the grand jury chose not to indict him.

Chinese, for the most part, fought only among themselves. Other than opium den rows, only three violent encounters occurred between Chinese and white men, and

45. Bodie *Daily Free Press*, 15 Feb. 1880.

46. Lyman, *Chinese Americans*, pp. 96–99; Barth, *Bitter Strength*, pp. 126–27.

47. Barth, *Bitter Strength*, p. 126.

48. Bodie *Daily Free Press*, 22 Jan. 1881.

49. *Daily Free Press*, 7 Feb. 1880; *Bodie Standard*, 24 July and 9 Oct. 1878.

two of those were provoked by intoxicated whites. In the first, a drunken miner punched a Chinese for no apparent reason.[50] The miner was arrested but subsequently released on a promise of future good behavior. A second drunk, a man named Babbitt, kicked in the door of a Chinese laundry late one night and began to tear the laundry apart.[51] The Chinese proprietors, asleep in a back room, were awakened by the commotion and rushed up front. One of the Chinese felled Babbitt with a flatiron, and another clubbed the drunk with a stick of wood. "A Chinaman," commented the *Daily Free Press*, "has a certain amount of back bone when it comes down to defending his own property, a fact which Babbitt is evidently familiar with, although it took a strong beating to make him believe it."

A laundry was also the scene of the third violent encounter. James Russell arrived at Hop Lee's laundry early one morning to pick up clothes that he had dropped off a few days before. Hop Lee looked over a stack of bundles and explained sadly that Russell's clothes were not there. His anger rising, Russell gave Hop Lee four minutes to produce the missing laundry. Hop Lee was unmoved and suggested that Russell leave. "Then it was that Russell's Christian meekness and forbearance entirely forsook him," said the *Daily Free Press*, "and he waded into the Chinaman and his associates."[52] Russell slammed one Chinese under a table, flattened another with a stool, and was about to tip over the stove when Hop Lee produced Russell's bundle of clothes. Hop Lee willingly let Russell go without paying.

One more confrontation should perhaps be mentioned, although it did not involve a Chinese and a white man. It did, however, involve a Chinese and a white man's dog. A "meek-looking" Chinese was passing the corner of Main and King streets when a white man set his dog upon him. When the dog took a nip at the Chinese's heels, the Chinese "suddenly drew from some mysterious place in his flowing garments a gun of prodigious size and blazed away at his tormentor."[53] Somehow the dog managed to escape unhurt. The Chinese continued on his way, "public sentiment appearing to be on his side."

Two Chinese were killed in violent encounters that remained mysteries, at least to the white authorities.[54] On the Tuesday night of 7 January 1879, Ah Chun was stabbed to death on King Street.[55] Ah Sow, a dishwasher in the Carson Exchange saloon who had left town, was implicated in the murder. He was arrested at Dogtown and was returned to Bodie for an appearance in justice court. The evidence against him was found to be insufficient to have him bound over for trial, and he was set free. No new evidence was ever produced, and Ah Chun's murder went unsolved. A second unsolved murder occurred some two months later, but the Chinese victim's body was not discovered until mid-April.[56] The body was found in a shallow grave about a mile below the Syndicate

---

50. *Bodie Standard*, 22 Feb. 1879.

51. *Bodie Standard*, 22 Dec. 1880; Bodie *Daily Free Press*, 17 Dec. 1880.

52. *Daily Free Press*, 26 Nov. 1879.

53. *Daily Free Press*, 28 August 1880.

54. The killings very possibly could have been tong related. The Chinese in Bodie were very reluctant to cooperate with white authorities, especially when the secret societies were involved.

55. *Bodie Standard*, 18 Jan. 1879.

56. *Bodie Morning News*, 18 April 1879.

mill. It had evidently been there for several weeks. Coyotes had eaten away the face, hands, and feet, making identification impossible. A bashed-in head indicated that death had not been due to natural causes.

The Chinese, like other residents of Bodie, committed crimes against property. These crimes were primarily burglary and theft, although there were a couple of instances of arson, and one of cruelty to animals.[57] Inasmuch as many burglaries and thefts went unsolved in Bodie, it is impossible to state the total number of these types of crimes that Chinese committed. Of the burglaries and thefts where the perpetrator was identified or apprehended, Chinese were responsible for about nine out of a total of some forty.[58] Another forty or so burglaries and thefts were committed by persons unknown. Whether the Chinese would have maintained their 22 percent share of the burglaries and thefts—some three times greater than their proportion of the population—if these other criminals had been identified is difficult to say.

The most common items stolen by Chinese thieves, as well as by their white counterparts, were blankets and wood, two necessary and scarce articles in Bodie. The Chinese were important figures in the firewood trade. They cut wood in the hills to the west of Bodie and packed it to town on mules. The firewood was then sold to Bodieites, who stacked it next to their cabins and stores for use in wood-burning stoves. A number of Bodieites suspected that some Chinese wood-packers sold wood by day and then stole it back by night for resale.

Sam Chung was the Chinese badman of Bodie. Chung, a member of the Yung Wah tong, spoke fluent English and had forsaken the traditional Chinese queue and dress for an American haircut and Western clothes. Because of his bilingual fluency, he often acted as an interpreter for justice and superior courts in cases involving Chinese. Chung was also Chinatown's leading businessman, owning a two-story building that contained a lodging house, restaurant, and laundry on King Street. It was this building, in fact, that first brought Chung notoriety.

Late one Tuesday night in mid-February of 1878, a fire broke out in Chung's building, and within minutes it was engulfed in flames.[59] Although volunteer fire fighters rushed to the scene, they could do nothing more than save the surrounding buildings. It was thought that a defective stovepipe in the roof of the kitchen had caused the conflagration.

All was not lost for Chung. He had wisely insured the building for fire and collected $5,000. The insurance company, not convinced that the fire was accidental, quietly began an investigation. In July 1878, Chung, along with two accomplices, was arrested for setting fire to his own building. The Mono County district attorney, relying on information provided by the Board of Underwriters of San Francisco, claimed that he had "evidence which will undoubtedly convict all of them." The evidence must have been less than convincing. During the next two weeks Chung's attorney, John McQuaid, succeeded in having charges against all three defendants dropped.[60]

---

57.   *Bodie Standard*, 14 August 1878; 9 and 23 Nov. 1881; Bodie *Daily Free Press*, 15 Nov. 1879; 27 Feb., 25 March, 14 April, and 2 Dec. 1880.

58.   These statistics were compiled from an exhaustive search of Bodie's four newspapers, the jail register, and the superior court records.

59.   *Bodie Standard*, 20 Feb. 1878.

60.   *Bodie Standard*, 10, 17, and 24 July 1878.

Sam Chung made headlines again when he shot and wounded Sam Wang, an opium den proprietor, and Ah Goon, on the Tuesday afternoon of 25 March 1879.[61] Chung disappeared from the scene of the shooting before police arrived, but he was later identified as the shooter and arrested. He was charged with assault with intent to commit murder and remanded by justice court to the custody of the sheriff. Unable to post bail of $3,000, Chung was taken off to the county jail at Bridgeport. A month later he was indicted by the grand jury.[62] But John McQuaid, again serving as Chung's attorney, got the case against Chung dismissed and he was released.

Chung was soon back at work, which now included vegetable farming behind his cabin on Rough Creek. Early on the Friday morning of 9 July 1880, Prudencia Encinos, "a well known and much respected Mexican," was driving his wood-laden mules by Chung's cabin when some of the mules strayed into Chung's vegetable garden.[63] Chung flew into a rage, grabbed a double-barreled shotgun, and blasted Encinos. Encinos was rushed to a doctor, but the wounded Mexican died that night.

Chung was arrested and lodged in the Bodie jail. When rumor spread that a party of vigilantes were planning to take him, Constable John Kirgan shackled Chung to a deputy and, under the cover of darkness, sent the pair to Bridgeport. A short time later, a dozen masked Mexicans arrived at the jail. Four of them rushed into the jail's front office and, brandishing revolvers, demanded that Kirgan hand over Sam Chung. Kirgan told them that Chung had been taken into the mountains and was heavily guarded. The Mexicans ordered the door to the cells opened and did not leave until they had identified each prisoner.

Sam Chung, safe in the jail at Bridgeport, retained Patrick Reddy as his attorney. In August, Chung was brought to trial in superior court. He appeared to have no chance of acquittal. "There is no doubt in the mind of any person at all familiar with the circumstances of the killing," commented the *Bodie Standard*, "that Sam Chung committed an unprovoked, cold-blooded and barbarous murder."[64] In a brilliant forensic display, Patrick Reddy put doubt in the minds of the jurors. The trial ended in a hung jury.[65]

The prosecution moved to have Chung retried, and he was indicted for murder a second time on 24 August.[66] Through deft legal maneuvers Reddy was able to delay Chung's retrial until April 1881.[67] The delay, as usual, proved beneficial for the defense. In the intervening time one key prosecution witness had died and another had left the state. The jury was again unable to reach a verdict, six jurors standing for acquittal and six for conviction. The prosecution, now believing that it would be impossible to win a conviction and that another trial would be an unjustified expense, asked the court to dismiss the charges against Chung.[68] The motion was denied and Chung went to trial

---

61. *Bodie Morning News*, 26 March 1879; *Bodie Standard*, 5 April 1879.

62. *Bodie Morning News*, 20 May 1879.

63. *Bodie Chronicle*, 10 July 1880; *Bodie Standard*, 10 July 1880.

64. *Bodie Standard*, 4 May 1881.

65. *Bodie Chronicle*, 21 August 1880; Minute Book, Criminal, Dep't No. 2, Superior Court, Mono County, p. 47, 15 August 1880.

66. Minutes, Criminal Cases, Superior Court, p. 41.

67. *Bodie Standard*, 13 April 1881.

68. *Bodie Standard*, 4 May 1881.

for a third time in mid-June 1881. This time the jury returned a unanimous verdict of not guilty.[69] Patrick Reddy had been his usual overwhelming self. "It is hardly necessary to state," said the *Bodie Standard*, "that in this Chinaman's case justice has not been done, neither has public sentiment been satisfied. But this is nothing new in Mono County, and now it only remains for Chung to settle down, behave himself and become a good American." He may have done just that. Never again did Sam Chung's name appear in Bodie newspapers or Mono County court records.

Bodieites joined in the general movement against the Chinese which swept California during the late 1870s and early 1880s. Their complaints against the Chinese were not unlike those voiced by other Californians.[70] Said the *Daily Free Press* on 14 February 1880:

> We reflect the sentiment of a large majority of the citizens of this coast when we say that we have no desire to see the Chinese ill-used or badly-treated in any way; but they are a curse to the people of the coast, and we do not want them here. They do not and cannot assimilate with Americans; they are a drain upon the interests of the country, as their accumulations are removed from our shores; they deprive our youth and women of the lighter employments, contributing to make hoodlums of the one, and in thousands of instances forcing the other from legitimate occupations; they have engrafted new and heretofore unknown vices upon thousands of people, and if given unlimited freedom to our shores they will in time overrun the entire country, and demoralize labor as effectually as they have already done on the coast.

This view apparently represented majority opinion in Bodie. Only a few months earlier, as part of a statewide election on the Chinese question, Bodieites had voted 1,144 to 2 against Chinese immigration.[71] It was later said that one of the two pro-immigration votes was cast as a "josh."

Bodieites also regularly voiced complaints against their own Chinatown. Opium dens, as was already noted, were considered the primary evil. Complaints were also lodged against the unsanitary conditions in Chinatown. The laundries dumped their dirty water in the streets and made no effort to drain it away. The stench that arose from the standing pools of wash water was said to be extremely malodorous, especially during summer months. It was also feared that the stagnant water would incubate disease. "A Chinaman," asserted the *Daily Free Press*, "is the most filthy creature in existence, and his warmest admirers and supporters are obliged to admit the fact if closely pressed."[72] The grand jury, as noted earlier, thought Chinatown a public nuisance because, among other reasons, "the filth, engendered in their hovels, threatens a pestilence."[73] The jury recommended that Chinatown be relocated outside of Bodie's town limits.

---

69. Minutes, Criminal Cases, Superior Court, p. 141, 17 June 1881; *Bodie Standard*, 22 June 1881.

70. See Lyman, *Chinese Americans*, pp. 54–85; Lyman, *Asian in the West*, pp. 19–24; Barth, *Bitter Strength*, pp. 129–56; Jacobus tenBroek et al., *Prejudice, War and the Constitution*, pp. 15–22.

71. *Bodie Morning News*, 6 Sept. 1879; *Bodie Standard*, 8 March 1882. California as a whole voted approximately 160,000 to 900 against Chinese immigration. The one-sidedness of the vote may have been due partly to the manner in which the ballots were printed. See Mary Coolidge, *Chinese Immigration*, p. 123.

72. Bodie *Daily Free Press*, 28 July 1880.

73. *Bodie Standard*, 13 August 1879.

Early in 1880 the California legislature passed a law that outlawed employment of Chinese by corporations and specified penalties for its violation.[74] Bodie's *Daily Free Press* endorsed the law, although it feared that the legislation might be declared unconstitutional. Even if that occurred, said the newspaper, the law still "will have done all that it was expected to do—call the nation's attention to the sentiment of the Pacific Coast." A ban on Chinese immigration would have satisfied the *Free Press*. When a bill was introduced into the California legislature early in 1881 which proposed to prohibit all employment of Chinese, the *Free Press* opposed it. "All that is really needed," argued the paper, "is to stop immigration, and gradually but surely Chinese labor would disappear from the coast."[75] Nevertheless, the *Free Press* did urge that Chinese opium dealers, gamblers, prostitutes, and badmen be deported.

Bodie held its first public meeting on the Chinese question in March 1882.[76] The "very respectable congregation of citizens" unanimously adopted a resolution that urged California's senators and representatives to secure congressional passage of a law prohibiting Chinese immigration. A bill that did just that, the Chinese Exclusion Act of 1882, was passed by Congress in early May and was signed into law by President Chester Arthur. When Bodie received news of the event, flags were unfurled, a cannon was fired, and a bonfire was kindled on Main Street.[77]

Two weeks later Bodieites held an evening meeting to discuss the Pacific Coast League of Deliverance, an organization that advocated banning the employment of Chinese and forcing their eventual repatriation. The league suggested that vigilante action might be used to achieve these two goals. Bodieites seemed to be in agreement with the league's goals, but were generally against its methods. Patrick Reddy was the evening's leading speaker in opposition to the league. Reddy argued that he was opposed to "doing violence to helpless slaves, who are not here at their own bidding. If we are to do violence, why be cowardly about it? Why not attack those who bring them here? If there is any boycotting to be done, do it in the right direction and strike like men."[78] Bodieites took Reddy's advice and refused to join the league. Nor was any organized white violence ever visited upon the Chinese of Bodie or any attempt made to relocate Chinatown.

By the summer of 1882 the Chinese question was rapidly becoming academic. The Chinese, like many others, were leaving Bodie in droves. The end of the year found Chinatown nearly deserted. "The members of the two great companies," reported the *Daily Free Press* on 15 December 1882, "have ceased to fight, the gong is muffled, and by midnight only the white opium fiend can be seen coming and going through the narrow street. Where two dollars was spent for the fatal drug two years ago, not two-bits are squandered now. The questionable glory of Chinatown has departed; its brightness has been obfuscated, and the buildings with all their nooks and crannies are covered with fuliginous matter."

The Chinese of Bodie, although they were regularly the objects of ridicule and occasionally abuse, never experienced any organized violence directed at them by

74. Bodie *Daily Free Press*, 14 and 20 Feb. 1880.
75. *Daily Free Press*, 15 Jan. 1881.
76. *Bodie Standard*, 8 March 1882.
77. *Bodie Standard*, 10 May 1882.
78. *Bodie Standard*, 24 May 1882.

whites. The only organized violence they experienced was their own tong warfare. Nor is there record of any individual white attacking a Chinese simply because he was a Chinese. This was certainly not the case in all western towns. Anti-Chinese riots and assaults on Chinese occurred in dozens of towns, including Los Angeles, San Francisco, Seattle, and Denver.[79] Moreover, the Chinese of Bodie seem to have been treated no differently from whites by the legal system. In the one case where white witnesses and Chinese witnesses gave contradictory testimony, the jurors accepted the word of the Chinese over that of the whites. The finest defense attorneys made themselves available to the Chinese, as well. The Chinese, on the other hand, normally did not make themselves available to the white authorities, especially when the secret societies were involved. The typical Chinese was a very reluctant witness even if he himself had been the victim of the crime.

Chinese carried guns and knives, just as did their white counterparts, and were not averse to using them. Most violence in Chinatown centered around its numerous opium dens, and many of the patrons of those dens were white. This, in the opinions of Bodie's newspapers, was probably the greatest sin of the Chinese: they supplied the opium that morally and physically degraded white men. The newspapers did not acknowledge that it was white men, the English, who supplied the Chinese with opium in the first place. Nor did they mention that Americans drank opium in the form of laudanum for its euphoric effects long before the arrival of the Chinese.[80]

Of the nine violent deaths associated with the Chinese or Chinatown, five were directly related to opium dens or opium. These five deaths were all of whites. Two of the whites were shot to death by other whites, two accidently overdosed on drugs, and one, a woman, committed suicide. The other four deaths saw a Chinese shot to death in a tong war (there may have been three other Chinese killed also), a Chinese fatally stabbed by another Chinese, a Chinese beaten to death by person or persons unknown, and a Mexican shot to death by a Chinese. Finally, it is interesting to note that for some unknown reason most of the violent confrontations in Chinatown occurred on Tuesday nights. Weekend nights were relatively quiet.

Bodie was home to nearly two hundred "Mexicans" during its heyday.[81] Some of the so-called Mexicans were actually native Californians who came from old California families and preferred to be called Californios and not Mexicanos.[82] The majority of Spanish-speaking Bodieites did come from Mexico, however, particularly the border state of Sonora. Mexicans had been coming to California mining strikes ever since James Marshall's great discovery in January 1848. They suffered considerable abuse and were the objects of occasional vigilante actions during the gold rush, especially in the Mother Lode towns of the southern Sierra.[83] Some were even forced to quit the camps. Many

79.   Lyman, *Chinese Americans*, pp. 54–85; Lyman, *Asian in the West*, pp. 22–23. California's most serious anti-Chinese riot occurred in Los Angeles on 24 October 1871. After a bystander and two police officers were killed in a tong war, a mob descended on Chinatown and killed at least nineteen Chinese. The death toll of Chinese was even greater at Rock Springs, Wyoming, on 2 September 1885. An argument between Chinese and white mine workers sparked violence in which twenty-eight Chinese were killed.

80.   Lyman, *Chinese Americans*, pp. 99–100.

81.   *Bodie Standard*, 18 Sept. 1878; Department of the Interior, Census Office, *Tenth Census*, p. 498.

82.   See Leonard Pitt, *The Decline of the Californios: A Social History of the Spanish-Speaking Californians, 1846–1890*, p. 7. Many of the Californios, especially the rancheros, liked to claim pure Spanish descent, although most of them had at least some Indian blood.

83.   Pitt, pp. 48–68.

American miners thought that the Mexicans, as foreigners, had no right to American mineral wealth. Others feared that the Mexicans would provide a pool of cheap labor and depress wages in the mines. On the other hand, freight shippers soon discovered that the Mexican *arrieros* (mule skinners) were unsurpassed as teamsters, and merchants quickly learned that the Mexicans spent their money more freely than most other men in the camps, especially the frugal New England Yankees.[84] Mexicans contributed to the cosmopolitan nature of mining-camp life—the Sonorans in their large sombreros, billowy white pantaloons, and sandals were colorful figures—and to the techniques and vocabulary of mining. The arrastra was introduced by Mexicans, and words such as *placer* and *Mother Lode* are Spanish in origin.

In Bodie most Mexicans worked as teamsters and wood-packers, and a few as miners. Unlike the Chinese, the Mexicans did not have a section of town that they could call their own. They did have a favorite haunt, however. Dozens of Mexicans could be found any night of the week buying dances, drinks, and sex at the Spanish, or Lower, dance house at the southern end of Main Street. Mexicans also engaged in two great celebrations during the year, Hidalgo Day in September and Cinco de Mayo in May.[85] The celebrations were organized by a group calling itself the Junta Patriotica Méxica de Bodie and featured horsemanship events in which gringos as well as Mexicans participated. In the main event a rooster was buried up to its neck in an open field. Riders then made passes at a full gallop and attempted to grab the poor bird by his darting head and pull him from the ground.

There was no organized violence directed at Mexicans in Bodie, nor does any Mexican seem to have been attacked simply because he was a Mexican. Nevertheless, there were three deadly confrontations between Mexicans and gringos. No reasons were given for the first two. In one, John McTigue mortally wounded Mateas Alcantra in a Saturday night shootout.[86] In the other, John Wheeler shot a Mexican dead in self-defense.[87] Although the *Bodie Standard* claimed that Wheeler was "entirely justified in the deed, " the dead man's friends swore they would kill Wheeler. None of them, however, chose to confront Wheeler openly, for he was known to be a crack shot. Instead, they tried to surprise Wheeler one night while he was sleeping at Silas Smith's warehouse. When Alcantra's friends attempted to pry open the back door of the warehouse, Wheeler awoke and called out, "What do you want?" "Come out here, you white-livered son of a bitch," one of the men answered. Wheeler concluded, said the *Bodie Standard*, "that it would not be proper to refuse such a pressing invitation, and to signify his acceptance, sent a pistol ball through the door as an advance courier. The Mexicans did not stop to explain whether the ball took effect or not; but it is to be sincerely hoped that it was not entirely wasted." Wheeler was not bothered again.

Robbery and honor were responsible for the final deadly confrontation between a Mexican and a gringo. On the Thursday night of 2 September 1880, John Hackwell, a thirty-year-old miner, found himself in the Spanish dance house.[88] There he met

---

84.   Pitt, p. 59.

85.   *Bodie Standard*, 8 May and 18 Sept. 1878.

86.   *Bodie Standard*, 17 April 1878.

87.   *Bodie Standard*, 19 Dec. 1877.

88.   *Bodie Standard*, 6 and 11 Sept. 1880; *Daily Free Press*, 5, 7, and 8 Sept. 1880.

"Spanish Dora," a native Californian who operated a brothel that adjoined the dance house. Dora was known for both her good looks, especially her "beautiful, large black eyes," and her vicious temper. It seems that Hackwell, thoroughly drunk and not very coherent, followed Dora to her brothel next door, passed out, and was robbed. He later awoke on the street and discovered that he was missing $15 and his gun, a British Bulldog.[89] He returned to the brothel and demanded that Dora produce the money and the gun. When she refused he slapped her across the face and said he would be back Saturday night.

John Hackwell was a man of his word. At about eight o'clock on Saturday night he left a group of friends who were viewing a body in Ward's mortuary and strode down Main Street toward Dora's. As Hackwell approached the Spanish dance house, a man suddenly emerged from the shadows and at point-blank range shot him twice in the chest. Hackwell slumped to the ground, and the assailant disappeared into the darkness. A couple of men rushed to the fallen Hackwell, raised his head up, and asked him who had done the deed. He was unable to reply and within a few minutes was dead.

Police, accompanied by John Rann, a woodchopper and a friend of Hackwell's, soon arrived at Spanish Dora's. There they found Dora and Manuel Castillo, an "elderly Spaniard" and well-known veteran of the trans-Sierra country. Dora denied having any involvement in the murder, but Rann insisted she be arrested and questioned. Castillo came to her defense and exchanged a few words with Rann. It was a futile effort. Dora was arrested and taken off to jail.

Rann spent the remainder of the evening drinking in Bodie's saloons. About one o'clock in the morning he entered Wagner's saloon. Waving a roll of bills in the air, he said he would give $100 for the name of the Mexican who killed Hackwell. Moments later Rann was called outside by Manuel Castillo and led around the corner of the saloon. Waiting there were town roughs Dave Bannon, Sylvester "Old Red" Roe, and James Flannery.

Castillo had no intention of identifying the killer and instead claimed that Rann had insulted him earlier in the evening. Realizing that he had no chance against the four men, Rann retreated into the saloon. When they followed him inside and backed him into a side room, he drew a gun and warned them to keep their distance. Flannery lunged for the gun and had just gotten his hand on the barrel when the gun discharged—whether accidentally or intentionally was disputed. The bullet blew off most of Flannery's little finger and struck Castillo in the groin. Castillo died shortly before dawn. The next day he was buried in what the *Daily Free Press* called the largest funeral "that has ever taken place in Bodie." The procession included a band, nearly every carriage and buggy in Bodie, and a hearse drawn by four horses.

Rann was arrested for the killing, but was later released when it was determined that he had acted in self-defense. Meanwhile, Spanish Dora continued to languish in jail. A witness asserted that he had heard her tell a couple of men on Saturday afternoon that she was going to have Hackwell killed when he came for his gun that night. Moreover, Dora had allegedly said that her cousin, Moreno Castro, would do the killing and that he would use Hackwell's own gun. Although this is probably precisely what oc-

---

89.   The British Bulldog was a .45 caliber (some were .44 caliber), five-shot revolver with a 4″ barrel. It was manufactured by P. Webley and Son in Birmingham, England, from 1878 to 1914. See Frederick Myatt, *The Illustrated Encyclopedia of Pistols and Revolvers*, pp. 97 and 101.

curred, no other witnesses came forward nor was any corroborating evidence produced. Spanish Dora was soon released, and neither she nor Moreno Castro was prosecuted for the murder.

Not all shootings ended in death. Professional gambler David Avery and Santiago Galindo began quarreling for some unknown reason one Friday night in the Spanish dance house.[90] Avery knocked Galindo to the floor and then drew a gun and shot the prostrate Mexican in the stomach. A number of men rushed for the exit; others drew their guns and waited for more action. Medical aid was summoned for Galindo, and minutes later a doctor arrived. The physician called it a miraculous escape; the bullet had missed all vital organs and had exited harmlessly.

Nevertheless, the Mexicans in the dance house were "greatly excited over one of their friends being so roughly handled and spoke in strong terms against the would-be slayer." Avery was arrested and lodged in the city jail. A week later he was examined in justice court along with several witnesses. The testimony of the witnesses was of such a conflicting nature that the judge discharged him. The freeing of Avery aroused little anger. After all, as the *Daily Free Press* expressed the thinking of the times, Galindo's gunshot wound was "not even of enough importance to confine him to his bed."[91]

There were only five other clashes between Mexicans and gringos, and none of them were considered serious affairs. A drunken brawl erupted in the Spanish dance house one December night; knives and revolvers were drawn, but the row ended peacefully when the gringos "beat a hasty retreat."[92] James Flannery, one of Bodie's roughest characters, used his revolver as a club to knock a Mexican tamale vendor senseless on the sidewalk in front of Magee's saloon. Flannery was arrested and later appeared in justice court; the outcome of the appearance was not recorded. A Mexican and a gringo who roomed together fell into an argument over ownership of their furniture after they had downed a bottle of whiskey one Saturday night. The argument developed into a fight, which left the participants bruised and their furniture "considerably broken up." In a dispute over a game of cards, a Mexican slashed a man named O'Brien with a knife. The wound was minor, and O'Brien refused to press charges. Finally, Joaquin Fontis attacked Alex Whitman with an ax. Evidently, Fontis did little damage, because he pleaded guilty in justice court and was simply fined $24.

Mexicans also had violent confrontations with other Mexicans in Bodie. Although weapons were normally used in these fights, only one death occurred. Early in June 1878, Jesus Revis and Antonio Valencia fell into an argument in front of Summers's butcher shop.[93] When Valencia slashed at Revis with a knife, Revis drew his revolver and shot Valencia. A few hours later Valencia died. Though conscious until the end, he refused to say anything about the fight. Revis was arrested, but was later released when it was determined that he had acted in self-defense.

A similar though less deadly fight occurred between John Gonzere and Joseph Garcia.[94] Garcia felled Gonzere with a blow from a revolver, then Gonzere sprang to his

90. *Daily Free Press,* 31 July 1880.

91. *Daily Free Press,* 10 August 1880.

92. The following incidents were reported in the *Daily Free Press* on 3 Dec. 1879, 20, 22, and 24 Jan., 4 April, 15 May, and 22 June 1880.

93. *Bodie Standard,* 5 June 1878.

94. *Bodie Standard,* 14 Nov. 1877.

feet and slashed Garcia across the forehead with a knife. They were both arrested and each was fined $25 in justice court. In a one-sided affair, an unarmed Antonio Martinez was stabbed by Nicholas Samonas.[95] Both men were drunk, and the two had a long history of animosity. Samonas was arrested, charged with assault with intent to commit murder, and lodged in the Bodie jail. Two days later justice court bound him over for action by the grand jury. His bail was set at $2,000. The grand jury, citing lack of testimony, chose not to indict Samonas, and he was discharged.[96]

Two Mexicans met at the corner of Main and King streets one Tuesday evening to settle a dispute over ownership of a woodpile. With knives as the chosen weapons, they fell to fighting immediately. Although one of the men was seriously wounded, the other escaped unscathed. An argument between two Mexicans in the Spanish dance house led to a fistfight. The fight spilled over into the street and left one of the men "severely bruised about the optics and nasal pertuberance."[97]

Mexicans were occasionally involved in crimes against property. Again, as with the Chinese, there is no way to determine if a Mexican committed a particular theft or burglary unless the criminal was apprehended or identified. Therefore it is impossible to know exactly how many thefts or burglaries were committed by Mexicans.

Only six instances of horse theft were known to have occurred in Bodie. Of these, Mexicans were responsible for two and gringos accounted for three; no person was ever caught or identified in the other horse theft. The first instance of horse theft by Mexicans saw two Mexicans, one of them a well-known teamster, gather several horses together in Bodie one night and slip quietly out of town.[98] A couple of deputy sheriffs were sent in pursuit, but the Mexicans made their getaway. In the second instance, ranch hand Manuel Rodriguez stole a horse from his former employer.[99] When he was arrested, Rodriguez admitted the theft, but argued that he had taken the horse in payment for wages. He was unable to prove his contention in court and was sentenced to one year in the state penitentiary.

In addition to horse theft, Mexicans were arrested for stealing coal oil and jewelry, and for cruelty to animals. A Mexican wood-packer was fined $10 for severely beating his overloaded mule, which had fallen down.[100] Antonio Martinez, "a man of bad character," was sentenced to six months in jail or a $500 fine for stealing several cases of coal oil from the warehouse of Page, Wheaton and Company.[101] Not having the money to pay the fine, Martinez went off to jail. For petty larceny—the stolen article is not mentioned—Frank Mendoza was sentenced to pay a fine of $40 or serve forty days.[102] A far luckier thief was a Mexican known only as "Little Dan."[103] He stole some $450 worth of jewelry from the bureau drawer of a Bodie woman and then tried to sell the jewelry in Aurora. When a potential buyer recognized the jewelry, Little Dan quickly

95. *Bodie Standard*, 11 Dec. 1878.

96. Records, A, District Court, Mono County, p. 344.

97. *Daily Free Press*, 28 July and 29 August 1880.

98. *Daily Free Press*, 4 Dec. 1879.

99. *Bodie Standard*, 17 August 1881.

100. *Bodie Standard*, 17 April 1878.

101. *Daily Free Press*, 27 July 1880.

102. *Bodie Standard*, 30 June 1879.

103. *Bodie Standard*, 20 Feb. 1878.

left town. Bill Withrow, who seems to have had a personal interest in the jewelry, was deputized and sent to track down the thief. At Wellington Station, some fifty miles north of Bodie, Withrow caught up with him and recovered all of the stolen property. With the jewelry in his possession, Withrow concluded that he had no further use for Little Dan and turned him loose. The *Bodie Standard* thought that although the action "may not have been exactly in accordance with law," it did save the county considerable expense.

Mugging, or "garroting," as it was known in Bodie, occurred occasionally. In at least three instances Mexicans were the victims of the mugging. Whether the muggings were also perpetrated by Mexicans is not known. The greatest loss was suffered by a Mexican who staggered out of the Bank Exchange saloon late one night and was knocked senseless by two men.[104] He recovered to find his pistol and $250 gone. Manny Quelos suffered a similar fate when he left the Fredricksburg Brewery and was also flattened by two men.[105] They relieved him of $30. Quelos thought the garroters might have been the same two men he had treated to drinks earlier in the evening in the Brewery. When Quelos paid for those drinks, the men had noticed that his money pouch was full of silver dollars. Muggers also knocked down and robbed a Mexican late one night in the Tuolumne Stables, causing the *Bodie Standard* to complain that the police never seemed to be out patrolling when garroting occurred.[106]

Bodie's Mexicans, then, were involved as participants, perpetrators, and victims in shootings, knife fights, horse thefts, burglaries, and muggings. They, like the town's Chinese, saw no organized violence directed at them. Nor did any individual suffer from violence simply because he was a Mexican. The legal system seemed to treat Mexicans just like everyone else. The severest criminal penalty meted out to a Mexican was a sentence of one year in the state penitentiary for horse theft. Horse thieves, Mexican or not, were not hanged. In the one instance in which a Mexican was implicated in the murder of a gringo, the Mexican was not even arrested, let alone prosecuted. Three Mexicans were shot to death in self-defense by gringos, one was shot to death by a Chinese, and one Mexican was shot fatally by another Mexican. Unlike the Chinese, who for some unknown reason had a penchant for becoming involved in violent confrontations on Tuesday nights, most Mexican violence occurred on the weekend nights of Friday and Saturday, and much of it was associated with the consumption of alcohol at the Spanish dance house or one of Bodie's saloons.

Indians played only a very minor role in violence and lawlessness in Bodie. This was in sharp contrast to the role they had played at Aurora. By the time of Bodie's boom, most of the Indians in the area had settled on the Walker River reservation. Nevertheless, small bands of Paiute still roamed the hinterland and occasionally came into Bodie. The federal census of 1880 counted some thirty-five Indians as permanent residents of the town.

Almost all Indian-related troubles involved alcohol, although there were a couple of exceptions. In one of those exceptions a band of Paiute threatened a group of Bodie woodchoppers on the eastern side of Mono Lake early in November 1877.[107] The

---

104. *Bodie Standard*, 4 Dec. 1878.

105. *Daily Free Press*, 1 August 1880.

106. *Bodie Standard*, 20 Jan. 1880.

107. *Bodie Standard*, 7 Nov. 1877.

25. By the time of Bodie's boom, most Paiute had settled on the Walker River reservation. Some still roamed the hinterlands, and a few lived on the edge of white settlements. The woman wearing the rabbit-skin shawl is "Old Talon," a Paiute shaman. A cradleboard, complete with sun shade, holds the infant on the right. (Credit: Southwest Museum)

Paiute said they would shoot every one of the woodchoppers—every "white squaw," as the Paiute put it—unless the woodchoppers cleared out. The *Bodie Standard* commented on 7 November:

> What has given rise to this sentiment, people are at a loss to conceive, unless it be the chronic jealousy of the red-skins on beholding the rapid growth of the white population, and contrasting the difference between their own debased condition with the continually increasing comforts and luxuries of the white settlers. If a little sense could be hammered into the clouded intellect of these red brothers and some of their chronic laziness thrashed out of them, they might some day be able to comprehend the laws of nature sufficiently and grow ambitious enough to induce them to work for a living like the rest of mankind, instead of frittering their time away in gambling and stretching their lazy carcasses in the sun's warm rays.

In spite of the venomous invective of the *Bodie Standard*, the Paiute had a very good reason other than "chronic jealousy" to threaten the woodchoppers. The Paiute depended for their very survival upon those trees that the whites were chopping down. The fruit of those trees, the pine nut, was a staple of the Paiute diet. The Paiute fully comprehended that the mining and ranching activities of the whites were causing the destruction of the few trees that dotted the mountain slopes of the trans-Sierra country.

The only fatal confrontation between an Indian and a white was also unrelated to alcohol.[108] Henry Martin, who operated the Bodie Ranch, located three miles east of Bodie on the road to Aurora, allowed a Paiute to pasture his horse on ranch property. When the horse died unexpectedly, the Paiute accused Martin of killing it and, not comprehending the meaning of the state boundary, went to Aurora to initiate legal proceedings against the rancher. At Aurora, the Paiute and several of his friends who had joined him were told that they must file the complaint in Bodie. Perhaps in the belief that they had been given the runaround, the Indians returned to the Bodie Ranch on the morning of 15 June 1880, and the Paiute said to Martin, "You kill my horse; guess I kill you." The Paiute drew his revolver, but Martin was ready with a double-barreled shotgun. As usual the shotgun won. Martin surrendered himself in Bodie and was lodged in jail. The *Daily Free Press* lamented the killing and said, "It is certainly a great pity that this should have occurred. The Indians hereabouts have heretofore been found very tractable, and no complaint could be made of them."

The day after the killing Henry Martin was brought before justice court and acquitted on a plea of self-defense. "The Indians were very much displeased at the result," noted the *Daily Free Press*, "and unless Martin is very cautious he may have trouble with some of the friends of the dead man." The trouble came not from friends of the Paiute, but from the Mono County grand jury. Disregarding the decision of Bodie's justice court, the grand jury indicted Martin for murder.[109] He went to trial in superior

---

108.   The following account is drawn from the *Daily Free Press* on 16 and 17 June 1880.

109.   Criminal Calendar, Dep't No. 2, Superior Court, Mono County, 13 July 1880.

court early in August, but the case was dismissed when the prosecution could produce no witnesses.[110]

Every other Indian problem, whether it involved whites or Indians only, was associated with the use of alcohol. The most serious incident was the attempted assassination of "Captain John," the "chief" of the Bodie and Mono Lake Paiute.[111] Two drunken Paiute set fire to Captain John's wickiup near the Noonday mine and shot at the chief as he came running out of the flaming hut. Constable Kirgan dispatched a couple of his officers to arrest the offenders, but the would-be assassins stole two of Captain John's horses and escaped.

There were also instances of drunken Indians committing petty thefts and ransacking cabins, wildly firing off their guns, fighting each other, and trying to cut off a Chinese's queue.[112] For the most part, however, drunken Indians usually just staggered around town until they passed out or were arrested and lodged in jail for "safe keeping." "There has not been a day," claimed the *Bodie Standard* on 2 August 1882, "but what Main Street becomes the thoroughfare of an inebriated Indian."

At least one of these evidently numerous drunken Indians was made the brunt of a cruel joke. One fine summer day a thoroughly intoxicated Indian was invited into an opium den by a group of Chinese, who offered him what they said was a pipe of tobacco. After a second pipe, he grew terribly ill and began to vomit. The Chinese then threw him into the street and sat down on the sidewalk to watch his agonies. "The Chinamen," said the *Bodie Standard*, "heartily enjoyed the huge joke they had played on the unsophisticated Indian."[113]

That it was Chinese who duped the drunken Indian was perhaps appropriate. Of eleven arrests for selling alcohol to Indians, four were of Chinese.[114] The others arrested included five whites and two Mexicans.[115] Moreover, Chinatown was repeatedly mentioned by drunken Indians as the place where they had purchased their liquor. Why the Chinese were so prominent in the illicit traffic is not known. Penalties for those caught selling liquor to the Indians were usually severe. Although one Mexican got off with only a $50 fine, one white man was sentenced to fifty days in jail, another to a hundred days, and a Chinese was fined $100 and sentenced to serve three months. Bodie's newspapers endorsed the stiff penalties and often called for stiffer ones.[116] When two drunken Indians at Big Pine cut the throat of one of their friends who had beaten

110. Register of Actions, Superior Court, Mono County, p. 14; Minute Book, Criminal, Dep't No. 2, Superior Court, Mono County, p. 38. It is not stated why the prosecution was unable to produce the witnesses, presumably the Indian friends of the dead Paiute. After 1872 California Indians could testify against white men in court. An 1851 California statute had previously proscribed their testimony. See Ferdinand Fernandez, "Except a California Indian: A Study in Legal Discrimination."

111. *Bodie Standard*, 30 June 1879.

112. *Bodie Standard*, 5 April 1879; 20 July 1881; 15 Feb., 12 April, and 2 August 1882; *Daily Free Press*, 19 Nov. 1880.

113. *Bodie Standard*, 20 July 1881.

114. *Bodie Chronicle*, 27 July 1878; *Daily Free Press*, 5 Dec. 1879, 3 March 1880; *Bodie Standard*, 15 Feb. 1882.

115. *Bodie Standard*, 14 August and 2 Oct. 1878; 20 April and 31 August 1881; *Daily Free Press*, 24 and 27 Feb. 1880.

116. *Bodie Chronicle*, 27 July 1878; *Daily Free Press*, 24 Feb. 1880; *Bodie Standard*, 20 and 27 April 1881.

them in a game of cards, the *Bodie Standard* argued that "the wrong throat was cut. It should have been that of the miscreant who sold the whiskey."[117]

The Indian in Bodie was not a threat. He was for the most part a pathetic drunk who had been robbed of his land, culture, and identity. When intoxicated he was often jailed for "safe keeping." Occasionally, an Indian would ransack a cabin, commit a theft, or get in a fight, usually with another Indian or a Chinese, but with a few exceptions, that was all.

There were no more than a handful of blacks in Bodie, and there was only one serious violent encounter that involved a black man. On the Friday morning of 21 November 1879, a man named Fox, the cook at the Gem Chop House, was busily preparing a customer's meal when Joe Davis, "a colored man," burst into the kitchen and attempted to stab him with a knife. Davis cut Fox's vest in half with one slash of the blade, but Fox escaped before more damage could be done. Fox could offer no reason for the attack, although the *Daily Free Press* noted that "Davis is considered a desperado and has had a good many fights, once fatally stabbing a man in Salt Lake."[118] A warrant was sworn out for the arrest of Davis, but there is no record of his ever having been brought to justice.

Chinese, Mexicans, Indians, and blacks, then, never experienced any violence directed at them merely because they were members of minority groups. Nor, with the exception of the Indians, who were prohibited from imbibing alcohol and who were often jailed merely because they were intoxicated, do they seem to have been treated any differently by either the civil or the criminal justice system. Their testimony was admissible in court and seems to have been evaluated no differently from testimony given by majority-group witnesses. Bodie's finest attorneys made themselves available to the minorities, and the sentences and fines that minority lawbreakers received were no different from those that other Bodieites received for similar offenses. Minority violence and lawlessness was not dramatically different from that of the majority group, but there were differences. Chinese evidently committed a disproportionate number of burglaries, thefts, and sales of liquor to Indians. The Chinese were also involved in more fights over women and in more brutal assaults on women. Mexicans resorted to the use of knives in fights more often than other groups, and committed a disproportionate number of horse thefts and sales of liquor to Indians. And Indians were arrested for public drunkenness at a rate far greater than that of other Bodieites.

117.   *Bodie Standard*, 27 April 1881.
118.   *Daily Free Press*, 21 Nov. 1879.

8

WOMEN, JUVENILES, AND VIOLENCE

Bodie was home to some five or six hundred women during its boom years. "There is probably not another mining camp on the coast," bragged the *Bodie Standard* on 31 May 1882, "that can boast of as many and handsome young ladies as Bodie." Nevertheless, women accounted for only about 10 percent of Bodie's total population.[1] Most of the married women had lived in other mining camps, and as a former resident of Bodie reminisced, "many of them, like their husbands, were of superior type. They, too, were notable for their breadth of view, warmheartedness, sociability, and for their good works."[2] Occasionally, groups of young women would be brought to Bodie from the East. One article in the *Bodie Standard* mentioned that six young ladies, ranging in age from eighteen to twenty-three, would be arriving soon and would "afford an excellent chance for our young men to marry and settle down in life, for upon the arrival of the fair sex—and with our present supply—any man ought to be satisfied."[3]

Still, the demand for young women exceeded the supply, and only a small number of Bodie men were able to find wives. As a consequence, prostitution flourished. Several dozen or more prostitutes lived in small cabins or in rooms attached to the brothels and dance houses that lined Bonanza Street, Bodie's red-light district. It was these prostitutes who accounted for most of the violence and lawlessness committed by or directed at women in Bodie. Profiles of the prostitutes reveal that their lives were invariably tragic, often violent, and occasionally cut short by suicide or, in one case, by murder.

Probably no prostitute led a life more filled with violence than did pretty and petite Rosa Olague, called the Castilian Cyprian or Spanish Maid by Bodie's newspapers. She had fights with men and with other prostitutes, and once attempted to take her own life. She first made headlines when she got into a fight with John Green in the Can Can restaurant on the Friday night of 14 November 1879.[4] She used a double-edged knife to

1. U.S. Department of the Interior, Census Office, *Tenth Census*, p. 108; *Bodie Standard*, 27 July 1881.
2. Grant Smith, "Bodie, Last of the Old-Time Mining Camps," p. 78.
3. *Bodie Standard*, 31 May 1882.
4. Bodie *Daily Free Press*, 15, 19, and 20 Nov. 1879; *Bodie Standard*, 19 and 28 Nov. 1879.

26.   *Attached to the brothels and dance houses that lined Bonanza Street were dozens of small rooms that served as living quarters for the prostitutes. Today the rooms are dilapidated but still standing. (Credit: California Historical Society)*

slash his face from forehead to chin. His nose was nearly cut off, and his "whole landscape presented a scene of blood and destruction." Rosa was arrested and charged with assault with intent to commit murder.

Four days later she appeared in justice court, the cynosure of a large crowd of spectators. Dressed in black with a white scarf around her neck, the still pretty though haggard brunette strode into the courtroom with a look of defiance on her face. "She's a wicked lookin' cat, ain't she," commented one spectator. In the justice court examination it was determined that Rosa had acted in self-defense and she was set free.

A week later Rosa was back in jail, this time for a drunken rampage in which she rousted prostitutes from several Bonanza Street brothels.[5] She took on Spanish Dora, a prostitute known for her beautiful eyes and vicious temper, on a Saturday night in March of 1880.[6] The two women threw punches and pulled hair until a police officer stopped the fight and arrested them. Four nights later Rosa attempted suicide by taking poison. A physician brought her back from near death. "Heaven knows," said the *Daily Free Press*, "she would be better dead than living a disreputable life."

Rosa was soon back on the job and fighting again. While she and her partner were dancing a waltz at the Spanish dance house they bumped into Amelia Torres and

5.   *Bodie Standard*, 28 Nov. 1879.

6.   *Daily Free Press*, 21 and 25 March 1880.

her partner. Amelia, "a modest unassuming senorita" who supported herself and her mother by working at the dance house, evidently only as a dance partner, asked Rosa for an apology. Instead, she received a blow in the face and a string of epithets. Although Amelia lodged a complaint of battery against Rosa, justice court heard several witnesses swear that Rosa had not lifted a hand and she was acquitted. "The life of a virtuous dancehouse girl," commented the *Daily Free Press*, "is not a merry one."[7]

Eleanor Dumont began her career not as a prostitute but as a gambler.[8] She arrived in Nevada City in 1854 and created a sensation when she began dealing twenty-one at the town's largest gambling establishment. The novelty of a woman gambler— and a pretty, stylishly dressed, twenty-year-old one at that—attracted a large number of players to her table. She did quite well, but she was as infected with wanderlust as were the miners. She joined rushes to British Columbia, Nevada, the Black Hills, Montana, and Idaho. There were few important mining camps in the Far West that she did not visit. "Probably no woman on the Pacific Coast is better known," said the *Bodie Standard*. She was known not only for her card playing but also for her dark eyes, warm smile, and good nature. She staked many a luckless miner and was able to cajole even the roughest characters. One night in Pioche she left her table and stepped into a crowd of drunken and quarreling miners who were brandishing revolvers. Laughingly reproaching them for their behavior, she cooled tempers and saved the men from a bloody shoot-out.

Eleanor arrived in Bodie during the spring of 1878 and began dealing twenty-one at the Magnolia saloon on Main Street. Although she was now in her mid-forties and had acquired the nickname "Madame Moustache," the *Bodie Standard* said, "She appears young as ever, and those who knew her ever so many years ago would instantly recognize her now."[9] Nevertheless, she was no longer a novelty and had little success at gambling. She seems to have resorted occasionally to prostitution for support. Early in September 1879 she borrowed $300 from a friend and promptly lost the money in a faro game. The next morning a sheepherder came across her body about a mile from town. Lying next to the corpse was an empty bottle of morphine. Eleanor Dumont, said the *Bodie Morning News*, was a female gambler who "bore a character of virtue possessed by few in her line. To the good-hearted women of the town must we accord praise for their accustomed kindness in doing all in their power to prepare the unfortunate woman's body for burial. Whatever else may be said of the class known as fallen women they are always to be found more generous, kind and forgiving than is the case with their more virtuous sisters."[10]

"French Joe" came to an equally tragic end. A prostitute with a strong temper, she was once fined $25 for "demolishing" a number of windows in the Sonora Consolidated dance house after an argument with the proprietress of the establishment. French Joe was surprised at the amount of the fine and thought "it was a great price to pay for so little sport."[11] She was later seen quite drunk, making her way along the Geiger Grade toll road toward Bridgeport. She was not seen alive again. In July 1881 a teamster, hauling wood on the Geiger Grade, found human remains not far off the road near Rough

7.   *Daily Free Press*, 9 June 1880.

8.   *Esmeralda Herald*, 13 Sept. 1879; *Bodie Standard*, 29 May 1878.

9.   *Bodie Standard*, 29 May 1878.

10.   *Bodie Morning News*, 9 Sept. 1879.

11.   *Daily Free Press*, 25 March 1880.

Creek. The tattered remnants of female garments and a switch of blond hair led authorities to believe that the remains were those of French Joe.[12]

Until her husband ran away with another woman, blond-haired "Mrs. Moore" was "a person of respectability and standing in San Francisco."[13] She resorted to prostitution to support herself and plied her trade in Aurora and Bodie, where she was well known among the "demi-monde." One bitterly cold night late in December of 1879 she appeared "out of sorts" when she retired to her room. Friends heard her pacing the floor for awhile and then all was quiet. An hour later they heard the report of a gun and rushed into her room. They found her "struggling in the agony of death with a bullet hole in her body." They also found the remains of a packet of morphine that she had taken. Evidently the drug had not been working fast enough.

Ellen Fair also turned to prostitution when she was abandoned by her husband in Virginia City.[14] She was frequently arrested for being drunk and disorderly. In 1878 she left Virginia City and began living a few miles outside of Bodie with a peculiar loner named Job Draper. The forty-five-year-old Draper had lived alone in the mountains for fifteen years before he took up residence with Ellen. He had a "hangdog, slovenly appearance" and wore a "full, ragged beard and long hair." Those who knew Draper said that he could never sleep for more than a few hours at a time because of what he called annoying phantoms. At night Draper would wander off into the hills and talk to imaginary spirits and goblins. Although he was obviously deeply disturbed, nobody considered him dangerous.

On the Friday night of 5 November 1880, woodchoppers Robert Keith and John Hay were returning to Bodie from Cottonwood Canyon when they came across Draper and Ellen camped alongside the road. From a short distance away, the woodchoppers watched a brutal and bizarre scene unfold. Draper was yelling at Ellen, accusing her of hiding his jug of whiskey. She was so drunk that she had trouble answering him. He continued to yell at her, threatening to beat her with a blacksnake whip. Then his mood suddenly changed. He apologized to her and helped her move closer to the campfire. Seconds later, he once more began yelling at her and gave her several blows with the blacksnake. Ellen screamed in pain and exclaimed, "Oh, Job, you're hurting me." Draper laid his whip aside and went off to gather sagebrush for the fire. Keith and Hay, their presence still unnoticed, picked up their gear and moved off to town.

The woodchoppers should have stayed a while longer. The next morning Ellen was found dead. Robert Hall, another woodchopper, passed by Draper's campsite just before sunrise and saw her battered corpse lying on a mattress. Draper said that she had fallen out of a wagon onto some rocks. Hall was hardly convinced. He rushed to town and reported what he had found. The coroner's jury and a justice of the peace reached Draper's campsite a little after noon. Draper was not in camp, but Ellen's body still lay on the mattress. The coroner's inquest began on the spot. While the inquest was in progress Draper returned to camp and, appearing totally unconcerned, sat down without saying a word. He remained silent throughout the proceedings. The inquest lasted until nightfall when the coroner's jury concluded that Ellen had come to her death at

12. *Daily Free Press*, 20 July 1881.

13. *Daily Free Press*, 30 Dec. 1879.

14. The following account is from the *Daily Free Press*, 9 Nov. 1880.

the hands of Job Draper. Draper was charged with murder and was escorted to the Bodie jail.[15]

Bodieites were shocked when they learned of the murder. There was even some talk of lynching. The *Daily Free Press* called Draper "a specimen of total depravity and the lowest type of the human brute." On Thursday, 11 November, Draper was examined in justice court and bound over for action by the grand jury. "The evidence that he did the horrible deed is convincing and overwhelming," said the *Daily Free Press* on the day of the examination, "and it is confidently hoped that an intelligent jury will pass a just verdict upon him and that the hangman will finish the job." In December the grand jury indicted Draper for murder and the court assigned Thomas Ryan and R. S. Minor to defend him.[16] Five months later he appeared in superior court and was found guilty—the precise charge he was found guilty of was not recorded—and sentenced to serve four and a half years in the state penitentiary.[17] Since the penalty was so light, it seems likely that he was convicted of manslaughter and not murder.

Mollie or Nellie Monroe was over forty years old, alcoholic, and addicted to opium when she arrived in Bodie. She had worked most of the mining camps of the trans-Sierra country. Her life did not improve in Bodie. Early in March 1880 Henry Olds clubbed her on the head with a stick of wood and attempted to rob her.[18] Two years later a man she had been drinking with began threatening her. Afraid to return home alone, she spent the night sleeping on a couch in a brothel. She never awoke. A combination of alcohol and opium had proved to be deadly. She was given a "Christian burial," though outside the fence of the Bodie cemetery.[19] Social ostracism for prostitutes extended even to the graveyard.

Holding the record for arrests and time in jail was Julia Hoffman. She began her career during the late 1850s in the mining camps of northern California, where "she was considered a belle and captured many hearts."[20] By the time she arrived in Bodie her beauty had faded badly, and the one-time "belle of Eureka," now forty-five years old, had become an alcoholic. Her trade did not thrive. In September of 1881 she was arrested for vagrancy and "the exposure of her person on a public street."[21] She was sentenced to serve ninety days on each charge but was released on 9 January 1882 after 122 days in jail. Two months later she was back in jail serving 13 days for public drunkenness. Early in April she got into a fight with the prostitute "Sailor Jack" and was given a sound thrashing and a black eye.[22] Both women were lodged in jail, but Julia was released after a day's confinement.[23] Sailor Jack was later convicted for assault.

15.   Jail Register: Bodie Branch Jail, 7 Nov. 1880.

16.   Minutes, Criminal Cases, Superior Court, Mono County, p. 90; Register of Actions, Superior Court, Mono County, p. 35.

17.   Minute Book, Criminal, Dep't No. 2, Superior Court, Mono County, p. 68.

18.   *Daily Free Press*, 8 March 1880.

19.   *Daily Free Press*, 24 Sept. 1882.

20.   *Bodie Standard*, 19 April 1882; *Daily Free Press*, 11 July 1882.

21.   Jail Register: Bodie Branch Jail, pp. 28 and 35.

22.   *Bodie Standard*, 12 April 1882.

23.   Jail Register: Bodie Branch Jail, p. 37.

On 16 April Julia was arrested for vagrancy and was lodged in jail once again.[24] The next day she appeared in justice court and was sentenced to serve sixty days in the county jail at Bridgeport. She was delighted that she would be released in time to celebrate the Fourth of July. During the last three Independence Days she had been in jail. She celebrated the Fourth without incident; then two days later she got into a fight with Kate Wise, "a female whose beauty and virtue," said the *Daily Free Press*, "have long since passed away."[25] The two "choice spirits of the almost forgotten past" fought "like royal Bengal tigers." They were arrested for disturbing the peace and lodged in jail.[26] Justice court acquitted Kate but found Julia guilty and sentenced her to an unspecified term in the county jail, "a resort," noted the *Free Press*, "that has often sheltered her."

The lives of Rosa Olague, French Joe, and Julia Hoffman demonstrated that prostitutes often fought each other. Rosa had at least three fights with other prostitutes, French Joe one, and Julia two. These and other fights between prostitutes normally did not have serious consequences; combatants were rarely injured. The fights certainly were not taken seriously by Bodie's journalists, who delighted in describing the action in what they thought was a humorous vein. Spectators often urged the fighting prostitutes on and were greatly disappointed whenever an officer arrived to separate the combatants.

Mademoiselle Albisu, "the 'handsomest woman in the world' and celebrated model artist," and Kittie Willis, "a dashing damsel" of Mollie Willis's "palace of folly and sin," had a long history of animosity.[27] Whenever they met on the street they would exchange offensive and disparaging remarks. Bodieites had long anticipated a good fight. On a warm August afternoon in 1880 the two prostitutes bumped into each other in the Wells, Fargo & Company's office on Main Street. "On meeting," said the *Daily Free Press*, "their eyes met and flashed fire. M'lle Albisu made a terrific dash at her enemy and gave her a stinger under the right ear, which left a red mark. This was followed by a right-hander on the cheek, which had the effect of knocking off about a spoonful of powder and paint." Kittie returned the blows, but without effect, and she retreated hastily from the office. Spectators relished the action and were about to make bets when the fight ended.

Nellie Ash caused spectators on Bonanza Street to "howl with excitement" when she pummeled another prostitute in a dispute over good taste in dress.[28] Nellie was fined $24 in justice court. Maude Bennett, "whose days of innocence have fled," attacked a prostitute who made some disparaging remarks about her beauty.[29] The fighters made "the hair fly, and the air was filled with loud and piercing yells." When they were finally separated they presented "a rather unbecoming appearance."

Sailor Jack had a reputation as a fighter. She did not disappoint Bodieites. Besides thrashing Julia Hoffman and blackening her eye, she attacked Mabel Hill and destroyed her switch of hair. Sailor Jack, said the *Daily Free Press*, "is a woman of judgement, that is she knows how to make one of her own sex unhappy. The glory of a woman is her hair, and as a switch of hair is a part and parcel of most women's make-up,

24.   Jail Register, p. 37; *Bodie Standard*, 19 April 1882.

25.   *Daily Free Press*, 11 July 1882.

26.   Jail Register: Bodie Branch Jail, p. 42.

27.   *Daily Free Press*, 3 August 1880.

28.   *Daily Free Press*, 9 Dec. 1879.

29.   *Daily Free Press*, 12 April 1881.

she bearded the lioness in her den and was arrested for acting so badly."[30] Unlike Sailor Jack, Nellie Grant disappointed Bodieites. Known as the "Carson Banger" in recognition of her many fights in Carson City, she had only one fight after her arrival in Bodie.[31]

Fights occasionally involved more than two prostitutes. Rosa Olague assaulted several prostitutes on one drunken rampage through the brothels of Bonanza Street. Another time three prostitutes, identified only as "two dizzy blondes and a decided brunette, all girls of happy natures," got into a heated discussion in their Bonanza Street brothel after sharing a bottle of gin. The discussion turned violent when a dispute arose over which one of them had the best lovers. "They got entangled in each other's hair," reported the *Daily Free Press*, "their little hands made sad havoc with their faces, and the midnight air was filled with expressions that sounded harsh in the extreme."[32]

Only once did prostitutes ever use weapons when fighting each other.[33] "Mrs. Hall," the madam of a brothel, was full of bourbon when she accused Jennie Lee, one of her working girls, of stealing four dollars. Jennie denied the alleged theft, but the drunken madam rushed upon her and attempted to slash her throat with a knife. Although Jennie warded off the blow, she was left with a deep gash on her arm. Hall was arrested, but what happened to her in justice court is not known.

If most of the violent encounters between prostitutes themselves were less than serious affairs, their violent encounters with men were usually just the opposite. Several prostitutes suffered beatings at the hands of men. Although the men were arrested for their assaults, their punishments typically amounted to a fine or a short jail sentence— punishments far less severe than if they had assaulted "respectable" women. Bodie's newspapers often treated the beatings humorously.

For "trying to destroy the good looks" of Johanna Albers and leaving "several respectable marks" on her face, as the *Daily Free Press* put it, Sam Farrell was arrested and fined $24 in justice court.[34] Jack Perry was arrested for beating Kate Wise so severely that her face looked like "a pan of sausage."[35] James McCarthy was lodged in jail for hitting Louise DuBarr, a "fat French damsel." The *Bodie Standard* thought he "whammed her most beautifully."[36] For striking Sailor Jack, "the brave old salt," Pat Shea pleaded guilty to assault and was fined $24.[37]

Men were not always convicted when assault was alleged. Ann Wheeler, "who claims to be a hard-working woman," said that when she went to Maggie McCormick's saloon to collect $20 that Maggie owed her, the bartender, Gabe Hall, bodily ejected her from the saloon.[38] Hall stated that Ann entered the saloon drunk and staggered into a back bedroom where she began to vomit. He further stated that he then "brought her vessels and medicine" and assisted her to the door. In the justice court trial, John McQuaid defended Hall, and R. S. Minor prosecuted. The courtroom was packed with

30. *Daily Free Press*, 16 May 1880.

31. *Daily Free Press*, 22 June 1880.

32. *Daily Free Press*, 20 Nov. 1879.

33. *Daily Free Press*, 9 Jan. 1880.

34. *Daily Free Press*, 29 Dec. 1879.

35. *Daily Free Press*, 23 Dec. 1882.

36. *Bodie Standard*, 5 April 1880.

37. *Daily Free Press*, 19 March 1880.

38. *Daily Free Press*, 8 Jan. 1880.

spectators, who came expecting that "a great deal of a delicate nature" would be revealed. The spectators were not disappointed. They enjoyed the trial so much that the judge ordered the courtroom cleared because of their noisy outbursts. The trial continued behind closed doors, where McQuaid evidently outshone Minor. Gabe Hall was acquitted, and Ann Wheeler was assessed for the court costs.

An unnamed prostitute, described only as "a lady well-known in Bodie," charged Charles Gray with battery.[39] She said that she had gone to Gray's house to show him jewelry she had for sale and that he had broken one of the pieces of jewelry while examining it. When she demanded that he pay for the damage, she said he hit her in the face and wrestled her to the ground. Gray told a different story. He claimed that she hit him in the face and tore his necktie off when he pronounced her a "bilk" and refused to pay for the damaged jewelry. He admitted grabbing her and wrestling her down, but said he had done so only to subdue her.

Despite Gray's protestations of innocence, he was arrested and brought to trial in justice court. The courtroom was again crowded with spectators eager for more racy testimony. This time they were disappointed. The case proved exceedingly dull. Defense attorney R. S. Minor and prosecuting attorney Frank Willard engaged in long-winded exchanges, which included "sarcastic remarks regarding each other's knowledge of law." Several members of the jury fell asleep; one sleeping juror accidentally tumbled out of his chair onto the floor. The testimony of several witnesses did nothing to relieve the courtroom ennui and was as much in favor of the defendant as the plaintiff. "Upon the jurymen being roused from their slumber," observed the *Bodie Standard*, "they retired to an adjoining room and soon returned a verdict of not guilty."

On two occasions prostitutes charged that men had attempted to rape them. Mable Gray, an alcoholic who was "wreckless in her manners," claimed that a man attempted to rape her on Main Street.[40] There were no witnesses to the alleged attempt, and Mable could not describe the attacker. In the only other incident, Kate Curran accused James McNamara of attempted rape.[41] The testimony of witnesses in justice court did not support her, and McNamara was acquitted.

In violent encounters with men, prostitutes fared well if they were armed.[42] Guns and knives were their favorite weapons. The gun made the prostitute a redoubtable combatant. In a confrontation on King Street, Daisy Livingstone, "a soiled dove of Bonanza alley," took a shot at an unidentified man. Though the bullet missed the man, it thoroughly frightened him and put him in full flight. Later on the same day, Martha Camp, as if not to be outdone by Daisy, chased a customer out of a brothel and fired five shots at him as he fled down Bonanza Street. The man's "hair stood on end, as he expected any second to be reduced to a state of perfect inutility." "Madame" Wicks, the proprietor of a brothel at the corner of Mill and Lowe streets, took a shot at "one of her numerous 'lovers,' " who was smashing brothel furniture. The gunshot brought an immediate halt to the man's furniture wrecking, and he was shortly arrested and lodged in jail.

39. *Bodie Standard*, 31 August 1881.

40. *Daily Free Press*, 10 Dec. 1879.

41. *Daily Free Press*, 25 June 1880.

42. *Bodie Standard*, 12 July 1882; *Daily Free Press*, 15 Jan. 1881, 7 July 1882.

As John Green could testify, Rosa Olague demonstrated that prostitutes also used knives effectively. Another prostitute who wielded a wicked knife was Ada Travis, "a good-natured blonde of Bonanza Avenue."[43] One Friday afternoon she sank a knife into gambler Edward Howe, who had come to her room for a visit. Although Howe was seriously wounded, Ada was not arrested.

Some prostitutes chose to use weapons other than guns or knives. One Friday afternoon Emma Douglas, wielding a hatchet, stormed into the Bodie House hotel and attempted to hack up the desk clerk, Mike Wilson.[44] While the occupants of the front room of the Bodie House "scattered like chaff before a strong wind," Wilson dodged the blows of Emma. He finally managed to disarm her, and the police took her into custody. She stayed in jail overnight and was released the next day on her own recognizance.

It was soon revealed that Wilson had incurred Emma's wrath because he had exposed her as the author of anonymous letters that certain Bodie men had been receiving. The language used in the letters, commented the *Daily Free Press*, "would make a cowboy blush with envy." On Monday afternoon, Emma appeared in justice court and was sentenced to pay a fine of $45 or serve forty-five days in jail. She had no money, so she went off to jail.

"Mrs. Brown," the madam of a brothel located opposite the Grand Central hotel on Main Street, found an ordinary chair to be an effective weapon against three unwanted drunken customers.[45] Using the chair as a club, she banged one man over the head, another across the jaw, and the third on the back. All three men ran for the street.

As a rule, the "decent" women of Bodie, said a one-time resident of the town, "lived quiet, uneventful, and thoroughly good lives."[46] They spent most of their leisure time organizing theatrical performances, dances, suppers, Sunday school picnics, sleighing parties, and similar diversions. The former resident continued:

> One of the remarkable things about Bodie, in fact, one of the striking features of all mining camps in the West, was the respect shown even by the worst characters to the decent women and the children. Some of the best families in town lived in the immediate neighborhood of Chinatown and the red-light district, and the women and children could not move out of their houses without passing saloons and all sorts of terrible places. Yet I do not recall ever hearing of a respectable woman or girl in any manner insulted or even accosted by the hundreds of dissolute characters that were everywhere. In part, this was due to the respect that depravity pays to decency; in part, to the knowledge that sudden death would follow any other course.[47]

Nevertheless, there were "respectable" women involved in violence. Husband and wife fights were the most common form of violence, with four reported clashes. Even these, though, were not very common, considering the several hundred married

43. *Daily Free Press*, 11 Sept. 1880; *Bodie Standard*, 18 Sept. 1880.

44. *Daily Free Press*, 2 and 4 Oct. 1881; *Bodie Standard*, 5 Oct. 1881; Jail Register: Bodie Branch Jail, pp. 28–31.

45. *Bodie Standard*, 28 July 1880.

46. Smith, "Bodie," p. 78.

47. Smith, pp. 78–79.

couples in Bodie. In three of the clashes, the husband was the aggressor; in the fourth the wife attacked the husband.

Thomas Treloar and C. M. Fahey were both convicted of battery for striking their wives.[48] The cause of Treloar's attack is not mentioned; Fahey was said to have been drunk and to have exploded over some trivial family matter. Thomas Keefe was charged with assault with intent to commit murder for threatening his wife with a bowie knife.[49] Keefe, a well-known carpenter who had a "generally good reputation," had been absent from Bodie for several months, working at Yankee Fork. Upon his return to Bodie, he learned that his wife had been unfaithful to him. She argued that he had deserted her. He struck her and allegedly threatened to kill her. In justice court, on a motion by the prosecuting attorney, the charge against Keefe was reduced to simple assault; the final disposition of the case is not mentioned.

In the one instance where the wife attacked the husband, a reporter from the *Bodie Standard* was present to record all the action. The reporter happened to be at the stage station when a black woman stepped off the morning stage and announced that she was looking for her husband. The husband, she said, was reported to be in Bodie and to be living with another woman. There were only about a dozen blacks in Bodie, so the husband was quickly identified as a black who lived in a tent on the edge of town and kept milk cows. The angry wife was delighted. With a small club in her hand and followed by a number of men who anticipated a good show, the woman marched off in the direction of the tent. "It would have been fortunate for him," said the reporter of the husband, "if a brass band had been secured to herald her approach to his tent on the flat, but alas! such was not the case; and between a screech and a howl she bounded in on the unsuspecting victim, and that club rose and fell pretty lively."[50] The wife stopped her attack long enough to notice a trunk containing a woman's clothes under her husband's bed. "She just grabbed that trunk," said the reporter, "and tossed it out the door like a stage driver does through freight." Her rage now spent, she cuddled up next to her battered husband, and the fully satisfied crowd of spectators, including the reporter, drifted away.

Women were also involved in violent encounters with men other than their husbands. Only one encounter had serious consequences. Late on the Thursday night of 8 January 1880, a Mrs. Martin was attacked by a club-wielding man on Main Street, just opposite the Esmeralda Brewery.[51] The assailant fractured her skull with a blow to the head and disappeared into the darkness. Medical aid was rushed to Mrs. Martin, but she appeared to have little chance of survival.

Suspicion for the attack rested upon Juan Brussell. When he was arrested at the Esmeralda Brewery he confessed to having paid Nick Meadows, described only as "a Swede," $5 to give Mrs. Martin a beating. Officers rushed to Meadows's cabin, broke down the front door, and found Meadows inside. One officer stuck a revolver in the suspect's face. While gazing into the muzzle of the gun Meadows confessed to the attack. He was arrested and lodged in jail. A few days later justice court bound him over to await

48.   *Bodie Standard*, 30 June 1879; *Daily Free Press*, 20 April 1880.

49.   *Bodie Morning News*, 24 and 25 Oct. 1879.

50.   *Bodie Standard*, 31 July 1878.

51.   *Daily Free Press, Bodie Chronicle, Bodie Standard*, all on 10 Jan. 1880.

trial in superior court and set his bail at $1,000.[52] When he could not raise the money, he was transferred to the county jail at Bridgeport.

Meanwhile, Mrs. Martin hovered between life and death for some time, but eventually recovered. At one point, the *Daily Free Press* erroneously reported that she had died.[53] When it was certain that she would survive, Meadows was indicted for assault with intent to commit murder and his case was placed on the superior court calendar.[54] With W. O. Parker serving as his attorney, Meadows repudiated his confession and entered a plea of not guilty. The trial, which was set for 29 January, had to be postponed when Mrs. Martin, the prosecution's principal witness, was unable to appear because of her condition. The trial was rescheduled for March. In the meantime, Parker took office as the new district attorney for Mono County, and the court appointed P. W. Bennett as Meadows's new counsel. Bennett became ill and was replaced by W. P. George. When the trial was finally held on 16 March, Meadows was found guilty of the lesser charge of battery.[55] He was fined $500 and sentenced to serve six months in the county jail. Before he began serving his sentence, he escaped from custody. Since his name does not appear in the records again, he evidently was never recaptured.

Only two other beatings of women occurred. C. C. Blair and his wife pummeled a Mrs. Orth for accusing them of stealing firewood.[56] Justice court found the Blairs guilty of assault and sentenced them to pay fines of $40 each or serve forty days in the county jail. In the other incident, Frank Argelaie was fined $25 for assaulting a woman identified only as a "Spanish lady."[57] He happily paid the fine, feeling he had gotten his money's worth.

A weapon could make a woman a formidable opponent. One September morning a dispute arose between a man and a woman over a city lot. The man had sold the lot to the woman, but he said that he had exempted the back portion of the lot from the deed. When he had a load of lumber dumped onto the lot and began to lay a foundation for a house, the woman ordered him off the property. However, as the *Bodie Standard* noted, since "he was a large man and she was a small lady, he concluded to tarry yet a while."[58] Realizing that talk was to no avail, the woman pulled out a six-shooter and, taking dead aim, again ordered the man to leave. This time he left, and in a hurry.

Even a broom was better than no weapon at all. Henrietta Schwartz was sweeping the sidewalk in front of her Main Street store when John Heilshorn came walking by one Fourth of July morning and, according to Schwartz, called her an "exceedingly disgusting name" and struck her. She countered by whacking him in the face with a broom, leaving his visage well marked. He then wrestled her to the ground, "to the delight of a mob of men across the way," said the *Bodie Standard*, "who generally delight in seeing the downfall of even a lady."[59] At that point the fight was stopped, and Heil-

52. *Daily Free Press*, 22 Jan. 1880.

53. *Daily Free Press*, 10 Jan. 1880.

54. Calendar of Criminal Cases, Superior Court, Mono County, 23 Jan. 1880.

55. Register of Actions, Superior Court, Mono County, p. 2; Minutes, Criminal Cases, Superior Court, Mono County, pp. 4, 5, 9, 12, 37–38.

56. *Daily Free Press*, 20 and 21 Nov. 1879.

57. *Daily Free Press*, 13 March 1880.

58. *Bodie Standard*, 4 Sept. 1878.

59. *Bodie Standard*, 12 July 1882.

shorn disappeared into the Occidental saloon. He was shortly arrested and charged with assault and battery. Four days later he appeared in justice court and, defended by Frank Drake, claimed he had acted in self-defense. Schwartz testified that she had hit him only after he had attacked her. Other witnesses were called to the stand, and they too gave conflicting testimony. The twelve men of the jury "agreed to disagree" and a mistrial was declared.

Women, other than the prostitutes already mentioned, also fought with other women. The most exciting row erupted in front of Boone and Wright's general store one December afternoon. In a dispute over a debt, two women pulled hair, kicked, "clawed and used vulgar language in a lively manner." Spectators loved the row. Whenever a successful blow was struck, they cheered in approval. The fight ended when one of the women was knocked through the store's front window. "When it comes down to fighting," commented the *Daily Free Press*, "women are like hens. Active operations do not last long. They start in without any preliminary sparring, and while it lasts is exciting in the extreme. . . . Pay days and fighting women make times interesting."[60]

In other fights a couple of women thrashed each other in a dispute over a borrowed flatiron; an alcoholic woman, armed with a club, shoeless, and in her normal drunken state, chased Bodie's schoolmarm out of the schoolhouse; and two sisters fought each other to a draw in an argument over a sewing machine.[61] This latter fight began with the husbands of the two sisters exchanging blows, but it wound up "like an old-fashioned hen fight, and the hair flew in all directions," when the women attacked each other. More than two hundred spectators enjoyed the action.

The most serious form of violence facing the women of Bodie was suicide. Prostitutes Eleanor Dumont, Mrs. Moore, and possibly French Joe committed suicide. Rosa Olague and an unnamed Chinese prostitute attempted suicide.[62] Three other women took their own lives, and two more made near-successful attempts. All but one of these women, prostitute or not, used some form of opium in taking or attempting to take their lives.

Nora Pine, a young woman of a "jovial nature," was the best-known and most determined victim.[63] Some Bodieites said she had a "sentimental attachment" for David Hitchell, a rough and unsavory character who had at one time served as a Bodie police officer. Others denied that she was involved with Hitchell. Nevertheless, after he was killed in an opium den shooting in June of 1881, she "repeatedly attempted suicide" by taking large doses of opium. Each time, a physician was able to revive her. On a Tuesday morning in August she tried again. A physician was rushed to her bedside. "You can't save me this time!" she laughingly exclaimed before she lost consciousness. The doctor tried several means to save her, including shocking her with a galvanic battery, but by early afternoon she was dead.

The suicide of Mrs. Thomas McCloud, the thirty-five-year-old wife of a miner and the mother of one child, may have been caused by an extramarital love affair.[64] Mrs. McCloud called at A. B. Stewart's drug store early one afternoon and asked for some

60.   *Daily Free Press*, 6 Dec. 1879.

61.   *Daily Free Press*, 8 April and 7 May 1880.

62.   *Bodie Standard*, 31 August 1881.

63.   *Bodie Standard*, 17 August 1881.

64.   *Bodie Standard*, 28 June 1882.

laudanum to relieve the pain of a bad toothache. A clerk filled a one-ounce vial with the drug, a tincture of opium, and Mrs. McCloud departed. She did not go home, but went instead to the cabin of a Mr. Cameron where she had spent many an afternoon. He was not at home; she let herself in, drank the vial of laudanum, and lay down on a bed to die. When he returned he thought that she was sleeping and did not disturb her. He finally became alarmed, however, and summoned a physician. She died shortly after the doctor's arrival. The coroner, Dr. D. L. Deal, thought that it was an obvious case of suicide and that an inquest was unnecessary. Perhaps in an effort to save the husband more grief, Deal attributed Mrs. McCloud's suicide to a "disordered brain."

Two other women used laudanum in suicide attempts, and both were revived by physicians.[65] Domestic troubles were responsible for one of the attempts; the cause of the other was "enveloped in mystery." Avoiding the uncertainty of laudanum, Mrs. J. G. Williams committed suicide by shooting herself in the head.[66] No reason was given for her suicide.

One woman died from the effects of an abortion. Bodieites awoke one morning to read of the death of Albertine Bush, "a young woman of handsome physique and a pleasing and impressive countenance" who, until shortly before her death, had run a boarding house with her brother. She had been ill for a week and had been under the care of her personal physician. When she died he said it was "from taking cold while suffering from a female complaint." Not everyone accepted his explanation. Her funeral was canceled and a postmortem examination was held. The examination revealed that an abortion had caused her death, but the coroner's jury, said the *Daily Free Press*, "could fix the horrible crime of murder on no particular person. . . . If this young woman placed herself in the hands of any person now living, as a subject for criminal practice, and that person endeavored and failed to deliver her of an unborn child, the truth ought to be known, and the guilty party brought to justice. The offense is one against God and humanity, and the penalty fixed by the laws of the State is severe but just."[67]

With only a handful of exceptions, then, prostitutes accounted for the violence related to women in Bodie. Of the thirty violent encounters between men and women, prostitutes were involved in twenty-five. When women fought women, prostitutes accounted for thirteen of seventeen fights. Only a few of either of these types of violent encounters had serious consequences. One, of course, did result in death; in that case the woman was a former prostitute and her murderer was insane. There was also one woman who nearly died from a clubbing and one who did die from a botched abortion. Three of the six women who committed suicide and two of the four who attempted it were prostitutes. Two of the suicide victims shot themselves (one of them had also taken morphine), and the others overdosed on opium or one of its derivatives.

For the women of Bodie, including the prostitutes of Bonanza Street, the threat of rape or robbery was virtually nonexistent. There were no reported cases of rape in Bodie. This does not necessarily mean that rape did not occur, since rape is a crime that has traditionally been underreported. Nevertheless, there was not even one report of rape in Bodie, and there is nothing to give the impression that rape did occur. There is, on the other hand, a considerable body of evidence that indicates that women were

65. *Bodie Morning News*, 8 August and 13 Sept. 1879.

66. *Bodie Standard*, 1 March 1879.

67. *Daily Free Press*, 16 March 1880.

generally free from crimes of all varieties and treated with great respect. There were two alleged instances of attempted rape, but in neither of these instances, both involving prostitutes, did testimony of witnesses support the allegations. Finally, only one robbery of a woman, that of a Chinese prostitute in her own room, is known to have occurred.[68]

Bodie's children, some 150 of them, contributed very little to lawlessness and violence in the town. Those who did contribute were exclusively teen-age boys. "Mining camp life," said a man who lived in Bodie as a teen-ager, "had a very unfavorable effect upon boys as they grew toward manhood; the example set by their elders could not have been much worse, and the doors of every kind of dissipation were wide open. The good women and the girls, on the other hand, lived their lives apart, respected and even revered. I recall with deep satisfaction the sweet, modest girls with whom I went to school in mining camps."[69]

Most teen-age boys in Bodie did not bother to attend school. Instead, they regularly congregated at the corner of Green and Wood streets and lounged about, smoking and gambling and occasionally insulting passersby.[70] They even had their own faro game set up in a cabin on Wood Street, and a few of the boys were known to sneak over to Chinatown to smoke opium. Several of the young roughs carried their own guns, although there is only one instance of a shooting: one of the boys shot himself in the thigh while practicing "quick draw" with a friend.[71] "If these boys are not looked after," said the *Daily Free Press* on 29 August 1880, "their end will be the penitentiary or gallows, and bring their parents into disgrace." The *Bodie Standard* thought the boys were educating themselves to replace Billy the Kid. "Two or three years will find them on the Mexican border," said the *Standard* on 27 July 1881, "unless the walls of the reform school close around them."

The young roughs were occasionally cited for playing pranks on businessmen, throwing mud on wash hanging from clotheslines, driving stock through vegetable gardens, and committing petty thefts.[72] On one occasion they disrupted a Chinese funeral. While Chinese mourners were carrying a corpse to the grave, the hoodlums carried off the feast of baked meats and delicacies that the Chinese had prepared as part of their traditional burial ceremony. The *Bodie Morning News* vehemently condemned the hoodlums and hoped that they would be identified and arrested.[73]

On another occasion the teen-age roughs entered the Bodie theatre through a second-story window, crowded into the balcony, and with various pranks and obscene language, disrupted the play that was in progress. A police officer climbed up to the balcony and quieted them, but as soon as he left they resumed their acts of hooliganism with renewed vigor. One boy was hung by his heels over a ground-level row of spectators, just inches above their heads. When a second boy was dangled over the audience, a portion of the balcony broke loose and crashed to the floor. Several persons were injured, though none seriously. In the resulting confusion the boys made their escape. "While all this was going on," noted the *Bodie Standard*, "an officer stood in the aisle quietly

---

68.   *Daily Free Press*, 21 July 1880.

69.   Smith, "Bodie," p. 79.

70.   *Daily Free Press*, 29 August and 16 Sept. 1880; *Bodie Standard*, 20 July 1881, 8 Feb. 1882.

71.   *Bodie Standard*, 27 April 1881.

72.   *Daily Free Press*, 18 Jan. and 29 August 1880.

73.   *Bodie Morning News*, 17 May 1879.

smoking a cigar."[74] Two months later the youths broke into the schoolhouse—the first time most of them had been inside the building—and overturned classroom furniture and marked the blackboards. This time the leader of the raiders was identified. He was arrested and brought before the justice of the peace. After a severe tongue-lashing, the boy was remanded to the custody of his parents.[75]

Although Bodie's newspapers accused youths of committing numerous petty thefts and burglaries, only once was a boy arrested for burglary. Charles Magee, "a boy not over fifteen years of age," was jailed for stealing fourteen boxes of cigars and a box of tobacco from W. A. Taylor's billiard hall and cigar store. Magee had stolen the cigars undetected, but was reported to the authorities when he tried to sell them to the proprietor of a saloon. The police then raided the boy's small cabin, where he apparently lived alone, and found the stolen articles. "Magee," asserted the *Bodie Standard*, "is one of a very bad gang of boys who live in Bodie. A year or more in reform school might have a tendency to increase their stock of good morals."[76] Magee spent a week in jail and was then examined in justice court. Unfortunately, there is no record of what happened to him after that.

Another two young hoodlums were caught during a burglary, but were not arrested.[77] A miner, returning home one August afternoon, spied the two boys racing from his cabin. He gave chase and, although the boys had a head start of three hundred yards, collared them. In their pockets he found his six-shooter, some jewelry, and eleven dollars in silver. He frog-marched the boys to their parents and told them of the burglary. The names of the boys were not revealed, nor were the police notified. Two other young hoodlums were identified as thieves, but were not apprehended. "The Kid" and "Windy" Clark stole a dozen blankets from the Bodie House hotel, sold them to a fence, and then "left for parts unknown."[78]

Complaints were often made against the young roughs for using obscene language in front of women and girls. "They use language," contended the *Bodie Standard*, "that would do justice to a confirmed Tar Flat hoodlum, or a hardened criminal."[79] Nothing was done to discipline the boys until Mrs. P. P. Molinelli took action. Late on the Thursday afternoon of 2 February 1882, Mrs. Molinelli, accompanied by Dr. J. W. Van Zandt, marched into the Wells, Fargo & Company office and repeatedly lashed John Davies, a twelve-year-old messenger boy, with a small horsewhip. Mrs. Molinelli said she punished the boy because he had used "the most vile and unmentionable language" when speaking to her daughter. The boy, suffering from several stinging welts, denied the accusation.[80]

When the boy's stepfather, Thomas Byrne, learned of the attack, he went straight to Dr. Van Zandt's office and demanded an apology. The doctor quickly complied, and the affair seemed to be settled. The mother of the boy, however, was not so easily satisfied. Armed with a whip, she now went to the doctor's office. She surprised

74. *Bodie Standard*, 20 Jan. 1880.

75. *Daily Free Press*, 31 March 1880.

76. *Bodie Standard*, 17 May 1882.

77. *Daily Free Press*, 5 August 1880.

78. *Daily Free Press*, 25 March 1880.

79. *Bodie Standard*, 8 Feb. 1882.

80. *Bodie Standard*, 8 Feb. 1882.

Van Zandt and lashed him a couple of times before he could wrest the whip away from her. Evidently, all was now considered even, and a month passed with no other incidents.

On the first of March the dispute flared again when the latest issue of the *Carson Tribune* arrived in town.[81] The newspaper contained a story written by Mrs. Molinelli and Dr. Van Zandt which Byrne thought insulted his wife. Byrne stormed into the doctor's office and this time, instead of demanding an apology, gave Van Zandt a severe beating. The next day, while the bruised and battered Van Zandt was recuperating with the aid of pain-killing opiates, Byrne was arrested and charged with assault with intent to do great bodily harm. He was later released on $500 bail. A day later he appeared in justice court and was bound over for trial in superior court. On 27 March he was tried, found guilty as charged, and sentenced to pay a fine of $60 or serve thirty days in jail.[82]

Three days after Mrs. Molinelli whipped Byrne's stepson, another woman had a confrontation with a group of young roughs.[83] The woman, an "independent if not dignified female" who owned a shop on Main Street, was hurrying to work when one of the boys made a remark about the way she walked. The woman pulled out a six-shooter, took dead aim at the boy, and "acted as though she would pull the trigger." The boy's knees buckled, and he fell over into a dry-goods box. Another boy dove into a snowbank, one jumped behind a post, and the rest scattered. This incident, not surprisingly, was the last occurrence of hoodlum harassment of pedestrians.

Bodie's young roughs, then, were known mostly for their insulting remarks, obscene language, and bad habits. They did commit a few petty thefts and burglaries, but no violent crimes. Their delinquent activities consisted almost entirely of youthful pranks and malicious mischief.

81.   *Bodie Standard*, 8 March 1882.

82.   Minute Book, Criminal, Dep't No. 2, Superior Court, Mono County, pp. 96, 114.

83.   *Bodie Standard*, 8 Feb. 1882.

9

IN ILLEGAL
PURSUIT
OF WEALTH

Not all Bodieites sought wealth through honest toil in the mines. There were those who robbed stagecoaches, stole horses, burglarized homes and businesses, committed petty thefts, and mugged people. Bodieites generally reacted strongly to these crimes, although the losses were usually not large and the total number of incidents was small. Cattle rustling and bank robbery, two crimes traditionally associated with the frontier, were unknown in Bodie. On the other hand, stagecoach robbery, a crime central to many Western novels and motion pictures, occurred with great regularity during the peak of Bodie's boom.

Bodie was connected to the outside world by stagecoach. The first regular stage service began during the fall of 1877, and by the spring of 1878 there were stages running daily between Bodie and the nearby hamlets of Aurora and Bridgeport and the more distant towns of Carson and Virginia. Stages also traveled over the Sonora Pass road to San Francisco—a forty-hour trip. The coach most commonly used by the stage lines of the trans-Sierra country as well as by those in other regions of the West was the Concord.[1] Named for the New Hampshire town of its manufacture, the Concord weighed nearly a ton and was pulled by four- and often six-horse teams. Passengers were treated to a relatively smooth ride. Two thick leather straps, called thorough braces, suspended the body of the coach between the axles and produced a rolling motion less tiring to those aboard than the jolting ride of a wagon. Nine passengers could sit on the front, middle, and rear seats inside the coach, and more could ride on the roof or up front with the driver. The coaches that arrived in Bodie during the great rush to the town in 1878 normally carried more than a dozen passengers.[2]

Handling a six-horse team pulling a one-ton Concord coach loaded with passengers and baggage was no mean task. The stage driver had to be a highly skilled teamster. He was a greatly admired and much respected figure in Bodie. The *Bodie Standard* commented:

> Many a man who has traveled much by stage through the mountains realizes how frequently his life may have been preserved through the ceaseless care and untiring dili-

---

1. For a comprehensive study of the stagecoach in the Old West, see Oscar O. Winther, *Via Western Express and Stagecoach.*

2. *Bodie Standard*, 18 Sept. 1878.

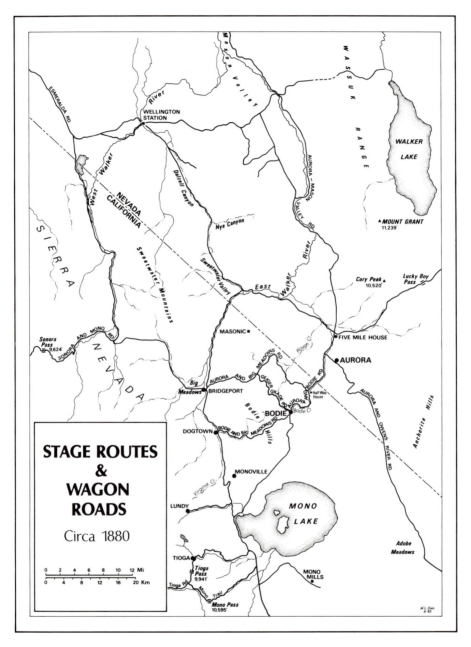

27.   Aurora and Bodie were connected to the outside world by several privately owned toll roads. Only the Sonora and Mono Road was built and maintained at public expense. (Cartography by Noel Diaz)

gence of the stage driver. No one but the accomplished reinsman can comprehend that on a dangerous grade a simple turn of the wrist of the left hand and a single touch of the silk near a leader's forearm has frequently saved an entire coach load of passengers from being hurled into eternity. Frequently in the mountains, and especially at such an altitude as surrounds Bodie, it is a fact that the stage driver takes his life into his own hands when he starts out on a route even but a few miles in length.[3]

The driver was usually at the reins for long hours, many of them at night, and had to negotiate his way over Bodie's tortuous mountain roads, which were both rocky and sandy, occasionally muddy, and often covered with snow in the winter. Only a few tall poles, stuck in the ground alongside the roads, helped guide the driver through snowdrifts. It is a credit to the drivers of the trans-Sierra country that few accidents occurred.

The driver had no responsibility to fight highwaymen. That was the job of special guards, known as shotgun messengers. The messengers were often armed not only with shotguns but also with Henry or Winchester rifles.[4] When a stage carried a bullion shipment, an "outside" messenger rode up top with the driver, and one or more "inside" messengers sat with the passengers. Although nearly every stage carried a Wells, Fargo & Company express box, which contained money and valuables, messengers rode only on those stages with bullion aboard. The bullion shipments could be enormous. During Bodie's boom years its stages carried an average of $250,000 worth of gold and silver bullion a month to the United States mint at Carson City.[5]

Not until more than a year after daily stage service began in Bodie was a stagecoach first stopped by a highwayman. At about one o'clock on the Monday morning of 12 May 1879, the Bodie-bound stage from Carson City was winding its way up a hill several miles outside Aurora when an armed highwayman, standing on a rocky hillside above the road, ordered the driver to halt and to throw down the express box.[6] The driver reined in the horses as he was ordered, and had almost brought the stage to a stop, when the road agent slipped on the hillside and sent several rocks crashing onto the road. The horses bolted, and before the would-be robber could recover, the stage was out of sight. It arrived in town an hour ahead of schedule.

A posse of officers rushed to the scene of the attempted robbery and tracked the highwayman into the rugged Bodie Hills. The officers soon had, or thought they had, the man surrounded. He was believed to be entrenched in a natural fortress of rocks; however, said the *Bodie Morning News*, since "the robber is known to be armed, and it being a matter of life and death with him, the officers fear to tackle his robbership."[7]

---

3. *Bodie Standard*, 12 April 1882.

4. The .44 caliber, lever action, brass-framed Henry rifle was designed by B. Tyler Henry and first produced by the New Haven Arms Company in 1860. The Henry used a rim-fire cartridge, fed from a 15-round tubular magazine. The 28 grains of black powder that the cartridge held proved too light a load for some of the long distances and big game of the West, but it was all that the thin-shelled rim-fire cartridge could safely hold. The rifle was modified and improved in 1866 and again in 1873 and carried the name Winchester after Oliver F. Winchester reorganized New Haven Arms. The 1873 model, known popularly as the .44–40, was not only stronger and lighter than the older models but it solved the range and impact problem by using a new center-fire cartridge which held 40 grains of powder. From 1873 until the end of production in 1923 over 720,000 .44–40s were manufactured. See George Madis, *The Winchester Book*.

5. Bodie *Daily Free Press*, 3 Nov. 1880, 5 Jan. 1881, 4 Jan. 1883; *Bodie Standard*, 2 August 1882.

6. *Bodie Morning News*, 13 and 18 May 1879.

7. *Bodie Morning News*, 18 May 1879.

28.   *"Frequently in the mountains, and especially at such an altitude as surrounds Bodie, it is a fact that the stage driver takes his life into his own hands." (Credit: Los Angeles County Museum of Natural History)*

The lawmen adopted a waiting game, hoping that hunger would eventually draw the man out. But he was not drawn out nor was he ever apprehended. Either the officers never actually had him surrounded or he slipped by their guard.

A year passed before the stage was stopped again. Then, on the Tuesday night of 8 June 1880, the Bodie-bound stage from Carson was halted in Dalzell Canyon by two shotgun-wielding, masked highwaymen.[8] They ordered the passengers to raise their hands and step out of the coach and warned that the first one of them who "batted his eye would be killed so dead that he would be ready to skin."[9] While one of the road agents stood guard with a double-barreled shotgun, the other relieved the driver, a man named Chamberlain, of his gold watch and took the Wells Fargo express box containing some $3,000 in coin. They also took several watches and about $100 in cash from the passengers. "The wretches," commented the *Bodie Chronicle*, "were ungallant enough to rob the only lady passenger, who was on her way to join her husband in Bodie."[10]

A posse of officers, messengers, detectives, and Paiute was sent after the robbers. The posse was gone several days and claimed to have tracked the highwaymen to Walker Lake and beyond before the trail turned cold. It must have been to the great chagrin of the posse, then, that just a week after the robbery, the same two highwaymen again halted the Bodie-bound stage from Carson in Dalzell Canyon.[11] Chamberlain,

8.   *Daily Free Press*, 10 June 1880; *Bodie Chronicle*, 12 June 1880.

9.   *Daily Free Press*, 10 June 1880.

10.   *Bodie Chronicle*, 12 June 1880.

11.   *Daily Free Press*, 16 June 1880.

who was again at the reins, was ordered in "polite but unmistakable firm terms" to throw down the express box. The highwaymen did not trouble any of the passengers this time and apologized to Chamberlain for taking his watch in the last robbery. They claimed they would return it, along with those watches they had taken from the passengers, at the first convenient opportunity. The highwaymen also told Chamberlain where he could find the express box, minus its contents, on his return trip. They said they did not want to put him to the trouble of having to search for it.

An hour later, Chamberlain met the Carson-bound stage from Bodie. The stage was carrying a consignment of bullion and had three messengers on board. Chamberlain informed them of the robbery and then drove on to Bodie. The messengers readied their guns for "active service," and a few miles down the road the stage entered Dalzell Canyon. It passed through without incident. Evidently, the highwaymen had no desire to tangle with the messengers, even though bullion, worth tens of thousands of dollars, was aboard the stage.

Three months later on the Monday night of 30 August 1880, George Finney, driving the Bodie-bound stage from Virginia City, thought he heard someone hailing him as he began the descent into Coal Valley.[12] But the stage was making considerable noise, as was a hilariously drunken passenger, and Finney continued down the grade. Seconds later he heard sounds that he was able to identify easily: the report of a rifle and the hum of a bullet as it whizzed by his head.

Finney ducked low and urged his horses onward. When he reached the stage station in the valley below, several men were sent in pursuit of the highwayman. They found his footprints near the top of the grade, where he had apparently stood waiting for some time. The prints indicated that the man wore a size six boot. His trail led over Mount Grant toward Walker Lake, then doubled back and disappeared.

On Thursday morning, just three days after Finney's narrow escape, two armed and masked men stopped the Carson-bound stage from Candelaria, a mining town some fifty miles southeast of Bodie. The highwaymen took the express box but left the passengers unmolested. Then on Saturday night it was the Bodie stage's turn again. As the Bodie-bound stage from Carson neared Sulfur Springs in Dalzell Canyon, two masked men with Henry rifles ordered the driver to halt. The driver was none other than the twice-robbed Chamberlain.[13] His eight passengers were not veteran victims, however. Two of them who were riding up top were slow to raise their hands. "Throw up your hands God damn quick," said one of the highwaymen, "or I'll blow your damn brains out!" The men's hands "went up lively." Chamberlain and the passengers were lined up and frisked for weapons—a revolver was found on one of the passengers—and then allowed to sit on the ground while one of the highwaymen rifled the express box. When he reported the take to his partner, the partner asked, "Is that all? Shall we go through the passengers?" "No," replied the first man, "I don't like to rob passengers." The highwaymen then allowed the passengers to climb back aboard the stage and returned the revolver to its owner. Chamberlain grabbed the reins, and the stage rolled off towards Bodie.

12.   Sources for the following accounts are the *Daily Free Press*, 7, 9, 17, 20 and 25 Sept. 1880; and the *Bodie Standard*, 6 and 11 Sept. 1880.

13.   There was some confusion over the stagecoach driver's name. The Bodie *Daily Free Press* called him Chamberlain in some articles and Cambridge in others. It is clear, however, that the newspaper is referring to the same man. See the *Daily Free Press*, 10 and 16 June, 7 Sept., and 9 Oct. 1880.

About three hours later, the stage met the Carson-bound stage from Bodie. This second stage had messengers Mike Toby and Tom Woodruff aboard. They were informed of the robbery but assumed that the highwaymen were long gone. Nevertheless, when the stage arrived at the scene of the robbery, Toby jumped to the ground to search for tracks left by the highwaymen. He found clear impressions in the dirt, and, somewhat to his surprise, they followed the road in a northerly direction. Toby climbed back aboard the stage, and the coach rolled on, stopping now and then so Toby could check the tracks.

When the stage reached a fork in the road, Toby climbed down again for a careful inspection of the ground. "You son of a bitch," a voice called out from the darkness, "you thought you'd sneak up on us, did you!" A shot rang out and a bullet whizzed by Toby. It struck the stage's lead horse in the head and killed the animal instantly. Toby dove underneath the stage and readied his rifle. "If you fellows fire a gun, we will murder every son of a bitch of you," said the voice. "Nobody is firing any guns," replied Toby. He quickly added, "What's the matter with you? If you want anything, come along." A man stepped out of the sagebrush onto the road. He was one of the highwaymen. Toby fired and the man dropped to the ground dead. The other highwayman, still hidden in the sagebrush, got off a revolver shot that blew a hole in Toby's arm. Toby's partner, Tom Woodruff, returned the fire and thought he hit his mark when the second highwayman appeared to fall into the sagebrush.

Toby was bleeding profusely, and Woodruff and a passenger helped him down the road to a ranch house. With both of the messengers gone, the remaining highwayman, who in fact had not been shot, emerged from the sagebrush and forced the driver, Billy Hodge, to hand over the express box. After securing its contents, the road agent disappeared into the darkness.

During the next week, Indian trackers, detectives, and messengers combed the hills for the man. Two suspects were taken into custody but later released when it was determined that they had not been involved in the robbery. Jim Hume, a detective employed by Wells Fargo, was busy in the meantime analyzing every scrap of evidence found on the dead highwayman. The dead man was of medium height, but his hands and feet were "exceedingly small and feminine in appearance." His boot was size six. He was obviously the man who had shot at George Finney in Coal Valley. Hume also learned from his inspection of the dead man, although the detective did not reveal it to anyone in Bodie, that the highwayman had been living in a lodging house on Minna Street in San Francisco.

On the Saturday night of 11 September 1880, Hume, accompanied by two detectives from the San Francisco police department, went to the house and had the landlady show them to the man's room. There they found several stolen articles and learned that the man's true name was Frank A. Dow. He had used three aliases: W. C. Jones and Frank Keefe or Keith. The detectives decided to keep the room under surveillance in the hope that the other highwayman might visit it. They were not disappointed. About eleven o'clock that night in came Milton (some reports say Lincoln) Anthony Sharp. He was immediately searched and found to have two guns, a morocco mask, $2,500 in gold coin secreted in a belt around his waist, two certificates of deposit for $300 from the First National Bank, and 150 shares of mining stock. Hume identified one of the guns as having been stolen from the express box of a stage. Sharp denied involvement in any stage robberies and said that the gun had been given to him by Dow.

Sharp was arrested and interrogated. Missouri-born and thirty-four years old, he was described as "part Cherokee and part French, possessing all the cunning of the former and all the intelligence of the latter race."[14] He said he had been on the Pacific Coast for twelve years and had earned a living as a miner. Most recently he had been in the trans-Sierra camps of White Pine and Pioche. The $2,500 in his money belt, he said, was the savings from his work in the mining camps. The authorities were not convinced, and they allowed detective Hume and messenger H. C. Ward of Wells Fargo to escort Sharp to Aurora for trial. They arrived with Sharp in tow on the Sunday afternoon of 19 September.

Although Hume thought that the evidence against Sharp was overwhelming and that a jury could not fail to convict him, Wells Fargo left nothing to chance and hired Patrick Reddy to handle the prosecution for the state.[15] With J. R. Kittrell defending Sharp, the trial began on the Thursday morning of 28 October. The case went to the jury on Friday afternoon, and on Saturday the jury brought in a verdict of guilty. Sentencing was deferred until 10 November because Sharp still had to be tried on a second indictment of assault with intent to commit murder for his shooting of messenger Mike Toby.

Meanwhile, Sharp was languishing in the Esmeralda County jail in Aurora and, according to the *Daily Free Press*, was thoroughly demoralized. "The heavy sentence that probably awaits him," said the *Free Press*, "has given him such a fit of blues that even the jailer scarcely knows him. His buoyant spirit is gone and his chances for any considerable life outside of prison walls is also quoted at a very low figure." The *Free Press* spoke too soon. Near sunset on the Tuesday afternoon of 2 November, the very day that the newspaper printed those words, Sharp tunneled through the brick wall of his cell and escaped. The escape left people shocked, not so much because Sharp tunneled through the wall of the jail—that had been done before, and Sharp picked the same spot—but because Sharp's ankles were shackled and a fifteen-pound ball was linked to one of them. Moreover, at the time of his escape the streets in the vicinity of the jail were crowded with voters. It was national election day, and the polls were located in the Aurora court house, a building which also contained the county jail. How Sharp escaped unnoticed through those crowds, shackled as he was, is a mystery.

A half-hour elapsed before the jailer discovered Sharp's empty cell, and perhaps another hour went by before a posse was organized to search for the fugitive. Sharp, meanwhile, was hobbling over Middle Hill and headed toward Adobe Meadows. At Five Mile Springs he stopped to free himself from the shackles. Using rocks, he pounded on the leg irons until the rivets fell out. For the next several days he cautiously worked his way south, camping at Adobe Meadows and then at Black Lake before turning east. On Sunday night he reached Candelaria, where he hoped to make contact with a friend. Instead, he was spotted sitting behind a boarding house near McKisseck's saloon and was arrested by police officer Alex McLean.

On Monday officer McLean escorted Sharp back to Aurora. This time the prisoner, looking much the worse for his escape, was securely locked in an iron cell. Three days later he appeared in court for sentencing. Although he asked the judge to "draw it mild," he was sentenced to serve twenty years in the Nevada state penitentiary.

14.   *Bodie Standard*, 6 Nov. 1880.

15.   Sharp's fortunes continued to be chronicled in the *Daily Free Press*, 9 and 31 Oct., 2, 3, 4, 5, 9 and 16 Nov., and 24 Dec. 1880.

Sharp still had another indictment to face, and the *Daily Free Press* predicted that he would "undoubtedly die in prison clothes, surrounded by his immediate convicts."

Sharp continued to make news from behind bars. He was featured in the *Police Gazette* in December. The woodcut likeness of him in the magazine was not flattering. "Sharp," said the *Daily Free Press*, "looks there as if he had just had a collar and elbow tussel [sic] with a barrel of Bodie whiskey, and got badly beaten. He has a bad eye, a villainous mouth, a frightful nose, ponderous jaws, big ears and a general expression of double distilled cussedness. If Sharp sees the picture he will commit suicide or kill the turnkey." A little more than a year later, the *Auburn Herald* reported that an unidentified man had dug up gold coins and watches near Sharp's cabin in Auburn. The *Bodie Standard* discounted the story and suggested that if Sharp did bury any of his loot, he must have buried it in Esmeralda County.[16]

Sharp's nemesis, Wells Fargo detective Jim Hume, also continued to make news. Three years after he captured Sharp, he apprehended another and more famous highwayman, Black Bart. Like Sharp, Black Bart also left evidence behind at the scene of one of his stage robberies, and the evidence, as it had in Sharp's case, led Hume to the highwayman's San Francisco apartment. Black Bart, again like Sharp, was convicted and sent to the state penitentiary.[17]

The killing of Frank Dow and the incarceration of Milton Sharp did not put an end to stage robbery. On the Saturday afternoon of 2 October 1880, while Sharp was languishing in the Aurora jail, the Mammoth-bound stage from Bodie was robbed.[18] The stage, driven by Frank Piercy, carried a Wells Fargo express box containing $800 in silver coin and another $700 in currency. Just as the stage neared the end of a stretch of deep sand about a mile north of King's ranch, a masked and Winchester-wielding highwayman ordered Piercy to halt. Another highwayman, armed with a double-barreled shotgun, watched from a short distance.

Piercy pulled the horses to a stop and together with a young Italian boy, the only passenger aboard, jumped to the ground. The boy burst into tears as the highwaymen leveled their guns at the pair. The boy was told to quit crying, that he would not be harmed, and Piercy was ordered to hand over the express box. Piercy quickly complied, and the highwaymen then allowed the stage to proceed. Hoping for help, Piercy drove hard to King's ranch but found all the ranch hands away on a hunting trip.

Less than two months later road agents struck again. Shortly before sunrise on the Thursday morning of 25 November 1880, the driver of the Bodie-bound stage from Carson spied two men standing alongside the road in the path of the oncoming stage.[19] Coincidentally, a passenger riding up top with the driver had remarked only a few minutes earlier that he would give $20 to have the pleasure of seeing someone attempt to

16. *Bodie Standard*, 29 March 1882.

17. Black Bart passed himself off in San Francisco as C. E. Bolton. His real name was Charles E. Boles. He came to California in the early 1870s after serving as an officer in the Union Army during the Civil War. For a while he taught school, but in 1875 turned to highway robbery. His first holdup was only meant to be a practical joke. He regularly left behind short poems, signed Black Bart, at the scene of his holdups. Through a laundry mark on a handkerchief that Black Bart dropped during a robbery, Wells Fargo detective Jim Hume was able to trace him to San Francisco and have him arrested. He was tried and convicted and served five years in the state penitentiary at San Quentin. Upon his release he disappeared and was never heard of again. See Joseph Henry Jackson, *Bad Company*, pp. 119–214.

18. *Daily Free Press*, 5 and 7 Oct. 1880; *Bodie Standard*, 9 Oct. 1880.

19. *Daily Free Press*, 28 Nov. 1880.

rob any stage he was on. The driver now replied to the passenger that he might get his wish. Sure enough, when the stage neared the men, one of them leveled a rifle at the passenger, and the other ran across the road to the driver's side. Then, strangely enough, he ran off into the sagebrush. Deciding that the highwayman had lost his nerve, the driver whipped his horses onward. The other highwayman, although he still had his rifle aimed, did not fire, and the stage rolled on unmolested. "It is to be hoped," commented the *Daily Free Press*, "that if these two make a second attempt, Toby, Ross or Ward [messengers Mike Toby, Y. A. Ross, and H. C. Ward] may be aboard to give them a good reception."

Only a few days later, on the Monday night of 29 November, a highwayman stopped the Bishop-bound stage from Bodie as the coach neared Bishop Creek. He forced a passenger to split open the express box, only to find that it was empty. Nevertheless, he did not rob the passengers and allowed the stage to proceed. Driver Jack Lynch could describe him only as "a very tall man with a very long gun."[20] "The probability is," noted the *Daily Free Press* a few days later, "that at the time both the robber and the gun looked longer to Jack than they really were." The tall highwayman, this time working with a partner, struck again on the Saturday night of 11 December. The robbers stopped the Aurora-bound stage from Bishop, cut open the U.S. mail sack, and stole all the letters.

Snowfalls early in the new year did not stop stage robbery. On the Wednesday night of 5 January 1881 the stage bound for Virginia City from Bodie was a few miles north of Aurora when driver George Finney spotted a rope stretched across the road in front of him.[21] He understood immediately what it meant. As he pulled the horses up a demand rang out: "Throw down the express box, you son of a bitch." Finney saw one man guarding him from the side of the road and a second man approaching the stage with a revolver in his hand. The revolver was aimed directly at Finney's head. The second man appeared rather nervous, and when he reached the stage he accidently fired the revolver. The bullet missed Finney—his second near miss in less than five months—but the report of the gun startled the horses. Finney exclaimed, "Keep quiet, boys, my horses are liable to turn. Wait a moment. I'm packed in here and if you will give me time I'll hand out the box."

After taking the meager contents of the express box, the revolver-armed highwayman dropped the rope and allowed the stage to pass. The two passengers, a man and a young woman, were not molested. Just a short distance down the road at the Five Mile House (present-day Fletcher), Finney reported the robbery, and two stage employees were dispatched to the scene. As they approached the spot, they thought they were in luck; the highwayman who had stood guard over the stage was still standing on the roadside. Surprisingly, as they drew closer he still did not move. Not until they were within a few feet did they realize that the supposed highwayman was actually a mannequin. Meanwhile, the real robber had made his escape.

After a half-dozen stage holdups in four months, there was an unexplained lull for nearly a year. Then, late in November 1881, as the stage neared Belleville, a mining town some forty-five miles east of Bodie, three armed, masked men stepped into the road, and one of them yelled, "Halt, you sons of bitches."[22] As the driver reined

---

20.   The tall highwayman was reported in the *Daily Free Press*, 4 and 14 Dec. 1880.

21.   *Daily Free Press*, 6, 7, and 9 Jan. 1881.

22.   *Bodie Standard*, 23 Nov. 1881.

29.   *The stagecoach driver George Finney, pictured here in 1880 hold-*
ing the reins of the four-horse team, was the target of highwaymen's bul-
lets twice. The driver of the other coach is Tom Petit. The Grand Central
Hotel, known as the Magnolia Lodging House until December 1879, is in
the background. (Credit: California State Library)

in the horses the same highwayman, who was visibly drunk, fired a shot at the boot of
the stage and ordered the messenger to step out. There was no messenger inside the
coach, however. Only a doctor, a miner, and prostitutes Tillie Swisher and Minnie Otis
were aboard.

The highwaymen took some $500 from the Wells Fargo express box, and then
the drunken road agent robbed the passengers of their money and jewelry. At this
point one of the prostitutes recognized him and cried, "Mr. Jesse Pierce, that is all I have
left, and it is not fair to leave me nothing." Pierce responded in what the *Bodie Stan-*
dard would describe only as "a very funny vein." The passengers were then ordered
back on the stage, and it rolled off toward Belleville. "Jesse Pierce," asserted the *Stan-*
dard, "has figured in other robberies, and can do the business in a clever manner when
perfectly sober."

The prostitutes were also able to identify another one of the highwaymen, "a
man of an unenviable reputation" named Hank Rogers. Within a few days of the robbery
both Pierce and Rogers were captured and lodged in the Aurora jail.[23] Their bail was
fixed at $9,000 each: $5,000 for robbing the express box and $4,000 for robbing the
passengers. Unable to raise the money, they languished in jail for nearly five months
awaiting the action of the Esmeralda County grand jury. The confinement broke Pierce's
spirit. On a Sunday in mid-April 1882 Pierce stabbed himself in the arm and would have

23.   The trials of Pierce and Rogers were reported in the *Bodie Standard* on 7 Dec. 1881; 19 April, 10 and
17 May, and 7 June 1882. The *Standard* often reprinted stories on the trials from the *Esmeralda Herald*.

bled to death had not officers interfered. "Jesse has been acting strangely of late," said the *Esmeralda Herald*, "as though he had as soon live as die. This was one of his freaks." A week later the grand jury indicted him and Henry P. Rogers for the stage robbery. Pierce, his fight gone, pleaded guilty to the charge and was sentenced to six years in the Nevada state penitentiary.

Unlike Pierce, Hank Rogers was not ready to quit. He retained none other than Patrick Reddy as his defense counsel and entered a plea of innocent. When Rogers's trial began in May, Reddy successfully challenged every potential juror summoned by the county sheriff. Reddy contended that the sheriff was prejudiced by reason of being a party to the prosecution. If Rogers were convicted, the sheriff would receive a reward from Wells Fargo. Reddy's successful challenges cost the county some $2,000 and delayed the trial until June.

When the trial resumed, the jurors heard witnesses—the passengers on the stage—testify that the masked man with Pierce was Rogers. Reddy somehow cast doubt on their testimony. The jurors deliberated for sixty hours without reaching a verdict; nine stood for conviction and three for acquittal. "To the majority of the community," said the *Aurora Herald*, "the disagreeing of the jury was certainly unexpected and occasioned much comment." Although Reddy had worked a small miracle, he could not get the charge against Rogers dismissed. The defendant was bound over for a second trial, and his bail was set at $16,000. Unable to raise such a sum, Rogers remained in jail. In October he went to trial, and the jury again failed to reach a verdict. This time he was discharged. Patrick Reddy had done it again.

The last stage robberies during Bodie's boom years occurred on consecutive days in late December 1881.[24] At about five o'clock on the Wednesday morning of 21 December, the Independence-bound stage from Bishop and Bodie was stopped by two masked, shotgun-wielding highwaymen. They took the Wells Fargo express box but left the passengers, two of whom had large sums of money on their persons, untouched. Early the very next morning the same stage, now with the express box chained in the boot, was ordered by a lone road agent to halt. In the darkness the driver of the stage did not see the shotgun the highwayman was carrying and yelled, "Get out of the way there, and damned quick, too!" Then he saw the shotgun. Its presence changed his attitude dramatically, and he brought the stage to a halt. The road agent, described only as a tall man, ordered the passengers into the road with their hands raised. He left them unmolested, however, and asked only for the express box. When the driver informed him that the box was securely chained to the stage, the road agent surprised the driver and passengers alike by producing an ax. He easily hacked the chain in two, took the box, and ordered the stage to proceed.

Although there was one more stage robbery in Bodie's history—in November 1889 the Hawthorne-bound stage from Bodie was robbed—these were the last of the robberies during the boom years. The robberies all had one thing in common. They were aimed not at the stages with the great bullion shipments but at the stages with the less valuable cargoes. The highwaymen evidently had no desire to tangle with the shotgun messengers who rode on the bullion stages, preferring instead to prey on the unguarded coaches. Only once did messengers and highwaymen exchange gunfire, and in that instance they met by chance. Also, nearly all the robberies occurred during hours of darkness, and the highwaymen always wore masks. Capture and identification of the

24. *Bodie Standard*, 28 Dec. 1881.

road agents was extremely difficult. In only two of the eleven robberies (and three attempted robberies) were arrests made. Perhaps this was not overly troubling to the general public. On only two occasions were passengers robbed. This respect for passengers extended to teamsters, for only twice were teamsters robbed.[25]

Next to stagecoach robbery, bank robbery is probably the form of robbery most popularly associated with the frontier West. Nevertheless, no attempt was ever made to rob either of Bodie's two banks. Neither the Mono County Bank, which was established in August 1877 and remained open through 1885, nor the Bodie Bank, which operated from the summer of 1878 until mid-1882, ever saw a robber. Bank officers and tellers normally were armed, and it would seem that robbers simply were unwilling to risk being shot.

Robbery of individuals—mugging, in today's vernacular, or garroting, as Bodieites termed it—occurred infrequently. During the town's boom years, only ten garrotings and three attempted garrotings were reported.[26] The first garrotings occurred in November and December of 1878 and caused the *Bodie Standard* to comment, on 11 December, "Among other metropolitan fashions we notice the favorite pastime of our cousins in San Francisco is becoming quite popular here among us. We refer to the cheerful and friendly system of garroting people on the street and robbing them of their money."

In nearly every case of garroting the circumstances were so similar as to be interchangeable: The victim had spent the evening in a gambling den, saloon, or brothel; he had revealed in some way that he had a tidy sum of money on his person; and he was staggering home drunk late at night when the attack occurred. The case of James Sunderland, a wood-hauler from Mono Lake, is typical.[27] During the Tuesday afternoon of 2 December 1879, Sunderland collected several bills, amounting to about $200, for wood. After making a few purchases around town, he headed for the faro tables. He lost considerably more than he won and drank heavily while he played. At about eleven o'clock he quit the tables—he still had $40 left—and staggered toward a friend's house near the Bodie brickyard. He had gone only a short distance before he was overtaken by two men, knocked to the ground, and relieved of his money. He was too drunk, the night was too dark, and the attack happened too quickly for him to describe the garroters. This scene was repeated with only minor changes ten times.

In three cases the garroters were foiled. A young miner who won big at the faro tables was set upon by three men as he walked home late one Friday night.[28] When one of the men drew a gun and ordered the miner to throw up his hands, the miner sprinted away. The man fired several shots but missed the fleeing target. A second foiled attempt saw a drunk with $90 on his person saved by three passersby.[29] And C. F. Reid made one garroter wish he had stayed home.[30] When the garroter told Reid to throw up his hands, Reid said "all right" and began raising them. As he did so he suddenly drew a foot-long

25. *Bodie Standard*, 29 March 1879; *Daily Free Press*, 14 Oct. 1880.

26. *Bodie Standard*, 4 and 11 Dec. 1878, 15 Feb. 1879, 20 and 28 Jan. 1880; *Daily Free Press*, 3 Dec. 1879; 20 and 25 Jan., 19 Feb., 30 April, 12 June, 1, 10, and 12 August 1880.

27. *Daily Free Press*, 3 Dec. 1879.

28. *Bodie Standard*, 15 Feb. 1879.

29. *Daily Free Press*, 10 August 1880.

30. *Daily Free Press*, 12 August 1880.

bowie knife from an inside coat pocket and drove the steel blade into the garroter's shoulder. The garroter let out a yell and took off running "like a deer." Reid gave chase but soon lost sight of the man. Nevertheless, Reid was satisfied. He felt certain he had "cut the man to the bone."

Bodie's newspapers were incensed by garroting. "This business of garroting," said the *Bodie Standard* on 15 February 1879, after the third such attack, "is getting a little too common. The parties engaged in it may wake up one of these fine mornings and find themselves hanging to the top of a liberty pole." After the sixth instance of garroting the *Daily Free Press* suggested, on 25 January 1880, that "everyone should go armed, so as to be equal to an emergency." Then, after the eighth attack, the *Daily Free Press* joined the *Bodie Standard* in urging vigilante action. "It is the history of every mining camp," commented the *Free Press* on 19 February 1880, "that a safety committee has had to be formed and some effective work performed in order to rid the place of hard characters. One or two examples have been sufficient to purify the place, and deliver it from the hands of treacherous men. Bodie is in this condition at present and the sooner a move is made the better." It is impossible to determine whether this talk of vigilante action had any effect on garroters. Nevertheless, after the *Free Press*'s comments only five more garrotings were attempted, and only two of them were successful.

The police were seemingly ineffective in controlling garroting. Three or four officers patrolled Bodie at night, and none of them ever made an arrest of a garroter or came to the rescue of a garroting victim. The mere presence of patrolling officers, though, may have been a deterrent. The *Bodie Standard* excoriated the night patrol on several occasions and claimed that the officers spent very little time actually walking their beats. In January 1880 the newspaper put an expensive chronometer on display in Ike Philip's saloon and offered it to the first garroter who caught an officer out in the street at night. "There appears," said the *Standard* on 28 January, "no other way of getting them together. We have never heard of them coming together, though it is darkly whispered that they do possibly meet in the back rooms and dark alleys after a successful garroting operation has been performed." Although no collusion between garroters and police officers was ever proved, a number of unsavory characters did serve on the night patrol. Three of them, Dave Hitchell, Sam Black, and Eugene Markey, were eventually dismissed from the force when rumors persisted that they cooperated with garroters. Hitchell was later shot to death in an opium den after he had threatened a man's life.

The robbery and murder of John Steigel did not follow the normal pattern of garrotings in Bodie. Steigel, a well and favorably known miner from Virginia City, came to Bodie in May 1879 with a "large amount of money" in his possession. A few days after his arrival, he was found shot to death about three miles outside of town. Steigel's body was "in a perfect state of repose, the head resting on a smooth rock, over which had been spread a handkerchief, the hands crossed on the chest, and a revolver resting loosely in his right hand."[31] One chamber of the revolver was empty, and there was a bullet hole in Steigel's temple. There were also several abrasions on his face, and his hands were bruised and lacerated; Steigel had evidently put up a good fight. His money pouch, with only ten cents in it, was found a short distance from the body.

It was speculated that Steigel had been lured away from town on some mining pretext and then attacked. The ritualistic arrangement of his body after his murder is unexplained. The *Bodie Morning News* thought the arrangement "shows a perfect aban-

31. *Bodie Morning News*, 13 May 1879.

donment of every feeling of humanity, and establishes the fact beyond question, that we have in our midst unhung murderers, who deserve death upon the nearest tree." Both the coroner's jury and the grand jury investigated the murder, but were unable to discover any clues. The grand jury did, however, recommend that the governor be requested to offer a reward for the arrest and conviction of Steigel's murderer or murderers.[32]

Besides occasionally falling victim to robbers, Bodieites also suffered from theft. Because of Bodie's severe winters—temperatures often dropped below zero—and the scarcity of timber in the immediate vicinity of town, firewood was always at a premium. As a consequence, some men found the piles of logs and kindling that lay next to nearly every cabin and store a temptation too great to resist. "There is a certain class of men in Bodie," commented the *Daily Free Press*, "who have a systematic dislike and contempt for those who pay out money for wood. They consider it a greater bit of extravagance than paying two bits for a five-cent cigar . . . they consider their neighbor's pile of fuel as common property, and require no invitation to help themselves."[33]

During the fall of 1879 firewood theft became such a problem that a group of citizens held a meeting to discuss ways of preventing losses.[34] Most suggested storing the wood in sheds or standing guard over it with shotguns. The *Bodie Morning News*, on 18 October, said that it was probably only a matter of time before the paper would receive word that one of the thieves "has been made the recipient of a few shares in a lead mine, and the Coroner will have some work to do." Nevertheless, no wood thief was ever shot, and only a half-dozen or so were ever caught.[35] If convicted, the wood thief could expect to pay a fine of $40 or serve forty days in jail. There was one wood thief who defended his actions by reciting the poetry of George Pope Morris. Said the man to the justice of the peace:

> *Woodman, spare that tree!*
> *Touch not a single bough!*
> *In youth it sheltered me,*
> *And I'll protect it now.*[36]

The justice noted, however, that the man did not spare the woodpile and gave him forty days in jail.

Blankets were stolen nearly as often as firewood. "The wood thief," said the *Daily Free Press* on 11 April 1880, "is beginning to have an important rival in the person of the blanket thief." The newspaper blamed the blanket thefts on the large number of "toughs and deadbeats" who had descended on Bodie. A month later, on 12 May, after two more blanket thefts, the *Daily Free Press* hoped that "some night a load of buckshot will be deposited where it will do the most good, and the frightful example may serve as a suitable scarecrow to many who are now on the fence waiting an opportunity to come

32. *Bodie Morning News*, 20 May 1879.

33. *Daily Free Press*, 10 Dec. 1879.

34. *Daily Free Press*, 10 Dec. 1879.

35. *Bodie Morning News*, 25 Oct. 1879; *Daily Free Press*, 1 and 27 Feb. 1880.

36. *Daily Free Press*, 27 Feb. 1880.

down and do a square night's robbing." Although there were probably a dozen instances of blanket theft—there is record of only eight such thefts, but several more are alluded to—only one man was ever convicted of the crime. For stealing two blankets John Dunavan was sentenced to serve fifty days in the county jail.[37]

Other than the aforementioned thefts of wood and blankets, there were fewer than thirty thefts reported in Bodie during the five years of its boom.[38] The armed state of the Bodie citizenry may have been a factor in holding the number of thefts to such a low figure. A good example can be found in the actions of Terrence "Teddy" Brodigan, one of the discoverers of Bodie's gold and a supplier of mountain-spring water to the town's hotels, restaurants, and saloons. A little after three o'clock one morning, Brodigan was awakened by the cackling of his chickens behind his house. Wearing only a night shirt but armed with a six-shooter, Brodigan opened the back door of his house just in time to see two men duck behind the chicken coop. The men, also armed with six-shooters, "threatened to shoot if Teddy advanced and Teddy threatened to shoot if they attempted to retreat."[39] The standoff lasted for nearly a half hour until two police officers arrived. The thieves "took to their heels," with the officers and a half-frozen Brodigan giving chase. By splitting up, the thieves managed to escape, but one of them dropped a mask and three dead chickens.

Another factor that may have inhibited theft was the strict punishment of thieves. For stealing one dollar from a card table, Ed Griffin was sentenced to serve twenty-five days in jail.[40] When Frank Mendoza pleaded guilty to a charge of petty larceny, he was given forty days in jail.[41] And Ambrose Gottenking, convicted of stealing a cheese from Silas Smith's general store, was sent to jail for an unspecified number of days.[42]

Although most theft in Bodie was classified as petty larceny, the "Bullion Robbery Case" was a notable exception.[43] When the Standard mining company began to notice bullion shortages at its mill during the late spring of 1880, it hired P. E. Davis, a San Francisco private detective, to investigate. His inquiry implicated Hank Morton, a battery feeder at the mill. Morton was accused of stealing thousands of dollars' worth of gold bullion from the mill over a period of many months. He allegedly had two accomplices in William Haight and Fred Smith. Just how much Morton was supposed to have stolen from the mill was variously estimated at anywhere from $10,000 to $40,000.

Morton and Haight were arrested early in August, lodged in jail, and later indicted by the grand jury for grand larceny. The Standard company retained Patrick Reddy to aid the Mono County district attorney, W. O. Parker, in the prosecution of the two men. Reddy got Haight to turn state's evidence, apparently in return for a

37. *Daily Free Press*, 6 Jan. 1880.

38. Jail Register: Bodie Branch Jail; *Bodie Standard*, 11 Sept. 1878, 30 June 1879, 30 March and 15 June 1881, 5 April 1882; *Daily Free Press*, 5, 6, and 7 Jan., 22 Feb., 17 March, 1, 14, and 29 April, 8 and 29 August, 3 and 23 Sept., 5 and 14 Oct., and 11 Nov. 1880; 1 March 1881.

39. *Bodie Standard*, 15 June 1881.

40. *Daily Free Press*, 6 Jan. 1880.

41. *Bodie Standard*, 30 June 1879.

42. *Bodie Standard*, 11 Sept. 1878.

43. *Daily Free Press*, 8 August 1880.

promise of reduced charges. Haight was allowed to post bail and was released from jail. But in December he fled across the state line to Aurora and disappeared.[44] Two months later, Davis, the private detective, caught up with Haight in Connecticut and returned him to Bodie.[45]

With Haight back in custody, Morton finally went to trial in superior court on 23 March 1881.[46] The unexpected happened: Haight recanted all of his earlier statements that implicated Morton in the bullion theft. The prosecution was shocked, and Reddy "favored Haight with a good tongue-lashing for his perfidy."[47] The judge was forced to dismiss the case against Morton. Morton, although elated, remarked that he had spent the last eight months in jail and was destitute. Upon hearing this, Reddy quietly handed him a $20 gold piece. For a time, the district attorney considered filing perjury charges against Haight, but a month later the would-be witness was discharged.[48]

Horse stealing and cattle rustling are probably the two forms of theft most commonly associated with the frontier West. There were hundreds of horses and thousands of steers in the general vicinity of Bodie. To the immediate west, Bridgeport Valley was home to some of the most productive stockfarms in the entire trans-Sierra, and to the south large herds of cattle grazed on the range lands of the Owens Valley. Between these two valleys dozens of ranches dotted the landscape. Despite this, there is no record of cattle rustling during Bodie's boom years, and only six instances of horse theft are recorded.[49]

Lawmen had little success in capturing horse thieves, and on one occasion a couple of deputy sheriffs were terribly humiliated. The deputies' troubles began when they were dispatched to the mining town of Marietta to arrest two horse thieves reported to be staying there. When the deputies arrived in Marietta, they discovered that the thieves had left town, headed for Aurora. The deputies climbed back in their saddles and headed off in pursuit.

Ten miles outside of Marietta they spotted the stolen horses in the corral of a way station. The station manager said that the two men who had ridden up on the horses were both inside and sound asleep and could be easily captured. Nevertheless, the deputies, said the *Bodie Standard*, "did not think themselves properly armed to attack highwaymen of such courage, having only two revolvers apiece, and asked the stationkeeper if he had a shotgun that he could lend them. The shotgun was furnished them, and then, to make sure that it was loaded, one of the sheriffs went and shot it off."[50] The report of the gun jarred the thieves out of their slumber and gave them all the warning they needed. Within seconds they came running out of the station with their guns drawn and captured two very surprised deputies. The thieves were last seen driving a buggy down the Carson road with the "brave sheriffs" roped in tow like a couple of horses.

If not humiliating to lawmen, the horse theft committed by Richard Lewis and

44. *Daily Free Press*, 17, 18, and 19 Dec. 1880.

45. *Daily Free Press*, 1 March 1881.

46. *Bridgeport Chronicle Union*, 26 March 1881; *Bodie Standard*, 30 March 1881.

47. *Bridgeport Chronicle Union*, 26 March 1881.

48. Minute Book, Criminal, Dep't No. 2, Superior Court, Mono County, p. 55.

49. *Bodie Standard*, 9 Oct. 1878, 29 March 1879, 17 August 1881; *Daily Free Press*, 4 Dec. 1879, 6 and 25 Jan. 1880; *Bodie Morning News*, 9 August 1879.

50. *Bodie Standard*, 29 March 1879.

Patrick Murphy was certainly frustrating.[51] The two men, enjoying a "bacchanalian" spree on New Year's Day of 1880, rented a two-horse sleigh from the Fashion Stables in Bodie and drove it two-thirds of the way to Virginia City before the snow thinned out. Undaunted, they unharnessed the horses and rode them the remaining distance. Bodie Deputy Sheriff J. A. Grant was sent after the two fun-loving characters. When he got to Virginia City, he had the local sheriff arrest the men for horse theft but was unable to obtain permission from the Nevada governor to take them back to California. They were subsequently released on a writ of habeas corpus, and Grant, realizing that further efforts to arrest them would prove futile, returned to Bodie.

Why Grant's request was rebuffed by the Nevada governor became clear a few days later when it was revealed that Lewis's brother-in-law was the superintendent of the Comstock's richest mine, the Consolidated Virginia, and a personal friend of the governor. The brother-in-law had convinced the governor that "it was only a bit of a spree that the boys were on." "The boys," said the *Daily Free Press*, "when they go on a spree ought not to carry off other people's property."

Horse thieves were not hanged, at least not in Bodie. The only two times that thieves were prosecuted and convicted, they received relatively mild sentences. George Box, "a noted horse-thief," was sentenced to serve six months in the county jail for stealing a mule, and Manuel Rodriguez one year in the state penitentiary for taking a horse belonging to his employer.[52]

Like theft, burglary was not a major problem in Bodie. Between 1877 and 1883, there is record of only thirty-two burglaries and eight attempted burglaries.[53] Seventeen of the burglaries were of homes and fifteen of businesses; the attempts were equally divided. The low number of burglaries is at least partly explained by the willingness of Bodieites to fight to protect their property.

Homeowners were especially willing to fight. When two burglars attempted to enter J. H. Vincent's house on Mono Street, Vincent grabbed a gun and sent them running. The *Bodie Morning News* applauded his action and gave the following advice about burglars: "Our people must be on their guard for this class of gentry, and if possible, when they call, treat them to a good dose of lead."[54] On another occasion an armed man returned to his cabin to find a Chinese burglar stealing a sack of flour. The burglar dropped the sack and ran for his life "followed by a shot from a revolver, which made him go over the ground like a three-minute horse."[55] Harry Bryan grappled with a Chinese burglar who had broken into his cabin, wrested a knife and a hatchet away from the intruder, and sent him running.[56] An employee of the Noonday Mill returned home early one day to find a man rummaging through his cabin. The mill worker chased the burglar through a back window and for a half mile across Bodie's hillsides before giving

51. *Daily Free Press*, 6 and 25 Jan. 1880.

52. *Bodie Standard*, 9 Oct. 1879, 17 Aug. 1881.

53. *Bodie Standard*, 20 Feb. and 25 Sept. 1878; 22 April 1880; 31 August, 9 Nov., and 28 Dec. 1881; 10 May 1882; *Daily Free Press*, 3 and 23 Dec. 1879; 6, 7, and 22 Jan., 18 Feb., 18, 25, and 31 March, 11, 14, and 28 April, 12, 22, and 23 May, 21, 27, and 28 July, 5, 7, 14, and 29 August, and 10 Oct. 1880; 30 Jan., and 9 and 22 Feb. 1881; *Bodie Morning News*, 29 July and 7 Sept. 1879.

54. *Bodie Morning News*, 29 July 1879.

55. Bodie *Daily Free Press*, 25 March 1880.

56. *Bodie Standard*, 9 Nov. 1881.

up the pursuit. "Those who witnessed the run," said the *Daily Free Press*, "say it was up to the gait of a Bodie livery team."[57]

It might be argued that there were so few burglaries of homes because they contained little of value to attract the burglar. This was not the case. Bodieites often kept large amounts of cash and valuable jewelry in their homes. In three of Bodie's home burglaries, losses of cash and jewelry were placed at over $500 and in two others at over $200.[58] These were losses equivalent to thousands of dollars today.

Burglaries of businesses, like those of homes, were prevented because men were armed and willing to fight. When a couple of burglars attempted to break open the door to the storeroom of the Standard mill, they inadvertently awakened an office clerk, W. A. Irwin, who slept there. Irwin sat up in bed and fired a shot from his British Bulldog revolver through the door. He then jumped out of bed and, reported the *Bodie Standard*, "looked out of the door just in time to see two men scampering away as fast as their legs could carry them. We are of the opinion that burglars will hereafter give the Standard mill a wide berth."[59] Two other attempted burglaries were also foiled because of the presence of armed men.[60]

Losses in the burglary of businesses normally did not amount to much. In only three cases did they exceed $50: the California Loan Office, a Main Street pawnshop, lost $700 worth of jewelry; the firm of Tower and Fullride, $75 worth of tea, coffee, and liquor; and a small jewelry store, $200 worth of merchandise.[61] Since most Bodie businesses carried insurance against such losses, these dollar-value estimates may have been exaggerated.

Bodie, then, suffered, although not seriously, from robbery, theft, and burglary. Stagecoach robbery was the most exciting and newsworthy of the larcenous crimes, but home burglary and garroting caused the greatest public outcry and occasionally provoked talk of vigilantism. The occurrence of these latter two crimes, however, never became common enough to cause Bodieites to resort to extralegal action. Only one man was ever killed for his money, and in that case the ritualistic arrangement of the corpse could possibly indicate that robbery was not the only motive for the man's murder. On the other side, only one robber, a highwayman, was ever killed, and the confrontation in which he died came about accidentally.

The total amount of robbery, burglary, and theft was really very small. The armed citizenry probably contributed to the limiting of the number of these crimes. On numerous occasions, burglars were scared away or shot at by an armed citizen. Bodieites seemed to have had no compunction about shooting robbers and burglars, even petty thieves, and the local newspapers regularly advocated doing so. Moreover, because of the presence of shotgun messengers, not one of the stages that carried the great gold and silver bullion shipments—valued in the tens of thousands of dollars—was ever stopped by highwaymen. Nor was any robber daring or reckless enough to challenge armed bank officers and tellers.

The police in Bodie were less than effective in stopping larcenous crimes. Some

57. *Daily Free Press*, 28 April 1880.
58. *Daily Free Press*, 22 Jan., 22 May, 21 July, and 7 August 1880.
59. *Bodie Standard*, 25 Sept. 1878.
60. *Daily Free Press*, 10 Oct. 1880; *Bodie Standard*, 28 Dec. 1881.
61. *Daily Free Press*, 31 March, 21 July, and 13 August 1880.

officers were even accused of aiding and abetting garroters. When thieves and robbers were arrested, tried, and convicted, their sentences were rather stiff by today's standards. Petty thieves were sent to jail for thirty or forty days, horse thieves for six months to a year, and highwaymen for six to twenty years. Since so few thieves or robbers were apprehended, let alone tried and convicted, it is difficult to say if these stiff penalties had much of a deterrent effect.

10

ROUGH
AND ROWDY

Bodie was a rough and rowdy town. Its streets were lined with saloons, gambling dens, and brothels, and it was populated mostly with young males. These men were adventuresome, aggressive, and tough. Some had fought in the Civil War, others had worked on the railroads, and nearly all were veterans of mining camp life in the West. More than half of them were foreign-born.[1] Ireland contributed the greatest number. The great majority of the native-born came from California and New York. Without wives and families for the most part, these young men made the saloon the most important social institution in Bodie. Nearly fifty watering holes were open and well patronized seven days a week. Most of the men drank and many of them drank heavily. Nearly all of them were armed. In such an atmosphere it is not surprising to find that rowdy behavior was the rule, that fights occurred frequently, and that the use of weapons in fights was not uncommon.

Rowdy behavior occasionally resulted in arrests for drunk and disorderly conduct or for disturbing the peace. In 1881, for example, there were nearly thirty arrests for these two offenses.[2] A man convicted of either offense could usually expect a fine of $25 or a sentence of twenty-five days in jail.[3] Significantly, the most severe sentence, thirty days in the county jail, was given to a drunk whose only crime was using "the vilest kind of language before ladies and children."[4]

A few of the arrests for disturbing the peace were for discharging firearms in the city streets. "It is customary among the lovers of pistol practice," said the *Bodie Standard* on 4 December 1878, "to engage in the sport in out of the way places or ranges, but with us here the recreation is carried on in our streets mostly at night." Although random shooting or "pistol practice" occurred almost nightly, no innocent bystander was ever hit and there were only three near misses. A police officer, Eugene Markey, was responsible for one of the three. On a drunken spree, he fired off several rounds, and one of

1. Department of the Interior, Census Office, *Tenth Census*, p. 498.

2. Jail Register: Bodie Branch Jail, pp. 10–30.

3. *Bodie Standard*, 19 June 1878, 18 Jan. 1879, 2 August 1882; Bodie *Daily Free Press*, 6 and 10 Dec. 1879, 16 and 18 March 1880.

4. *Daily Free Press*, 14 April 1880.

them narrowly missed a bartender's head.[5] A mother and daughter were startled when a bullet buried itself in the outside wall of their house only inches from the open window where they were seated.[6] And the thickness of a door saved the editor of the *Bodie Standard* from possible death.[7] The journalist was at home seated in a chair and leaning against the inside of his front door when a stray round from a Colt Lightning revolver struck the outside of the door directly opposite his back.[8]

Bodie's newspapers occasionally scolded the shooters for endangering the lives of others and urged stricter law enforcement. "It is true," said the *Bodie Standard* on 11 September 1880, "that the present condition of society in Bodie warrants, if it does not force, the carrying of firearms as a matter of self protection against the lawless element in our midst. There is no necessity, however, for them to endanger the lives and property of others by carelessly discharging their weapons." The *Bodie Morning News* said, on 24 October 1879, that it thought that the "playfully disposed individuals should be taught a severe lesson when captured, and made acquainted with the inside of a jail." And the *Daily Free Press*, on 26 May 1880, hoped that "a few heavy fines would dampen this sort of enthusiasm."

Despite these editorial admonishments, random shooting continued to occur almost nightly. After all, there was no law that specifically prohibited discharging a firearm in Bodie. Shooters could be charged only with drunk and disorderly conduct or disturbing the peace. Moreover, most Bodieites, including police officers and justices of the peace, simply did not consider "pistol practice" a very serious problem. Shooters were only occasionally arrested, and the heaviest fine ever imposed was $25.[9] When police made a rare effort to crack down on the practice on New Year's Eve, 1879, even one of the town's newspapers that usually advocated strict enforcement complained. "As soon as the firing began," commented the *Daily Free Press* on 2 January, "several over-zealous officers made attempts to quell the enthusiasm, which was quite out of place considering the time and place. A few celebrators had their pocket pieces taken from them, and felt that human liberty had been done away with."

This sort of rowdy atmosphere in Bodie was conducive to fighting. Fistfights and gunfights occurred with alarming frequency. Nearly all of these fights resulted from personal feuds, challenges to the pecking order in a saloon, careless insults, or affronts to personal honor. Only a few fights occurred as a result of disputes over property or women.

Fistfights could occur any day of the week, but they were especially likely to erupt on weekend nights. The *Bodie Morning News*, on 28 October 1879, described a typical Saturday night:

> The latter half of Saturday night was a wild one. The consumption of bug juice was something wonderful. Fighters were as thick as blackbirds in a rice field, and

---

5. *Bodie Morning News*, 25 Oct. 1879.

6. *Bodie Standard*, 10 August 1881.

7. *Bodie Standard*, 11 Sept. 1880.

8. The .41 caliber Colt revolver was first produced in 1877. Called the Lightning, it was Colt's first double-action or "self-cocker" revolver. It became popular throughout the West and was the favorite of Henry McCarty, better known as Billy the Kid. See Elmer Keith, *Sixguns by Keith*, pp. 29–30.

9. *Bodie Standard*, 18 Jan. 1879, 2 August 1882.

were accommodated almost to a man. The down-town dance houses were scenes of numerous pugilistic passages, and pistols were several times drawn to enforce fistic arguments. No one had his measure taken, however, for a wooden overcoat, though the prospect at times looked as if it would develop into a bonanza for the Coroner and undertakers, but simmered down to a few rich "pockets" of broken noses and black eyes. . . . Such little pleasantries as firing off pistols were frequently indulged in during the course of the night, and the Sabbath dawned while the boys were having a high old time generally.

On 20 April 1880 the *Daily Free Press* described a Sunday night in a similar manner:

> Instead of remaining in their rooms and reading moral books, a great many citizens were on the rampage Sunday night. . . . In a saloon at the upper end of town a party of Mill Creekers pitched into a single man, and were knocking him about in a lively manner, when a Standard reporter, out of mere sympathy for suffering humanity, made a gallant charge for the victim. In all probability the S.r. would have been among the killed, wounded and missing had not a reserve force rushed to the rescue. . . .
>
> Several sons of old Erin were unruly in a place further down town. A knockdown was the result of a long argument, followed by a round of drinks.
>
> Continuing on down the street the excitement increased. At one time it looked as though an undertaker would be blessed with a victim. . . . The officers were plentiful but the arrests were few. For this they were called hard names. The private citizen considers an officer the most useless person in the world, until his own head is being split open, and is rescued by that public servant, from the hands of a tough.

The typical fistfight took place in a saloon on a weekend night and resulted from a challenge as to who was the better man. More often than not, one or both of the participants had been drinking. A representative example was a fight between a brawler from Reno and a Bodie miner, which occurred one Saturday night in 1880. The brawler arrived in Bodie on the afternoon stage and, noted the *Daily Free Press*, wasted no time in making "a terrific howl about being the best man in town."[10] Early in the evening he walked into a saloon, drank a glass of whisky, and said, "I made all the toughs of Reno take a back seat and from the looks of things, I'm boss here." A miner named Sullivan took exception to the remark, and "before the bar-keeper had time to wipe the glasses the Reno 'desperado' was on the floor, and in a moment more was out on the sidewalk." Left with a battered eye and a split lip, he "looked very demoralized."

Fistfighting was not restricted to any particular social or occupational group in Bodie. There are examples of doctors, lawyers, and businessmen fighting, as well as miners, teamsters, and woodchoppers. Dr. T. J. Blackwood, who had arrived in Bodie in 1877, making him the first physician in town, had an argument with John Greenwood and "battered him up considerably."[11] During a civil trial in superior court the plaintiff, A. B. Stewart, and the attorney for the defendant, John Kittrell, came to blows.[12] Kit-

10. *Daily Free Press*, 7 March 1880.
11. *Daily Free Press*, 25 March 1880.
12. *Bodie Standard*, 27 April 1881.

trell was initially cited for contempt of court and fined $250, but after an eloquent speech on his behalf by Patrick Reddy, the fine was remitted. George Callahan, the proprietor of the Can Can restaurant and the owner of a lodging house, thoroughly pummeled a miner who had refused to pay a bill and had bragged that "no ten men in town" could make him pay.[13]

Even an impostor made a name for himself among the ranks of Bodie's fistfighters. On a Thursday night in 1882 "a rough looking fellow" entered a saloon and announced to the score of patrons that he was Billy the Kid and that he could stand any man in the room on his head. This boast caused half of the men in the saloon to retreat through the back door. "The balance of the select company of tax payers and Christian statesmen," said the *Bodie Standard*, "advanced on the bogus Billy the Kid, and when he struck the sidewalk it sounded as though Berliner had hit a base drum. When the man got up he explained that his name was simply John Smith and that his father went by the same name."[14]

The most notorious of Bodie's brawlers was Mike McGowan, known as the Man Eater.[15] McGowan had earned his sobriquet in Virginia City, where he delighted in chomping on the ears and noses of his foes. He obviously received his share of defeats, however, because his head was described as having been "beaten all out of shape." McGowan was a cook by trade and a very good one at that—when he was sober. Too often, though, he was "in his cups" and the terror of the town. In Bodie he managed to chomp on Sheriff Peter Taylor's leg, chase a man down Main Street with a butcher knife, break a pitcher over a waiter's head, threaten to chew off the justice of the peace's ears, eat a stray bulldog, and engage in several fistfights. The Man Eater was finally given a choice of a long jail term or exile from Bodie. He chose the latter and wound up back in Virginia City, where he was arrested for vagrancy. "This must be a mistake on the part of the authorities," said the *Bodie Standard*, "for Mike has a visible means of support. He has an upper and lower row of teeth."[16]

Fighting with fists, and in some cases teeth, did not satisfy all Bodieites. Weapons were often used. Guns were far more popular than knives, but there were six knife assaults other than the nine minority-related incidents already mentioned. A rough with the curiously appropriate name of John Cropley was responsible for two of the assaults.[17] For inflicting minor wounds on two different men in separate incidents, he was sentenced to pay a $50 fine or serve fifty days in jail. Since Cropley was unable to pay the fine, the sheriff escorted him to the county jail at Bridgeport. Another knife-wielder, not named and said to have "struggled hard to lessen the amount of whisky on sale in various saloons," was arrested and lodged in the Bodie jail for attacking "Winnemucca Jack" Edwards.[18] Edwards blocked the knife attack with his hands and suffered several cuts and the loss of a finger.

13. *Bodie Standard*, 14 Sept. 1881.

14. *Bodie Standard*, 8 March 1882.

15. *Bodie Standard*, 15 July, 9 Oct., and 29 Dec. 1880; *Daily Free Press*, 3 Sept., 10 Oct., and 29 Dec. 1880.

16. *Bodie Standard*, 29 Dec. 1880.

17. *Bodie Standard*, 29 May 1878.

18. *Bodie Morning News*, 14 August 1879.

One man was stabbed not with a knife but with a miner's candlestick.[19] James Murphy suffered a punctured lung when William White, his partner in the Stanford Consolidated, sank the sharp point of a miner's candlestick into his chest during a heated argument over ownership of some shares of mining stock. White became so distraught over having stabbed his partner that he attempted to slash his own throat. Bystanders prevented him from making anything more than a few scratches. Murphy recovered from the stabbing, and White, although initially arrested and lodged in jail, was released when Murphy failed to file a complaint.

Not just roughs, drunks, and miners were knife wielders. John McQuaid, one of Bodie's most prominent attorneys, always carried a knife for protection. One afternoon he alighted from a buggy in front of the Mammoth saloon and was approached by Thomas Muckle, a stonecutter, said to be in a slightly "oiled" condition.[20] Muckle berated McQuaid over a money matter and then punched him in the eye. The lawyer responded with a knife thrust into Muckle's rib cage and left the stonecutter with a painful if not serious wound. McQuaid was arrested and tried in justice court for assault with a deadly weapon, but won acquittal on a plea of self-defense.

The night after Muckle's wounding, Ed Jackson came running into the Rosedale saloon yelling that he had just been stabbed.[21] His shirt was bloody, and he appeared to have two frightful gashes on each side of his throat. Constable John Kirgan was summoned and, on seeing the wounded man, cried, "Great God, who's done this?" Kirgan then pulled out a revolver from one pocket and a pair of handcuffs from another and exclaimed, "Damn you fellows. Some of you go and get a doctor. You'd stand around like knots on a pine log, and let a man bleed to death." The patrons of the Rosedale saloon were unmoved, however, and not one stirred. When Kirgan looked about incredulously, a few men burst into laughter. Kirgan began to suspect the obvious and took a closer look at Jackson's neck wounds. He found they were dripping not blood but red paint. With a violent outburst of profanity, Kirgan swore that he would jail Jackson for the ruse. The constable soon relented, however, joined in the laughs, and ordered drinks for the house.

Only one of the six knife assaults resulted in a death.[22] The fatal assault had its origin in an argument that erupted between Thomas Travis and Thomas Dillon in a Chinese opium den on the New Year's Eve night of 31 December 1879. During the dispute, said the *Daily Free Press*, Travis called Dillon "all the vile epithets that a dirty, vulgar tongue could give utterance to."[23] Travis's "lady friend," a prostitute named Dolly, joined the attack on Dillon with "remarks too obscene to appear in print." Profane verbal abuse was not enough for Travis, though. He struck Dillon in the face with an opium pipe and threatened him with a gun. Police officer David Hitchell, who was present in the opium den—he seems to have spent much of his time in opium dens— and until now had only watched the dispute, entered the fray and disarmed Travis.

19. *Daily Free Press*, 25 Feb. 1880.

20. *Bodie Standard*, 26 Nov. 1879; *Daily Free Press*, 22 Jan. 1880.

21. *Bodie Standard*, 26 Nov. 1879.

22. *Daily Free Press*, 5 and 9 Jan., 22 Feb., 19, 20, 21, 23, 24, and 25 March 1880; *Bodie Standard*, 5, 6, and 8 Jan. 1880.

23. *Daily Free Press*, 23 March 1880.

Undaunted, Travis declared that he would kill Dillon, or Dillon would kill him, within a week.

Four days later on the Saturday night of 3 January 1880, Travis was standing in front of the Rosedale saloon bragging about his confrontation with Dillon. "Yes, I hit the son of a bitch," said Travis. "We Eureka boys generally get away with whatever we go after."[24] Later that evening Travis had an opportunity to prove it. At about one o'clock in the morning he spied Dillon standing in front of the Opera House dance hall smoking a pipe. Accompanied by John Mulligan, Travis approached Dillon, pulled out a gun, and exclaimed, "Now, you Irish son of a bitch, you must fight." Before Dillon could answer, Travis stuck the gun in Dillon's stomach and pulled the trigger. The gun misfired. Dillon did not give Travis a second chance. He wrestled him to the snow-covered ground, drew a knife, and plunged it into his chest. Police officers Eugene Markey and Samuel Black happened upon the scene almost immediately and pulled Dillon off Travis. While Black led Dillon away, Travis, who had been helped to a sitting position, grabbed his gun and shot Dillon in the back. Both Dillon and Travis were now carried into the dance house. Travis was dead within five minutes.

Although seriously wounded, Dillon was carried off to jail, where he was charged with murder and locked in a cell. Doctors could treat his wound only superficially. The bullet that had struck him in the back was lodged against his spine and they dared not operate. Dillon's discomfort was increased by his confinement in the city jail. The *Bodie Standard* suggested he be removed to the county hospital. "It would be a great deal better, and more humane," said the *Standard*, "if authorities would provide a different place for prisoners in Dillon's condition. It hardly seems right to keep a man, whatever his offense, who is hovering between life and death, with the floor of such a place as our calaboose for his bed."[25] Despite these conditions, Dillon improved day by day. A week after the shooting he was eating heartily, walking about his cell for short periods, and smoking his pipe, which he filled with opium as often as tobacco.

When questioned about his killing of Travis, Dillon claimed self-defense and said he had no fear of conviction on the murder charge. Nevertheless, he retained the very best legal counsel in the trans-Sierra, Patrick Reddy. The prosecution, meanwhile, built its case primarily on the testimony of John Mulligan, with some support from officer Sam Black. Mulligan contended that Dillon had been the aggressor, and that it was Dillon, not Travis, who had drawn the gun.

On 18 March Dillon's examination in justice court began. Mulligan was the first witness to testify. As was expected, he put all the blame for the affair on Dillon. But then Reddy cross-examined Mulligan and, noted the *Daily Free Press*, "the sagacious lawyer cornered him on several occasions."[26] By the time Mulligan got off the witness stand both his testimony and his character appeared seriously flawed. The next day, Black, now a former police officer, testified. During cross-examination Reddy first established that Black and Travis had been friends and then "gave him such a game as he never experienced before, and he must have lost considerable flesh while going through the trying ordeal. His memory was defective, and Mr. Reddy was repaid by catching 'him

24. *Daily Free Press*, 23 March 1880.

25. *Bodie Standard*, 6 Jan. 1880.

26. *Daily Free Press*, 19 March 1880.

out' several times."[27] Reddy now called the Bodie town constable, John Kirgan, to the stand and asked him why Black had been dismissed from the police force. When Kirgan replied that Black had been fired because of persistent rumors that he cooperated with garroters, what little remained of Black's credibility vanished.

During the next two days, Reddy had several defense witnesses testify, including Dillon himself. The prosecution was unable to discredit any of the testimony. Final arguments were heard on 23 March. Although the district attorney's argument was brief, Reddy's "occupied some time in delivery, and was closely listened to by a large audience. His plea for the discharge of Dillon was strong and eloquent. The law, bearing directly on the case in question, was liberally quoted and elucidated to His Honor."[28] The following day the justice of the peace, R. L. Peterson, ruled that on the evidence submitted a jury would never convict Dillon of murder. But, he added, if the prosecution thought they could produce more evidence at a later date, Dillon would be held to answer. When the prosecution said they could not, Peterson dismissed the charge of murder against Dillon and discharged him. Dillon thanked Reddy and left the courtroom a happy man. "During the evening," noted the *Daily Free Press*, "many friends congratulated Dillon on his being set at liberty. He was about town until a late hour."[29]

In mid-July, three and a half months after he was discharged by justice court, Dillon was indicted for murder by the Mono County grand jury.[30] The jury's action came as a surprise; no new evidence seems to have been produced. Dillon was arrested and lodged in the county jail at Bridgeport. He did not remain there long. On 20 July Patrick Reddy moved in superior court to have him released and the charge of murder dismissed. The court granted the motion and Dillon was freed for good.[31]

If Bodieites only occasionally resorted to the use of knives, they regularly used firearms. More often than not, however, they preferred to simply brandish their guns. "Weapons," recalled a Bodieite, "were oftener drawn than used. Most men that carry guns like to get them out on slight provocation, but they loath to use them. More than once, I have seen a whole crowd of men with their guns drawn and not a shot fired."[32] Several incidents can be cited to support this contention. In a brawl in a Main Street dance house on the Monday night of 20 October 1879, "pistols were drawn," said the *Bodie Morning News*, "fists used, and a good deal of hard swearing indulged in. It was a lively scene for a while, and at one time it seemed as if the Coroner would get a job out of it, but the fracas finally ended with only a black eye and two or three bloody noses as casualties."[33] Less than a week later, guns were again drawn but not used in another dance house row.[34] A brawl in the Spanish dance house a month later saw revolvers brandished but not fired.[35]

27.   *Daily Free Press*, 20 March 1880.

28.   *Daily Free Press*, 24 March 1880.

29.   *Daily Free Press*, 25 March 1880.

30.   *Bodie Standard*, 15 July 1880.

31.   Minute Book, Criminal, Dep't No. 2, Superior Court, Mono County, p. 11; Register of Actions, Superior Court, Mono County, p. 15.

32.   Grant Smith, "Bodie, Last of the Old-Time Mining Camps," p. 71.

33.   *Bodie Morning News*, 22 Oct. 1879.

34.   *Bodie Morning News*, 28 Oct. 1879.

35.   *Daily Free Press*, 3 Dec. 1879.

Men did not have to be in crowds to brandish firearms. Andy Donahue got "uproariously" drunk one Sunday night, waved a Colt Navy revolver about, and threatened to "take the town."[36] James Cohan brandished a revolver in front of Phillips and Moore's saloon on a Christmas Eve night and expressed "an ardent desire" to shoot anyone connected with the saloon; and angry, revolver-brandishing James Courtney sent the proprietor of "a well known restaurant" running out of his establishment.[37] More than a dozen other instances of individuals brandishing firearms can be cited.

Bodie newspapers generally reported gun-brandishing incidents in a light-hearted, tongue-in-cheek vein. When a reporter from the *Bodie Morning News* learned that there were two men facing each other with guns drawn in Wagner's saloon, "he rushed headlong into the saloon, when horrible to relate, they put up their weapons and we had no man for breakfast, thereby spoiling a fine local."[38] In another incident, when a police officer attempted to disarm a man brandishing a six-shooter, the gun discharged. The bullet, noted the *Bodie Standard*, "landed in McLaughlin's boot and shoe store, demoralizing a last."[39]

This less than serious treatment of gun-brandishing reflected the attitude of police officers and judges. Brandishers were often not arrested. The heaviest fine ever imposed on a brandisher amounted to only $40, and in that instance the offender thought the fun he had had was well worth the fine.[40] Depite the rather casual attitude of Bodieites toward brandishing firearms, the act was, of course, only a trigger-pull away from a shooting. Perhaps Bodieites were casual about brandishing a gun because shooting and shoot-outs occurred with alarming frequency. Bodie was, in the vernacular of the day, a shooter's town.

There were some fifty separate incidents of shootings and shoot-outs, other than those already mentioned in connection with minorities and women, in Bodie between 1877 and 1883.[41] Six of these incidents were suicides or accidental shootings, eight were the result of property disputes, one was caused by adultery, and a few had their origins in family quarrels or arguments between neighbors. In stark contrast to Aurora, politics was never a factor in Bodie shootings or shoot-outs.

Eight Bodie men committed suicide. Of these, three ended their lives with gunshots, and they all did so during 1879, a year when Bodie was booming and the outlook for the future was bright.[42] Thomas Barlow, "a man enjoying good health, a lucrative position and means at his disposal," shot himself to death on the Friday night of 11 July 1879.[43] He left behind a brief suicide note addressed to the head of the Bodie

36. *Bodie Standard*, 9 Oct. 1878.

37. *Bodie Standard*, 25 Dec. 1878.

38. *Bodie Morning News*, 3 April 1879.

39. *Bodie Standard*, 12 April 1882.

40. *Bodie Standard*, 25 Dec. 1878.

41. "Shootings," as used here, includes those instances in which an intended victim was shot at but not actually hit, as well as those instances in which the bullet found its mark. "Shoot-out," of course, denotes shooting by the two or more parties involved.

42. A total of five Bodie men committed suicide in 1879, and only one in 1880, 1881, and 1882, respectively. Three took overdoses of laudanum and one of strychnine; three shot themselves; and one threw himself down a mine shaft. *Bodie Morning News*, 31 May, 12 July, 20 Sept., 2 and 10 Oct. 1879; *Daily Free Press*, 11 Nov. 1880; *Bodie Standard*, 17 August 1881, 7 June 1882.

43. *Bodie Morning News*, 12 July 1879.

Freemasons, which listed his possessions and concluded, "You and the brothers please put me under. Goodbye. Success to the cause." John Bassett, a devoted husband and father of two children, put a British Bulldog revolver to his head on the Wednesday night of 1 October 1879 and fatally shot himself.[44] Bassett had a steady job at the Maybelle mine, and the only explanation offered for the suicide was a possible condition of temporary insanity brought on by a fall a week before.

Just a little more than a week after Bassett committed suicide, D. H. Denton, a thirty-nine-year-old miner who had been ill with pneumonia for several days, picked up a revolver lying near his bed and, according to a report in the *Bodie Morning News*, "fired two shots into his brain."[45] An attendant who had been caring for the pneumonia-stricken Denton happened by a short while later and found him dead. Denton was described by his boss at the Syndicate mill as a sober, steady, and much respected workingman and the last person he "would suspect doing such a rash act as committing suicide." Nevertheless, no one seems to have disputed the coroner's finding of suicide or questioned how Denton could have shot himself twice in the head.

Three other Bodie men shot themselves. In these cases, however, the shootings were accidental and the men were only wounded. L. A. LaGrange accidentally shot himself in the leg while practicing a quick draw in the Bodie shooting gallery.[46] A man "somewhat under the influence of liquor" winged himself in the calf when he accidentally discharged a derringer as he pulled it out of his hip pocket. And George Mann accidentally shot himself in the jaw while inspecting a revolver that had misfired.[47]

In only one accidental shooting was a man other than the shooter wounded.[48] A. Fried, an affable and corpulent wholesale liquor salesman from San Francisco, was accidentally shot in the shoulder by H. H. Moody, a clerk in the Bodie post office, while the two were riding the Bodie stage to Aurora. Moody was intoxicated at the time and apparently was handling his gun carelessly when it discharged. Nevertheless, Moody was arrested, charged with assault with intent to commit murder, and lodged in the Aurora jail. The district attorney at Aurora, now little more than a way station on the Bodie line, evidently was in need of cases to prosecute. When Moody's trial came up, Fried, regarding the shooting as purely accidental, did not appear to testify, and the district attorney was forced to move that the defendant be discharged. The district court judge granted the motion, and an elated Moody was set free. Fried, meanwhile, recovered rapidly from the wound, although the bullet remained lodged under his collarbone. Six months later the *Bodie Standard* noted that Fried was entirely recovered and "as jolly and obese as ever—weighing something over 200 pounds."[49]

Real property was a factor in eight of Bodie's shootings and shoot-outs.[50] Disputes over a city lot and a ranch site accounted for two shoot-outs, and conflicting mining claims for the other six. The city lot, located on Main Street, was claimed by

---

44. *Bodie Morning News*, 2 Oct. 1879.

45. *Bodie Morning News*, 10 Oct. 1879.

46. *Bodie Chronicle*, 12 June 1880.

47. Both instances reported in the *Bodie Standard*, 8 June 1881.

48. *Daily Free Press*, 15 Oct. and 21 Nov. 1880; *Bodie Standard*, 13 April 1881.

49. *Bodie Standard*, 13 April 1881.

50. One of these eight instances of property-related shootings and shoot-outs led to vigilantism and is discussed in chapter 12.

both John Wheeler—an expert marksman who had already shot to death one man—and J. L. Blethens.[51] On the Wednesday night of 19 December 1877, Blethens dumped a load of lumber on the lot and the next day began fencing the property. That night Wheeler arrived at the scene and started to dismantle the day's work and throw the lumber into the street. Blethens decided that the ground was worth a fight. From be-hind a wagon, he emptied both barrels of a shotgun at Wheeler. The blast missed. Wheeler drew a revolver and got off two shots at Blethens before the latter, without attempting to reload his shotgun, ran off down the street and disappeared into a house. Both Wheeler and Blethens were arrested, but no charges were filed and they were soon released.

The delivery of a load of lumber also precipitated the shoot-out over the ranch site.[52] On the Friday afternoon of 11 June 1880, James Hurley employed T. M. Post to deliver lumber to property he had preempted in Mill Creek canyon. When Post arrived at the property he found Robert Dalzell there waiting for him with a cocked revolver. Dalzell said that the land was his. It seems that both Dalzell and Hurley had filed preemp-tion claims for the land with the United States Land Office in Bodie. Post was not there to argue, especially with a revolver pointed at him, and he prudently left without trying to unload the lumber.

Post returned the next day, accompanied by Hurley and Richard Hammond. As they told the story, Dalzell was there waiting for them, and he opened fire with a Henry rifle. Hammond was slightly wounded, but he, along with Hurley and Post, re-turned the fire. When the shooting stopped, Dalzell lay dead on the ground. Hurley, Hammond, and Post surrendered themselves to the authorities and a week later were indicted for murder by the grand jury.[53] The ultimate charge called for the ultimate legal defense, and the three men wisely retained Patrick Reddy.[54]

Hurley's superior court trial came up first, just a month and a half after the shoot-out. On 30 July the case went to the jury; after hours of deliberation the jurors were unable to reach a verdict.[55] The district attorney moved that Hurley be discharged on the grounds that a conviction could not be obtained. The judge granted the motion, and the first of Reddy's three clients was set free.[56] Five days later, a second jury was out only fifteen minutes before it returned a verdict of not guilty in the trial of Hammond. Only two more days passed before another jury found Post not guilty.[57]

These verdicts were reported without comment by the *Daily Free Press* and the *Bodie Standard*, but the *Bodie Chronicle* was quick to express its outrage. Commented the *Chronicle* on 7 August:

> It seems that Dalzell was not murdered, after all the fuss that was made about his death for Hurley, Hammond and Post, who were known to have killed him, have

51. *Bodie Standard*, 26 Dec. 1877.

52. *Daily Free Press*, 13 and 15 June 1880; *Bodie Chronicle*, 12 June 1880.

53. *Daily Free Press*, 23 June 1880.

54. Criminal Calendar, Dep't No. 2, Superior Court, Mono County, 10 July 1880.

55. *Daily Free Press*, 31 July 1880.

56. Minute Book, Criminal, Dep't No. 2, Superior Court, Mono County, p. 22; Register of Actions, Su-perior Court, Mono County, p. 21.

57. Minute Book, Criminal, Dep't No. 2, Superior Court, Mono County, pp. 29, 34.

been tried for his murder and acquitted! If three men shoot another to death, it is not murder but a pleasant pastime in the mountains—unless it can be proven that the three had conspired to kill their man. Out of all the murders committed in this county in the past two years, not a murderer convicted! What laws; what a country and what a peoples!

Perhaps the *Chronicle* should have added: and what an attorney! Patrick Reddy was simply unbeatable. Moreover, the *Chronicle* had conveniently forgotten that on 12 June it had reported that Dalzell had fired the first shots.

Although all mining claims had to be carefully surveyed and staked, disputes arose occasionally. Most of the disputes were settled in the courtroom, but six were resolved by gunfire. Three of these (one of which will be discussed later in connection with vigilantism) had fatal consequences, one resulted in the wounding of a man, and in two others the participants escaped unscathed.

Late in August 1878, a dispute arose over the "Yosemite ledge," located just south of the hoisting works of the Blackhawk mine.[58] The Blackhawk had bought the ledge from Phil Reilly, but Reilly claimed he still owned a portion of it and, together with Jack O'Hara, Tom O'Brien, and a man named McDonald, began sinking a shaft into the ledge on the Sunday morning of 25 August. At noon they finished work for the day, and all but O'Hara left for an afternoon in town.

"Colonel" Sam Ferguson, the superintendent of the Blackhawk mine, thought the time propitious to reclaim the ledge. Holding a revolver in his hand, he walked down to the ledge and ordered O'Hara off the property. O'Hara, also armed with a revolver, said he was just working for wages and did not want a fight and that he intended to stay put until his employer, Phil Reilly, returned. The thirty-four-year-old Irish-born O'Hara, a veteran of mining camps in Montana, Idaho, Nevada, and California, was an expert marksman. He pointed out an old oyster can lying on the ground off in the distance and then shot it full of holes. Ferguson got the message.

Early in the evening Reilly returned to the ledge. His arrival did not go unnoticed. Ferguson stepped out of the Blackhawk's office, located in a cabin next to the hoisting works, and yelled a warning to Reilly: Leave or be shot. Before Reilly could respond O'Hara yelled back that if shooting was desired then he would "like a twist." Ferguson again backed down. Reilly offered to negotiate the disputed claim, but Ferguson said there was nothing to discuss.

On Monday morning Reilly approached the Blackhawk office and called for Ferguson. The superintendent remained inside the cabin and told Reilly that if he came any closer he would be shot. Reilly, reportedly intoxicated, pulled open his shirt, exposed his chest, and dared Ferguson to shoot. Ferguson sent one of his men out to persuade Reilly to leave. Reilly left but said he would be back to work on the ledge the next morning.

As promised, Tuesday morning found Reilly, along with O'Hara and the others, back at the Yosemite ledge. Ferguson had been waiting for them. From the Blackhawk's cabin, he and several of his men opened fire with Henry rifles. Their target was the feared gunman of the Yosemite group, Jack O'Hara. O'Hara was hit in the stomach, the side, and the hand and fell to the ground with his intestines protruding through a hole in his abdomen. Reilly and the others shot back and under the cover of their own fire

58. *Bodie Standard*, 28 August 1878.

carried O'Hara to a cabin at the Tioga mine. They summoned medical aid for the horribly wounded O'Hara, but Dr. J. L. Berry could do little for him other than amputate a finger that had been badly damaged by a bullet. O'Hara was not given much time to live, but he struggled on until one o'clock the next morning before he died.[59]

Neither Ferguson nor any of his men were arrested for the killing. An inspection of the ground indicated that the Yosemite ledge was just within the Blackhawk claim and that Reilly and the others were, therefore, claim jumpers. "The jumpers," said the *Bodie Standard*, "have been taught a lesson which it is hoped will not soon be forgotten. It is not a very pleasant affair when a man must hold his property with a Henry rifle and it is to be hoped that the prompt action of our citizens in this matter will cause it to be the last case of the kind in Bodie."[60] It was not.

Just a week later on the Tuesday night of 3 September 1878, John Enright and James Harrington began arguing over a mining claim as they stood at the bar in the Bank Exchange saloon.[61] Although Enright, a forty-six-year-old veteran of mining camps in Idaho, Nevada, and California, worked as a shotgun messenger, he was generally considered a quiet, inoffensive man. For the last several days, however, he had been drinking and drinking hard. Harrington had earlier warned him not to trespass on a certain piece of ground, but Enright now claimed that the ground was his and that he would go on it if he pleased. Hearing that, Harrington punched Enright in the face. Enright did not return the blow but said he would get his gun and settle the matter. Harrington pushed him out the saloon door, saying, "Now go get your gun. I'll be here."

About fifteen minutes later Enright returned. He walked into the saloon and yelled, "Where is that son of a bitch?" When he spotted Harrington, he pulled out a British Bulldog revolver and fired. Almost at the same time Harrington drew his own Bulldog and drilled Enright through the chest with the first shot, and the shoulder with the second. Enright dropped to the saloon floor and exclaimed, "I'm dead." Within seconds he was. Harrington looked at his victim and said, "It's done and I'm sorry for it. I had to do it to save my own life." Harrington was arrested and the next day appeared in justice court. The examination revealed that he had acted in self-defense, and he was discharged.[62]

Revolvers were resorted to again just before daylight on the Saturday morning of 5 April 1879 when two miners could not agree on the ownership of a claim.[63] A half dozen rounds were fired before one of the men was slightly wounded, and they considered the matter settled. A reporter who arrived on the scene said that the men, who refused to give their names, "appeared perfectly satisfied with the result." George Macartney and his partner, a miner named Hogan, found gunfire less than satisfying. They were working on their claim on the Saturday afternoon of 19 November 1881 when three rounds fired from a rifle whizzed past their ears. They immediately concluded to call it a day's work and quit. "It is uncomfortable to work," noted the *Bodie Standard*, "when bullets are flying in the air."[64]

59. *Bodie Standard*, 4 Sept. 1878.
60. *Bodie Standard*, 4 Sept. 1878.
61. *Bodie Standard*, 4 and 11 Sept. 1878.
62. *Bodie Standard*, 11 Sept. 1878.
63. *Bodie Morning News*, 5 April 1879.
64. *Bodie Standard*, 23 Nov. 1881.

The laws of the Bodie mining district decreed that on the first day of each new year claims that had not been worked sufficiently would become eligible for relocation. New locators occasionally had confrontations, and at least once a small war almost erupted. About midnight on the New Year's Eve Friday of 31 December 1880 a group of men attempted to relocate the Brooklyn Consolidated.[65] The men arrived at the mine only to find another group of relocators already there. The firstcomers were well entrenched. They were standing on a plank platform, which they had built over a plug of ice that had sealed off the mine shaft. The ice had formed about five feet below ground level, so the men could stand on the planks with only their heads and rifles showing. It was a nearly perfect redoubt. Words were exchanged between the two groups, then rifle fire. The latecomers were driven off but returned several times during the night, hoping to catch the entrenched relocators off guard. This game, with an occasional shot fired, continued the next night—Saturday—and also on Sunday night. The mining recorder of the Bodie district would not be out to inspect and register the relocators' claim until Monday morning.

On Sunday night the entrenched relocators found themselves faced with a new enemy, the cold. To keep from freezing to death, they removed the center planks of their platform and built a fire on top of the ice. The heat from the fire warmed the relocators but also began to melt the ice, faster than was expected. All of a sudden the men heard a terrifying crack, and the ice plug broke loose. They jumped onto the only two planks that they had driven into the walls of the shaft and watched the rest of the platform fall 175 feet to the bottom of the shaft. A few hours later the recorder arrived and registered their hard-fought-for relocation. The mine turned out to be a bust.

Men outnumbered women in Bodie by nine or ten to one. Competition for the few females available must have been fierce, yet there were only two shootings that were unquestionably the result of love triangles. The second of these (the first will be discussed later in connection with vigilantism) involved L. E. Tubbs, a well-known attorney from Benton, and William W. Barnes, one of the trans-Sierra country's leading newspaper publishers.[66] Tubbs and Barnes were friends, and Tubbs had reportedly loaned Barnes "considerable sums of money" to see his newspapers through difficult times. Tubbs was also friends with Mrs. Barnes, "a lady of education and refinement," the mother of five children, and the sister of C. N. Harris, one of Nevada's most prominent judges.[67] Barnes suspected that his wife, a lady of refinement or not, was romantically involved with Tubbs.

January of 1882 found Tubbs staying at the Mono House hotel in Bodie. On the Monday afternoon of the thirtieth, Barnes learned that his wife was also at the hotel. He grabbed his British Bulldog revolver, rushed up to Tubbs's room, and pounded on the locked door. None other than Mrs. Barnes opened it. The enraged husband stepped into the room and saw Tubbs, with his coat off, sitting on a bed. "I've got you!" exclaimed Barnes as he pointed his gun at Tubbs. Mrs. Barnes grabbed her husband's gun arm and held it long enough for Tubbs to throw a bear hug on him. The two men wrestled their way out of the room and into the hallway, with Tubbs hanging on to Barnes from behind

65.   *Daily Free Press,* 4 Jan. 1881.

66.   *Bodie Standard* and *Daily Free Press,* 1 Feb. 1882.

67.   *Bodie Standard,* 1 Feb. 1882; Myron Angel, ed., *History of Nevada,* facing p. 340.

and preventing him from turning around and shooting. But Barnes was a resourceful fighter. Although his arms were pinned to his sides and he was facing away from Tubbs, he managed to stick his gun between his legs and shoot Tubbs in the thigh. He then pulled his gun arm free and pointed the Bulldog over his shoulder directly at Tubbs's heart and fired again. The bullet shattered Tubbs's vestpocket watch but did Tubbs himself little damage. Tubbs cried that he had been shot and ran into the street.

Barnes did not give pursuit but instead surrendered himself to the authorities. He was lodged in jail and charged with assault with intent to commit murder.[68] Tubbs's leg wound proved superficial, and he was up and about the next day. In early March, Barnes was tried in superior court for the assault on Tubbs and found not guilty.[69]

Two shoot-outs occurred as the result of quarrels between families. One saw Mike Gilmore and his Green Street neighbor, identified only as "a Cornishman," exchange three or four shots in front of their houses. Although neither of them was hit, they retired from the field of battle "seemingly well pleased with their exercise and its effects."[70] The other shoot-out was the climax of a long-standing feud between the Murphy and Lester families, who lived next door to each other on Standard Avenue.[71] One Saturday afternoon, family heads John Murphy and James Lester met behind their houses and opened fire at each other with revolvers. Lester's first two shots missed their mark and so did Murphy's first. Murphy's second shot, however, hit Lester in the head and he fell to the ground. Murphy rushed toward his vanquished foe, and Lester slowly raised his revolver to fire again. Murphy told him to drop the gun or he would kill him. Lester dropped the gun. Murphy picked up the six-shooter and, now with a revolver in each hand, walked downtown and surrendered himself to Sheriff Andy Showers.

Miraculously, Lester's wound proved neither fatal nor even serious. The bullet had struck him near the temple on the right side of his head, penetrated under his scalp, and exited over his right ear without doing any serious damage. Murphy was examined in justice court and was discharged when it was decided that he had acted in self-defense.

One shooting was the result of a domestic quarrel. Frequent squabbles between Felix Cronyn, an "industrious" miner, and his wife, "a woman whose temper is almost certain to be bad," made the couple the object of neighborhood gossip on Standard Avenue.[72] On a summer morning in July of 1882 one of their squabbles turned violent. Although Mrs. Cronyn was not incapable of defending herself, her brother—Jerry Mahoney, who was living at the Cronyn house—rushed to her aid and punched Cronyn. Mahoney then grabbed a carving knife and chased Cronyn into a bedroom. Cronyn locked the bedroom door and pulled his Colt Navy revolver out of a trunk. When Mahoney started to kick in the door, Cronyn fired a shot through the bottom of the door in hopes of scaring him away. The bullet passed through Mahoney's left calf and lodged in his right leg. An artery was severed, and although he was bleeding profusely, Mahoney walked downtown to Dr. W. H. Rogers's office for treatment. Rogers applied a tourniquet to Mahoney's leg and had the wounded man taken to the county hospital. He was

68.   *Bodie Standard*, 1 Feb. 1882; Jail Register: Bodie Branch Jail, p. 32.

69.   *Bodie Standard*, 8 and 15 March 1882.

70.   *Bodie Standard*, 5 April 1882.

71.   *Bodie Standard*, 24 May 1882.

72.   *Bodie Standard*, 26 July 1882.

later reported to be recovering nicely. In the meantime Cronyn was arrested, not for the shooting—that was considered self-defense—but for battery on a complaint filed by his wife. The outcome of the case was not reported.

Numerous shootings, then, as well as several stabbings and almost nightly fistfights made Bodie a rough town. The free flow of whiskey, the discharging of guns in city streets, and the brandishing of firearms made it a rowdy town. Property disputes, arguments between neighbors, domestic quarrels, accidental discharges, and suicides accounted for nearly twenty shootings and shoot-outs in Bodie. In these incidents seven men were killed and another eight wounded. As high as these figures are, there was, as we shall see, another category of shootings and shoot-outs in Bodie that put even more men in the town cemetery and left even more wounded.

11

THE BADMEN
OF BODIE

The majority of Bodie's shootings and shoot-outs were not caused by disputes over mining claims or real estate, or by love triangles, domestic quarrels, and arguments between neighbors; they were the result of what might be called reckless bravado: a willingness to exchange gunfire over a careless remark, an insult, or a challenge to fighting ability. Reckless bravado—often encouraged by the consumption of alcohol—was demonstrated, not just by roughs or badmen, but also by generally law-abiding and hardworking miners, teamsters, carpenters, and wood-choppers, and an occasional attorney or businessman.

Still, the badman accounted for more than half of Bodie's shootings or gunfights caused by reckless bravado. The personal characteristics of the badman—characteristics shared to a large degree by many men on the mining frontier—invariably produced a violent reaction to an insult or a challenge. The badman was proud and confident, brave to the point of recklessness, and willing to fight to the death. He was usually young and single, and well traveled. He moved from one mining town to the next as each experienced its boom times. When he worked, if it was not as a professional gambler, it was usually as a gunman for a mining company, a police officer, a bartender, or a miner. He spent much of his time in saloons drinking and gambling, and there occurred most of his gunfights. He was always "heeled," or armed with a revolver. The piece was most often a Colt—the Lightning, or "self-cocker," as it was commonly called, was the preferred model. The badman normally carried his gun not in a holster but in a coat or hip pocket, or simply tucked into his waistband. He was always ready to use the weapon and he frequently did. His targets were mostly other badmen. The old, the weak, the female, and the innocent were generally left untouched. "There has never yet been an instance," said the *Daily Free Press* on 7 January 1880, "of the intentional killing of a man whose taking off was not a verification of the proverb that 'He that liveth by the sword shall perish by the sword.' "

Harry Dugan fit the profile of the badman well. He arrived in Bodie in 1878 and took a job behind the bar at Phillips and Moore's saloon on Main Street. He quickly won a reputation as an affable but tough bartender who was not afraid to trade blows with unruly patrons. The *Bodie Standard* called him "a man of good impulses, but reckless and quarrelsome when under the influence of whisky."[1]

1. *Bodie Standard*, 20 March 1880.

The Friday night of 17 January 1879 found Dugan tending bar at Phillips and Moore's as usual.[2] A dozen or more men, including John Muirhead, stood at the bar drinking. Muirhead was not in a good mood. Over the past year he had twice suffered terrible injuries in mining accidents. First his forearm was blown off in an explosion, and then, after being fitted with a hook prosthesis and returning to work, he slipped and fell eighty-five feet down a mine shaft.

Into the saloon walked a prostitute and a male companion. They ordered a round of drinks and asked a few acquaintances to join them. Without being invited, Muirhead pushed his way into the group and reached for a drink. The prostitute protested his presence and said she drank only with friends. Muirhead took offense and advanced toward the woman "with the evident intention of assaulting her." His advance was stopped short. Dugan clubbed him on the head with a revolver and sent the belligerent miner reeling through the saloon door. "I'll get even with you," growled Muirhead as he staggered away.

The incident had all but been forgotten when Muirhead returned to the saloon at about two o'clock in the morning and asked for the man who had struck him. Dugan responded immediately, "If you were struck in here, I'm the man that done it." Hearing that, Muirhead drew a revolver, aimed at Dugan, and opened fire. Two rounds narrowly missed the bartender, but several others were well wide of their mark. One of them tapped a barrel of ale and another knocked a cigar out of a bystander's mouth, leaving the frightened man clenching an inch-long stub between his teeth.

Dugan, meanwhile, drew his own revolver and returned the fire. One round grazed Muirhead's head and left the stump-armed miner with a scalp wound. Other rounds drove him out of the saloon and shattered the glass panes of the watering hole's front door. As Muirhead retreated down Main Street Dugan calmly walked over to the bystander who had had his cigar shot out of his mouth and gave him a new one. Dugan casually noted that the stub of the original was not long enough to relight.

Both Muirhead and Dugan were later arrested and charged with battery.[3] Dugan was examined by R. L. Peterson, justice of the peace, and was discharged when neither Muirhead nor any other witnesses appeared to testify against him. A few days later Justice Peterson examined Muirhead. Again, no witnesses appeared for the prosecution, not even Dugan or the cigar-smoking bystander, and Muirhead was discharged. Evidently, Muirhead and Dugan felt that the shoot-out had satisfactorily concluded their dispute.

Less than two months later, Harry Dugan was involved in a bloodier duel.[4] Late on the Friday night of 14 March 1879, a "friendly talk" between Dugan and Frank Black, a recent arrival from Virginia City, heated up. Both men drew their revolvers and opened fire. Several shots later, Black, closely pursued by Dugan, retreated into the Bonanza saloon. Once inside, said the *Bodie Standard*, "the belligerents emptied their pistols at each other with the rapidity of lightning at short range—firing some six shots—and then closed in on what seemed a death struggle for a few minutes."[5]

The men were finally separated by deputy constable Patrick Phelan. Dugan was

2. *Bodie Standard*, 18 Jan. 1879.

3. *Bodie Standard*, 18 and 25 Jan. 1879.

4. *Bodie Morning News*, 15 and 18 March 1879; *Bodie Standard*, 22 and 29 March 1879.

5. *Bodie Standard*, 22 March 1879.

found to have been shot through the upper chest, and Black through the arm and the leg. Jim Broderick, a bystander, had been hit in the back by a stray round. Dugan and Black were arrested and, because of their wounded conditions, were taken to their own lodgings. Dugan was spitting up blood—the round that had struck him had perforated one of his lungs—and his condition was considered critical. Black, although shot twice, was in no apparent danger. The bystander Broderick was in the best condition. The bullet that had hit him in the lower back had damaged nothing but flesh, and the wound was described as unimportant.

The night after the gunfight found the Bonanza saloon crowded with men. They were busy playing billiards, drinking, and discussing the shoot-out when suddenly the sound of gunfire rang out and smoke filled the air. The Bonanza patrons, many of whom had narrowly escaped being hit by stray bullets the night before, stampeded for the exit. "Some of them," said the *Bodie Standard*, "went so far and so fast they have not been heard from since."[6] When the smoke cleared, it was discovered that the loud bangs which had stampeded the men had actually been the sound of exploding Chinese cherry-bombs set off by a practical joker.

Black and Broderick made rapid recoveries from their wounds. So did Dugan, surprisingly enough. He, like Black, was "in close confinement in his room" awaiting an examination in justice court. But on the morning of 24 March, only ten days after he was shot, he slipped out of town.[7] Constable John Kirgan telegraphed a report of the escape to surrounding towns, but nothing was heard of Dugan until a year later when news reached Bodie that he had been shot through the stomach in a gunfight in Silver Cliff, Colorado. His chances for survival were reportedly slim. Assuming that he would soon be dead, the *Bodie Standard* said, on 20 March 1880, "It was a foregone conclusion that he would die 'with his boots on.' "

Billy Deegan was a Bodie rounder with a fearsome reputation. Powerfully built, he spent his days working in the Standard mine, and his nights drinking, gambling, and fighting in Bodie saloons. When drinking, he was, said the *Daily Free Press*, "one of the most desperate and dangerous characters in Bodie."[8] First arrested for assault during the spring of 1879, he was released on a writ of habeas corpus and soon renewed his saloon brawling.[9] His greatest rampage began on the Wednesday night of 15 December 1880 when he accidentally shot Adelia O'Neill, his landlady, with a Colt Lightning.[10] Her wound was minor and she refused to press charges. Deegan, meanwhile, walked downtown to the Bank Exchange saloon and " 'ginned up' to the point of frenzy." When Deegan seemed about to demolish the saloon, the bartender drew a gun and held him at bay until police officers Joe Farnsworth and James Monahan arrived. They led Deegan out of the Bank Exchange and up Main Street, and urged him to go home. He walked off, saying that he would kill the officers before morning.

Deegan got as far as the Comstock saloon. He stepped in and, with his hand on his Colt Lightning, threatened to "clean out" the establishment. He left without doing any damage and proceeded to Gunn's saloon. There he brandished his gun and

6.   *Bodie Standard*, 22 March 1879.

7.   *Bodie Standard*, 24 and 29 March 1879. Prisoners were afterward confined in jail even if wounded.

8.   Bodie *Daily Free Press*, 17 Dec. 1880.

9.   Records, A, District Court, Mono County, p. 423, 24 April 1879.

10.   *Daily Free Press*, 17 Dec. 1880; *Bodie Standard*, 22 Dec. 1880.

threatened to shoot the bartender. At one point he stuck the barrel of the Colt in his own mouth and said that he had "a notion to take one ball" himself. Officers Farnsworth and Monahan arrived, and while Monahan attempted to persuade the drunken Deegan to put his gun away Farnsworth rushed the wild brawler and wrestled him to the floor. The officers managed to subdue him only by beating him into unconsciousness.

Deegan was taken to jail, and a doctor dressed his police-inflicted head wounds. The next day, Deegan appeared before Justice Peterson on a charge of disturbing the peace. He pleaded guilty and was fined $25.[11]

Two months later Deegan was in trouble again. The Tuesday night of 22 February 1881 found Deegan, Dan Weir, Bill Cunningham, Pat Desmond, and Andy Donahue in the back room of the Snug saloon playing cards and drinking whiskey.[12] At about half-past eleven Deegan and Weir, an engineer at the Goodshaw mine, began arguing. Deegan pulled out his six-shooter and struck Weir in the face with it. Donahue, a game-legged man who was never without a heavy cane, came to Weir's aid and used the cane to club Deegan on the head. The blow knocked Deegan to the floor and left him stunned. Nevertheless, he managed to point his gun at Donahue, who was standing above him, and fire. Donahue was hit in the groin and he fell to the floor. Weir, meanwhile, drew a gun and fired at the prostrate Deegan.

At this point police officers Richard O'Malley and Jack Roberts came running into the room. Seeing Weir standing with a gun in his hand and Deegan and Donahue lying on the floor, O'Malley drew a revolver and, as he put it, "turned her loose." He fired two or three shots at Weir before calling it quits. Some of Weir's clothing was shot away, but Weir himself was left unscathed. The others were less fortunate. Donahue had been seriously wounded; Deegan had a minor wound; and Pat Desmond, who along with nearly everyone else in the saloon had run for the door when the shooting started, had had his earlobe blown away by a stray round.

Donahue was lifted from the pool of blood in which he lay and rushed to the hospital. Dr. Henry Robertson examined Donahue's wound. "Am I going to die?" asked Donahue. "Well, Andy, it is a rather bad wound. It may prove fatal and it may not," replied Robertson. "If I am going to die, I want to make the statement that Deegan shot me," said Donahue. He then described the entire fight, but evidently would have remained silent if he had been assured that he would live.

For the next several days Donahue hovered between life and death before his condition stabilized and he began to recover. Meanwhile, Billy Deegan had not been taken into custody. Said the *Daily Free Press* on 25 February, three days after the shootout:

> The officers displayed a great deal of stupidity on Tuesday night in allowing those engaged in the shooting in the Snug Saloon to escape from their clutches. They would have exercised some judgement if they had marched them to the lockup. As yet none of them have been taken in. It is said that a warrant has been issued for the arrest of Deegan, but Kirgan has not succeeded in finding him. It is remarkable with what vigilance our officers avoid arresting a man after he has committed a murderous act. There are a great many officers in town, more than can be counted on one hand, yet they are not up to business. If there is one reason more than another why an organization [of

11.   *Daily Free Press*, 18 Dec. 1880.

12.   *Daily Free Press*, 24 Feb. 1881.

vigilantes] . . . should exist in a community of this kind, it is to perform the duties which the officers and the so-called law neglects. There is a great deal in will power, and some officers can do more than others when they are so disposed.

Deegan was not interested in waiting around town to see if the police would eventually take action. Shortly after the shoot-out he left Bodie and in early April was reported in Tombstone, Arizona.[13] While there he was involved in several fights, one of them with police officer Bill Withrow, another former Bodieite.

A couple of years later Deegan returned to Bodie and gave the town, then in a precipitous decline, a final few thrills, including its last gunfight. On 30 July 1883, he was arrested on a charge of disturbing the peace for firing a gun on Main Street, and on 12 January 1884 he was arrested again on the same charge for a fight in the Temple saloon.[14] His adversary in the saloon brawl was none other than his old enemy Joe Farnsworth. Deegan had evidently made at least one new enemy since his return, however. At five o'clock on the morning of 18 March 1884, Deegan and Felix Donnelly met on Main Street and dueled at long range. Although they exchanged some nine shots, neither man was hit and, said the *Bodie Evening Miner* later that day, "not even a by-stander was killed."

Dave Bannon was a man who, in the vernacular of the day, had gone bad.[15] Having first tasted mining camp life in Gold Hill, Nevada, Bannon arrived in Bodie late in 1878 at the age of twenty-three. In Gold Hill Bannon had earned the reputation of "a quiet, industrious young man," and his first months in Bodie seemed to confirm that estimation of his character. He worked hard in the mines and did extra duty as a volunteer fireman. By late 1879, however, he found himself unemployed and began spending more and more time in saloons and loafing about with James Flannery, a gambler and a rough. Bannon's sister, "a very estimable person" who lived in Bodie also, evidently had little influence over her brother.

Associating with Flannery first got Bannon into trouble with the law in late January 1880.[16] He was with Flannery when the rough knocked Florentine Herrera senseless and allegedly attempted to rifle his pockets. Bannon was arrested along with Flannery for attempted robbery but was found innocent in a justice court examination. Herrera died a month after Flannery flattened him; his death, though, was said to be from natural causes.[17] By the end of March, Bannon was in trouble again. This time he and Flannery, along with a third rough, Mike Noonan, were arrested for, as the *Daily Free Press* put it, "thumping some of their fellow citizens."[18] More fights and disturbances followed, and by spring Bannon was well established as a town rough. Nevertheless, he continued to serve as a volunteer fireman and was regarded as one of the "best and most efficient" members of the Pioneer Hook and Ladder Company No. 1. There was no doubt that Bannon could do two things well—fight fires and fight.

13.   *Tombstone Epitaph*, 1 April 1881, as reprinted in the Bodie *Daily Free Press*, 7 April 1881, and the Bodie *Standard*, 13 April 1881.

14.   Bodie Justice Court Record, pp. 72–73, 126–29.

15.   *Daily Free Press*, 22 Jan. 1881.

16.   *Daily Free Press*, 20, 22, and 24 Jan. 1880.

17.   *Bodie Standard*, 17 Feb. 1880.

18.   *Daily Free Press*, 30 and 31 March 1880.

Deciding to capitalize on his fighting ability, Bannon met the heavyweight wrestling champion of Bodie, Rod McInnis, in a match for a purse of $200.[19] McInnis, employed as a miner at the Standard, was a skillful wrestler and an impressive physical specimen. At 180 pounds, he was hard and muscular. He was also quick and agile; he could spring off one leg and kick an object hanging eight or nine feet above the floor with the same leg.[20] With Con Driscoll, a veteran professional wrestler from San Francisco, as referee, and the Miners' Union Hall filled with spectators, the match began. The first fall went to McInnis, as was expected, but Bannon took the second. After a long struggle, McInnis won the third fall and the match. Nevertheless, Bannon had made a memorable debut in the ring.

In August Bannon was hired as a special officer to help maintain order at the Bodie heavyweight wrestling championship between Rod McInnis and Eugene Markey.[21] The sports of the town had bet heavily on Markey. When it became obvious that Markey was going to lose, they had Bannon and Robert Whitaker, another special officer, stage a fight.[22] The two officers drew their revolvers, waved them wildly about, and exchanged epithets. The crowd stampeded out of the Miners' Union Hall, and the match had to be called.

A month later Bannon was involved in a confrontation that ended in death.[23] He was one of those, as was James Flannery, with Manuel Castillo when the old Californio was shot and mortally wounded by John Rann in Wagner's saloon. Bannon was lucky on that occasion, for he could have been hit by Rann's wild shot as easily as Castillo.

Perhaps the incident had a sobering effect on Bannon. Shortly after Castillo's death, he found steady employment at the Standard mine and for the next four months did not miss a day's work. And a day's work was twelve hours, and the workweek was six days. But then, a few weeks into the new year, he went on a drunk and missed his shift at the mine. Just past two o'clock on the Friday afternoon of 21 January 1881, he reeled into the Dividend saloon.[24] Several friends of Bannon were in the saloon, including Ed Ryan, a professional gambler and Civil War veteran who had lived in the mining camps of the Far West since the end of the war. Bannon found Ryan leaning against the chop counter and drinking a whiskey cocktail in an effort to soothe a hangover.

Ryan, evidently in a playful gesture, grabbed the lapel of Bannon's coat. The lapel had previously been slightly torn and Ryan's grip now increased the rent. Bannon flew into a rage and punched Ryan in the face. Ryan reeled backwards into the chop counter, but he regained his balance and reminded Bannon that they were friends and claimed that there was no reason for the blow. "You damn son of a bitch," Bannon replied. "You've fooled with me long enough. You tore my coat once before." Bannon then punched Ryan again and pulled out a British Bulldog. Holding the gun in his right hand, Bannon threw several more blows at Ryan with his left.

Seeing the scuffle from the sidewalk in front of the Dividend, officer James

---

19. *Daily Free Press*, 21 May 1880.

20. *Bodie Standard*, 21 June 1880.

21. See p. 115.

22. Whitaker was killed a month later in the Comstock Saloon. See pp. 127–28.

23. See p. 141.

24. The *Daily Free Press* reported what followed, on 22, 25, 26, and 28 Jan. and 6 Feb. 1881.

Monahan rushed into the saloon and tried to pull Bannon away. With Bannon momentarily distracted, Ryan, who until now had been afraid to reach for a gun, pulled a sawed-off Colt revolver out of his back pocket. A moment later Bannon broke loose from Monahan, and now Bannon and Ryan, both with guns drawn, fell together in a desperate struggle. The fight continued for nearly a minute, with the men grappling, punching, and shooting. Finally, they separated and staggered off in opposite directions. Ryan fell against the swinging doors of the Dividend's entrance and tumbled onto the sidewalk. Blood dripped from a wound in his left hand and oozed from a hole in his side. Bannon stumbled through the swinging doors that led to the saloon's cardroom and dropped unconscious to the floor. A bullet hole in his lung and a round lodged in his neck caused blood to gush from his mouth and nose. His breath came in labored gasps. Fifteen minutes later he was dead.

Bannon's sister "became almost frantic with grief" when she learned what had happened. His friends, especially members of Bodie's volunteer fire department, were saddened but perhaps not shocked by his early demise. His body was displayed at Ward's mortuary on Saturday, and on Sunday his funeral was held. The procession began at his sister's house and, led by the Pioneer Hook and Ladder Company No. 1, wound its way to the graveyard. The volunteer firemen unanimously resolved that "our brother fireman David Bannon . . . was always prompt and fearless in the discharge of his duty, fearing no danger and shirking no responsibility."

Ryan, meanwhile, was clinging to life, just barely. One bullet had injured his hand, and another had perforated his left lung—missing his heart by a fraction of an inch—and had lodged underneath his shoulder blade. He was spitting up blood, was unable to swallow any food, and had difficulty breathing. Although he was in intense pain, he refused to take morphine or other pain-killers. He said several times that he did not want to be under the influence of a drug when death came. He drifted in and out of consciousness and hovered near death for several days before he slowly began to improve. By Tuesday afternoon he was fully conscious and coherent for the first time since the shoot-out on Friday. He said that he had been able to recognize the many friends that had come to see him but that everything else seemed like a dream. In his semiconscious state he had fancied that he had been shot by highwaymen during a stage robbery. Now he remembered the gunfight with Bannon clearly and asked about Bannon's condition. When informed that Bannon was dead, Ryan expressed great regret that he had been forced into the fight.

Ryan continued on the mend, heartened by a coroner jury's verdict that he had acted in self-defense, and strengthened by the removal of the bullet from underneath his shoulder blade. Fighting off pneumonia, he was hobbling about on crutches by the end of April.[25] He eventually made a full recovery and returned to his "sporting" ways. When Bodie declined, he drifted off and was last reported in Tuscarora, Nevada.[26]

Jesse Pierce was a Bodie gambler and notorious rough who supplemented his earnings at the tables by robbing stages. The Tuesday night of 30 March 1880 found Pierce drinking and dancing in the Miner's Exchange dance house on Main Street.[27] When the musicians took a break, Pierce sauntered over to the rear of the establishment

---

25. *Bodie Standard,* 27 April 1881.

26. *Daily Free Press,* 15 Feb. 1883.

27. *Daily Free Press,* 31 March 1880.

30. *Many a badman wound up buried in Bodie's graveyard. The large marble monument at the right was erected by Bodieites in the fall of 1881 in honor of the assassinated president James Garfield. High Peak and Bodie Bluff can be seen in the background and below them what remained of the town of Bodie in 1950. (Credit: California Historical Society)*

and leaned against a door which opened into prostitute Kittie Wells's room. Growing restless, Pierce yelled to the musicians, "Strike up a lively tune, and I'll show you how to dance."

Just then Kittie opened her door and pushed past Pierce to the dance floor. "Who are you shoving," remarked Pierce. "This is my door and my room, and I have a right to get out," responded Kittie. Pierce then called her what the *Daily Free Press* would only describe as a disagreeable name. When she told him to take it back, he repeated it, told her he was not afraid of her man, and threw her to the floor. Kittie's boyfriend, Sam Black, a police officer who had recently been discharged from the force for his alleged cooperation with garroters, rushed up and pulled Pierce away. Black began to help Kittie to her feet, but Pierce drew a .41 caliber Colt Lightning and shot him in the side. Officer Bill Withrow, on the scene in the dance house, disarmed him and marched him off to jail.

For several days Black hovered near death.[28] The bullet had entered his right side and ranged upward to the left side of his neck. He was bleeding internally, and the doctors gave him little hope of survival. But survive he did. With the loving care of Kittie, he was up and about in a few weeks.

Meanwhile, Pierce was charged with assault with intent to commit murder and formally indicted by the grand jury.[29] But he was freed on bail and managed to have his trial delayed until June 1881, when, on a motion by his attorney, he was discharged.[30] Even before Pierce was discharged, however, he was involved in another shooting. A short time after he shot Black, he shot and wounded miner Johnny Allen in front of the Dividend saloon.[31] This latter shooting was perhaps an obvious case of self-defense, because Pierce was not arrested.

Pierce's career as a badman was nearly at an end, however. Late in November 1881 he and two other men robbed the Bodie stage as it neared the mining town of Belleville.[32] A prostitute who was traveling on the stage recognized Pierce, and he was soon arrested. Eventually convicted for the robbery, he spent the next six years in the state penitentiary.

Patrick Carroll was never known to have declined an offer to fight. His fighting and brandishing of firearms got him arrested in Bodie more than once.[33] His attorney, Thomas P. Ryan, got him back out on the streets, and back into the mines. Carroll was a miner and a member of the Miners' Union.

As the Fourth of July 1880 approached, it appeared that the Miners' Union would not march in Bodie's annual Independence Day parade.[34] The grand marshal of the upcoming parade was a staunchly anti-union man, and the miners voted not to participate. Carroll had voted with the majority. But then the union, evidently caught up in the festive spirit of the holiday, decided to reconsider its decision. On the Sunday

---

28. *Daily Free Press*, 2 April 1880.

29. *Daily Free Press*, 17 July 1880; Calendar of Criminal Cases, Superior Court, Mono County, 15 July 1880.

30. Minute Book, Criminal, Dep't No. 2, Superior Court, Mono County, p. 69.

31. *Bodie Standard*, 30 March 1881.

32. See pp. 173–75.

33. *Daily Free Press*, 8 Jan. 1880.

34. *Bodie Chronicle*, 10 July 1880; *Bodie Standard*, 7 July 1880.

night of 4 July 1880 (the parade was scheduled for Monday the fifth) a special meeting was held in the Miners' Union Hall. The debate over participation was heated, and Carroll was said to have become "abusive and insulting" to those who favored marching in the parade. Finally, union president J. P. Shaughnessy had Carroll ejected from the hall. It took five men to do it.

Carroll ambled away from the union hall, then returned a short while later and attempted to gain entry. Several guards scuffled with him and pushed him away from the door and off the sidewalk into the street. This was finally too much for Carroll. He drew a Colt Dragoon and fired. At almost the same time, the guards drew their guns and fired. Carroll missed. Two of the guards, William Lemon and Eugene Godatt, did not. Carroll was hit by several rounds, and minutes later was dead. The next day the union marched in the parade while Carroll's body lay in a coffin at Kelly and Carder's mortuary. On Tuesday afternoon the union had Carroll buried, and a day later the coroner's jury determined that Lemon and Godatt had acted in self-defense. "Carroll is said to have been a bad man," noted the *Bodie Chronicle*, "and his sudden taking off is not regretted by those best acquainted with him."

Pat Shea and John Sloan were two roughs whose poor aim saved each other's lives.[35] Ill feeling had existed between the two men for several days when Shea walked into Magee's saloon early one Sunday morning and found Sloan, the bartender, counting the proceeds of the night's business. The roughs exchanged a few uncomplimentary words, and then Sloan leaped from behind the bar and took a swing at Shea. The blow missed, but Sloan did succeed in pushing Shea through the saloon door onto the sidewalk. Sloan then drew a gun and, from not more than a few feet away, fired twice without hitting Shea before the gun malfunctioned. Shea, meanwhile, drew a Colt Lightning and returned the fire. One round blew off Sloan's coat collar and two others missed Sloan entirely. Constable Kirgan arrested the gunfighters and then let them go on bail. They appeared in justice court two days later, pleaded guilty to disturbing the peace, and were fined $15 each. Both would be arrested again, Sloan for helping George Watkins shoot to death special officer Robert Whitaker, and Shea for striking prostitute Sailor Jack.[36]

Thomas Hamilton was another rough saved from an early demise by poor aim.[37] Early one Sunday evening he got into an argument with Thomas Keefe while the two were standing together on the sidewalk near Kingsley's livery stable. Keefe, a rough who had "acquired some notoriety by having a very remarkable head put on him on two or three occasions," drew a gun, pointed it at Hamilton, and fired. The bullet entered Hamilton's coat on the left side, passed through his vest and shirt, grazed his stomach, and buried itself in the lining of his coat on the right side. This was Hamilton's second narrow escape. A year before, he had been shot in the neck, but not seriously wounded, during a gun battle between the Owyhee and Jupiter mining companies.[38]

There was often little difference between Bodie's badmen and Bodie's lawmen. Several roughs served as deputy constables, or police officers, as they were more commonly called. "An exchange says," noted the *Daily Free Press* on 3 December 1879, "that the police force here is made up almost exclusively of hard cases." Officers occa-

35.   *Daily Free Press* and *Bodie Standard*, 1 Dec. 1879.

36.   See pp. 127, 155.

37.   *Daily Free Press*, 26 Oct. 1880.

38.   See p. 230.

sionally had to be dismissed from the force for misconduct. In one instance, three officers were dismissed when they were alleged to have cooperated with muggers.[39] Considering the character of Bodie's officers, it is surprising that, with the exception of those officers involved in stopping the Sam Sing and Yung Wah tong battle, only five of them were ever involved in shootings and only one fired his gun while on duty. All these instances of officer-involved gunplay seem to have been caused by reckless bravado.

All Bodie police officers carried revolvers, although most of the time they used them as clubs rather than firearms. A deputy constable, Richard O'Malley, was an exception. Besides shooting at Dan Weir during the brawl between Billy Deegan and Andy Donahue in the Snug saloon, O'Malley was a participant in Bodie's most classic gunfight.

The early morning hours of Thursday, 15 July 1880, found O'Malley and fellow officer James Monahan out patrolling Bodie's streets.[40] While the officers were checking Boone and Wright's general store at the corner of Main and Green, Bob Watson and George Center happened by. Center, a young miner who worked at the hoisting works on Bodie bluff, was "quiet when sober," noted the *Daily Free Press*, "but when full of liquor he is a sweeping whirlwind on the down hill grade." He was now "comparatively full" and armed with two Colt Lightnings.

Watson stopped to talk to the officers, but when Center turned up Green Street, O'Malley decided he had better follow him. Near the intersection of Green and Wood streets, Center took it on his own to greet the break of day with a two-gun salute. O'Malley caught up with Center and found him standing in the street with his hands in the pockets of his overcoat. "You've been shooting. Give me your pistols," demanded O'Malley. Center pulled his hands out of his overcoat pockets. Each hand held a Colt. "No son of a bitch will take my pistols," he exclaimed.

O'Malley made a move for Center, and the inebriated miner aimed the revolvers at him. Looking into the muzzles of the guns, O'Malley slowly backed away. When he was some fifteen feet from Center, O'Malley went for his own Colt Lightning. Center opened fire, but his drunken aim was wild. One bullet ripped through O'Malley's coat, another ricocheted off his gun, and six others missed entirely. O'Malley was a bit more accurate. One of the five rounds that he fired hit Center in the leg and another struck him in the hand. "As things go lately," said the *Daily Free Press*, "it was rather poor shooting. But perhaps it is better as it is. The officer is of the opinion that it was red-hot as long as it lasted, and Center shares the same opinion."

Center was carried to jail, where a physician dressed his wounds. The gunfighting miner was charged with nothing more than disturbing the peace and released. There were those who thought Center was perfectly justified in shooting at O'Malley. "The question now agitating the public mind is: What right had the officer to demand Center's pistol?" said the *Bodie Chronicle*. "There is no law in this State against carrying concealed weapons, and as we have no town incorporation and town ordinances to prevent the discharge of firearms within town limits, it strikes us that there is no authority vested in any one to compel a citizen to give up his arms, unless he has committed a felony. Officers should be sure that they have the law on their side before acting."

Eugene Markey, a six-foot-two rough weighing 240 pounds, held a remarkable number of responsible positions in Bodie. During 1879 he was fire warden and chief engineer of the volunteer fire department, quarter-master sergeant of Bodie's national

39. *Daily Free Press*, 19 Feb. and 20 and 21 March 1880; *Bodie Standard*, 28 Jan. 1880.

40. *Bodie Standard*, 15 July 1880; *Daily Free Press*, 16 July 1880; *Bodie Chronicle*, 17 July 1880.

guard company, and a police officer.[41] In this latter capacity he twice disarmed men with drawn revolvers and once took a knife away from a wild drunk who had slashed one man and was about to attack others.[42]

Markey was known to go on a drunken spree occasionally. Late in October 1879 he went on one that lasted nearly three days and ended with his shooting up the Senate saloon.[43] One of his bullets penetrated the saloon wall and just missed the head of the bartender in the saloon next door. When another officer arrived and asked about the shooting, Markey explained that he had only been having "a little fun." Markey was not arrested, but he did remain out of sight for the next day or two; one report said he had left town. Markey was soon back patrolling Bodie's streets and was one of the arresting officers at the scene of the Thomas Travis killing early in January 1880.[44] Shortly afterward, however, Constable John Kirgan dismissed Markey from the force for his rumored cooperation with garroters.[45]

Markey's famous wrestling match with Rod McInnis occurred in August 1880. Three months later, Markey made news in Bodie for the last time when he got into a gunfight with Dick Prentice, "one of the bad men of the Comstock." The shoot-out left Prentice wounded in two places and Markey untouched. "The friends of Eugene Markey," said the *Daily Free Press* on 5 November, "never suspected that he had any considerable nerve or would fight when a bluff was made. But this recent difficulty with Dick Prentice . . . demonstrated that he would stand up when the proper time came."

William Withrow did not begin his career in Bodie as a police officer, but he ended it in that capacity. Withrow arrived in town late in 1877 and for a time operated a saloon on Main Street with T. H. Moore. Withrow first made a name for himself during February 1878 when, serving as a special deputy, he tracked down "Little Dan," a Mexican jewelry thief.[46] A few months later he and a number of other Bodie businessmen joined forces to build a horse-racing track on the flat south of town. By the end of 1878 he had left the saloon business and had gone to work for Wells, Fargo & Company as a shotgun messenger.

The life of a shotgun messenger perhaps did not agree with Withrow. He gradually grew ever more ill-tempered and began feuding with various individuals, particularly Charles Slade. Slade had come west in the mid-1860s and had made a living as a professional gambler. He had a large number of friends among the "sporting fraternity" in the mining towns of the Far West, and the *Daily Free Press* called him "a genteel, good-natured man when sober."[47] He had not been in Bodie long, however, when, in January 1879, he was shot by Burns Buchanan.[48] Slade recovered quickly from the

---

41. *Bodie Morning News*, 21 and 29 August and 25 Oct. 1879.

42. *Bodie Morning News*, 18 July and 14 August 1879.

43. *Bodie Morning News*, 25 Oct. 1879.

44. See p. 189.

45. *Bodie Standard*, 28 Jan. 1880; Bodie *Daily Free Press*, 19 Feb. and 20 and 21 March 1880.

46. See p. 146.

47. *Daily Free Press*, 3 Feb. 1880.

48. *Bodie Standard*, 18 Jan. 1879; *Bodie Morning News*, 20 May 1879. Buchanan was arrested and charged with assault with a deadly weapon. He was set free on a $1,000 bond to await action of the grand jury. In May the jury declined to indict him, and the charge against him was dismissed.

wound and had no further difficulties with Buchanan. Then Withrow began feuding with Slade.

The cause of the feud was known only to the close friends of Withrow and Slade. Slade's friends repeatedly warned him to stay away from Withrow and let the troubles die out; Slade nevertheless agreed to meet with Withrow to settle their differences. The Saturday night of 31 January 1880 found the two men in deep discussion in the faro room of the Comstock saloon.[49] The discussion grew heated, but friends managed to keep the two separated. Near midnight Withrow got up from the table where they were seated and remarked as he left, "Keep away from me now, or I'll give you the gun."

Slade disregarded the warning and followed Withrow to the door of the faro room. Withrow turned, pushed a gun into Slade's stomach, and fired. Slade staggered back to the middle of the faro room, stood there perfectly straight and quiet for a moment, then cried, "He shot me" and keeled over. Withrow walked out of the saloon and disappeared down the street.

Medical aid was summoned but little could be done for Slade. By early morning the thirty-four-year-old gambler was dead. A telegram related the tragedy to his mother, a resident of Carlisle, Illinois. She replied with the simple request that her son be buried in Bodie. The poor woman had lost her husband, Slade's father, only a short while before when he was shot to death in Missouri.

Just prior to Slade's Tuesday afternoon funeral, the coroner's jury rendered its verdict: Charles Slade came to his death at the hands of William Withrow. But Withrow was nowhere to be found and had not been seen since the shooting on Saturday night. Police officers searched Bodie's side streets and deserted cabins but found no clue to his whereabouts. "It seems strange," said the *Daily Free Press* on Tuesday, "that a man can shoot another in the rear part of a room crowded with people, and deliberately walk out and down the street unmolested. It is supposed that he remained in town over night, and left early in the morning. . . . Some think he is still in town, but this is hardly probable. Withrow, among his own class, was considered a good-hearted fellow, generous in money matters, and ever willing to help a man who was out of means. For the past six months he has grown rather ill-natured, and has lost much of his accustomed good nature." Slade would have agreed.

On Thursday a letter arrived from Bishop stating that Withrow had been seen there on Monday.[50] The correspondent was a former resident of Bodie, and the *Daily Free Press* thought the information reliable. If it were, Withrow was probably long gone. But two days later, on Saturday, a Bodie deputy sheriff walked into Justice Peterson's courtroom with Withrow in tow.[51] The deputy said he found Withrow walking down the street. Withrow claimed he had not left town and had been ready to be taken into custody at any time.

Then another surprise rocked Bodie. When Withrow was examined in justice court, no witnesses could be found to testify that they had actually seen Withrow shoot Slade. Even Slade did not implicate Withrow. According to the district attorney, who

49. *Daily Free Press,* 1 and 3 Feb. 1880.
50. *Daily Free Press,* 6 Feb. 1880.
51. *Daily Free Press,* 8 Feb. 1880.

was present when Slade died, the gambler only said, "We had a quarrel and he shot me." Slade left the "he" unidentified. Justice Peterson could do nothing more than release Withrow. "Under ordinary circumstances," noted the *Daily Free Press*, "he would have been held, and he is remarkably fortunate in being discharged without even a trial." But the *Bodie Standard* took an opposite point of view when it noted that Withrow was "warmly congratulated by a host of friends, of all classes, upon his discharge from such an ugly accusation."[52]

Bill Withrow, as if being rewarded for fatally shooting Charles Slade and for being released without trial, was now hired as a Bodie police officer. He seems to have done a satisfactory job and was responsible for disarming and arresting Jesse Pierce after Pierce shot Sam Black. Withrow stayed in Bodie until the summer and then left for Arizona.[53] He eventually reached Tombstone, where he found work as a police officer.[54]

Officer Jack Roberts worked the night patrol regularly. He was not known to be trigger happy, and he effected most of his arrests with a minimum of violence. One Bodieite called him "a thoroughly reliable officer and a pleasant, kindly man."[55] Nevertheless, he made at least one serious enemy, Jack Myers. Roberts had known Myers, a tall, thin, blond-haired and blond-mustached rounder, first in Virginia City and later in Bodie. The men were bitter enemies.

The Saturday night of 28 May 1881 found Roberts and a couple of his friends drinking at the bar of the Comstock saloon.[56] Just at midnight, in walked Myers. Unaware of Roberts's presence, Myers headed toward the end of the bar. He never got there. Roberts drew a revolver and blasted him back against the saloon's swinging doors. Hit by four bullets, Myers was still able to draw a gun and fire one wild shot before he fell to the floor. "Oh, my God!" he cried. Within seconds he was dead.

Frank Viles, a deputy constable, arrested Roberts and took him to jail, where he was charged with murder and locked in a cell.[57] The next day the coroner's jury held an inquest. There was no difficulty in establishing that Roberts killed Myers, for Roberts had already admitted as much. But several witnesses testified that a day or two before the shooting they had heard Myers threaten to kill Roberts.

On Wednesday evening Roberts was examined by Justice A. M. Phlegar.[58] Again, witnesses testified that Myers had threatened to kill Roberts. Phlegar decided that Roberts's actions were justified and had the officer discharged. The people of Bodie, said the *Daily Free Press*, are "satisfied Roberts did about as most men would do under the circumstances." Another supporter of Roberts later claimed that Myers was planning to rob the Mono Bank and that killing Roberts was part of the plan. "He dogged Roberts," said the man, "until the latter thought it was time to put a stop to the business. Roberts was justified in shooting Myers like a dog, and the people upheld him."[59] So did

52. *Bodie Standard*, 7 Feb. 1880.

53. *Bodie Standard*, 13 April 1881.

54. *Tombstone Epitaph*, 1 April 1881, as reprinted in the Bodie *Daily Free Press*, 7 April 1881, and the Bodie *Standard*, 13 April 1881.

55. *Bodie Standard*, 22 June 1881.

56. *Daily Free Press*, 29 May 1881.

57. Jail Register: Bodie Branch Jail, p. 26, 29 May 1881.

58. *Daily Free Press*, 3 June 1881; *Bodie Standard*, 8 June 1881.

59. *Bodie Standard*, 22 June 1881.

Bodie's lawmen. Roberts stayed on the police force and continued working the night patrol until Bodie's boom days were over.[60]

Frank Viles served as a police officer in Bodie during 1881 and 1882. He seems to have maintained a rather low profile until he incurred the wrath of Ed Loose, a Bodie pioneer who had arrived in town in 1876. The two men had been feuding for several days when, late on the Saturday night of 8 April 1882, Loose and several friends found Viles in the cardroom of the Standard dance house.[61] Loose, six feet and two hundred pounds, made a charge for Viles and threw several punches before the men were separated. The friends of Loose then dragged him off to the Occidental Hotel and told him to call it a night.

Instead, Loose stole out of the hotel and returned to the Standard. Viles was standing at the end of the bar. When the two men spotted each other, they drew their guns and closed for action. Before they collided, Loose got off a shot that missed. Then as they fell to the floor fighting, Viles fired. The round struck Loose in the side and exited through his back. He was really through for the night this time.

Loose was helped back to the hotel, and Dr. W. H. Rogers treated the wound. The next day Loose was moved to his brother's house and was said to be in "a very comfortable condition." He recovered quickly and resumed a mining career that lasted into the twentieth century. Viles was not held for the shooting and remained on the police force. He was last mentioned in August 1882 when he arrested a man for firing off a shotgun from the rear door of a saloon.[62]

As can be seen from the actions of George Center and Ed Loose, reckless bravado was certainly not confined to badmen or police officers. Numerous times the men participating in shootings and shoot-outs were simply average workingmen: miners, teamsters, mechanics, carpenters, woodchoppers. These men spent most of their waking hours working at their jobs. Yet they too went about armed, spent many leisure hours in saloons, and were ready to fight to the death for a challenge to their bravery or even for a slight offense. The distinction between badman and average citizen often blurred.

Consumption of alcohol was frequently a factor—the predominant factor on several occasions—in the gunfights that involved average Bodieites. The fighting parties usually had been drinking, and it seems likely that fights would have been considerably less frequent had alcohol not been available. The men themselves often blamed liquor for a fight. If the intoxicated fighters were friends, they routinely refused to cooperate with authorities, preferring instead, even if wounded, to simply let the matter drop.

John T. O'Connor followed such a course of action.[63] Late one night O'Connor and two of his friends, Mooney and Maguire, were involved in such a boisterous argument in the Bank Exchange saloon that the bartender asked them to leave. While they were continuing the argument on the sidewalk in front of the saloon, a shot rang out. O'Connor slumped to the ground with a bullet in his chest. Officer Eugene Markey, standing a short distance away, rushed to the scene and arrested Mooney and Maguire. But the wounded O'Connor would not identify the shooter and blamed no one "but the

60. *Bodie Standard*, 22 Feb. and 10 May 1882.

61. *Daily Free Press*, 11 April 1882; *Bodie Standard*, 12 April 1882.

62. *Bodie Standard*, 2 Aug. 1882.

63. *Bodie Standard*, 1, 27, and 29 August 1879; *Bodie Morning News*, 2 August 1879.

curse of too much whisky."[64] O'Connor survived and later went to San Francisco to have the bullet removed.

On another occasion, John Ryan shot a carpenter named Kelly in a drunken row at Clearwater Station on the road to Bridgeport.[65] Kelly, though seriously wounded, recovered rapidly and evidently made no attempt to have Ryan prosecuted. Similarly, Maurice McCormick shot a man named Cassidy during a drunken brawl in the Shamrock saloon.[66] The bullet entered Cassidy's jaw and lodged in the back of his neck. Perhaps because of its small caliber, the bullet seems to have done little serious damage. McCormick was arrested and two days later was examined in justice court. Cassidy did not appear in court to testify, and police officers were unable to locate him. Three men who had witnessed the shooting were in court, but each "displayed a remarkable lack of knowledge" when it came his turn to testify. McCormick was promptly discharged.

Witnesses proved equally uncooperative following a shoot-out in the middle of Main Street.[67] The two men involved in the gunfight began their dispute while drinking in a saloon. They first exchanged blows and then fought their way into the street and exchanged shots. Although a reporter from the *Bodie Morning News* found "some two or three hundred men" at the scene, no one seemingly could identify the gunfighters.

A man who was shot at during a drunken argument in a Main Street saloon perhaps best expressed the attitude of Bodieites toward drinking, gunfighting, and friendship. When asked why he refused to identify the shooter, he said, "Oh, he's a friend of mine, and I don't want to have him arrested. You see he is drunk and don't know what he is doing. He's a first rate fellow when he's sober but he'd shoot his best friend when he's drunk."[68]

Even if friendship encouraged those shot at to forgive and forget and prevented them from testifying against a shooter, flying bullets were still dangerous. Innocent bystanders were often lucky to escape unscathed. When Harry Butts fired a shot at a man named Galvin during an argument in the Magnolia saloon, the bullet traveled through the saloon's main room, perforated a pane of glass in the front door, and carried into the street without touching a soul. Noting that it was fortunate indeed that no innocent party was killed, the *Bodie Morning News* proffered an alternative to wild saloon shootings. "It would be better were the old practice of duelling revived," the newspaper urged, "as then the parties in interest would take the open field and the result would be fatal only to themselves, and outsiders might be spared."[69]

A fight in a Bonanza Street brothel demonstrated that there were reasons other than friendship for refusing to testify against a shooter.[70] The affray began when Charles Price, a man who did "Chinese work" at the brothel, took offense at a remark made by a brothel customer. The customer, identified only as a man "very respectably connected in Virginia City and Sacramento," had accused Price of trying to "ring in" on food and

64. *Bodie Standard*, 1 August 1882.

65. *Bodie Standard*, 10 July 1878.

66. *Bodie Standard*, 16 Oct. 1878.

67. *Bodie Morning News*, 8 July 1879.

68. *Bodie Standard*, 8 June 1880.

69. *Bodie Morning News*, 25 April 1879.

70. Bodie *Daily Free Press*, 1 April 1881; *Bodie Standard*, 6 April 1881; Jail Register: Bodie Branch Jail, 30 March 1881.

refreshments meant for the customer's favorite prostitutes. In an attempt to soothe Price's hurt feelings, one of the prostitutes gave him a piece of pie. Price took the pie, threw it against a wall, and said, "I can whip any son of a bitch in the house."

The customer responded to the challenge. He grabbed a wine bottle and broke it over Price's head, splitting the janitor's scalp wide open. Price was undeterred. He laid hold of the customer and together they tumbled onto a sofa. While they were grappling and punching, Price managed to draw a gun and fire. The round drilled a hole through the left thigh of the customer but did not take the fight out of him. He wrested the gun away from Price and shot him in the arm. The bullet broke Price's radius.

The fighters separated, and the customer ordered Price out of the brothel and gave him a kick to help him on his way. When deputy constable Frank Milburn heard of the affray, he went in search of Price. Two hours later he found him. "Price refused to be arrested and showed fight," said the *Daily Free Press*, "but the officer sprang at him, overpowered him and took him to jail." Price was charged with assault with a deadly weapon, but, when brought up before justice court a few days later, he was promptly discharged. The "very respectably connected" customer, evidently fearing publicity, did not appear in court to testify.

The cases of Scott Westside, Peter Savage, and Sammy Oulette demonstrated that even when the victim of a shooting testified, the shooter was usually discharged from custody following an examination in justice court. Scott Westside lived with his mother in a house on the south side of Bodie.[71] One summer evening Mike McCann, "somewhat under the influence of liquor," paid the Westsides a visit. A woman neighbor of the Westsides was also visiting. After a few rounds of drinks, she remarked that her husband seldom if ever drank strong liquor. The comment ignited McCann. He called her a damned liar and said he had drunk with her husband many times. Westside remonstrated with McCann and told him he had better go home. "I will go home when I damn well please," responded McCann.

Westside grabbed McCann and tried to throw him out of the house. But being much the stronger of the two, McCann soon had Westside pinned to the floor. Westside pulled a hand free, however, drew a derringer, and fired. The bullet hit McCann in the left side, glanced off a rib, and exited a few inches from where it had entered. The wound convinced McCann to call it a night. Shortly after the shooting, Westside was arrested, charged with attempted murder, and lodged in jail. A friend quickly bailed him out. Two days later Westside was examined in justice court and discharged.

Early one June evening French Canadian Peter Savage came upon his wife and a fellow countryman, "Frenchy" Mace, arguing in Mace's store.[72] Savage waited only long enough to hear his wife's version of the argument before drawing a gun and opening fire. One round struck Mace in the lower back, another grazed his chest, and a third missed him entirely. Though wounded, Mace never lost his composure. When a reporter from the *Daily Free Press* arrived on the scene, he found that "the coolest man in the crowd appeared to be a Frenchman, who was covered with blood, but who was moving around in the most unconcerned manner."[73]

71. *Daily Free Press*, 10 and 12 August 1881; *Bodie Standard*, 17 August 1881; Jail Register: Bodie Branch Jail, p. 28, 8 August 1881.

72. *Daily Free Press*, 10 and 22 June 1880; *Bodie Chronicle*, 12 June 1880; *Bodie Standard*, 10 and 11 June 1880.

73. *Daily Free Press*, 10 June 1880.

Savage was arrested and lodged in jail. It looked as if he could be in serious trouble, especially when a rumor spread that Mace was partially paralyzed and not expected to live. Savage made the right move and retained defense counsel Patrick Reddy. A week later Savage appeared before Justice Peterson. The examination was long and thorough and saw several witnesses take the stand. At its conclusion Savage was, noted the *Daily Free Press*, "acquitted of all blame in the matter. From the testimony it was evident Savage was in the right, and the discharge of the prisoner met with general approval."[74]

Sammy Oulette came to the defense of his mother.[75] Mrs. Oulette owned a small saloon next door to the Virginia restaurant on Main Street. One night she got into an argument with a drunken man named Graham, who claimed she had robbed him of a twenty-dollar gold piece after he had passed out. Holding a beer mug in one hand and brandishing a revolver in the other, he called her a thief and, according to Mrs. Oulette, fired a shot at her. Graham denied firing the shot. Whether inflamed by the name calling or returning the fire, Sammy Oulette took a shot at Graham. The bullet glanced off Graham's head and left him with a scalp wound and a severe concussion. Officer Patrick Phelan arrested young Oulette later that night, but when the case came up before Justice Peterson, the boy was discharged.

Justice Peterson, who later became a deputy district attorney for Mono County, routinely discharged defendants in shooting cases if the shooting occurred during a fight or a threat of a fight and little or no harm was done. Only occasionally did he bind over defendants for trial in a higher court. Peterson may have been the most lenient of Bodie's justices because he himself carried a gun and was not averse to using it. On one occasion he took a shot at a man during a dispute in the Temple saloon. The bullet lodged harmlessly in the arch above the saloon's swinging doors.[76]

In only one instance in which a man was wounded in a shooting caused by reckless bravado did the case go to a higher court. The trouble that led to the shooting began about two o'clock on the morning of the Fourth of July 1882 when Sam Howarth, a "well-known" carpenter, and James Leonard met in the Parole saloon.[77] They exchanged a few heated words and then Leonard remarked, "I am not your equal physically." "I will give you any kind of a game you want," replied Howarth.

Bartender Tom Woodruff jumped between the men and tried to restrain them, but Howarth drew a gun, reached over Woodruff's shoulder, and shot Leonard in the face. The bullet struck Leonard just under his left eye and lodged in the back of his head. With blood running out of his left ear, Leonard was taken to his room, and doctors were rushed to his bedside. It seemed certain he would die.

Leonard struggled against death day after day. A week after the shooting, doctors W. H. Rogers and D. Walker located the bullet and extracted it through Leonard's left ear. "The operation," noted the *Daily Free Press*, "was performed without the use of chloroform or ether, after which the patient was very much prostrated."[78] Although

74. *Daily Free Press*, 22 June 1880.

75. *Bodie Standard*, 11 Dec. 1878.

76. *Daily Free Press*, 29 Oct. 1882.

77. *Daily Free Press*, 6, 12, 18, 21, 25, and 26 July, 10 August, and 6 Dec. 1882; *Bodie Standard*, 12, 19, and 26 July, and 2 August 1882.

78. *Daily Free Press*, 18 July 1882; see also the *Bodie Standard*, 19 July 1882.

Leonard's hearing in his left ear was destroyed, the operation was otherwise a success, and a few weeks later he was up and about.

Sam Howarth, meanwhile, was arrested shortly after the shooting, charged with assault with intent to commit murder, and lodged in jail.[79] It was the second time that he had been in jail in a little more than a week. On 26 May he had been jailed for disturbing the peace.[80] On that occasion he had spent only a few hours behind bars. Now he languished in jail for two weeks before he was examined by Justice Phlegar. The justice bound Howarth over for trial in superior court and set his bail at $1,500. He was released from custody when his attorney, Patrick Reddy, furnished the money. Reddy managed to have the trial delayed until early December. Then Reddy pleaded that his client had acted in self-defense. The key defense witness, R. M. Aldridge, testified that immediately before the shooting, when Howarth and Leonard were quarreling, Leonard had his right hand on the pocket of his coat "in a threatening attitude." The jury deliberated only half an hour before returning a verdict of not guilty.[81]

Only once was a Bodieite shot and wounded by an unknown assailant.[82] William McLaughlin, a woodchopper and Bodie rounder of long standing, had made at least one serious enemy during his saloon sprees. On a December evening in 1878 he was standing in the doorway of his cabin on a ranch outside of town when the roar of a shotgun blast came from behind a nearby tree. A load of buckshot ripped into his side and left him wounded seriously.

McLaughlin had not seen the gunman, but a man named Thompson, who evidently had had some trouble with McLaughlin earlier, was arrested, charged with the shooting, and then released on his own recognizance. Apparently, the authorities could produce no evidence against him, because he was not subsequently prosecuted. McLaughlin, meanwhile, was nursed back to health by Joe Hunt and his wife, the keepers of Mormon Station on the Bodie road to Bridgeport. McLaughlin was soon back chopping wood and, during his leisure hours, drinking in Bodie's saloons. A year after being shot, he made news again when he got into a fight with a bartender in a Main Street saloon. He lost and, with the bartender's help, landed on the sidewalk in front of the saloon "as if he weighed a ton."[83]

Bill McLaughlin was lucky to have survived the shotgun blast. Equally lucky were James Leonard, Mike McCann, and all the other Bodieites who had suffered only wounds or who had narrow escapes to talk about as a result of shootings or gunfights. Seven Bodieites—not counting those badmen already discussed—had no such luck. Reckless bravado for them meant death.

On the cold winter night of 15 January 1878, James Blair and John Braslin met in the street in front of the Standard Hotel and startled boarders with a six-shooter duel.[84] Although Blair was shot through the left arm on the first exchange, he continued firing and hit Braslin several times. Braslin, known as U.P. (for Union Pacific) Jack, died almost immediately. He was thirty years old. Blair did not have long to savor his

79. Jail Register: Bodie Branch Jail, p. 41, 4 July 1882.

80. Jail Register, p. 39, 26 May 1882.

81. Minute Book, Criminal, Dep't No. 2, Superior Court, Mono County, pp. 130–31, 144–46, 149–50.

82. *Bodie Standard*, 11 Dec. 1878; *Bodie Chronicle*, 21 Dec. 1878.

83. *Daily Free Press*, 24 Dec. 1879.

84. *Bodie Standard*, 23 Jan. and 13 Feb. 1878.

victory. Surgery was performed on his wounded arm, and part of the humerus was removed. The operation was deemed a success, but while recuperating the twenty-eight-year-old Blair caught pneumonia and died. It was the only time that both parties to a gunfight died as a result of the shoot-out.

The early morning hours of Thursday, 13 June 1878, found Patrick Gallagher's Shamrock saloon crowded with men.[85] Some stood at the bar drinking Irish whiskey, others were at the chop counter eating fried steaks, while several huddled around the gambling tables playing faro. Alex Nixon, the popular and powerfully built thirty-one-year-old, Irish-born president of the Bodie Miners' Union, treated the men at the bar to a round of drinks. When they had finished, Tom McDonald offered to buy the next round. But he found himself out of pocket change and asked the bartender, T. C. O'Brien, to lend him a dollar. Nixon objected and handed McDonald the dollar himself. The action offended McDonald. Heated words were exchanged, and then, when McDonald said he was the better man, Nixon unleashed a vicious blow that caught McDonald under the right eye and sent him tumbling to the floor.

Terrence Brodigan, a deputy constable and the son of one of the discoverers of Bodie's gold, grabbed Nixon from behind and tried to restrain him. The union president wheeled about and said, "Do you want any of it? Don't throw your hand behind you, for I am heeled. But I don't want any trouble with you for you are a constable." By now McDonald had gotten to his feet and was leaning against the bar. He said to Nixon, "It's pretty hard for a man to be knocked down, get a black eye and cut face for nothing." "You're a son of a bitch for letting me do it, even if I do weigh twenty pounds more than you," replied Nixon.

The dark-complexioned, thirty-five-year-old McDonald was over six feet tall and no small man himself. Nevertheless, he stepped back, drew a revolver, and asked Nixon, "Will you give me even chances?" "Yes, by God," answered Nixon.

O'Brien, now out from behind the bar, seized McDonald by the arm, and officer Brodigan caught hold of Nixon. But Nixon struggled free and drew a revolver from his hip pocket. At the same time McDonald pulled his arm out of O'Brien's grasp. Both men opened fire. Nixon's first shot missed McDonald by inches, but McDonald's hit Nixon in the side. "My God, boys, I'm shot. Run for a doctor," exclaimed the big miner as he staggered back and fell to the floor. As he lay there with blood running out of a hole in his side, he fired two more shots at McDonald. They missed. One of the bullets was found the next day embedded in a head of cabbage in the restaurant next door. McDonald returned the fire. The rounds tore holes in the wooden planks of the Shamrock's floor but left Nixon untouched. It hardly mattered. Less than two hours later Nixon died from the effects of McDonald's first shot.

On Friday, hundreds of Bodieites, including John Nixon, the brother of the deceased, viewed Nixon's body as it lay in a coffin in the Miners' Union Hall. Late in the afternoon, a funeral procession, said to be the "largest turnout ever seen in Bodie," made its way from the union hall to the cemetery. With F. K. Bechtel, a prominent mine owner and judge, conducting the graveside service, Alex Nixon was laid to rest, some six thousand miles from his native County Tyrone. Tom McDonald, meanwhile, was arrested, charged with murder, and lodged in jail. On Thursday afternoon, he appeared before D. V. Goodson, justice of the peace. But the justice decided it was "impracticable to examine him at this time" and had him transferred to the county jail at

85. *Bodie Standard,* 19 June 1878.

Bridgeport for "safe keeping." Finally, on 24 June, McDonald appeared in justice court again. This time he was remanded to the custody of the sheriff to await action of the grand jury.[86] His bail was set at $2,500. He remained in jail at Bridgeport another four days before a group of friends raised the money and bailed him out.[87] When the grand jury met two months later, the jurors declined to indict McDonald, and the charge against him was dropped.[88]

On the Wednesday afternoon of 26 February 1879, Henry Heif, a stocky, German-born miner who worked at the Red Cloud, and George Taft, an engineer at the South Bulwer, began quarreling over "some trifling matter."[89] Neither man had a reputation for violence, but when Taft lashed Heif with an "opprobrious epithet," the German miner threatened to kill him if he did not retract the insult. Taft refused but was sufficiently shaken to stop by the office of the justice of the peace and discuss the matter. Taft found Justice Peterson and Sheriff P. B. Taylor there and asked them if, under the circumstances, he would be justified in killing Heif on sight. They said no and then sent officer James Grant to talk to Heif. Grant located the thick-set miner and searched him in vain for a weapon. Heif later said he had anticipated the officer's arrival and had hidden his revolver.

The next night found Heif shopping in Gillson and Barber's general store on Main Street. He purchased a pair of gum boots, tucked them under his arm, and stepped out of the store onto the sidewalk. Suddenly he was confronted by Taft. "You said you would kill me, did you?" cried Taft as he drew a revolver and opened fire. One bullet hit Heif in the wrist and another missed him entirely. Heif dropped his newly purchased boots, pulled a revolver out of his pocket, and fired back. One of his six shots hit Taft in the shoulder and another drilled the Bulwer engineer through the heart. With blood running out of his mouth and nose, Taft staggered into the street and fell on his face dead. Another man, Con Sullivan, was also lying in the street with a bullet hole in him. He had been passing along the sidewalk when the firing began. A stray round had hit him in the back, and he had fallen into the street at the feet of a woman who had just stepped out of the Bodie Pharmacy. Heif looked at the bodies in the street, dropped his gun, and ran to Justice Peterson's office where he surrendered himself. Constable Kirgan arrived shortly afterward and took Heif to jail.

Meanwhile, friends of Sullivan, a miner at the Standard, carried him into the Bank Exchange saloon and then to his room. This was the third time he had been wounded in a shoot-out to which he was not a party, and only the year before, his brother had been shot to death in Virginia City. He was bleeding internally and suffering acutely. Suspecting that this time he would not recover, he sent for his wife, who was in Virginia City. He struggled on through the night and the next day, but just before sunrise on Saturday morning the thirty-six-year-old native of County Cork, Ireland, died. His wife was still en route to Bodie. When her stage reached Aurora, she was notified of her husband's death. She collapsed in the coach. Later that day the coroner held an inquest over Sullivan's body, but the jury was unable to determine who had fired the fatal shot.

Other stray rounds had less serious consequences. Frank McAvoy, a clerk in

86.   Records, A, County Court, Mono County, pp. 332–33.

87.   *Bodie Standard*, 3 July 1878.

88.   *Bodie Standard*, 9 Oct. 1878.

89.   *Bodie Standard*, 1 and 8 March 1879; *Bodie Chronicle*, 8 and 10 March 1879.

Gillson and Barber's, came running to the front of the store on hearing the first shots. But when a bullet crashed through the store window, whizzed by his head, and blew a hole in a can of lobster—splashing the juice in the can over his face—he spun around and ran back to the rear of the store for cover.

The examination of Heif began in Justice Peterson's courtroom late on Saturday afternoon and continued into Sunday. The start of Sunday's session was delayed when the district attorney, George Whitman, arrived drunk. Major Foote was appointed to replace the intoxicated prosecutor, and the examination got under way. Testimony seemed to support Heif's plea of self-defense, but Justice Peterson decided to have Heif held in custody on a charge of murder to await the action of the grand jury. The next day, Heif was taken to the county jail at Bridgeport. There he stayed until 2 May when his attorney had him brought before H. L. Leavitt, the county judge, on a writ of habeas corpus.[90] Judge Leavitt ordered Heif released from custody. Two weeks later the grand jury declined to indict him and said, "We do not believe that a trial jury could convict the said Hief [sic] upon said evidence, and we believe the discharge of the said Hief was justifiable and correct."[91]

The Monday night of the Fourth of July 1880 found Main Street crowded with celebrating men.[92] Canadian-born James Kennedy, a popular twenty-eight-year-old woodchopper employed at the Booker mine, and several others were standing in front of Patrick Fahey's Mono Brewery—a saloon known for its County Cork whiskey—when William Baker stepped out of the saloon next door. Kennedy and Baker had exchanged words earlier, and now as Baker passed by, Kennedy reached out and tipped Baker's hat. Without saying a word, Baker drew a revolver and shot Kennedy in the stomach. The woodchopper fell to the ground and crawled into the Mono Brewery. From there he was carried to his room, where Dr. Robertson removed the bullet and dressed the wound. In the meantime, Baker was arrested and lodged in jail.

Kennedy put up a valiant struggle for his life, but infection set in and on Wednesday afternoon he died. His friends were saddened and angered by his death, and some of them threatened vigilante action. The authorities responded by secretly transferring Baker to the county jail at Bridgeport. Three days later Baker was indicted for murder, and on 24 August his trial began in Mono County superior court. He was defended by the best, Patrick Reddy.

Reddy contended that Kennedy had made the first move for a gun and that Baker had acted in self-defense. The prosecution put several witnesses on the stand who testified to the contrary, but Reddy managed to cast doubt on much of their testimony. By the afternoon of the second day of the trial the jurors were full of reasonable doubt. One juror was also full of whiskey. Reddy called for a mistrial, but the judge simply told the juror if he showed up intoxicated again he would be jailed. On 27 August, after four days of trial and an afternoon of reasonably sober deliberation, the jury found Baker not guilty.[93]

William Page, a thirty-five-year-old Vermont-born teamster, drove his wagon

---

90. Records, A, County Court, Mono County, p. 367; *Bodie Morning News*, 20 May 1879.

91. *Bodie Morning News*, 20 May 1879. Heif's name was often spelled Hief.

92. *Bodie Chronicle*, 10 July 1880; *Bodie Standard*, 6, 7, 10, and 15 July 1880; *Daily Free Press*, 15 Jan. 1881.

93. Minutes, Criminal Cases, Superior Court, Mono County, pp. 41–54; Register of Actions, Superior Court, Mono County, p. 13; Criminal Calendar, Dep't No. 2, Superior Court, Mono County, 9 July 1880; *Daily Free Press*, 28 August 1880; *Bodie Standard*, 27 and 28 August 1880.

into Bodie on the Friday evening of 15 October 1880 and, after concluding his business, went out on the town.[94] Sometime during the night he arrived at a dance house on King Street. He stayed there dancing and drinking for several hours. About two o'clock in the morning he and his dance partner were bumped by Pat Keogh and his partner. Page, who was by then "somewhat in liquor," responded to the bump by making a "threatening remark" to Keogh.

A fight appeared imminent. Another teamster, a man nicknamed Shorty, jumped between the two men and told Page to calm down, that Keogh, a miner at the Syndicate, was a friend. Page remarked that since Keogh was Shorty's friend, it was all right, but otherwise he might have slapped Keogh across the face. Upon hearing the latter comment, Keogh "made some insulting remark and used an opprobrious epithet." Page reached for his gun but was too slow. Keogh outdrew him and shot him through the temple. Page fell to the floor dead, and Keogh walked out of the dance hall unmolested. Justice court later determined that Keogh had acted in self-defense.

William Page and ten other Bodieites had paid the ultimate price for a show of reckless bravado. During Bodie's boom years, reckless bravado accounted for some thirty-five shootings and shoot-outs. Adding these figures to the already mentioned incidents related to Chinese, Mexicans, Indians, women, and property produces a total of some seventy shootings and shoot-outs in which nearly thirty men were killed and another two dozen or more wounded. Without a doubt, Bodie was a shooter's town. It was the home of the badman. It was also the home of many average workingmen who used guns to resolve their differences.

With so many shootings, it is no wonder that the gunfighting men of Bodie soon had a reputation known throughout the West. Helping to spread this reputation were journalists from more established towns who realized that the exploits of the "badmen of Bodie" made great copy. These journalists, in the best Western tradition, loved hyperbole. As a consequence, the badmen of Bodie soon became legendary figures.

E. H. Clough of the *Sacramento Bee* probably did more than anyone else to publicize the badmen. His first story, entitled "The Bad Man of Bodie," appeared on 1 June 1878 and featured a character called Washoe Pete. "I'm bad," cried Pete in the Cosmopolitan saloon. "I'm chief in this yer camp, and I ken lick the man that says I ain't. I'm a raging lion of the plains, an' every time I hit I kill. I've got an arm like a quartz stamp, an' crush when I go fur a man. I weigh a ton an' earthquakes ain't nowhere when I drop."[95] In a later article Clough attempted to describe the badman more fully. He wrote:

> One of the peculiarities of a Bad Man from Bodie is his profanity. A Bad Man from Bodie who never used an oath is as impossible as perpetual motion or an honest election in Nevada. This trait is especially noticeable whenever he kills a man or endeavors to kill one. Whenever you hear of a man from Bodie who did not swear when he pulled his gun you may depend upon it that he is base metal, a tenderfoot, a man from Pioche, or Cheyenne, or Leadville. The oath of the Bad Man from Bodie is like the cheerful warning of the rattlesnake. And like that warning the blow follows close upon its heels. . . . Whenever a Bad Man from Bodie dons his war paint and strikes the bloody trail of carnage, he is prepared for every contingency. His little gun nestles cosily

94. *Daily Free Press*, 16 and 17 Oct. 1880; *Bodie Standard*, 16 Oct. 1880.

95. *Argonaut*, 1 June 1878; *Bodie Standard*, 28 August 1878.

in his right hand coat pocket, the latter being lined with velvety buckskin to prevent the hammer from catching and frustrating his purpose of converting his enemies into full fledged angels. Meeting an eligible candidate for a place in his graveyard, he emits his stereotyped oath and blazes away. . . . I have seen him leap upon a billiard table and shout his defiance in the following stirring manner: "Here I am again, a mile wide and all wool. I weigh a ton and when I walk the earth shakes. Give me room and I'll whip an army. I'm a blizzard from Bitter Creek. I can dive deeper and come up drier than any man in forty counties. I'm a sand storm mixed with a whirlwind, and when I hump myself I tear. I'm a wild hog from Texas and it's about my time to bristle. I was born in a powder house and raised in a gun factory. I'm bad from the bottom up and clear grit plumb through."[96]

During the next few years newspapers in San Francisco, San Jose, Santa Rosa, Stockton, and Reno, as well as Sacramento, carried stories on the badman of Bodie. Bodie's local newspapers worried about the effect of such attention on the town's reputation. Commented the *Daily Free Press* on 7 January 1880:

> The desperate straits to which newspaper writers are often driven to find subjects upon which to comment, or objective points for their wit, not infrequently lead them to build upon a slight foundation of fact a structure so different from what it should be that the truth is entirely lost sight of, and an utterly incorrect idea is given. Especially is this the case with reference to Bodie, and the manner of its treatment at the hands of the press of the Coast. We do not misstate the facts when we say that Bodie has the reputation abroad of being a fearfully and wonderfully bad place, and withal decidedly unhealthy. When the witty paragrapher of one of our metropolitan contemporaries has touched up all the live topics of the day, and still lacks a little of filling the space in his department of his paper, he dashes off a few lines about the "bad man of Bodie" and his exploits.

Despite such comments, California and Nevada newspapers continued to carry stories about the badman of Bodie. Although Bodie newspapers noted that the stories were aprocryphal or greatly exaggerated, this did no good. The legend had taken root.

Bodie newspapers also tried to make the badman stories look ridiculous by exaggerating them to the point of outrageous hyperbole. When the *Gold Hill News*, after carrying a story about a killing in Bodie, asked, "Why can't a man get along in Bodie without fighting?" the *Bodie Standard* replied, on 25 December 1878, "It must be the altitude. There is some irresistable power in Bodie which impels us to cut and shoot each other to pieces. . . . The clashing of revolvers up and down Main Street can be constantly heard, and it sounds as if we were enjoying a perpetual Chinese Fourth of July. Scarcely a man in town wears a suit of clothes but has more or less holes in it. . . . Yes, it is sad, but only too true, that everybody must fight that comes to Bodie." When the *Tybo Sun* reported that "a Bodie man never has two disputes with the same man; this is explained by the fact that he kills him at first quarrel," the *Standard* replied, on 5 April 1879, that "the *Sun* omitted to mention that the Bodie man always eats his victim

96.   *Sacramento Bee*, 12 Oct. 1880; *Bodie Standard*, 16 Oct. 1880.

after killing him." Bodie's most clever response came in the summer of 1881, at a time when Bodie had begun to decline. Said the *Daily Free Press* on 10 June 1881:

> Some of the newspapers are commenting upon the number of shooting scrapes that occur in Bodie and argue that the town must be bad. To be sure here is something of a shooting gallery, and there is a man for breakfast not unfrequently, but what are we to do? Times are dull, money scarce and the weather miserable. Under such a condition of affairs there must be some inexpensive recreation provided for the people. Six-shooters are of no account unless they can be used, and coffins will warp and be unfit for occupancy if allowed to stand a great while in an undertaker's room. In India mothers throw their children into the river when the number is too large, and nothing is said about it, but when Bodie is overcrowded and a man is put out of the way to make room for a new arrival, a great howl goes up and we are called a "hard crowd."

As Bodie's decline gained momentum and more and more Bodieites began showing up in other western towns, the badman of Bodie stories took a new direction. Now almost every gunfighter or rough was said to be a badman from Bodie. Newspapers in Bodie received reports from all over the West of former Bodieites shooting up towns. Often the reports had misidentified the badman's former place of residence. Said one defendant in a Stockton courtroom:

> I have been doubly mortified, your honor, by the reputation the press of this city has established for me through their glaring "bad man from Bodie" head lines. I am popularly suspected of carrying a nitroglycerine magazine in each pocket; of having a large and ugly-shaped knife in each boot and a brace of pistols in my belt a la Bodie bad men. You may judge of my pain at being obliged to bear this reputation, which I cannot sustain, when you hear that I have never been in Bodie.[97]

Nevertheless, a surprisingly large number of Bodieites were involved in shooting affrays in other towns. Harry Dugan was fatally wounded in a shoot-out in Silver Cliff, Colorado, and Billy Deegan, shortly after arriving in Tombstone, Arizona, was arrested for fighting by another erstwhile Bodieite, Bill Withrow.[98] Bill O'Farrell shot up the Mammoth saloon in San Francisco and wounded the bartender in the head after an argument with the "mixologist."[99] William Driscoll, another former Bodieite and a friend of O'Farrell, wrested the gun away from O'Farrell, and four police officers marched the badman from Bodie off to the city jail. "On the way down," noted the *San Francisco Call*, "Bill got out his knife and made a desperate attempt to carve Officer Flynn."

Joe Rowell died in a gunfight in Butte City, Montana. "Joe shot his adversary five times before he unbuckled his buckles," noted the *Daily Free Press*. "While in Bodie he was a quiet man, but noted for his 'sand.' "[100] Johnny Burrows, while defending a

97. *Daily Free Press*, 2 June 1880.

98. *Bodie Standard*, 20 March 1880; *Tombstone Epitaph*, 1 April 1881, as reprinted in the Bodie *Daily Free Press*, 7 April 1881, and the *Bodie Standard*, 13 April 1881.

99. *San Francisco Call*, 6 May 1881, as reprinted in the *Bodie Standard*, 18 May 1881.

100. *Daily Free Press*, 3 Jan. 1882.

claim near Tombstone, Arizona, was hit by six bullets and died of his wounds. "He did some good work before biting the dust," said the *Daily Free Press.* "He shot one man through the left lung, another in the hip, and a third through the neck."[101] Mike Gracy killed a Texas cowboy in a saloon shoot-out in El Paso.[102] And a man named Brown left Bodie to become known as the "Mendocino Outlaw." Among other crimes, he became notorious for killing a member of a constable's posse.[103]

The badmen of Bodie certainly were not responsible for all the gunfights in the West, as some newspapers liked to claim, but the badmen did seem to participate in more than their share.

101.   *Daily Free Press,* 13 Jan. 1882.
102.   *Daily Free Press,* 29 Jan. 1882.
103.   *Bodie Standard,* 19 April 1882.

12

VIGILANTISM

Bodie experienced vigilantism on three different occasions. The first outbreak resulted from a labor strike, the second from a gun battle over conflicting claims on Bodie Bluff, and the third from a murder. The circumstances and results of these outbreaks were very different, yet there were characteristics common to all: violence, military-like organization and discipline of the vigilantes, and noninterference on the part of lawmen.

First came the labor strike. The Miners' Union and the Mechanics' Union were the only two unions of any importance in Bodie. Most of the members of the Mechanics' Union were "hoisting engineers" who operated the equipment that lowered and raised men in the mine shafts. At all but two mines the engineers received $4.50 for working a twelve-hour day.[1] During February 1879 they began calling for an eight-hour shift at $5 a day.[2] They contended that the twelve-hour shift left them exhausted, thus endangering the lives of the miners, and that $5 a day was no more than fair compensation for their skilled work. The mining companies, noting that only two or three mines in the district were paying dividends, claimed that the eight-hour demand, which would require three shifts a day, was a prohibitively expensive proposition. The companies further argued that many of the hoisting works were powered by "donkey engines," which required little skill to operate. The engineers and the companies were obviously at loggerheads.

On the Wednesday morning of 12 February 1879, some 125 members of the Mechanics' Union met in the Miners' Union Hall and voted to strike. They filed out of the hall and fell into a company formation in the street. With military precision, they marched up Main Street and Standard Avenue to the mines on Bodie Bluff. Beginning at the south end of the Bluff and working their way northward, the engineers first visited the Champion, then the South Standard, the Addenda, and several others. "At all of these mines," said the *Bodie Standard* that day, "some understanding was arrived at, by

---

1. *Bodie Standard*, 12 Feb. 1879.

2. The eight-hour workday was regarded as an alarmingly radical idea by the conservatives of the late 1870s. The strongest proponent of the shorter workday as well as other labor reforms was Denis Kearney, the dynamic and fiery leader of the Workingmen's party. See Ralph Kauer, "The Workingmen's Party of California," and Henry George, "The Kearney Agitation in California."

which they continued running." In most cases the "understanding" was a period of grace granted by the union to the various mine superintendents, giving them time to confer with the mine owners.

When the strikers arrived at the Goodshaw and the Queen Bee, they found that the superintendent of the two mines, Thomas Buckley, had anticipated their arrival and had closed the mines for the day. Frustrated by Buckley's action, the striking engineers marched on to the Mono. Here they found that superintendent George Daly had locked the doors to the hoisting works, unfurled an American flag, and prepared for a shoot-out. Daly absolutely refused to negotiate with the strikers or to allow them into the mine to talk with the Mono's engineers. His bellicose attitude and intransigence inflamed the strikers. Some of them even considered attacking the Mono and forcibly carrying off the engineers. For a time it looked as if a battle would erupt, but cooler heads prevailed and the strikers marched on. By early afternoon every mine on the Bluff, except the Mono and Standard, had shut down.

Thursday morning found the streets of Bodie crowded with miners who had been forced out of work by the engineers' strike. Many of the miners sympathized with the engineers, but the Miners' Union had, as yet, taken no action. The mine superintendents spent the early morning in a closed meeting. A *Standard* reporter could learn only that the meeting ended with the superintendents agreeing "upon some plan of action." The plan itself remained confidential. Meanwhile, out on the streets the tension mounted. Heightening that tension was George Daly's display of the American flag. The engineers were infuriated by Daly's suggestion that their strike was somehow un-American. "It is a singular fact," said the *Bodie Standard*, "that the flying of that flag has given more umbrage than any other thing since the commencement of the strike."[3] The day ended with the Mechanics' and Miners' unions and the mine superintendents all in separate meetings.

The next day saw the first and only real violence of the strike. The object of the violence was, not surprisingly, the defiant George Daly. His life was an American success story. Born in Australia of Irish immigrant parents, he himself had immigrated to San Francisco while still "quite young."[4] There he learned the printer's trade and in a few years rose to be foreman of the *Alta California*'s printing shop. He was prominent in his craft as a nonunion man, and was one of those most instrumental in destroying the power of the San Francisco Typographical Union. He crossed the Sierra in 1870 and took charge of the printing of Virginia City's *Territorial Enterprise*. He subsequently purchased the newspaper.

At the same time Daly was also investing in Comstock mines and acquiring an intimate understanding of mining. He soon left journalism to become the superintendent of the Erie Consolidated and Florida mines. He did such a good job that a group of San Francisco investors, several of whom were former members of William Ralston's "ring," sent him to Aurora in 1877 to reopen the Real Del Monte mine.[5] The investors thought that the Del Monte, a producer of fabulous quantities of gold and silver in the early 1860s, could be brought back to life by sinking a new, deeper shaft. The project failed—there were simply no new veins of ore to be found—and in 1878 Daly moved to

3.   *Bodie Standard*, 14 Feb. 1879.

4.   *Bodie Standard*, 24 August 1881.

5.   *Bodie Standard*, 24 August 1881; Joseph Wasson, *Account of the Important Revival of Mining Interests in the Bodie and Esmeralda Districts*, pp. 51–53.

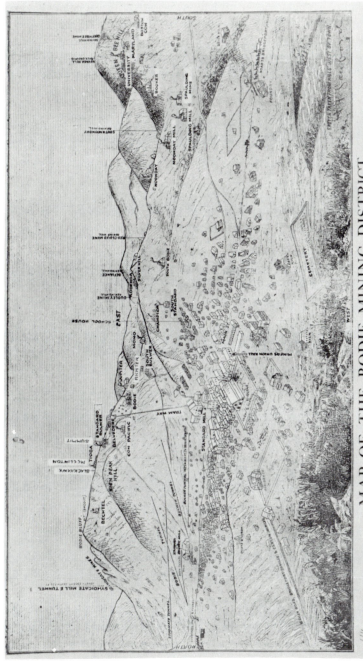

MAP OF THE BODIE MINING DISTRICT.

A Birdseye View of the Mining District and the Town of Bodie, Mono County, Cal.

31. *H. F. Sanford drew this sketch of Bodie in November of 1879 for the San Francisco Daily Stock Report. The Mono and Jupiter mines can be clearly seen in the upper center of the sketch, as can the Miners' Union Hall almost directly below them on Main Street. (Credit: Bancroft Library)*

Bodie to become superintendent of the Mono. Now, after a year in Bodie, he found himself in a confrontation with the Mechanics' Union.

When Daly finished his breakfast on Friday morning and stepped out of the Palace restaurant, he was met by a formation of men standing in the street.[6] Their leader, Phil Mahar, stepped up to Daly and asked him to come along with them to a meeting at the Miners' Union Hall. "What meeting? Miners or Mechanics?" asked Daly. "Mechanics' Union," replied Mahar. "I have nothing to say to the Mechanics," said Daly. "What I had to say was said at the Mono hoisting works on Wednesday. I'm not going." "Men, do your duty," ordered Mahar. Two men seized Daly, and the engineers then marched to the union hall. But just as they were about to enter the hall, Daly wrenched free, drew a revolver, and sprang into the street. Taking aim at Mahar, Daly cried, "I'll kill the first man that attempts to lay a hand on me!"

Knowing Daly to be a man of his word, Mahar and the other engineers made no attempt to stop the gun-wielding superintendent as he backed into Gillson and Barber's general store. One of the men did yell a word of warning to Daly, though. "All right, young man," said the striker, "you're heading for it. You'll get plugged yet." The striker was right. Daly was eventually shot to death, but under circumstances far different from those that could have been expected. For the time being, Daly had stopped Bodie's first vigilante action dead in its tracks.

The *Bodie Standard*, although emphasizing that it was not anti-union, vehemently denounced the actions of the striking engineers. Commented the *Standard* on Friday afternoon, 14 February 1879:

> The demonstration on the streets this morning, in which an attempt was made to force Mr. George Daly to go where he did not wish to go, was unlawful and illegitimate, and no organization can afford to defend it. Whatever may be thought of the policy which that gentleman has pursued, in keeping his flag flying from the Mono hoisting works, which is thought by the mechanics to be simply an aggravation—one thing is certain: He has the *right* to do it. It is his great American privilege to wave the American flag whenever and wherever it suits his humor. Further, he is under no obligation to go to any sort of meeting against his own wishes, and he is entitled to regard with suspicion any attempt to force him to do so.
>
> The Mechanics' Union is composed principally of hard-working, industrious men, but like all organizations of the kind, it evidently has rash and foolish men in its ranks who will, and indeed have, brought it into disrepute. Let the Union, in common with all who love the American principal [sic] of law and order, discountenance such acts. The original question of the eight-hour shifts and wages has become shadowed in the far more important question of whether we shall have law and order. . . . We say that order must and shall be maintained, and that if one drop of blood is shed in this crisis, the perpetrators will be held to rigid accountability and a swift retribution.

On Friday afternoon the Miners' Union finally took action. The miners adopted, although less than unanimously, a resolution disclaiming any connection with, or responsibility for, the action of the engineers.[7] Furthermore, the miners declared that

6. *Bodie Standard*, 14 Feb. 1879.
7. *Bodie Standard*, 15 Feb. 1879.

the Mechanics' Union had acted "ill-advisedly," that it had not given the superintendents proper notice, and that there were nearly a thousand miners who were out of work and bearing "the brunt of a fight in which they had no hand." The miners then appointed a fifteen-man committee to confer with the superintendents.

The Mechanics' Union, in an attempt to salvage something out of the strike, now restricted the demand for an eight-hour shift to only those mines that were paying dividends. The proffered compromise had no effect. The superintendents met with the Miners' Union committee on Friday evening and won the miners' support for a return to work at prestrike conditions. The Mechanics' Union, without the support of the miners, could do nothing more than accept the superintendents' ultimatum. George Daly's hard-line stance had carried the day. But George Daly himself had won hundreds of new enemies.

Shortly after the strike Daly became superintendent of a second mine, the Jupiter. The mine was a consolidation of two earlier claims, the Savage and the East Savage, and was owned and heavily financed by the same group of powerful San Francisco investors who owned the Mono.[8] On the Jupiter's southern boundary was the Owyhee, a claim owned by a small group of Bodie miners.[9] There was some question about where the Jupiter claim ended and the Owyhee began.

Late on the afternoon of 11 August 1879, Daly returned from a visit to the Del Monte to find a note from his foreman, Joseph McDonald, saying that a group of men were sinking a shaft on the south end of the Jupiter claim. Early the next morning Daly rode to the site and found Patrick Reynolds and several other Owyhee men at work.[10]

"Well boys, what are you doin'?" Daly asked. "We're sinking a shaft," replied Reynolds. "What do you call this?" continued Daly. "The Owyhee," said Reynolds. "We call this the Jupiter," remarked Daly. "You do, eh?" responded Reynolds. "The Jupiter ain't got any ground here." "Well, I am playing this for the Jupiter," said Daly.

The battle of words intensified, and Daly ordered the Owyhee men off the property. They refused, saying that the ground could be purchased but that they would not be driven off it—not as long as guns would hold it. Daly remarked that he and his men also had guns.

A couple of days later, Daly returned to the disputed ground with C. L. Anderson, the local deputy United States mineral surveyor.[11] Anderson found that the Owyhee men were, in fact, sinking their shaft on Jupiter ground and that a survey marker he had erected two months earlier was missing. Daly accused the Owyhee men of removing the marker and told them he would have a new one erected and it would be protected by guards armed with shotguns. Shortly thereafter, Daly went to see John Goff, one of the owners of Owyhee. Goff, an Irish immigrant and a veteran of the Civil War, was a shift boss at the Bodie mine and a popular member of the Miners' Union. When Daly asked him to quit the disputed ground, Goff reportedly said that if the Jupiter

---

8. See pp. 107–8.

9. The Owyhee owners were John Goff, Patrick Reynolds, Patrick McDermott, Thomas Hamilton, John Fitzgerald, and Patrick Lowney. The name Owyhee was a common phonetic rendering of Hawaii. Owyhee can be found as a place-name today in northern Nevada, southeastern Oregon, and southwestern Idaho. The name in that tri-state area derives from several Hawaiians, or Owyhees, who disappeared from a fur-trapping brigade and were presumably killed by Indians.

10. *Bodie Standard*, 10 Oct. 1879.

11. *Bodie Standard*, 10 Oct. 1879.

wanted the property they could buy it for $4,500 or take the Owyhee to court. Daly rejected the offer to purchase the property and allegedly added, "Ammunition and guns are cheaper than law." "Go to hell," Goff supposedly responded.

Words were exchanged for another week, and then, on the Friday night of 22 August 1879, while the Owyhee men were in town, Daly had his men fill the Owyhee shaft with dirt and move a small cabin onto the top of the shaft. [12] Sometime later that night the Owyhee men learned what had happened and, armed with rifles, returned to their claim. They took up a position in the cabin of Peter Burke, which was located about two hundred feet south of the Owyhee shaft, and fired a few shots at the newly erected Jupiter cabin. The Jupiter men returned the fire, and desultory rifle shots were exchanged for an hour or two.

Then, just before sunrise on Saturday morning, the Jupiter men crept out of their cabin, separated into three groups, and charged the Owyhee cabin. The assault took the Owyhee men completely by surprise. They were quickly overrun and two of them were wounded. John Goff was shot through the head and Tom Hamilton through the neck. Hamilton's wound miraculously proved not serious; Goff, with part of his skull blown away and a portion of his brain protruding from the hole, died two hours later. The Jupiter men, who had had only one man slightly wounded, marched the rest of the Owyhee men into town and turned them over to deputy constable Eugene Markey. Markey refused to take charge of the "prisoners" and they were set free.

The news of the killing of John Goff spread rapidly through Bodie and left many citizens outraged. The outrage for some came from the fact that Goff had been killed as the result of actions taken by a mining company and that those actions stemmed from a property dispute, something that should have been settled in the courts. As the *Bodie Morning News* put it on 24 August:

> No man or company should attempt to take or retain by force what he or they believe to be theirs by right of purchase or other means of acquirement. We have laws made and provided for such cases, officers sworn to execute the same, and we hold there is no excuse for violence and bloodshed on either side. The merits of this case will be settled in the Courts—we mean the right of ownership—but the death of John Goff is another matter. . . . The *News* will always be found on the side of law and order, and will never waver in its opinion as to the proper manner of protecting rights of property, which we hold to be through the Courts, and not with shot guns and pistols.

The outrage for others came from the fact that not only was Goff gunned down as the result of actions taken by a mining company but that those actions were ordered by George Daly. This was certainly true of the miners. By late Saturday afternoon several hundred of them had gathered at the union hall. "Without a dissenting voice," they passed a motion which declared that George Daly would be hanged if he dared show himself in Bodie. [13] The miners then filed out of the hall, marched up to the hillside location of the early-morning battle, posted armed guards, and took "formal possession" of the disputed ground. Before leaving, they set the Jupiter's small cabin ablaze and sent it crashing down the hillside.

12. *Bodie Morning News*, 24, 26, and 27 August 1879; *Bodie Standard*, 10 Oct. 1879.

13. *Bodie Morning News*, 24 August 1879.

George Daly would have preferred to stay and fight, but he acceded to the
wishes of his friends and quietly left the Bluff. He spent the next two weeks in Virginia
City and Carson City.[14] In the meantime, he and the Jupiter men who had participated
in the fight were charged with the murder of John Goff. Their examination began on
the Wednesday morning of 10 September 1879 in Judge H. L. Leavitt's courtroom in
Bridgeport.[15] Patrick Reddy and R. H. Lindsay represented Daly and his men, and
Thomas Ryan appeared for the state. The preponderance of the testimony, including
that of the U.S. mineral surveyor C. L. Anderson and the Bodie mining recorder,
George Macartney, supported Daly's contention that the Owyhee men were trespassers.
The examination was completed on Friday afternoon, and Judge Leavitt took the case
"under advisement." The next morning the judge announced that he had found George
Daly and the Jupiter men not guilty. The grand jury also investigated the Jupiter-Owyhee
fight, and it too exonerated Daly and his men.[16]

Daly returned to Bodie a few days after he was acquitted and resumed his duties
as superintendent of the Jupiter and Mono mines. Union miners were outraged. On the
Saturday night of 20 September 1879, they met at the union hall and adopted a resolution that banished George Daly and the Jupiter men who had participated in the Owyhee
fight. Printed copies of the resolution were posted about town and delivered to the *Bodie
Morning News* and the *Bodie Standard*.[17] The resolution read:

NOTICE
HALL OF THE BODIE MINERS' UNION

September 20, 1879—10 P.M.

The following resolution was adopted: That George Daly, Joe McDonald,
Barney McDonald, George Harber, Joseph Burnett, James Murphy and William Andrews be ordered outside the limits of the Bodie Mining District within 12 hours from
the date of this notice.

J. P. SHAUGHNESSY, President
M. CULLINAN, Rec. Secretary

Daly quickly had a rejoinder printed and distributed. It read:

TO ALL GOOD CITIZENS

The lawless element of the Bodie Miners' Union have passed a resolution
ordering me and several men in the employ of the Jupiter Company to leave camp within
twelve hours. We have been, by the laws of our country, declared innocent of any crime
or wrong doing; we are American citizens, and as such are entitled to pursue our respec-
tive avocations free from molestation, and this right we *propose to maintain*, and we call
upon all good and true men in the community to assist us in so doing, and in quelling

14.　*Bodie Morning News*, 23 Sept. 1879.

15.　*Bodie Morning News*, 12 and 13 Sept. 1879; Virginia City *Territorial Enterprise*, 17 Sept. 1879; *Bodie
Standard*, 10 Oct. 1879.

16.　*Bodie Morning News*, 23 Sept. 1879.

17.　The miners' resolution and Daly's rejoinder were published in the *Bodie Morning News* and the *Bodie
Standard* on Monday, 22 Sept. 1879.

the turbulent element now disturbing the peace of this community. It is our belief that this obnoxious and violent resolution is NOT the sentiment of the *majority* of the Bodie Miners' Union, most of whom we believe to be good and true men, but it is merely the voice of the mob, and will be repudiated by every good man in the Union.

GEORGE DALY

Not waiting to see just how many "good and true men" came forward to support him, Daly gathered together some twenty well-armed Jupiter men early Sunday morning and erected barricades around the Jupiter mine. Portholes were cut in the barricades to allow fire in every direction, ammunition was stacked high, and men were strategically positioned. Daly would fight. Meanwhile, the union miners held another meeting and voted 500 to 3 not to rescind or modify their resolution of banishment.[18] By midmorning Bodie was in a state of fevered excitement.

With a small battle about to erupt on the Bluff, a number of Bodie's leading figures issued a call for a citizens' meeting at the fire station. By 11 A.M. the station was filled to overflowing with people. R. M. Folger, publisher of the *Bodie Chronicle*, proposed the formation of a vigilance committee. Instead, at the suggestion of Patrick Reddy, a nine-man committee was chosen to mediate the dispute. The committee first trekked up to the Jupiter, where it passed through a line of sentries, and talked to Daly. Daly said that he was a free American citizen, that he was armed to defend his rights, and that he did not propose to leave Bodie on any consideration. The committee next conferred with the Miners' Union, which proved to be equally intransigent.

Hour after hour the committee, hoping for a breakthrough, passed back and forth between the union hall and the Jupiter. Finally, three of Daly's friends, one of them attorney Patrick Reddy, convinced Daly that if a battle did occur there would be no end to private assassinations and reprisals and that the warfare could destroy Bodie. Daly decided to capitulate. The union allowed Daly and the others named in the banishment resolution an initial forty-eight hours to attend to their business affairs and thereafter twenty-four hours in town once a month. The union also guaranteed them freedom from molestation and insults when they were in town.[19]

Daly had acceded to the wishes of his friends and capitulated, but he was no less defiant. On Monday, in an open letter to the citizens of Bodie, he recounted the events of the preceding several days, asserted his rights as an American citizen, and concluded:

The situation was a grave one, and though feeling that the principle involved was such that it warranted me in asserting it, even at the expense of my life, I well knew that a precipitation of hostilities would cause great, and perhaps *irreparable* injury to the camp, and also cause the ruin of many good citizens. This view was urged by my friends so strongly that I at last consented to submit to great personal injustice, and for the general welfare of the whole community to retire (if I could do so honorably) from the contest. This I have done, and the peace resulting is attributable to the *influence of my friends* instead of the *threats of my foes*. It is my sincere wish that this peace be a lasting one,

18. *Bodie Morning News*, 23 Sept. 1879.

19. *Bodie Morning News*, 23 Sept. 1879; *Bodie Standard*, 22 Sept. 1879.

and that never again in Bodie will an enlightened American citizen be compelled to purchase the peace of the community by the sacrifice of his own independence.[20]

On Tuesday night a large crowd gathered to watch Daly, the McDonald brothers, Joseph Burnett, James Murphy, William Andrews, and George Harber leave Bodie. The crowd was subdued and well-behaved. No threat of violence was made, nor were any insults hurled at the departing men. The next day Bodie had returned to normal. "It is to the credit of the people generally," said the *Bodie Morning News*, "that the angry passions aroused during the recent troubles have been quieted and subdued. A stranger to walk through the streets of Bodie to-day would never imagine that but a short time ago men were arrayed against each other in deadly hate, and prepared, on the slightest provocation, to precipitate a bloody encounter."[21] But the *Bodie Standard* argued that the price paid for peace was too high.[22] It said:

> Peace now hovers over the Bodie Bluff. Our devoted people, devoted to the business of money making . . . can, once more, regulate the entire attention of their minds and bodies to their several pursuits. It is true that half a dozen men have been compelled to leave town. Some of them have families here, wives and children. When we contemplate how easily peace is obtained by simple sacrifice of the honor and manhood of the community, we can but think of the Revolutionary Fathers as an absurd lot of stubborn old fools; they fought eight years to establish American Liberty. Could anything be more ridiculous? They should have appointed a Citizens Committee and then they might have had peace. How more sensible the conduct of the citizens of Bodie who would see American Liberty to the devil before they would fight eight minutes for it. Let us have peace.

During the entire Jupiter-Owyhee affair, the official agencies of law enforcement were conspicuously absent. Neither the Mono County sheriff nor the Bodie town constable or any of their officers participated in any of the proceedings. Moreover, the Bodie National Guard had just been organized and presumably could have been called into action. The newspapers, usually quick to publicize the inefficiency and incompetence of the police, never once asked why the police were not involved nor mentioned the National Guard.

Although George Daly was banished from Bodie, his career was in no way harmed.[23] He first went to Aurora and employed the banished Jupiter men at the Real Del Monte. Then, in late October, several mining companies sent him to New York to represent, ironically enough, the Bodie mining district. While in New York he made a number of important contacts with eastern capitalists and renewed his acquaintance with George Roberts, a powerful San Francisco investor. At Roberts's behest, Daly became

---

20. Daly's letter was published in the *Bodie Standard* on Monday, 22 Sept. 1879, and in the *Bodie Morning News* the following day.

21. *Bodie Morning News*, 24 Sept. 1879.

22. *Bodie Standard*, 23 Sept. 1879.

23. *Bodie Morning News*, 24 Sept. 1879; Bodie *Daily Free Press*, 19 Sept. 1880, 13 March and 7 April 1881; *Bodie Standard*, 16 March, 13 April, 24 August, and 7 Sept. 1881; *Bridgeport Chronicle-Union*, 8 Oct. 1881.

superintendent of the Little Chief mine in Leadville, Colorado, early in 1880. One of his first moves as the new superintendent was to hire all the banished Jupiter men.

Daly was highly successful in Leadville. In his eight months as superintendent of the Little Chief, the mine produced record yields, and he made $60,000 for himself. Although he was a redoubtable and bitter foe of the Leadville Miners' Union, he was very popular with the men at his own mine. As a token of their esteem, they presented him with an expensive gold watch when he left the Little Chief to become superintendent of the Robinson in September of 1880. As in Bodie, Daly had the ability to inspire fierce loyalty among his own men and, at the same time, to create bitter enemies in the ranks of the union.

Daly's stay at the Robinson, claimed to be "the largest and richest mine in Colorado," included a violent confrontation with the miners' union. Whether or not Daly was ordered to leave Leadville—as one report asserted he was—the spring of 1881 found him in New Mexico purchasing and developing mining properties for George Roberts. Daly now faced a new foe, marauding bands of Apache. In August he set out with a group of thirty-six soldiers and civilians to track one of the bands. On the Saturday afternoon of 20 August, the whites, with Daly in the lead, followed the Apache into a canyon some forty miles northwest of Deming. Suddenly, the Indians opened fire from ambush. Daly and four others were blown out of their saddles and killed. George Daly, said the *Bodie Standard* on 7 September, "was a born leader, but died with a myriad of enemies—all of his own making."

George Harber, one of the banished Jupiter men who had followed Daly to Leadville, also was shot to death in 1881, not by Apache but by a deputy sheriff, McIlhenny.[24] Nine days later, McIlhenny was shot and mortally wounded by an unknown assassin. Joseph and Bernard McDonald may have been involved. They were close friends of Harber and were openly gleeful when McIlhenny died. Joseph, who had become the superintendent of the Robinson upon Daly's departure for New Mexico, wrote to the Bodie *Daily Free Press* and informed the newspaper that Harber's death had been avenged. McIlhenny, said Joseph, "took one of Winchester's latest improved pills, which gave him a severe case of belly ache, of which he died the next day, and peace and quietness have since reigned in Robinson [the Robinson mining district], notwithstanding the fact that the Robinson mine is superintended and run by 'Bad Men from Bodie.' "[25]

The departure of George Daly and the Jupiter men from Bodie did not put an end to vigilantism, but it did produce a new cast of characters. Johanna Londrigan, Thomas Treloar, and Joseph DeRoche now took center stage. Raised in Providence, Rhode Island, Johanna Londrigan left home in the late 1860s to live with a married sister in Chicago.[26] In 1876 she moved to San Francisco and two years later, after a brief stay in Virginia City, opened a laundry in Bodie and took up residence at the American Hotel. At the hotel she met Thomas Treloar, a Cornish miner who had been in the West for a dozen years. The *Daily Free Press* described Treloar as "a small, harmless man, but little more than half-witted, from the effects of a fall of 225 feet down a mine at Virginia City."[27]

24.   *Daily Free Press*, 13 March and 7 April 1881; *Bodie Standard*, 16 March and 13 April 1881.

25.   *Daily Free Press*, 7 April 1881; *Bodie Standard*, 13 April 1881.

26.   *Daily Free Press*, 15 Jan. 1881.

27.   *Daily Free Press*, 15 Jan. 1881.

On the Thursday afternoon of 2 January 1879, Thomas Treloar and Johanna Londrigan were married. When John Brophy, who owned Bodie's only auction house and knew the couple intimately, asked Johanna why she had married "that little half-witted fellow," she allegedly responded, "Oh, I married him for that endowment policy on his life, which will be due in a couple of years; and then I will have the money."[28] Treloar had had his life insured for $1,000 on the "endowment plan" with the New England Life Insurance Company in 1871, and the original investment plus interest would be due in 1881.

The Treloars had marriage problems from the very beginning. Treloar suspected that Johanna had a lover in Joseph DeRoche, a French-Canadian who owned the Booker Flat brickyard on the south side of Bodie and a two-story brick house downtown.[29] DeRoche had known Johanna for a dozen years or more. They had first met in Chicago in the late 1860s and now renewed their friendship in Bodie. DeRoche had a wife and three children back in Chicago, living with her parents.[30] Although she wrote regularly to him, he rarely answered her letters.

DeRoche and Johanna were occasionally seen together at Brophy's auction house, and gossip had it that they were romantically involved. They claimed that they were only friends and that Treloar had no cause for his jealousy. From time to time, Treloar quarreled with DeRoche about Johanna and about business matters. He also quarreled with Johanna, sometimes violently. Six months after they were married, Treloar struck Johanna during an argument and was subsequently convicted of assault.[31]

On the Thursday night of 13 January 1881, Johanna was employed to help cater a ball given by a Bodie social society at the Miners' Union Hall. At about eleven o'clock, Treloar, dressed in denim work clothes, appeared at the union hall and asked the doorman for Johanna. She was summoned, and the Treloars stepped outside and conversed "in a low tone of voice" for a few minutes. Johanna then reentered the hall, and Treloar disappeared down the street. An hour and a half later, Treloar returned to the hall just in time to see his wife dancing a quadrille with none other than Joseph DeRoche. "I told my wife not to dance with that man, and she said she wouldn't," exclaimed a visibly agitated Treloar to the doorman. "I want to get her away."[32]

The doorman warned Treloar not to create a disturbance in the hall. Treloar turned to "Captain" G. S. Morgan, who was standing nearby, and told him that Johanna had been untrue and that he intended to kill DeRoche. Morgan went inside and informed DeRoche of the threat. DeRoche said he would shoot Treloar if the Cornishman made an aggressive move. DeRoche then stepped outside and exchanged a few words with Treloar. Minutes later DeRoche entered the hall and told Morgan that he had "run Treloar off with a gun."

The ball ended a short time later, and Treloar returned to the hall to meet his wife. For some unknown reason, he left the hall with DeRoche, and the two walked off down Main Street. As they approached Kilgore's meat market, they passed G. W. Alexander and E. S. Butler. Alexander, who had been a floor manager at the ball, turned to Butler and said, "That's the two gentlemen who are likely to have trouble about the wife

28. *Daily Free Press*, 15 Jan. 1881.
29. *Daily Free Press*, 15 Jan. 1881. DeRoche's name was often spelled DaRoche in Bodie newspapers.
30. *Daily Free Press*, 18 Jan. 1881.
31. *Bodie Standard*, 30 June 1879.
32. *Daily Free Press*, 16 Jan. 1881.

of the smaller man." Alexander and Butler watched as Treloar and DeRoche neared the corner of Main and Lowe. Treloar stepped off the sidewalk into the snow-covered street. DeRoche fell a step behind and pulled a .38 caliber, double-action Forehand and Wadsworth out of his pocket.[33] He put the revolver to the back of Treloar's head and fired. The Cornishman pitched forward into the snow. Blood gushed from a hole behind his left ear.

Alexander and Butler raced down the street to the fallen Treloar. Butler grabbed DeRoche's gun and cried, "What did you shoot that man for?" "Because he jumped me—see where he scratched me," replied DeRoche. The answer surprised Alexander and Butler. Neither man had seen Treloar make any move toward DeRoche. Nevertheless, they looked DeRoche over carefully. They found no scratches. At this point Deputy Sheriff James Monahan arrived and arrested DeRoche. DeRoche had a different story for Monahan. He told the officer that Treloar had drawn the gun and that he, DeRoche, had only attempted to wrest it away. The gun, DeRoche claimed, discharged accidentally.

Meanwhile, Johanna Treloar finished her work at the hall. Since her husband was nowhere to be found, she asked T. A. Stephens, an attorney and the committee chairman for the ball, and his wife to escort her home. As the three of them neared the corner of Main and Lowe they saw officer Monahan with DeRoche in custody coming toward them. Johanna, fearing that there must have been a fight, ran forward. DeRoche spotted her and exclaimed, "Mrs. Treloar, I have killed your husband." "Good God!" gasped Johanna. Stephens tried to restrain her, but she managed to struggle free and rush to her husband's side. Treloar lay in a pool of blood, beyond help and near death. The blood was turning the snow a deep crimson. Minutes later, without having uttered a word, Treloar died.

Monahan arrived at the Bodie jail at about two o'clock in the morning and turned DeRoche over to Constable John Kirgan and Deputy Constable Sam Williamson.[34] DeRoche was charged with murder and locked in a cell. Two hours later, Deputy Sheriff Joe Farnsworth, who had been on night duty and had sampled too much whiskey while patrolling the saloons, rushed into the jail and said that there would be a lynch mob there in less than twenty minutes. Farnsworth volunteered to take DeRoche to a secret location—the deputy suggested his own room at the Standard boarding house—where the prisoner would be safe until the vigilantes lost their enthusiasm.[35]

Constable Kirgan concurred with Farnsworth's plan, and Williamson hurried back to DeRoche's cell and unlocked the door. "What are you going to do with me—hang me?" asked DeRoche. "No. We are trying to save you," replied Williamson. Williamson handcuffed DeRoche and turned him over to Farnsworth. With DeRoche in tow, Farnsworth hurried to his room at the Standard and had the prisoner lie down on the room's one bed so that his ankles could be shackled. But one of the shackles had sprung shut, and Farnsworth was forced to return to the jail for the key. He left the

---

33. Forehand and Wadsworth produced five-shot revolvers in a variety of calibers and barrel lengths from 1871 to 1890 in its Worcester, Massachusetts, plant. See Frederick Myatt, *Illustrated Encyclopedia of Pistols and Revolvers*, p. 138.

34. Jail Register: Bodie Branch Jail, p. 12, 15 Jan. 1881; *Daily Free Press*, 15 and 16 Jan. 1881.

35. This was not an unprecedented procedure. Sam Chung, who had killed Prudencia Encinos, and William Baker, who had killed James Kennedy, both had been removed from jail to other locations for safekeeping when vigilante action was threatened. See pp. 136, 220.

Standard's landlady and a boarder in charge of DeRoche, with his police whistle to blow if there was trouble. With key in hand, Farnsworth was soon back at the Standard. He shackled DeRoche and, after talking to the prisoner for a while, fell into what the *Daily Free Press* described as "the profound sleep of the inebriated."[36]

Constable Kirgan had ordered Farnsworth to have DeRoche back at the jail at seven o'clock in the morning, but the hour passed without the appearance of the deputy sheriff. Kirgan grew steadily more uneasy as the minutes ticked away. Finally at eight o'clock he walked over to Farnsworth's room. There he found the deputy sheriff sound asleep, and DeRoche was nowhere in sight. Kirgan awakened Farnsworth and asked him what had become of DeRoche. Farnsworth said he did not know. Mentally noting that the lynch mob that Farnsworth had warned of had not materialized, Kirgan then suggested to Farnsworth that perhaps he had been involved in a conspiracy to allow De-Roche to escape. Farnsworth strongly denied the suggestion and claimed that quite the opposite was true—that he had indignantly refused a $1,000 bribe from DeRoche in exchange for freedom and that when he had gone to sleep DeRoche was lying on the bed securely handcuffed and shackled.

By the time the coroner began an investigation of the murder on Friday afternoon, the entire town had learned of the murder and of DeRoche's escape. Bodieites were outraged over both events. Treloar was considered a quiet, peaceable man, and he had never been known to carry a gun. Also, it was obvious to Bodieites that Treloar suffered from brain damage received in his fall down the mine shaft, and a few people considered it just as obvious that Treloar's wife was unfaithful. Treloar was not a rough or a badman. He was simply a small, likeable miner who had never been quite the same since his fall.

Before nightfall squads of men, who were said to be "in dead earnest," were searching the town not only for DeRoche but also for Farnsworth. "Farnsworth must produce the murderer or take the consequences," cried the searchers. "It was difficult to determine," said the *Daily Free Press* the next day, "whether the feeling was more intense against the assassin or the officer who let him escape." The men searched until four o'clock the next morning—through the two-story brick building where DeRoche lived, the jail, brothels, saloons, warehouses, and vacant cabins and buildings—without success.

The coroner's jury spent two days carefully investigating the case and examining more than a dozen witnesses, including eyewitnesses G. W. Alexander and E. S. Butler. Both Alexander and Butler testified that they had clearly seen the entire event and that DeRoche had, without provocation, shot Treloar in the back of the head. The coroner's jury also took time to grill Constable Kirgan.

"Do you think, Mr. Kirgan, even if there were a Vigilance Committee, prisoners would be safer outside than inside jail?" asked the coroner. "I do," replied Kirgan. "Then do you not think that it's a great extravagance to build jails at all?" said the coroner. Kirgan did not reply.

On Saturday night the jury rendered its verdict. It found that Thomas Treloar was killed by Joseph DeRoche and that the killing was "a willful and premeditated murder."[37] The jury further found that Constable Kirgan was "guilty of gross neglect of duty in allowing the prisoner to be removed from jail" and that Deputy Farnsworth was "crim-

36. *Daily Free Press*, 15 Jan. 1881.

37. *Daily Free Press*, 16 Jan. 1881.

inally careless in allowing the escape of the prisoner." The *Daily Free Press* made even stronger accusations. "The insufferable stupidity of Kirgan in allowing his prisoner to be taken away," argued the *Press* on Sunday, 16 January, "should forever bar him from holding an office of trust in the county. The people ask that both Farnsworth and Kirgan be removed from places of public responsibility. The taxpayers and citizens generally have no further use for Farnsworth as an officer. If he did profit by DeRoche's escape, they certainly do not want him; and if he did not, he is altogether too innocent and childlike for the place." The murder itself, said the *Press*, was "so cold-blooded and cowardly, and was committed for a purpose seemingly so base and sordid, and under precedent circumstances so revolting to every impulse and sensibility of manhood, that it has stirred the blood of every human being in Bodie to the very springhead of the fountain."

Meanwhile, on Saturday afternoon, Treloar's funeral was held at the Miners' Union Hall. The hall was packed with members of the Miners' Union and the Bodie Fire Department; Treloar had been a member of both organizations. F. M. Warrington, a Methodist minister, conducted the services, and he did nothing to abate the rising fever of vigilantism in Bodie. The greater part of his sermon concentrated on the murderer and the crime, not on Treloar. Warrington described the "babe on its mother's breast, then the boy, the young man almost imperceptibly diverging from the moral path pointed out by his mother, then the hardened man, and next the assassin and the fugitive from justice." Warrington appealed to God to put his hand upon sin and strike down the arm of the assassin. He concluded, "If a man have an irresistible impulse to take another man's life, I say let the law have an irresistible impulse to put a rope about his neck [Warrington was simultaneously demonstrating the operation] and take the life from his body. But keep cool, and under all circumstances be men."[38]

By the time the funeral had ended no fewer than two hundred vigilantes were again searching Bodie for DeRoche and Farnsworth. The vigilantes operated like the military veterans some of them were. They were organized into squads, had their own elected officers and a chain of command, and went about their business in a quiet and orderly, but determined, manner. Farnsworth managed to avoid them only with the help of his friends, one of whom was Ned Reddy, Patrick Reddy's younger brother. Ned and the other friends kept Farnsworth well concealed until night fell and then hid him in a buggy and drove furiously to Aurora. There they put him aboard the stage for Carson City. "His departure," noted the *Daily Free Press* the next day, "was a most timely movement on his part."

At about half-past six, Mrs. Archie McMillan, who lived on Lowe Street just a half block from where the murder occurred, heard what sounded like a man crawling through her woodpile. She grabbed a pistol and headed for the yard. The gun discharged accidently. The bullet struck her in the hand but damaged nothing more than flesh. Sheriff P. B. Taylor arrived and discovered that an area had been excavated under the woodpile and that a man had been lying there. The man's footprints were tracked through the snow into the street, but there they merged with others and were lost. On the chance that the man—thought by many to be DeRoche—might return, guards were secreted around the woodpile, and the entire block was surrounded.

At nine o'clock the vigilantes regrouped and held a meeting at the Headquarters saloon. After a brief discussion, they decided on a new strategy—a roundup and

38.   *Daily Free Press*, 16 Jan. 1881.

interrogation of DeRoche's French-Canadian friends. Three squads of vigilantes were dispatched to conduct the roundup, and they soon had several of the French-Canadians imprisoned at Webber's blacksmith shop on Mill Street. The prisoners "were handled rather roughly and several threatened," but none seemed to know of DeRoche's whereabouts.

Near midnight a saloonkeeper named DeGerro was brought into the blacksmith shop. Feigning not to understand much English and to be nothing more than a casual acquaintance of DeRoche, DeGerro at first was able to fend off the inquisitors. But it soon became apparent that he was not telling all he knew. At that point, noted the *Daily Free Press*, "a thoughtful man procured a rope and threw it over a beam. DeGerro was informed that if he did not tell where DeRoche was a hanging party would be inaugurated. Still the man hesitated to divulge, and it was not until the boys began to make such remarks as, 'Pull him up,' 'Grease the rope so that it won't make any noise,' 'Fix up the noose,' etc., that he unfolded himself."[39]

DeGerro revealed that his brother owned a wood ranch some eight miles from town and that DeRoche was hiding there. A squad of ten vigilantes was dispatched to the ranch. The vigilantes took DeGerro with them and told him that if they found he had "put them off the track" he would not return to Bodie—at least not alive. A hard ride through crisp night air and over snow-covered ground brought the vigilantes and DeGerro to a ramshackle wood-and-adobe cabin that served as ranch headquarters. The vigilantes surrounded the cabin and called for DeRoche. DeGerro's brother opened the door and stepped outside into bright moonlight. He found himself confronted by a half-dozen armed men with their weapons leveled. "His hair arose on his head and stood up like the quills on a fretful porcupine," said the *Daily Free Press*, "and, rushing out, he cried, 'Let me get out of this.' His progress was stopped by a six shooter, and he stood trembling."

Moments later DeRoche came through the door, crying "Hang me! Hang me!" The vigilantes told him that they had come not to hang him but to return him to jail. They put him on a horse and began the ride back to Bodie. On the way he recounted the events of the past two days. He again claimed that Treloar drew the revolver and that it had accidentally discharged when he, DeRoche, tried to wrest it away. He also said that Farnsworth told him that he would be lynched by a mob if he did not escape. Therefore, when Farnsworth fell asleep, said DeRoche, he worked his way over to Farnsworth's side and slipped the keys to the handcuffs and the shackles out of the deputy's pocket. He then opened the locks, stole out of the boarding house, and walked all the way to DeGerro's ranch.

The vigilantes arrived back in Bodie just before seven o'clock on Sunday morning and, as they had promised, returned DeRoche to jail.[40] By nine o'clock the news of DeRoche's capture had reached almost every person in Bodie, and by noon there were hundreds of men milling about Main Street. A meeting was held in front of the Bodie House hotel, and the case of the prisoner was discussed. Many men urged that DeRoche be hanged immediately, while others argued that the law be allowed to take its course. But as time wore on indignation over Treloar's murder grew and the crowd began moving toward the jail. Into the street jumped Patrick Reddy. He brought the crowd to a halt and in "a speech of some length" cautioned the assembled men to do nothing rash and

39. *Daily Free Press*, 18 Jan. 1881.
40. *Daily Free Press*, 18 Jan. 1881; Jail Register: Bodie Branch Jail, p. 12.

promised that the law would, if properly administered, deal with DeRoche severely and justly. "General" John Kittrell, an attorney, and William Irwin, the president of the Bank of Bodie, then joined Reddy and echoed his sentiments. No leader arose to oppose Reddy and his two supporters, and "the immense throng gradually cooled down."[41]

Shortly after Reddy had calmed the crowd, the Sunday edition of the *Daily Free Press* came off the presses with an editorial that probably did much to fan the flames of outrage again:

> The criminal history of Bodie has been a peculiar one. There have been many foul murders committed since the revival of affairs here, yet there have been no convictions. . . . A number of red-handed murderers have been brought to trial, but their nonconviction was due to stupid and easily influenced juries. In this respect the people are to blame. When a man is put on trial and twelve men can not have the heart to punish him, it is no fault of the law. The past has demonstrated the fact that the exertions of a vigilant and faithful lawyer have more to do with the framing of a verdict than the plain, cold facts developed in the case.

At two o'clock in the afternoon, DeRoche was marched to justice court for his examination.[42] He appeared frightened at seeing the hundreds of angry men, but nevertheless walked with a firm step up the street and into the courtroom.

"You are entitled to secure counsel," Thomas Newman, justice of the peace, told DeRoche. "I'll take Pat Reddy," said DeRoche. "I'm engaged for the prosecution," replied Bodie's ablest defense attorney. A surprised and disheartened DeRoche turned to John Kittrell and said, "Then I'll take you."

The testimony given in the subsequent examination did not differ materially from that given before the coroner's jury. At half-past six o'clock court was recessed, and DeRoche, under heavy guard, was returned to jail. When court reconvened, G. W. Alexander was put on the stand. He testified, as he had before the coroner's jury, that he saw DeRoche pull a revolver out of his pocket and put the gun to Treloar's head and fire. Treloar, said Alexander, had made no move toward DeRoche and, in fact, was not even looking at him. After the testimony of one more man, a doctor who had examined Treloar's body, court was adjourned until Monday morning, and DeRoche was returned to jail.

Several hundred Bodieites reckoned that DeRoche had had enough justice. They met at Webber's blacksmith shop and, after a "long and deliberate" discussion, concluded that DeRoche should hang. At about half-past one on Monday morning, the men, some of them masked and some not, marched up to the jail, surrounded it, and began shouting: "DeRoche—bring him out—open the door—hurry up." Constable Kirgan looked out the jail window and saw several hundred armed vigilantes. Evidently deciding that the occasion called for discretion, Kirgan yelled, "All right boys. Wait a moment. Give me a little time." A few seconds later Kirgan opened the door, and five vigilante officers entered the jail. They found DeRoche in his cell, fully aware of what this untimely visit meant. Nevertheless, it was some time before they had DeRoche dressed and brought him outside. The delay caused the men outside to grow restless,

41. *Daily Free Press*, 18 Jan. 1881.
42. *Daily Free Press*, 18 Jan. 1881.

especially after a few vigilantes suggested that the law officers probably had removed DeRoche from the jail. "If this had been the case," said the *Daily Free Press*, "what would have followed can only be imagined."

DeRoche appeared at the door wearing light-colored pants, a calico shirt, a canvas jacket, and a look of "dogged and defiant submission" on his face. With a firm step he descended the stairs of the jail and walked into the street. His gaze was fixed firmly on the ground and he did not say a word. "Fall in!" commanded the vigilante captain. The vigilantes assembled in company formation and, at the bark of a second command, marched DeRoche to Webber's blacksmith shop. In front of the shop stood a large hoisting frame, used for raising wagons and stagecoaches while they were being repaired. "Move it to the spot where the murder was committed," ordered the captain of the vigilantes. A dozen men picked up the hoisting frame and carried it to the corner of Main and Lowe streets. They set it down on the very spot where Treloar fell.

DeRoche was led underneath the frame, and a rope was placed around his neck. He stood there stoically and even helped adjust the knot of the noose to prevent it from rubbing his ear. His hands and feet were tied and he was asked if he had anything to say. "No, nothing," he replied. A moment later he was asked the same question again, and a French-speaking bystander was requested to receive the reply. "I have nothing to say, only, O God," said DeRoche.

Snow had just begun to fall, and the moon, which had shone brightly earlier in the night, shed a pale glow on the improvised gallows. "Pull him," ordered the vigilante captain. Instantly DeRoche was jerked several feet off the ground. His eyes closed, his legs twitched, and then all was still except the slow pendulum swing of his body. The vigilantes remained perfectly silent, except for the vigilante captain, who ordered, "Keep back and give the man all the air possible."

After a lapse of two or three minutes a man, who had come upon the crowd from the rear, broke the silence with a clear, sharp call: "I will give a hundred dollars if twenty men connected with this affair will publish their names in the paper tomorrow morning." The voice was immediately recognized as that of a person whom the *Daily Free Press* would only call "a leading attorney." Shouts of "Give him the rope," "Put him out," and similar cries drowned out the attorney—who could have been none other than Patrick Reddy—and he retreated "as dignified as the exigencies of the case would admit of." Not surprisingly, no one else was brave enough to protest the actions of the vigilantes. Law enforcement officials—the county sheriff and the town constable and all their deputies—were once again conspicuously absent.

While DeRoche was still hanging from the hoisting frame, a note was pinned to his chest. The note read: "All others take warning. Let no one cut him down. Bodie 601."[43] For the next ten or fifteen minutes men came forward and read the note by the light of matches that they struck. After DeRoche had been hanging for some twenty minutes, his heart beat rapidly for a brief period and then stopped. The coroner was summoned and, on examining the body, pronounced DeRoche dead. H. Ward, an undertaker, was then allowed to cut the body down and take it to his mortuary. "All members of the Bodie 601 will meet at their rendezvous," the vigilante captain sang out. In a moment the intersection of Main and Lowe streets was deserted. "DeRoche," said the

43. A Virginia City vigilance committee first used the numerals 601. It was copied by vigilance committees in the Nevada towns of Eureka and Hiko as well as in Bodie.

Daily Free Press, "died game. He was firm as a rock to the last and passed out into the unknown without a shudder."

Monday afternoon the coroner summoned a jury to investigate the death of Joseph DeRoche. Within minutes the jury rendered its verdict: "The deceased came to his death at the hands of persons unknown to the jury."[44] Meanwhile, DeRoche's body lay in Ward's mortuary. A large number of people came to view the body, but no one came to claim it. "It is a rare instance," said the *Daily Free Press*, "when a man lives in a place for years and at his death no friend volunteers to see that his remains are properly buried." As a result, the county conducted DeRoche's funeral. It also paid for it. The real estate that DeRoche had owned was heavily mortgaged, and his personal effects were worth little. The only items of value that DeRoche left behind were the ropes that bound his hands and feet and the noose that encircled his neck. Pieces of the ropes and the noose were eagerly sought as souvenirs.

Deputy Sheriff Joe Farnsworth, meanwhile, was a prisoner in the Carson City jail. When he had first stepped off the stage on Sunday, he had been arrested by the local sheriff on charges preferred via telegram by Bodie authorities. On Monday the Carson sheriff received a second telegram from the Bodie authorities, saying that DeRoche had been captured and tried by Judge Lynch and that Farnsworth could be released. The telegram also said that "Farnsworth had better not return to Bodie, the prevailing sentiment regarding him being anything but favorable."[45]

The next day the *Daily Free Press* expressed some of the prevailing sentiment when it suggested that "the altitude of this section is not good for an officer who betrayed his official trust and allowed a murderer to escape. According to medical statistics Los Angeles, Santa Barbara, or some other Coast town has more health to the square inch than a place 8,500 feet above the sea."[46] Farnsworth responded to the *Press*'s comments immediately. In a letter to the newspaper he absolutely denied having aided DeRoche and concluded, "I took the man away to save his life, and was as anxious as any man in Bodie to produce him; but deemed it best to leave while there was so much wild excitement over the matter, as no man's life is safe when a mob have become bent on his destruction. It is claimed that I received money to let him go. I challenge the production of the proof. I left Bodie without a dollar."[47]

Farnsworth returned to Bodie sometime during the next few months and all seems to have been forgiven. He became a regular participant in Bodie wrestling tournaments and at 170 pounds was said to be as "quick as a cat, and . . . a perfect master of the Greco-Roman style of wrestling."[48] He was eventually arrested and brought into court, not for anything to do with DeRoche's escape, but for a brawl with Billy Deegan in the Temple saloon.[49]

Joe Farnsworth was not the only Bodie lawman to suffer, at least temporarily, as a result of DeRoche's escape. Constable John Kirgan lost one of his two jobs. Kirgan was both town constable and jailer of the Bodie jail. As jailer he was appointed by the

44.   *Daily Free Press*, 18 Jan. 1881.

45.   *Daily Free Press*, 20 Jan. 1881; Carson City *Daily Appeal*, 18 Jan. 1881.

46.   *Daily Free Press*, 18 Jan. 1881.

47.   *Daily Free Press*, 21 Jan. 1881.

48.   *Bodie Standard*, 14 Dec. 1881.

49.   Bodie Justice Court Record, pp. 126–29.

county sheriff and carried the title of deputy sheriff. Reacting to community pressure and *Daily Free Press* editorials, Sheriff P. B. Taylor dismissed Kirgan from his post as jailer and appointed in his place Patrick Roan, a two-year resident of Bodie and a former sheriff of Douglass County, Nevada.[50] Kirgan continued to serve as town constable, an elective post, until March, when his sulky overturned on Main Street and he was fatally injured.[51]

With DeRoche hanged, Farnsworth in temporary exile, and Kirgan replaced as jailer, Bodie began to return to normal—normal, that is, for Bodie. Editorial comment in the days following the hanging strongly supported the actions of the vigilantes. After summarizing the murder, escape, trial, and hanging, the *Daily Free Press* said, on 18 January:

> These events are sufficiently terrible to produce a lasting effect upon the minds of all before whom they have been enacted. That effect can but be a salutary one. . . . We are not quick to advise a resort to unlawful methods even to obtain justice. But there are times in the history of nations, States, communities and individuals when a revolution is necessary. There is a struggle for mastery between the right and the wrong, the good and the bad, which breaks forth beyond the bounds of ordinary procedure. The horror stricken DaRoche, as he stood beneath the improvised gallows on Main street, suffering as he doubtless had a thousand deaths in his flight, capture and seizure by the committee, was not there for the sole reason that he had killed Treloar—though that was reason enough. He stood there as the fit representative of the Spirit of Murder. . . . The miserable wretch has now gone before a Higher Court . . . and we dismiss him to his fate.

The Virginia City *Territorial Enterprise* voiced similar sentiments on 20 January.

> The summary hanging at Bodie of the Frenchman DaRoche by the Vigilantes of that reckless camp will probably have the effect of checking if not crushing out the spirit of lawlessness which has so long terrified its people. When the officers of the law persistently fail to do their duty, and the courts, established for the promotion of justice, prove themselves unequal to the task, it is time for the people to rise in their majesty and vindicate the first great law of self-preservation. . . . Deplore, as we may, that condition of society which requires the gathering of a mob to execute the decrees of justice, it is an improvement over that other high state of civilization which allows murder to run riot in a community and allows assassins to walk the streets unharmed.

There were those in Bodie who disagreed with the actions of the vigilantes. "Since the sudden taking off of DaRoche by a mysterious collection of citizens," said the *Daily Free Press* on 18 January, "the toughs, rounders, dead beats, pimps, opium fiends, four-time losers, broken down gamblers, garroters, the he prostitutes and the outcasts generally have not hesitated to put in their protest against the deed." But not all who

50. *Daily Free Press*, 20 Jan. 1881; Myron Angel, ed., *History of Nevada*, p. 377.

51. *Daily Free Press*, 9 March and 2 April 1881.

protested the deed were dissolute characters. Some ninety Bodieites met at the music hall on the Wednesday evening of 19 January and formed the Law and Order Association.[52] Robert Fouke was elected president of the association, Leo Scowden secretary, and Ed Loose sergeant-at-arms. All three men were pioneer Bodieites and respected members of the community. Scowden, in fact, had been responsible for surveying and laying out Bodie Township. Featured speakers at the meeting were attorneys Patrick Reddy, John Kittrell, and Selden Hetzel. All members of the association pledged to aid and protect officers of the law in the discharge of their official duties, and to assist by legal means in the suppression, detection, and punishment of crime.

On Saturday night the association met again, this time in Justice Peterson's courtroom.[53] When a reporter from the *Daily Free Press* tried to gain entry to the meeting, he was stopped on the steps leading to the courtroom by Eugene Markey and Sylvester Roe and told that the meeting was private. The reporter nevertheless persisted and knocked on the courtroom's door. Ed Loose, the sergeant-at-arms, opened the door "a little more than the width of his own nose" and refused to allow the reporter to enter. The reporter did see enough, however, to conclude that the meeting was devoted to cigar smoking and drinking and not to the business of law and order.

When the Gold Hill *News* heard about Bodie's law and order association, it commented, "Such organizations amount to about as much as St. Paul said faith did without works. . . . Law and order bluffs hard, telling what it is going to do, but 601 [601 was a popular designation for vigilance committees in Nevada] goes right ahead and does what it proposes without telling it all to the newspapers beforehand. In fact, it is a peculiarity with 601 that newspapers never have a chance to publish their intentions, but only their achievements."[54] The *News* seems to have been right about Bodie's law and order association. The association faded from the scene after its first two meetings. But, then, so did Bodie's 601. Although there were more than a dozen shootings after Treloar's murder, the vigilance committee was never heard of again.

Vigilantism, then, was no stranger to Bodie. The first outbreak was nothing more than an attempt to carry off George Daly and perhaps intimidate him into capitulating to the striking engineers. The second saw Daly and the Jupiter men banished from Bodie for killing John Goff, and the third ended with DeRoche hanging from a wagon hoist for murdering Treloar. Probably the most striking features of these outbreaks of vigilantism were the military-like organization and discipline of the vigilantes and the absence of the law enforcement officials.

While the vigilantes were certainly violent and impassioned, they never operated as an unruly, reckless mob. They were determined but generally quiet, orderly, and highly disciplined. They had a definite chain of command, were organized into companies and squads, and fell into ranks and marched wherever they went. A considerable number of Bodieites, especially members of the Miners' Union, were veterans of the Civil War. These men obviously carried their military experience with them into the vigilante activity.

Neither the Mono County sheriff nor the Bodie town constable or any of their officers ever attempted to interfere with the vigilantes. Nor was the Bodie National

52. *Daily Free Press*, 20 Jan. 1881.

53. *Daily Free Press*, 23 Jan. 1881.

54. Gold Hill *News*, date unknown, as reprinted in the Bodie *Daily Free Press*, 9 Feb. 1881.

Guard ordered into action. Attorney Patrick Reddy did stop the advance of a mob—not the vigilantes—on the jail, and he also confronted the vigilantes after they had hanged DeRoche. But the motion-picture image of the courageous sheriff facing down the vigilantes is contradicted by Bodie's experience. The vigilantes who hanged De-Roche would have hanged or shot to death any man who stood in their way. While Reddy was able to stop a leaderless mob, no one could have stopped the well-organized and disciplined vigilantes, and no one was willing to sacrifice his life in a futile attempt.

Less easily understood was the nearly complete lack of action on the part of the institutions of justice—justice and superior courts and the coroner's and grand juries—to investigate the extralegal actions of the vigilantes. The only effort in that direction—a dishonest effort at that—came when the coroner held an inquest over DeRoche's body. The coroner's jury quickly decided that DeRoche had come to his death at the hands of "persons unknown to the jury" and let the matter drop. Nor did the justice system try to do anything to reverse the banishment of George Daly and his men. This was even more surprising because the banishment was not just a one-time event to be buried and forgotten, it was an ongoing condition.

The explanation for the noninvolvement of the justice system seems to lie in the great popularity of the hanging and the banishment. While many men had been shot to death in Bodie, their passing did not seem to trouble most Bodieites. The death of Treloar was different. It violated the sensibilities of everyone. Treloar was not a bad-man or a rough, or even a gun-packing rowdy. He was simply a small, brain-damaged miner who was considered anything but a threat. When DeRoche shot him in the back of the head and the testimony of two eye-witnesses eliminated any claim to self-defense, DeRoche's fate was sealed. Bodieites knew that the court system favored defendants—no killer had ever been convicted—and were unwilling to let the law take its course. Ironically, DeRoche won some degree of respect from the vigilantes. While he had committed a cowardly murder—so cowardly that it provoked a vigilante response—he was not a coward. He contradicted the motion-picture image of the craven murderer sniveling and pleading for his life. In the words of the *Daily Free Press*, DeRoche was firm as a rock to the last and died game.

The vigilante response to the killing of John Goff was produced by factors considerably more complex than those that brought forth the vigilantes in the Treloar killing. The two most important factors seem to have been the nature of the dispute between the Jupiter and the Owyhee and the personalities involved. The dispute was over property—the kind of dispute that Bodieites, miners or not, thought should have been settled in the courts—and the principal actors in the drama were the hated George Daly and the popular John Goff. Probably no man in Bodie was more hated by the miners than George Daly. While he was intelligent, dedicated, and recklessly brave, he was also dogmatic, uncompromising, and belligerent. But most of all he was bitterly and aggressively antiunion.

Then, also, Daly was the representative of big business. The Mono and Jupiter mining companies were controlled by enormously wealthy and powerful San Francisco investors. The average Bodieite had no love for the powerful few in the city by the bay who manipulated Bodie mining stock with corrupt but ingenious dexterity and who all but ignored mine accidents that killed and injured dozens of Bodie miners each year.[55]

55. See p. 108.

John Goff, on the other hand, was a fitting example of the Bodie miner. Goff was a popular shift-boss at the Bodie mine, a leading member of the Miners' Union, and a respected Civil War veteran. Moreover, the claim that he died defending, the Owyhee, was owned and worked by a small group of struggling, local miners, including Goff himself. The Owyhee miners, right or wrong in their claim to the disputed ground, were considered the undeniable underdogs and, as such, won the sympathy of many a Bodieite. It also seems likely that the Miners' Union saw the dispute between the Jupiter and the Owyhee in a larger context. Inasmuch as the late 1870s was a time when San Franciscan Denis Kearney was at his popular best, railing against the dangers and abuses of monopolistic capitalism and fighting for workers' rights, the union miners probably perceived the dispute as, among other things, a contest between big business and the workingman.

Thus the vigilante response to the killing of John Goff, and the popularity of Daly's banishment, seem to have been the products of several factors. The property-related nature of the dispute and the personalities involved were undoubtedly paramount, but the underdog nature of the Owyhee miners and the metaphorical clash of big business and workingman were perhaps important factors also.

13

THE HERITAGE OF
THE TRANS-SIERRA
FRONTIER

The trans-Sierra frontier was unmistakably violent and lawless, but only in special ways. Whereas bank robbery, rape, racial violence, and serious juvenile crime seem not to have occurred, and robbery, theft, and burglary occurred relatively infrequently, shootings and shoot-outs among roughs, badmen, and miners were fairly regular events. Vigilantism visited Aurora once and Bodie three times, and warfare between Indians and whites was a bloody reality—mostly for Owens Valley ranchers and the Second Cavalry—during Aurora's boom years. Thus the violence and lawlessness that the trans-Sierra frontier experienced was generally confined to a few special categories and did not directly affect all activities or all people. The old, the young, the unwilling, the weak, and the female—with the notable exception of the prostitute—were, for the most part, safe from harm. If, as many popularly assume, much of America's crime problem stems from a heritage of frontier violence and lawlessness, then it is ironic that the crimes most common today—robbery, theft, burglary, and rape—were of no great significance and, in the case of rape, seemingly nonexistent on the trans-Sierra frontier.

Robbery was as often aimed at stagecoaches as at individuals. There were eleven robberies and three attempted robberies of stages during Bodie's boom years and possibly an equal number during Aurora's heyday. At the same times there were ten robberies and three attempted robberies of individuals in Bodie and a somewhat smaller number in Aurora. When highwaymen stopped a stagecoach, they usually took only the express box and left the passengers unmolested. Passengers often remarked that they had received only the most courteous treatment from the highwaymen. Only twice were passengers robbed. In the first instance the highwaymen later apologized for their conduct, and in the second instance the robbers were drunk.

Stage robberies were almost exclusively nighttime events. Only one occurred during the day. The stages carrying the great bullion shipments were not the targets of the highwaymen. The highwaymen had no desire to tangle with the two or more shotgun messengers who always rode on the bullion stages, preferring instead to prey on the unguarded coaches. Only once did messengers and highwaymen exchange gunfire—a messenger was wounded and a highwayman killed—and in that instance they met by chance. Several of the highwaymen lived in San Francisco and crossed into the trans-

Sierra country only to rob stages. Not more than three highwaymen were ever apprehended, and only two of those were convicted of robbery. The only deterrent to stage robbery seems to have been the shotgun messengers.

Next to stagecoach robbery, bank robbery is probably the form of robbery most popularly associated with the frontier West. Yet, although Aurora and Bodie together boasted several banks, no bank robbery was ever attempted. Most of the bankers were armed, as were their employees, and a robber would have run a considerable risk of being killed. If highwaymen were unwilling to stop the messenger-guarded stages, then who would wish to take the even greater risk of robbing a bank?

There were only ten robberies and three attempted robberies of individuals—other than those robbed as part of a stage holdup—in Bodie during its boom years, and there seem to have been even fewer in Aurora during its heyday. Nevertheless, the few robberies that did occur outraged the citizens and in Bodie provoked talk of vigilantism. In nearly every one of these robberies the circumstances were so similar as to be interchangeable: The robbery victim had spent the evening in a gambling den, saloon, or brothel; he had revealed in some way that he had on his person a tidy sum of money; and he was staggering home drunk late at night when the attack occurred.

Again, it would seem that in both Aurora and Bodie more robberies might have occurred if the citizens had not gone about armed and ready to fight. It is revealing that nearly all robbery victims were staggering drunk when attacked. A man in anything resembling a sober state was simply too dangerous to rob. The presence of police officers patrolling the streets at night may also have deterred some robbers, although no officer in Bodie ever made an arrest of a robber or came to the rescue of a robbery victim, and several officers were dismissed from duty for alleged cooperation with robbers.

Bodie's total of twenty-one robberies—eleven of stages and ten of individuals—over a five-year period converts to a rate of 84 robberies per 100,000 inhabitants per year.[1] On this scale—the same scale that the Federal Bureau of Investigation uses to index crime—New York in 1980 had a robbery rate of 1,140, Miami 995, Los Angeles 628, San Francisco–Oakland 521, Atlanta 347, and Chicago 294.[2] Equaling Bodie's rate of 84 was Santa Rosa, California.[3] The lowest rate of robbery among U.S. cities was Bismarck, North Dakota's 7.5.[4] The rate for the United States as a whole, including small towns and rural areas, was 243.[5] Thus Bodie, even with its stagecoach robberies included, had a robbery rate significantly below the national average in 1980.

Unfortunately, it is impossible to compare Bodie's rate of robbery—or rates of any other crimes—directly with those of eastern towns during the nineteenth century. All crime studies of the eastern towns are based on numbers of arrests and not on numbers of offenses.[6] It is generally conceded that, except in the case of murder and manslaugh-

---

1.   This rate was arrived at by dividing the total number of robberies (21) by the span of years over which they took place (5) and multiplying by the factor (20) necessary to convert Bodie's average population during those years (5,000) to the 100,000 population norm used by the FBI Crime Index.

2.   U.S. Department of Justice, Federal Bureau of Investigation, *Uniform Crime Reports: 1980* (Washington, 1981), pp. 61, 64, 73, 76, 81. All figures have been rounded off.

3.   *Crime Reports,* p. 81.

4.   *Crime Reports,* p. 62.

5.   *Crime Reports,* p. 17.

6.   See, e.g., Roger Lane, *Violent Death in the City: Suicide, Accident, and Murder in Nineteenth-Century Philadelphia.* Lane briefly discusses the problems of using numbers of arrests rather than numbers of offenses,

ter, numbers of offenses are many times greater—often four or five or more—than numbers of arrests.[7] Bodie's experience certainly confirms this. For the great majority of offenses in Bodie there were no arrests.

Nevertheless, comparisons can be made by extrapolation of the numbers of arrests. For example, Boston's robbery arrest rate for the years 1880 through 1882 was 23.[8] If four robberies were committed for every one arrest—a ratio based on FBI statistics for 1980—then Boston's robbery rate was 92. During the same years Salem, Massachusetts, had a robbery arrest rate of 13, giving it a robbery rate of 52.[9] Thus it would seem that Boston and Salem had robbery rates roughly comparable—considering the estimation and projection involved—to Bodie's rate of 84. But it would also seem, since stagecoach robberies accounted for about half of Bodie's robberies, that the individual was more likely to be robbed in Boston or Salem than in Bodie.[10]

Just as the heavily armed messengers prevented robbery of the bullion stages, and the armed citizenry discouraged robbery of individuals, the armed homeowner and merchant discouraged burglary of home and business. Between 1877 and 1883, there were only 32 burglaries—17 of homes and 15 of businesses—in Bodie. Again, Aurora seems to have had fewer still. At least a half-dozen attempted burglaries in Bodie were thwarted by the presence of armed citizens. The newspapers regularly advocated shooting burglars on sight, and several burglars were, in fact, shot at. Moreover, Bodieites, even when not armed, were willing to fight intruders.

Bodie's five-year total of 32 burglaries converts to an average of 6.4 burglaries a year and gives the town a burglary rate of 128 on the FBI scale. In 1980 Miami had a burglary rate of 3,282, New York 2,661, Los Angeles 2,602, San Francisco–Oakland 2,267, Atlanta 2,210, and Chicago 1,241.[11] The Grand Forks, North Dakota, rate of 566 and the Johnstown, Pennsylvania, rate of 587 were lowest among U.S. cities.[12] The rate for the United States as a whole was 1,668, or thirteen times that for Bodie.[13] Boston's burglary arrest rate from 1880 through 1882 was 87, and Salem's was 54.[14] A conversion factor of 7—a figure based on FBI data—gives these towns burglary rates of 609 and 378, rates three to five times greater than that for Bodie.

Theft was not a major problem in Aurora or Bodie. Bodie had some forty-five instances of theft, and most of the theft was for firewood and blankets. Included in this

on pages 56–57. See also Roger Lane, *Policing the City: Boston 1822–1885*; Eric Monkkonen, *Police in Urban America, 1860–1920*, and *The Dangerous Class*; Theodore N. Ferdinand, "The Criminal Patterns of Boston Since 1849," and "Politics, the Police, and Arresting Policies in Salem, Massachusetts, Since the Civil War."

7. For the disparity between offenses and arrests in 1980, compare pp. 41 and 191 of the *Uniform Crime Reports: 1980*. The following ratios of offenses to arrests can be extrapolated from the data: robbery 3.8 to 1; burglary 7.3 to 1; theft 6.0 to 1; rape 2.6 to 1. (All figures have been rounded to the nearest tenth.)

8. Ferdinand, "Criminal Patterns of Boston Since 1849," p. 93.

9. Ferdinand, "Politics, the Police, and Arresting Policies in Salem," p. 579.

10. Boston's robbery arrest rate in the period 1880–1882 was the lowest of the years 1855 through 1900. In 1883–1884, e.g., the robbery arrest rate was 31; in 1880–1882 it was 23. See Ferdinand, "Criminal Patterns of Boston Since 1849," p. 93.

11. *Uniform Crime Reports: 1980*, pp. 61, 64, 73, 74, 76, 81. All figures have been rounded off.

12. *Crime Reports*, pp. 68 and 70.

13. *Crime Reports*, p. 23.

14. Ferdinand, "Criminal Patterns of Boston Since 1849," p. 94, and "Politics, the Police, and Arresting Policies in Salem," p. 579.

total of forty-five thefts are six instances of horse theft. Only two horse thieves were ever caught, and they were punished far less severely than would traditionally be supposed; one of them was sentenced to serve six months in the county jail, and the other to serve one year in the state penitentiary. Although there were thousands of head of cattle to the west of Aurora and Bodie in the Bridgeport Valley and to the south in the Owens Valley, cattle rustling, except for Indian depredations during the warfare of the 1860s, did not exist.

Bodie's forty-five instances of theft give it a theft rate of 180. In 1980 Miami had a theft rate of 5,452, San Francisco–Oakland 4,571, Atlanta, 3,947, Los Angeles 3,372, New York 3,369, and Chicago 3,206.[15] Lowest theft rates among U.S. cities were those of Steubenville, Ohio, at 916, and Johnstown, Pennsylvania, at 972.[16] The rate for the United States as a whole was 3,156, more than seventeen times that for Bodie.[17] Boston's theft arrest rate for 1880 through 1882 was 575, Salem's 525.[18] A conversion factor of 6—a factor consistent with the FBI data—gives the towns theft rates of 3,450 and 3,150.

Thus Bodie's rates of robbery, burglary, and theft were dramatically lower than those of most U.S. cities in 1980 and were as low as or significantly lower than those for Boston and Salem from 1880 through 1882. Even if four or five times as much robbery, burglary, and theft occurred in Bodie but went unreported in the newspapers and unrecorded in the jail register and court records, Bodie would still have had rates dramatically lower than those for most U.S. cities in 1980. In comparison with nineteenth-century Boston and Salem, Bodie's rate of theft would still be many times lower, its burglary rate about equal, and its robbery rate higher.[19] Aurora seems to have had rates lower than Bodie—the available evidence so indicates—but because of the incomplete nature of the sources such a conclusion must remain speculative.

Institutions of law enforcement and justice certainly were not responsible for the low rates of robbery, burglary, and theft. Rarely were any of the perpetrators of these types of crime arrested, and even less often were they convicted. Many law officers had less than zealous attitudes about their work, and some operated on both sides of the law; gang-leader John Daly and several of his men served as officers in Aurora, and several Bodie officers may have cooperated with robbers. When a man *was* arrested, chances were good that he would not be convicted. Because so few men were convicted of these crimes, it does not seem that the normal punishment—imprisonment in jail or the penitentiary—could have served as much of a deterrent.

The citizens themselves, armed with various types of firearms and willing to kill to protect their persons or property, were evidently the most important deterrent to larcenous crime.[20] Full employment may also have served as something of a deterrent.

15. *Uniform Crime Reports: 1980*, pp. 61, 64, 73, 74, 76, 81. All figures have been rounded off. Auto thefts are not included in these figures. The FBI lists auto thefts in a separate category.

16. *Crime Reports*, pp. 70 and 83.

17. *Crime Reports*, p. 27.

18. Ferdinand, "Criminal Patterns of Boston Since 1849," p. 96, and "Politics, the Police, and Arresting Policies in Salem," p. 580.

19. It is certainly likely that some burglaries and thefts went unreported in Bodie, but this would be true also of nineteenth-century Boston and Salem and of U.S. cities today. On the other hand, because of the violent nature of robbery, it is unlikely that many robberies went unreported in Bodie.

20. In an effort to deter crime, several small towns in the United States enacted laws during 1982 requiring their citizens to own firearms. Kennesaw, Georgia, a town with a population of 5,400 and located some 35

Aurora, where few were without jobs, seems to have had slightly less larcenous crime than Bodie, where many suffered periodic unemployment. Perhaps the most intangible of the possible deterrents was the optimistic attitude of Aurorans and Bodieites. They had hope. And while men have hope, no matter what their circumstances are, they are less likely to commit crime.

Aurora and Bodie women, other than prostitutes, suffered little from crime or violence. In Bodie from 1878 through 1882 there were only some thirty violent encounters between men and women, and prostitutes were involved in twenty-five of them. When women fought women, prostitutes accounted for thirteen of seventeen fights. Only a handful of either of these types of violent encounters had serious consequences. Just one resulted in death, and in that case the woman was a former prostitute and her murderer was insane. There was also one woman who died from the effects of an abortion, and another who nearly died from a clubbing.

A very obvious double standard existed in Bodie. While the "decent" women were treated with the greatest deference, prostitutes were socially ostracized and generally shown no respect. Newspapers often treated beatings of prostitutes humorously, and the attitude of police and judges was only slightly better. Men who assaulted prostitutes were usually arrested for their attacks, but their punishments were far less severe than if they had assaulted "respectable" women. The double standard extended even to the graveyard. Prostitutes who died in Bodie were buried outside the fence of the graveyard.

The greatest threat facing women in Bodie was suicide. Six women killed themselves during the town's boom years, and four others tried to do so.[21] The six deaths give Bodie an extraordinarily high female suicide rate of 24.[22] From 1868 through 1872 Philadelphia had a female suicide rate of only 2.0, and the United States during the 1970s had female suicide rates that all fell between 6 and 7; in 1978 the rate for females was 6.3.[23] The difference between Bodie's rate and those of nineteenth-century Philadelphia and the United States today would be even greater if the figures were based only on populations of women rather than on total populations. Women normally represent about half of the population; in Bodie they made up only some 10 or 12 percent. Accounting for this difference would give Bodie an astounding female suicide rate of 100 or more. Prostitutes contributed disproportionately to the high rate. While they constituted considerably less than half of the female population, they committed half of the suicides.

Bodie women were six or seven times more likely to kill themselves than were Bodie men.[24] The opposite was true in Philadelphia during the 1870s; for every one

miles from Atlanta, was the first to do so. Four months after Kennesaw's gun law was enacted, the town's mayor insisted that the law was having the desired effect. "It's accomplished everything that we'd hoped," he said. "We wanted to let the criminal element know that it was not safe for them here." The number of burglaries has declined dramatically in Kennesaw since the passage of the law, but it is obviously too early to draw firm conclusions from the experiment. See the *Los Angeles Times*, 23 July 1982.

21.   There may have been more than six suicides, but the evidence is ambiguous. For example, one prostitute took some opium and alcohol, allegedly to relax after a fight with a man. She died from the drugs, and her death was considered the result of an accidental overdose. It could easily have been suicide.

22.   Bodie averaged 1.2 female suicides per year between 1877 and 1883, or 24 per 100,000 population.

23.   Lane, *Violent Death in the City*, p. 29; U.S. Bureau of the Census, *Statistical Abstract of the United States: 1981*, pp. 75, 77, 79.

24.   Eight Bodie men committed suicide—two more than women—but men outnumbered women by nine to one in Bodie. Bodie's male suicide rate was 32, but drops to about 19 when adjusted for a population base that was over 85 percent male. In 1978 the suicide rate for males in the United States was 19.0. See *Statistical Abstract of the United States: 1981*, p. 75.

woman who killed herself more than five men took their own lives.[25] The opposite is also true in more recent times. During the 1970s (the ratio is much the same for the 1950s and 1960s) males in the United States killed themselves at a rate three times that of females.[26]

Although Bodie's female suicide rate was extraordinarily high, there was nothing unusual about the methods the women employed to kill themselves. Two shot themselves to death, and the other four overdosed on some type of drug or ingested poison. Much the same holds true today. In 1978, for example, some 36 percent of female suicides were committed with guns, and about 41 percent with drugs or poison.[27]

If suicide was a serious threat to women, rape and robbery were not. Only one woman, a prostitute, was robbed in Bodie, and there were no reports of women having been robbed in Aurora. There were also no reported cases of rape in either Aurora or Bodie. This does not necessarily mean that rape did not occur, since rape is a crime that has traditionally been underreported. Nevertheless, there was not even one report of rape, and there is nothing to suggest that rape may have occurred. On the other hand, there is a considerable body of evidence that indicates that women, other than prostitutes, were only rarely the victims of crime and were generally treated with the utmost respect. There were two cases reported in which attempted rape was alleged. In neither of these cases, both involving prostitutes, did testimony of witnesses support the allegations.

Aurora's and Bodie's records of no rapes and thus rape rates of zero were not matched by nineteenth-century Boston or Salem. From 1880 through 1882 Boston had a rape arrest rate of 3.0 and Salem 4.8.[28] A conversion factor of 2.6—a figure consistent with FBI data in 1980—gives the towns rape rates of 7.8 and 12.5. Nor are Aurora's and Bodie's rates matched by any U.S. city today, although in 1980 Johnstown, Pennsylvania, had a rate of only 5.7.[29] Close behind were Steubenville, Ohio, at 6.2; Bismarck, North Dakota, at 6.3; and Lancaster, Pennsylvania, at 6.4.[30] At the other end of the scale was Los Angeles with more than five thousand rapes in 1980 and a rate of 75.4.[31] Miami had a rate of 67.0, San Francisco–Oakland 64.0, Atlanta 62.3, New York 43.3, and Chicago 30.0.[32] The rape rate for the United States as a whole in 1980 was 36.4.[33]

Juvenile crime is not even mentioned in Aurora; in Bodie it was almost entirely of the youthful prank and malicious mischief variety. The most frequent complaint against the teen-age roughs in Bodie was their use of obscene language. Their drinking, smoking—mostly tobacco but occasionally opium—and gambling were also causes of complaint. They committed a few petty thefts and burglaries, but no violent crimes. By contrast, youth today commit a significant percentage of the violent crime in the United

25. Lane, *Violent Death in the City*, p. 29.

26. *Statistical Abstract of the United States: 1981*, pp. 75 and 77.

27. *Statistical Abstract*, p. 79.

28. Ferdinand, "Criminal Patterns of Boston Since 1849," p. 91, and "Politics, the Police, and Arresting Policies in Salem," p. 579.

29. *Uniform Crime Reports: 1980*, p. 70.

30. *Crime Reports*, pp. 62, 71, 83.

31. *Crime Reports*, p. 73.

32. *Crime Reports*, pp. 61, 64, 74, 76, 81.

33. *Crime Reports*, p. 14.

States. In 1980, 9 percent of the arrests for murder, 15 percent of those for rape, and 30 percent of those for robbery were of persons under the age of eighteen.[34] Moreover, there is simply no comparison between Bodie's gang of teen-agers who loitered at the corner of Green and Wood streets and today's youth gangs. In Los Angeles county alone, youth gangs were responsible for 351 homicides in 1980.[35]

Aurora and Bodie had sizable populations of Chinese and smaller but also significant populations of Mexicans, yet there was no racially motivated violence in either town. Moreover, Chinese and Mexicans seem to have been treated no differently by the legal system than were other Aurorans and Bodieites. In the one case in which white witnesses and Chinese witnesses gave contradictory testimony, the jurors accepted the word of the Chinese over that of the whites. Attorneys made themselves available to the Chinese and Mexicans, and Patrick Reddy, Bodie's ablest lawyer, defended Sam Chung, the Chinese badman, more than once. When convicted of crimes, Chinese and Mexicans suffered penalties similar to those meted out to other Bodieites, and non-Mexican whites were punished no differently for their crimes against minorities than if they had committed them against anyone else. Despite this seemingly equal treatment, Mexicans and especially Chinese often preferred to avoid dealing with the justice system. Mexicans, as the murder of John Hackwell, the attempted murder of John Wheeler, and the attempted kidnapping of Sam Chung demonstrated, sought to personally avenge what they thought to be wrongs. Chinese let the secret societies handle most of Chinatown's problems. The authorities quickly learned that if both the victim and the perpetrator of a crime were Chinese, they could expect little or no cooperation, even from the victim himself.

The Chinese and Mexicans carried guns and knives, as did nearly everyone else on the trans-Sierra frontier, and were not averse to using them. Minority crime was not greatly different from that committed by the majority. The most spectacular difference, at least in Bodie, was the tong warfare of the Chinese. The Chinese were involved in a disproportionate number of burglaries and thefts, instances of selling liquor to Indians, and fights over and assaults on women. Mexicans also sold more than their share of liquor to Indians and committed a disproportionate number of horse thefts.

In Aurora and Bodie then, Chinese and Mexicans were not the targets of racially inspired violence. Women were not the victims of rape nor, for the most part, any kind of assault. And larcenous crime was of no great importance. In most ways the towns were not violent or lawless places. But when it came to men fighting men, Aurora and Bodie were unmistakably violent. Fistfights were nightly occurrences and gunfights were not infrequent. Some of these fights resulted from disputes over property and women; a few, from political differences; a handful, from domestic quarrels or arguments between neighbors; but most, from disputes over who was the better man, affronts to personal honor, careless insults, and challenges to pecking order in the saloon. For the most part, the parties involved in these fights were willing participants. Many of them belonged to that class of western frontiersmen known as badmen: proud, confident, and recklessly brave individuals who were always ready to do battle and to do battle in earnest. But most of them were simply miners, teamsters, carpenters, and woodchoppers.

Thirty-one Bodieites and no fewer than seventeen Aurorans were shot, stabbed, or beaten to death, mostly in fights, during the boom years. Because the record

34. *Crime Reports*, p. 202.

35. *Los Angeles Times*, 3 Dec. 1981.

for Aurora is incomplete, it is very possible that more than seventeen Aurorans were victims of homicide.[36] The large majority of these killings would fall today into the FBI's category of murder and nonnegligent (voluntary as opposed to accidental) manslaughter.[37] Of Bodie's thirty-one killings probably twenty-nine qualify for such categorization.[38] This would give Bodie a murder and nonnegligent manslaughter rate of 116 on the FBI scale. Aurora, with sixteen of its seventeen recorded killings qualifying, would have a rate of 64.[39]

No U.S. city today comes close to matching Bodie's rate of 116 or even Aurora's 64. In 1980 Miami led the nation with a rate of 32.7.[40] Las Vegas, Nevada, was a distant second at 23.4, followed closely by Los Angeles at 23.3.[41] New York had a rate of 21.0, Chicago 14.5, Atlanta 14.4, and San Francisco–Oakland 11.7.[42] A half-dozen cities had rates of zero.[43] The rate for the United States as a whole in 1980 was 10.2, a rate less than one-eleventh that for Bodie.[44]

Nor do eastern cities during the nineteenth century seem to have had rates more than a fraction of Bodie's. From 1880 through 1882 Boston had a murder and manslaughter (Boston police did not consistently distinguish between negligent and nonnegligent manslaughter) arrest rate of only 3.8 while Salem recorded a 0.0.[45] Since murder and manslaughter are two crimes for which arrests usually equal or occasionally even exceed offenses, there was probably little difference between Boston's and Salem's rates of arrest and rates of offenses.[46] From 1874 through 1880 Philadelphia had a homicide rate of 3.7, and its overall rate for the second half of the nineteenth century was 3.0.[47]

36.   There could have been as many as thirty-one homicides in Aurora. See note 21, p. 76. Two other factors would appear to have contributed to Aurora's lower total of killings. First, the hanging of John Daly and three members of his gang and the banishment of dozens of roughs and badmen early in 1864 caused killings to drop off at a time when the town itself had more than a year of real life left. And second, although both towns had peak populations of something over 5,000, Bodie maintained the peak for three of its five boom years, whereas Aurora maintained it for only two.

37.   The FBI defines murder and nonnegligent manslaughter as "the willful (nonnegligent) killing of one human being by another." Inclusion of offenders in this category is based solely on police investigation and not on the determination of a court. Justifiable homicides, defined as "the killings of felons by law enforcement officers in the line of duty or by private citizens," are not included. See *Uniform Crime Reports: 1980*, p. 7.

38.   The two exceptions would be shotgun messenger Mike Toby's killing of highwayman Frank Dow, and the killing of bystander Con Sullivan, who was struck by a stray round during a gunfight.

39.   The shooting of Lee Vining may have been accidental.

40.   *Uniform Crime Reports: 1980*, p. 74.

41.   *Crime Reports*, pp. 72 and 73.

42.   *Crime Reports*, pp. 61, 64, 76, 81.

43.   *Crime Reports*, pp. 62, 68, 71, 78, 82. The towns were Bloomington, Indiana; Grand Forks, North Dakota; Great Falls, Montana; La Crosse, Wisconsin; Provo, Utah; and Sioux City, Iowa.

44.   *Crime Reports*, p. 7.

45.   Ferdinand, "Criminal Patterns of Boston Since 1849," pp. 89 and 90, and "Politics, the Police, and Arresting Policies in Salem," p. 579.

46.   Oftentimes several members of a gang are arrested for one murder. As a result, in Los Angeles in 1981, e.g., numbers of arrests for murder far exceeded numbers of murders. See the Los Angeles Police Department's annual publication *The Statistical Digest*. Nationwide in 1980, numbers of murders exceeded numbers of arrests for murder, but only by a small margin. See *Uniform Crime Reports: 1980*, pp. 41 and 191. In Bodie numbers of arrests for murder exceeded the numbers of murders.

47.   Lane, *Violent Death in the City*, pp. 60 and 79. Since Lane bases his homicide rate on numbers of indictments for homicide and not on numbers of homicides, the actual homicide rates were probably slightly higher than 3.7 and 3.0. Lane discusses the problem of determining homicide rates on pp. 56–59.

Aurora and Bodie seem to have been matched in homicide rates only by other western frontier towns. Although studies have not been done that calculate homicide rates for other frontier towns, a look at the numbers of homicides that did occur in several of the towns suggests that their rates were, like those for Aurora and Bodie, very high. Virginia City had eight homicides during the year and a half following its founding in 1859.[48] In 1876, the year of its birth, Deadwood had four homicides.[49] Ellsworth, one of the Kansas cattle towns, had eight homicides during the twelve months following its establishment in 1867, and Dodge City, the queen of the cattle towns, had nine in its first year, 1872–1873.[50] Since the populations of all these towns were small—never more than two or three thousand during the first year—their homicide rates would seem to have been very high. By contrast, Oakland, California, a western but by 1870 no longer a frontier town, had only two homicides during the entire first half of the 1870s, and its population was more than 11,000 in 1870 and nearly 25,000 in 1875.[51]

Several factors would appear to be responsible for the high rates of homicide in Aurora and Bodie. First, the towns' populations were composed mostly of young, healthy, adventurous, single males who adhered to a code of conduct that required a man to stand and fight, even if, or perhaps especially if, it could mean death. Courage was admired above all else. Ironically, these men had come to the West for a materialistic end—to strike it rich—and yet their value structure emphasized the nonmaterialistic values of honor, pride, and courage. Alcohol played a major role as well. These men imbibed prodigious quantities of whiskey. Sobriety was thought proper only for Sunday school teachers and women.

If the character of the men and their consumption of alcohol made fighting inevitable, then their side arms often made fighting fatal. While the carrying of guns probably reduced the incidence of robbery, burglary, and theft, it undoubtedly increased the number of homicides. Although a couple of homicides resulted from beatings and a few from stabbings, the great majority resulted from shootings. With or without the gun, Aurorans and Bodieites would still have fought, but without the gun their fights would not have been so deadly.

The citizens of Aurora and Bodie were generally not troubled by the great numbers of killings, nor were they very upset because only one man was ever convicted by the courts of murder or manslaughter. They accepted the killings and the lack of convictions because those killed, with only a few exceptions, had been willing combatants, and many of them were roughs or badmen. The old, the weak, the female, the innocent, and those unwilling to fight were rarely the targets of attacks. But when they *were* attacked—and murdered—the reaction of the citizens was immediate and came in the form of vigilantism.

Contrary to the popular image of vigilantes as an angry, unruly mob, the vigilantes in both Aurora and Bodie displayed military-like organization and discipline and went about their work in a quiet, orderly, and deliberate manner. The vigilance committees that were formed after the murder of William Johnson in Aurora and Thomas

---

48. Myron Angel, ed., *History of Nevada*, pp. 343–44.

49. Harry H. Anderson, "Deadwood, South Dakota: An Effort at Stability," p. 47.

50. Robert R. Dykstra, *The Cattle Towns*, p. 113. Ellsworth and Dodge City never again had as many homicides as they had in their first years, although Ellsworth had five in 1873 and Dodge City had five in 1878.

51. Lawrence M. Friedman and Robert V. Percival, *The Roots of Justice: Crime and Punishment in Alameda County, California 1870–1910*, pp. 27 and 29.

Treloar in Bodie—the Citizens' Safety Committee and the Bodie 601—had as members some of the towns' leading citizens as well as the support of the local newspapers. In both towns the vigilantes waited until the coroner's jury had rendered a verdict before they acted. At no time did any officer of the law attempt to interfere with the actions of the vigilantes. Moreover, the after-the-fact investigations of the vigilantes by the grand jury in Aurora and the coroner's jury in Bodie resulted in nothing more than justifications of vigilantism.

The Citizens' Safety Committee and the Bodie 601 fit the model of "socially constructive" committees of vigilance.[52] In each case they were supported by a great majority of the townspeople, including the leading citizens; they were well regulated; they dealt quickly and effectively with criminal problems; they left the towns in more stable and orderly conditions; and when opposition developed, they disbanded. The committees made no attempt to interfere with the regular institutions of law enforcement and justice in matters that were unrelated to the killings of Johnson and Treloar. Unlike some other vigilante movements, most notably San Francisco's Committee of Vigilance of 1856, the vigilantes in Aurora and Bodie had no political motives.[53]

The vigilance committees were organized, not because there were no established institutions of law enforcement and justice, but because those institutions had failed, in the eyes of the vigilantes, to provide justice. That was not greatly troubling when the homicide victim was a rough or a badman or a man who had chosen to fight, but it was unacceptable when the victim was an innocent party. While killers were invariably arrested and charged with murder, most were discharged after an examination in justice court. In Bodie some forty men were arrested for murder (on three different occasions more than one man was arrested for the same murder) but only seven of these men eventually went to trial in superior court. The rest were either discharged after an examination in justice court or not indicted by the grand jury. Of the seven who were tried all but one—the insane Job Draper—were found not guilty.

Defense attorneys were surprisingly capable, and one, Patrick Reddy, was unquestionably brilliant. Reddy defended two men in justice court examinations and five men in superior court trials on charges of murder. Although the evidence against his clients appeared incontrovertibly damning on two occasions and strong on four others, Reddy never lost a case. One strategy commonly employed by Reddy, and by other defense attorneys, was delay. Since the population of the mining towns was largely transient, a postponement of a trial often meant the loss of prosecution witnesses. The tactic Reddy and the others employed most often to cause delays was disqualification of jurors. In one case Reddy managed to disqualify the entire jury. Jurors were difficult to replace. Aurorans and Bodieites found an endless number of excuses for not serving as jurors, and the county sheriffs regularly mentioned the trouble they had in producing the requisite twelve good and true men. For this reason judges refused to excuse potential jurors if they were familiar with a particular case and instead dismissed them only if they thought they could not be fair-minded.

Defense attorneys also had an important advantage over their colleagues who represented the state. Prosecutors in criminal cases had to prove, as they have to today, not only that the preponderance of the evidence indicated that a defendant was guilty

52.   Richard Maxwell Brown, *Strain of Violence: Historical Studies of American Violence and Vigilantism*, p. 118.

53.   Brown, pp. 134–43. See also Hubert Howe Bancroft, *Popular Tribunals*, vol. 2.

but that the defendant was guilty beyond a reasonable doubt. Moreover, all twelve jurors had to be so convinced. Defense attorneys often were able to place a reasonable doubt in the mind of at least one member of the jury and have a mistrial declared. This usually meant months of delay. The first two murder trials of Chinese badman Sam Chung, for example, ended in hung juries. When he was tried a third time, a full year after the murder, one key prosecution witness had died and another had left the state. Chung was found not guilty.

Also working to the advantage of the defense was the attitude of Aurorans and Bodieites. They thought that a man was fully justified in killing another man if that other man had threatened the first man's life. This held true even if some time had elapsed between the threat and the murder, as the murders of William Carder in Aurora and Jack Myers in Bodie demonstrated. Since the men of the trans-Sierra frontier were known to be men of their word, there was no such thing as an idle threat. Also, since fights were serious business and often proved fatal, any move that a man made during a confrontation which the other man involved in the dispute might interpret as a move for a gun justified that other man's drawing his gun and firing.

If the attitude of the people and the law itself stacked the odds in favor of the defense, so too did the attorneys themselves. The most capable attorneys, such as Patrick Reddy, John McQuaid, and Thomas Ryan, were in private practice and not, except when pressed into service, in the employ of the state. The defense attorneys regularly outshone the prosecutors. Patrick Reddy's performances in court were legendary. Known for his devastating cross-examinations of prosecution witnesses, he was also known to quote the law to the prosecutors, a tactic that brought roars of approval from spectators and left prosecutors chagrined. On the trans-Sierra frontier murder convictions were hard to come by.[54]

Two forms of violence and lawlessness existed in Aurora which were unknown in Bodie, political violence and warfare between Indians and whites. Political violence in Aurora was due entirely to the California-Nevada boundary dispute and the Civil War. The editors of Aurora's two newspapers, one Unionist and the other Copperhead, bore the brunt of this violence. They were both shot once and threatened many times, not by mobs, as occurred elsewhere in California during the Civil War, but by individuals. Aurora was a border town, both literally and figuratively, and political divisions ran deep during the Civil War years. Republican and Democratic clubs were organized almost as soon as the town was established, and there was even a group of Confederate sympathizers who, for a time, held regular meetings and rallies. Fistfights over political disputes were common, and voting frauds and other irregularities were not unknown.

Unlike Aurora, Bodie experienced no politically inspired acts of violence or lawlessness. Bodieites generally paid little attention to national politics—the Civil War was only a memory—and almost none to local politics—the California-Nevada boundary had been established. The only political issue that consistently aroused large numbers of Bodieites, at least Irish Bodieites, was England's continued occupation of Ireland and her oppression of the Irish. Bodie boasted a local chapter of the Land League of Ireland, and the chapter's meetings regularly filled the Miners' Union Hall to overflowing.

---

54.   Other frontier regions had similar experiences. Few men were ever convicted of murder. See Angel, *History of Nevada*, pp. 341–42; Anderson, "Deadwood, South Dakota," p. 46; and Dykstra, *Cattle Towns*, p. 129.

Warfare between Indians and whites occurred on the trans-Sierra frontier only during Aurora's boom years. This warfare cost the lives of no fewer than two hundred Indians and thirty whites; perhaps another hundred Indians and whites were wounded. It was not the activities of the miners that precipitated the warfare but those of the ranchers. It is conceivable that the miners and the Indians could have lived together in amity. Once the cattlemen began stocking the range lands of the trans-Sierra, however, warfare was inevitable. Cattle grazing meant less forage for the indigenous animals, whose numbers began to decline as the numbers of steers increased, and the destruction of native plants, whose seeds and roots were the staple of the Indian diet. The Indians of the arid and inhospitable trans-Sierra country had always suffered from a precarious food supply. With white encroachment that food supply was reduced even further, and the Indians had little choice but to prey on cattle and become beef eaters or starve. When a cowboy riding herd in the Owens Valley shot an Indian cattle rustler, the warfare began.

The Indians of the trans-Sierra country fought much as Indians fought elsewhere in the American West. They excelled at hit-and-run raiding and laying ambushes, but had no unity of command, logistical support, or sense of strategy. They were, after all, family men fighting in defense of their homeland, not professional soldiers. They were nearly always outgunned, and they suffered continually from food shortages. Destruction of Indian food caches, a favorite tactic of the whites, was tantamount to destroying the Indians themselves.

The warfare saw cruelty and savagery on both sides. Indians tortured their white (and in one case black) captives to death and gave no quarter to white noncombatants, including women and children. Whites shot down Indian women and children on more than one occasion and twice summarily executed Indian prisoners. If both the Indians and the whites were responsible for cruelty and savagery, ultimate responsibility for the conflict lay with the whites. They were trespassers on Indian lands. They were the invaders, the aggressors. From the perspective of the whites, however, there appeared to be ample room for settlement. They did not comprehend that the Indians were already, as required by the needs of a hunting and gathering people, making maximum use of the land. Nor did the whites comprehend that stocking the range lands with cattle would force the Indians either to drastically alter their way of life or to fight against encroachment by whites. Most Indians chose to fight.

By the time of Bodie's boom most of the Indians of the trans-Sierra frontier had been removed to reservations. A few small bands still roamed the hills, but it was almost impossible to eke out an existence. Woodchoppers had denuded most hillsides of trees and with them the pine nut, a staple of the Indian diet. Some three dozen Indians lived in Bodie, but they were not important figures in violence or lawlessness. For the most part they were pathetic alcoholics who would occasionally ransack a cabin, commit a theft, or get in a fight, usually with another Indian or a Chinese. When drunk they spent much of their time in jail for "safe keeping," as the authorities termed it. The Indian had been robbed of his land, his culture, and his identity, all within the span of a few years, and the results were devastating.

The violence and lawlessness that visited the trans-Sierra frontier most frequently and affected it most deeply, then, took special forms: warfare between Indians and whites, stagecoach robbery, vigilantism, and gunfights. These activities bear little or no relation to the violence and lawlessness that pervade American society today. Serious juvenile offenses, crimes against the elderly and weak, rape, robbery, burglary, and theft were either nonexistent or of little significance on the trans-Sierra frontier. If the trans-Sierra frontier was at all representative of frontiers in general, then there seems to be little justification for blaming contemporary American violence and lawlessness on a frontier heritage.[55]

The experience of the trans-Sierra frontier also demonstrates that some long-cherished notions about violence, lawlessness, and justice in the Old West—especially those created by motion pictures and, still worse, television—are nothing more than myth. Probably the most glaring example of myth conflicting with reality is that of the gunfighter. Film and television imagery suggests that a quick draw was the critical factor in a gunfight and that shooters were deadly accurate. In Aurora and Bodie the critical factor was not a quick draw but accuracy, and although some gunfighters were deadly accurate—from fairly long range Irish Tom Carberry shot one man between the eyes and another in the heart—most were not. Shooters missed their targets more often than they hit them, and there were fights in which six-shooters were emptied at close range with no one being hit. There were many reasons for the inaccuracy of a shooter. The fights often occurred in crowded saloons where a shooter's arm was bumped or grabbed, the lighting was dim, the shooter was often intoxicated, and guns malfunctioned and misfired.

Shooters normally carried their guns not in a holster but in a pocket or tucked into a waistband. While the revolver most often used was a Colt, the popular model during Bodie's heyday was not the Peacemaker but the Lightning, and fifteen years earlier during Aurora's boom it was the Navy or Dragoon.[56] Gunfights were almost always between private citizens; lawmen were rarely involved. Only once did a lawman—Richard O'Malley in Bodie—participate in a one-on-one gunfight with another man.

Other film and television images also contradict reality on the trans-Sierra frontier. Indians never launched attacks on soldiers, civilians, or stagecoaches which could prove costly to themselves. The Indian did not risk suffering great losses. Bank robbery did not occur, and stagecoaches carrying great bullion shipments were not stopped by highwaymen. Guards on stages—the shotgun messengers—exchanged gunfire with highwaymen only once. Women, even prostitutes, rarely ventured into saloons. For the most part, the saloon was an all-male preserve. Alcohol was not the only popular intoxicant. Opium was plentiful and widely used, and addiction to opium, among whites, was not rare. Prostitutes were often addicted to both alcohol and opium.

Institutions of law enforcement and justice were well established, and defendants were entitled to every protection that they receive today. Defense attorneys were highly capable and sophisticated and won acquittals for most of their clients. Horse thieves were not hanged; they were sentenced to short jail or prison terms. Although minorities were certainly the objects of some abuse and varying degrees of social ostracism, they were treated equally and fairly by the criminal justice system. Jailbreaks were rare—only one in Bodie and two in Aurora. Vigilantism was the product not of hyster-

55. America's frontier heritage has often been blamed for contemporary American violence and lawlessness. See, e.g., James Truslow Adams, "Our Lawless Heritage"; R. W. Mondy, "Analysis of Frontier Social Instability"; Mabel A. Elliott, "Crime and the Frontier Mores"; Gilbert Geis, "Violence in American Society"; Joe B. Frantz, "The Frontier Tradition: An Invitation to Violence."

56. The Colt Peacemaker was not mentioned even once as the revolver used in a gunfight in Bodie. This does not necessarily rule out its use. On several occasions the guns used were not identified, but when they were, the Lightning, or "self-cocker" as it was called, was named most often. The Peacemaker was definitely not used in Aurora during its boom years—the gun was not manufactured until 1873.

ical torch-waving mobs but of highly organized and disciplined bodies of men. Lawmen did not take heroic stands against vigilantes; they stood aside or cooperated. The murderers hanged were not sniveling cowards at the end but brave men.

The trans-Sierra frontier, then, did not give us the basis for much of the motion picture and television portrayal of the Old West, nor does it seem to have fathered the violence and lawlessness that plagues America today. But it certainly did give us warfare between Indians and whites, highwaymen, prostitutes and gamblers, opium smokers, vigilantes, pistol-packing women, a Chinese tong battle and a Chinese badman, a brilliant one-armed lawyer who never lost a case, a gang of badmen, and gunfighters aplenty.

APPENDIX: SCHOLARLY ASSESSMENTS OF FRONTIER VIOLENCE

A review of the scholarly literature that focuses on frontier violence indicates that although most authors think that the frontier was violent and lawless, some—particularly those writing in more recent times—argue that it was not especially violent or lawless. In the historiographical essay that follows I have tried to include the most significant works that represent the two viewpoints. (See the Bibliography for full publishing data for each work reviewed.)

THE FRONTIER WAS VIOLENT

James Truslow Adams, in "Our Lawless Heritage" (*The Atlantic Monthly*, Dec. 1928), contends that lawlessness has been one of the most distinctive American traits. The United States is English in origin, says Adams, and yet "England is the most law-abiding of nations and ourselves the least so" (p. 732). It is impossible to blame the lawlessness on immigrants from other nations because "the overwhelming mass of them were law-abiding in their native lands." Something, then, in the American environment caused the immigrants, whether from England or elsewhere, to become lawless. Although Adams argues that several factors were responsible for the transformation, he claims that the frontier "has been of prime importance in many respects." On the border of civilization, says Adams, life was rough and there was little recognition of law. Remote from the courts and authorities of established communities, the frontiersman had not only to enforce his own law, but also to choose those laws he would observe. Thus while he was shooting or hanging horse thieves, for example, he was also disregarding laws that required payment of debt to older settlements. This attitude, concludes Adams, brought about disrespect for the law itself and contributed to a legacy of lawlessness and violence that persisted long after the frontier had disappeared.

R. W. Mondy, in "Analysis of Frontier Social Instability" (*Southwestern Social Science Quarterly*, Sept. 1943), examines the forces that caused social instability on the American frontier. The frontiersman, Mondy notes, found no stable social order waiting in the wilderness to receive him. There was only a "child society" lacking the requisite complex of organized habits, sentiments, and social attitudes, a circumstance not unlike that of the French Revolution. The absence of a structured society allowed and even forced the frontiersman to act independently and to work out social relationships on his own initiative. The result was a lack of law and order. Life, concludes Mondy, became the property of the individual, and not of society. "Violent death came often and there was little respect for life itself" (p. 177).

Also contributing to the social instability of the frontier, says Mondy, was the type of people who moved there: the adventurous, eccentric, and lawless, including "counterfeiters, desperadoes, robbers, and horse thieves." These misfits and criminals slowed the evolution of a civilized social order and promoted lawlessness. Still another contributing factor was isolation. First, there was the physical isolation of a sparsely populated area where the distance between families was great and travel difficult. Then there was the isolation caused by cultural barriers: the lack of education, reading material, wealth, and social standing. Conflict between Indians and whites intensified the isolation and instability of the frontier. Violence between the two races became an "awful realism." Taken together, social instability, isolation, the character of the migrants, and the conflict with the Indians frustrated the establishment of law and promoted violence.

Mabel A. Elliott, in "Crime and the Frontier Mores" (*American Sociological Review*, April 1944), contends, like James Truslow Adams, that much of America's present-day criminal behavior may be traced to a lawless heritage from the frontier. The frontier culture, argues Elliott, had little or no respect for or patience with formal legislative controls. The pioneer moved into the wilderness "where a man could exist without tribute to tax collectors, or law makers, and if he moved fast enough he did not need to defer even to his neighbor's opinion." Here, especially on the mining and cattle frontiers, developed an exaggerated sense of individualism encouraged by the lack of legal, religious, and educational institutions. The presence of few women and the absence of the stabilizing influences of family life fostered the establishment of brothels, gambling houses, and saloons. The "distorted sex ratio . . . was undoubtedly a factor in crime rates" on the frontier, where shootings and quarrels over the attentions of the prostitutes were common (p. 189). Also promoting violence were the consumption of great quantities of alcohol, a sense of honor that allowed no insult to go unchallenged, the vast sums of money afloat in the West because of insufficient banking facilities, and the often tenuous difference between outlaw and lawman. This last factor frequently forced citizens to organize vigilance committees, which often precipitated violent clashes.

In the popular mind, the frontier has evidently always stood for America at its most violent. Some scholars also accept this concept without question. Gilbert Geis, in "Violence in American Society" (*Current History*, June 1967), takes a cursory glance at violent crimes and some of their causes. Geis's conclusions are, with one exception, tentative and speculative. The one exception is striking. "What is it then," asks Geis, "that may be said with certainty about crimes of violence in the United States? We can report with some assurance that, compared to frontier days, there has been a significant decrease in such activities" (p. 357). Geis offers no documentation for this statement. He assumes not only that the frontier was violent but that the frontier was more violent than the American society of the 1960s.

Joe B. Frantz, in "The Frontier Tradition: An Invitation to Violence" (*The History of Violence in America*, 1969), contends that violence is only one facet of the frontier heritage. There were other and positive legacies, but the frontier, claims Frantz, "not only condoned but actually encouraged the idea and practice of violence . . . which undoubtedly plays a role in shaping 20th-century American attitudes" (p. 151). The frontiersman, notes Frantz, faced danger as a matter of course. Courage and self-reliance were necessary. Thus the bold and strong were the first to move into the wilderness. Veterans of the American Revolution, the War of 1812, the Mexican War, and the Civil War, who had tasted action and could not return to the discipline of the settled world, sought out the frontier. To it they took their combat training and a penchant for direct action. The frontier also attracted the rootless and the drifters, who were often desperate men.

In addition to attracting strong and violent types of people, says Frantz, the frontier also developed too swiftly for the institutions of law and order to keep up. The six-gun or the rope replaced judicial procedure. The subtleties of law and order escaped the frontiersman, who favored direct and immediate punishment of the wrongdoer. But the trouble with vigilantism "is that it has no stopping place." Men grow accustomed to taking the law into their own hands and continue to do so even after legal institutions have been established. This practice has continued down to present days, thinks Frantz, so Americans "burn down a ghetto, they loot and pillage, they bury three civil rights workers beneath a dam, or they shoot a man in Dallas or on a motel balcony in Memphis" (p. 140). Also contributing to frontier violence, says Frantz, were land-use conflicts (for example, cowboy against sheepman, and cowboy against nester) and racism (for example, white against red or yellow).

Not all authors who fall into the frontier-was-violent category discuss frontier violence in general essays, as do Frantz and the others reviewed thus far. Some focus on a specific frontier region, such as west Texas or the range lands; others investigate a particular form of violence, such as gunfighting or vigilantism. W. C. Holden is among these authors. In "Law and Lawlessness on the Texas Frontier, 1875–1890" (*Southwestern Historical Quarterly*, Oct. 1940), he demonstrates that there was plenty of violence and lawlessness on the west Texas frontier but notes that some forms of crime were nonexistent. While horse stealing brought the death penalty, says Holden, fatal shootings resulting from "fair fights" were not seriously regarded, stage holdups and train robberies were frequent and taken for granted, drunkenness and fighting were pastimes, and prostitution was condoned. However, petty thievery and burglary were unknown; people never locked the doors of their houses or businesses—other than banks—or even bothered to put locks on the doors in the first place. Mutual trust and one's word were better than any contract, loans were made without question, and hospitality was a reality.

Holden's narrative takes on an almost romantic aura. Shooting up a town was a favorite pastime of cowboys from some of the tougher outfits. Dogs, lazing on front porches, and windows were usually the only casualties from these hell-bent sprees. A cowboy who had successfully "taken a town" was usually accorded folk-hero status for his skill and daring. Stage holdups in which the highwaymen entertained the passengers while divesting only the wealthy male riders of their money and jewelry, train robberies that included exciting leaps from rapidly moving mail cars onto waiting horses, and neatly executed bank "heists" are also recounted by Holden. These robberies evidently did not bother most citizens. "At no time do we read of spontaneous demonstrations, grim-faced posses, or the relentless hunting down and hanging of robbers" (p. 196).

Harry Sinclair Drago, in *The Great Range Wars: Violence on the Grasslands* (1970), focuses on conflict over the use of range lands. Although in his introduction he plays down the amount of violence on the grasslands, in the chapters that follow he recounts with considerable readability one violent and bloody confrontation after another. Beginning with the shotgun death of Fred Leigh in Jack Ryan's saloon, Drago proceeds through the Cheyenne burning of Pat Hennessey at the stake, the battle at Palo Duro, the Comanche killing of Oliver Loving, the Lincoln County, Pleasant Valley, Fence Cutting, and Horse Thief wars, the Johnson County insurrection, and much more. There were parts of the range lands, says Drago, where the only effective law was "the law a man carried on his hip" (p. 93). In the Southwest "range thievery was a recognized profession," and the 1870s and 1880s in "outlaw ravaged Arizona" were "the blazing decades" (p. 93). Although New Mexico was sparsely populated, "it is doubtful if anywhere else in the United States so many men were indicted for murder" (p. 72). To say that Montana territory was lawless "would be to imply that it had laws that were being flouted; actually there was no law" (p. 206).

Drago never explains the disparity between his introduction and the rest of his book. Nor does he account for specific contradictions: in his introduction he claims that "very few serious confrontations" between sheepmen and cattlemen occurred and that none deserve "the name of war," yet later he says that "innumerable conflicts occurred between cattlemen and sheepmen" and "fewer than half a dozen deserve to be called wars" (pp. v and 256). These are, perhaps, minor flaws in an otherwise fine work, but they could lead someone looking only at the introduction to misconstrue the study.

Numerous authors have written about the gunfighters of the Old West. Reviewing their works presents one of the thorniest problems in the historiography of frontier violence. Gunfighter literature is massive in extent, and much of it is contradictory. Nevertheless, some general trends can be noted. Authors writing in the 1920s and 1930s, such as Walter N. Burns in *The Saga of Billy the Kid* (1926), Stuart N. Lake in *Wyatt Earp: Frontier Marshal* (1931), and William E. Connelley in *Wild Bill and His Era* (1933), tended to exaggerate the exploits of the gunfighters and even to romanticize and ennoble them. A generation later, authors such as Frank Waters in *The Earp Brothers of Tombstone* (1960), Kent Ladd Steckmesser in *The Western Hero in History and Legend* (1965), and Joseph G. Rosa in *The Gunfighter: Man or Myth?* (1968) portrayed the gunfighters as less than noble characters who were concerned primarily with self-preservation at whatever cost. The number of men killed by the gunfighters is also, for the most part, considerably reduced by the revisionist historians of the 1960s.

Nevertheless, all authors do agree that the gunslingers were involved in a considerable amount of violence. Some early authors claim, for example, that Billy the Kid killed twenty-one men, whereas revisionists contend that such an estimate is exaggerated and revise it downward to "only" six or seven. Similarly, the kill-totals of Wild Bill Hickok, Bat Masterson, and other gunslingers have been reduced. The controversy over the gunfighters is far from dead, however. Gary L. Roberts, in "The West's Gunmen" (*The American West*, Jan. and March, 1971), a provocative and penetrating review of gunfighter literature, reverses the trend of the 1960s and claims that the revisionists overreacted and that the earlier claims for the gunmen might be closer to the truth. Roberts argues that the revisionists have been so obsessed with the destruction of what they think is gunfighter myth that they misuse sources and, in turn, create a new myth of their own.

From this controversy one point emerges: the gunfighters, regardless of whose estimate is accepted, were involved in an extraordinary amount of killing. However, none of these authors really demonstrates whether this violence was typical of the frontier as a whole or was only typical of the gunfighters themselves. To explain how the gunslinger-outlaw was developed, these authors fall back upon the same explanations for the presence of violence on the frontier that were proffered by the other frontier-was-violent authors. Joseph G. Rosa's explanation in *The Gunfighter* is representative of the majority of these authors.

The trans-Mississippi West, says Rosa, "was a harsh, rugged, and often desolate land, to be conquered only by those strong enough and brave enough to face it and tame it" (p. 14). But before the new land could be settled, it had to be fought for. Indian wars were part of the westward movement. Still, pioneers came to the West by the thousands, pulled there by the wealth that the West had to offer and pushed there by post–Civil War economic pressures. Criminals were also pushed and pulled to the West, and "outlaw activity became a problem." Law and order were slow to follow the westward surge of settlement, and the frontiersman was forced to make his own laws and to dispense justice on the spot. But the outlaw had the advantage. His chance of capture and punishment was remote, since he could simply disappear into the wilderness for a time. Communication was extremely limited, and months might pass before information about a wanted man could be circulated. Then, too, there were few lawmen. Most of the time it was a matter of the individual citizen's defending himself and pursuing his attackers. Occasionally, citizens formed vigilance committees, which often acted hastily, overreached themselves, and contributed more to violence than to law and order.

Other factors promoting violence, says Rosa, were an extraordinary number of saloons, gambling dens, and brothels, conflicting interests between cattleman and sheepman, battles over range lands among cattle barons, fights between cowboy and farmer, and conflict over the use of barbed wire. One last factor was the six-shooter, the "instrument of the lawman as well as the lawless." The rifle had been the weapon of the colonial and trans-Appalachian frontiers; the six-shooter was the weapon of the plainsman and horseman in the trans-Mississippi West.

Although much has been written on vigilantism, Richard Maxwell Brown's *Strain of Violence* (1975) is perhaps the best general study of the topic. The tradition of American vigilantism, says Brown, began with the Regulator movement in the South Carolina backcountry in 1767 and has continued to the present day. There have been well over three hundred vigilante movements, notes Brown, which have inflicted no fewer than seven hundred fatalities and administered corporal punishment to thousands of others. Although vigilantism was not restricted to the frontier, it was especially prominent there because pioneers, without recourse to established institutions, often felt compelled to take the law into their own hands in order to establish an orderly and stable society. The presence of outlaws and "marginal types," coupled with weak and ineffectual law enforcement, frequently created social chaos. Vigilantism both solved the problem of disorder and had symbolic value as a clear warning to outlaws and a reaffirmation of the sanctity of the deeply cherished values of life and property.

The frontiersman, argues Brown, desired new opportunities and not social innovation. His primary goal was improvement of his economic position and replication of the type of community from which he came. Re-creation of the old community was not difficult for such groups as the Mormons and the Puritans, who migrated to the frontier en masse; for most others difficulties abounded. Disorder and chaos were the rule. Gold-rush San Francisco, for example, was a polyglot of diverse people, and thus the reestablishment of the old community structure and its values was impossible. Disorder resulted and vigilantism followed.

The main reason for vigilantism on the frontier, claims Brown, was inadequate law enforcement. The law that existed was highly localized, pinned down to the immediate vicinity of a town. The mobility of the sheriff depended on the ability of his horse. A fugitive with a lead was difficult, if not impossible, to catch. Trails quickly disappeared into the wilderness. An ineffectual judicial system also contributed to vigilantism. For lack of proper jails, the accused frequently escaped. It was not difficult for outlaws to hire false witnesses, pack or intimidate juries, and bribe officials. Convictions were few, and the frontiersman often saw the guilty go free. Lack of public funds was another factor in promoting vigilantism. The typical frontier town could not afford to support an adequate police force or to finance the chase, capture, jailing, trial, and incarceration of outlaws. Vigilantism was regularly praised for the great expenditures it saved.

The classic era of frontier vigilantism ended by 1900, notes Brown. However, a tradition of "neo-vigilantism" lives on. Examples include the McCarthyism of the early 1950s, and the self-protective patrol groups of the 1960s and 1970s operating in urban neighborhoods beset by crime or racial problems. The ideology of vigilantism, which stresses popular sovereignty, self-preservation, and the right of revolution, continues to attract Americans even though frontier rationales for vigilantism have disappeared.

THE FRONTIER WAS
NOT ESPECIALLY VIOLENT

Thomas M. Marshall, in "The Miners' Laws of Colorado" (*American Historical Review*, 1919–1920), analyzes the organization of mining districts, the election of officers, and the ordinances that were adopted in early Gilpin County, Colorado. The local mining camps, such as Central City, Black Hawk, and Nevada City, concludes Marshall, were rather orderly settlements even in their very first years. Marshall bases his conclusions primarily on his inspection of the laws that the miners enacted, laws that in some districts forbade the operation of saloons, gambling dens, and houses of prostitution. This could not have been Bret Harte's Wild West, argues Marshall. Enactment of laws, however, is only the first step toward the establishment of order. Marshall neglected to study the agencies empowered to enforce the laws.

Lynn I. Perrigo, in "Law and Order in Early Colorado Mining Camps" (*Mississippi Valley Historical Review*, June 1941), supplies such information. The agencies of the law, says Perrigo, were vigorously active, and, if not entirely successful, were as effective as could be expected in those virile mining camps. There was never a time, concludes Perrigo, when any of the camps resembled "a traditional 'Wild West' settlement." Perrigo seems surprised to discover how orderly the camps were considering the circumstances: guns were plentiful; gambling, drinking, and prostitution were common; a lawless element was present in the camps; and some ethnic tension existed.

The miners were all well armed with rifles, revolvers, and bowie knives. During the first couple of years in the life of each camp the miners usually wore their revolvers strapped to their belts. Even boys as young as thirteen were known to carry guns. And yet violence and bloodshed, says Perrigo, were uncommon. To be sure, killings did occur, but they were almost always in "fair" fights: fair in the sense that the combatants faced off against each other and then fought. The average citizen enjoyed great security of both person and property. "We could go to sleep in our cabins," noted one miner, "with our bag of gold dust under our pillows minus locks, bolts or bars, and feel a sense of absolute security" (p. 46). Despite laws in some camps which proscribed gambling houses, saloons, and brothels, notes Perrigo, such establishments were commonplace. Nevertheless, they do not seem to have promoted much violence. The camps also had more than their share of "the lawless element," but the problems from this "element" were infrequent. Finally, although some ethnic tension between Irish and Cornish miners was evident, after only one major disturbance they resolved their differences and lived in amity.

Perrigo does not directly concern himself with the reasons for the lack of crime. He reports the "what" and not the "why" of law and order in the mining camps, and occasionally he seems to imply through his use of quotes that swift punishment of offenders deterred crime. If a man killed another in a fair fight, a Perrigo-quoted miner notes, the victor was taken to the saloon and bought a drink. However, if a man murdered another in cold blood, he was immediately tried, convicted, and hanged. Another miner claimed that "crime was of rare occurrence because punishment, like an avenging nemesis, was sure to follow" (p. 46).

Perrigo offers three explanations for the reputation of lawlessness and violence these camps acquired: stories of the early years have grown with repeated telling; the romantic efforts of writers tend to enlarge the pictures; and the residents of one camp contributed to the bad reputation of other camps—miners regularly boasted of the virtues of their own camp and described others as steeped in vice and disorder. According to Perrigo, then, the mining camps of Gilpin County, Colorado, earned undeserved reputations and were really not especially violent or lawless. But were they, he asks in conclusion, shining exceptions in the West or were they representative?

Michael N. Canlis, in "The Evolution of Law Enforcement in California" (*The Far-Westerner*, July 1961), contends that frontier California was not a lawless and disorganized territory, as "the romantic reports" would have us believe. Americans, like their "Anglo-Saxon forebears," says Canlis, had a passion for organization, regulation, and law, and carried this passion with them to the diggings. In the Mother Lode, they put their principles of law and order into practice and eliminated "many of the common ills of new settlements in many foreign lands" (p. 2). Crime was simply not much of a problem in the mining camps. Even though the miners lived almost in the open with their valuables exposed, crimes were infrequent. The most important deterrent to crime, maintains Canlis, was swift and certain punishment. Because of the absence of jails, punishment took three forms: whipping, banishment, and death. Other deterrents were the easy acquisition of gold and full employment.

Although Canlis fails to mention the numerous outbreaks of vigilantism in the Mother Lode country and throughout California in general, he does take notice of the San Francisco vigilance committees of 1851 and 1856. While admitting that the committees eliminated "some disreputable and despicable characters," he asserts that "there can never be any justification for their [the committees'] overall acts in a society as well organized as San Francisco was at this time" (p. 13). However, Canlis notes that the committees were also well organized and had impressive constitutions and written codes. The committees described the reasons for their existence and their plans of action. Nevertheless, concludes Canlis, "it is strange indeed that the constituted government of the time did not put down by force . . . this group which had taken the law into its own hands" (p. 13).

Robert R. Dykstra, in *The Cattle Towns* (1968), finds that the Kansas cow towns, like Perrigo's Colorado mining towns, were not especially violent or lawless. Dykstra, while analyzing the urban impulse of frontier Abilene, Wichita, Caldwell, Ellsworth, and Dodge City, discovers that during the years 1870–1885 only forty-five homicides occurred, an average of just 1.5 homicides per cattle-trading season. The greatest number of killings in any one of those years was five, at Ellsworth in 1873 and at Dodge City in 1878. These statistics seem to indicate that the cattle towns were not particularly violent. However, a note of caution is appropriate. Dykstra compiled his statistics exclusively from the local newspapers, and he limited his homicides to only those which occurred within the city limits of the five towns. Also, and perhaps most important, he does not begin counting homicides for his table of "Cattle Town Homicides" until "the first full shipping season in which each town existed as a municipality" (p. 145). Therefore, many of the towns' homicides are not included in the table, since all of the communities had been established a year or two or more before they had a full cattle-shipping season. Ellsworth, for example, had eight homicides during the twelve months following its establishment in 1867, and Dodge City had nine (some report twelve, and one resident claimed fifteen) in its first year, 1872–1873 (p. 113). Yet Dykstra does not include these homicides in the table, or others which occurred before 1872 in Ellsworth or before 1876 in Dodge City.

Cowboys, gamblers, and lawmen were the usual victims of shootings in the cattle towns. Many of the foremost gunfighters visited the towns during their heydays, but of those notorious characters, only John Wesley Hardin, Wild Bill Hickok, and Wyatt Earp are known to have actually killed anyone. Such figures as Bat Masterson, Clay Allison, Doc Holliday, and Ben Thompson were there, but they participated in none of the killings.

Dykstra also finds little violent conflict between Texas drovers and hinterland farmers. The cattle towns initially saw their futures only as depots for buying, selling, and shipping Texas longhorns to eastern markets, and the local farmer was considered a nuisance because of his damage claims against the drovers and his demand for the quarantine of the splenic-fever-carrying longhorns. But sodbusters who protested the movement of herds by their farms were not gunned down by wild cowboys. Conflicts between the farmers and the drovers and the farmers and the entrepreneurs of the towns were generally resolved without violence, and the business community of each town continually promoted programs—with drover cooperation—which mollified rural hostility.

Deadwood has long been used as the example of a violent western mining town. However, Harry H. Anderson, in "Deadwood, South Dakota: An Effort at Stability" (*Montana, The Magazine of Western History*, Jan. 1970), contends that the violent aspect of Deadwood's past has been greatly overemphasized. Anderson focuses primarily on those factors which made significant contributions to Deadwood's stability and permanence during 1876, the year of the town's infancy. Only four killings and not a single lynching, notes Anderson, occurred in 1876. One of the killings, however, was that of Wild Bill Hickok. Other crimes, such as public drunkenness, assault, and disturbing the peace, occurred, admits Anderson; generally, however, the atmosphere in Deadwood was one of stability and order. The attitude of the miners toward crime was similar to that of citizens of other mining towns. Killers went unpunished if the fight had been a fair one. One gunslinger was permitted to go free after convincing the court that although he had fired the first shot in the fight, he had not been the first to reach for a gun.

Brothels, gambling houses, and saloons were not only tolerated, says Anderson, but encouraged by inexpensive licensing fees. For example, lawyers and butchers, much to their chagrin, paid fees equal to those of the saloons. The saloon-licensing fee was deliberately kept low because the Black Hills were still a part of the Sioux Reservation and the liquor dealers were, therefore, subject to federal arrest and prosecution. Nevertheless, the miners demanded their amusements. During 1876, twenty-seven saloons, fourteen gambling houses, and twelve brothels were established.

Anderson's argument for order and stability in Deadwood has some weaknesses. He records only the fatal shootings during 1876, not the total number of shooting incidents, which might reveal a more accurate picture of the violent nature of the community. Also, he emphasizes that "only" four killings occurred, without appreciating that those four killings would give Deadwood—considering its small population during its first year—an enormously high homicide rate. In addition, although he refers to violence in Deadwood's hinterland, he fails to take it into consideration even though that violence was in the immediate vicinity of the town and probably connected with it.

Frank Prassel, in *The Western Peace Officer* (1972), examines various types of law enforcement personnel and their activities in seventeen western states and concludes that frontier violence has been greatly exaggerated. Indeed, argues Prassel, "it would appear that, in the American West, crime may have been more closely related to the developing urban environment than the former existence of a frontier" (p. 21). The much-heralded western peace officer, says Prassel, actually faced fewer problems than did peace officers elsewhere. Crimes such as drunkenness, disorderly conduct, and petty larceny were common enough, but the westerner usually "had to look elsewhere for news of murder, rape, and armed robbery" (p. 22). The westerner, concludes Prassel, "probably enjoyed greater security in both person and property than did his contemporary in the urban centers of the East" (p. 22).

Why, then, has the West earned a reputation for violence and lawlessness? For primarily two reasons, answers Prassel: first, because of the general absence of disorder the occasional exploits of outlaws received special notoriety; and second, through literature, motion pictures, and especially television the violent aspects of the West have been overemphasized.

Although Prassel argues that crime was more closely related to the developing urban environment than the frontier, he thinks that "considering the factors present [on the frontier] it is surprising that even more murders, assaults, and robberies did not occur" (p. 23). Elsewhere Prassel specifically delineates "the factors present": conflict between Indians and whites; the wide-open spaces of the West, which could put men beyond the reach of the law; the armed citizenry; the individualistic, adventuresome frontiersman; the abundance of saloons, gambling houses, and bordellos; and competition for grazing lands. It would appear, then, that Prassel has accepted the conventional wisdom about the frontier: that certain factors peculiar to the frontier, or at least exaggerated on the frontier, were responsible for promoting lawlessness and violence on the frontier. And yet Prassel suggests that the frontier was not especially lawless or violent. Could it be that some of the unique frontier conditions—for example, the wide, open spaces or the armed citizenry—instead of promoting violence actually militated against it?

W. Eugene Hollon, in *Frontier Violence: Another Look* (1974), contends that frontier lawlessness was primarily the result, rather than the cause, of America's violent society. The frontier, Hollon believes, "was a far more civilized, more peaceful and safer place than American society is today" (p. x). Violence in America has been a problem more related to postfrontier urban development than to the Old West. How, then, did the frontier earn a reputation for violence? According to Hollon, the frontier to most Americans and Europeans was an image of spaciousness, fertility, abundance, and freedom. And since the frontier was a kind of poetic image, its extreme aspects tended to be exaggerated: the good was very good, and the bad very bad. Westerners themselves were partly responsible for the creation and perpetuation of this image. They emphasized the spectacular and violent events and blew them entirely out of proportion. Like any newly emerging people searching for identity, westerners "have had to make do with what little historical material they have had to work with" (p. 196). As Walter Prescott Webb has noted, cowboys were made knights, cowmen kings, saloons museums, and boot hills shrines. Violent characteristics of westerners were often turned into virtues. The outlaw became a legendary hero. In literature and legend, if not always in fact, the outlaw operated independently, got what he wanted with his own two hands, and performed spectacular deeds. Since Americans like to view themselves in such terms, this myth has refused to die. The result, concludes Hollon, is an overemphasis on the violent side of the frontier and an underemphasis on the peaceful and orderly side.

But Hollon himself contributes to the "overemphasis." After nine chapters devoted to violence in the West, he offers the reader just one chapter about the relative tameness of the West and provides no comparative statistics about eastern areas. Nevertheless, the arguments that Hollon presents in his concluding chapter are impressive in their logic. But he does not give them enough support to counterbalance, let alone reverse, what he has done in the first nine chapters. Why he does not provide more evidence and data from the "other side of the coin" seems clear. His nine chapters devoted to shoot-outs, stage holdups, train robberies, lynchings, cattle rustling, and claim jumping are fascinating reading. His one chapter on the nonviolent West does not generate the same kind of excitement. This is not Hollon's fault. He writes with great skill and style and is among the most readable of historians. But it is to say that frontier violence has infinitely greater appeal to the reader than frontier calm.

Although Hollon is convinced that the nineteenth-century eastern city and modern society were and are more violent than the frontier West, he nevertheless, like Prassel, notes several factors that should have made the West violent. The frontiersman was remote from the courts and authorities of established communities, he enforced his own laws, he faced a wilderness, he confronted a foreign culture, he was armed. Land, game, fur, minerals, timber, grass, and water would go to the swiftest, strongest, and most intelligent. "It is miraculous," says Hollon, "that the last and largest frontier region in the United States was settled in as orderly a fashion as it was" (p. 125).

The work of Hollon and others who believe that the frontier was not especially violent has made a major impact on scholars but does not seem to have caught the attention of the general public. *Westways*, a magazine published by the Automobile Club of Southern California, did, however, publish a short article in 1978, "Wilding the Tame West" by W. H. Hutchinson, which reflected the views of these authors, especially Hollon, and utilized Dykstra's homicide statistics for the cattle towns.

The scholarly literature on violence and the frontier suggests several observations. The frontier-was-violent authors are not, for the most part, attempting to prove that the frontier was violent. Rather, they assume that it was violent and then proffer explanations for that alleged violence. These explanations are based on conditions that the authors think were peculiar to or exaggerated on the frontier and to the personality traits of the frontiersman himself. The authors reason that it must have been the unique frontier conditions and the frontiersman's personality that caused the violence. The frontier-was-not-especially-violent authors, while contending that there was relatively little violence on the frontier, nevertheless indicate that the unique frontier conditions which the frontier-was-violent authors enumerate were present, and they believe that those conditions *should* have caused violence. That those conditions did not do so suggests that they might have actually promoted peacefulness—though none of the frontier-was-not-especially-violent authors proposes such a connection.

Several of the frontier-was-violent authors suggest that Americans are prone to violence because they have inherited a tradition of violence from the frontier experience. This belief is, of course, widely shared by the general public. Yet, despite the currency of this notion and the implications it has for all Americans, none of the authors has attemped to compare, in anything more than a very casual manner, frontier violence and today's violence, let alone demonstrate a causal relationship between the two. Nor has any one of them attempted to compare frontier violence and lawlessness with that which occurred contemporaneously in the East.

All of the authors—whether they conclude that the frontier was violent or not especially violent—have a major characteristic in common. Their conclusions are not based on a thorough investigation of *all* forms of violence and lawlessness in the West or even in a particular town or region. Most of the authors focus on the exploits of the most notorious gunfighters, such as Billy the Kid, Wild Bill Hickok, and Bat Masterson, or on the most spectacular incidents, such as the Graham-Tewksbury feud, the Johnson County war, and the Sand Creek massacre, or on certain crimes, such as homicide and robbery. These authors provide a less than complete—in some cases a highly selective and perhaps unrepresentative—picture of frontier violence and lawlessness. Moreover, because of the incomplete nature of their studies, they are generally unable to extrapolate meaningful statistical data relative to frontier crime. And, for the most part, no attempt has been made to study the criminal justice system of the frontier, to follow the arrest and prosecution of lawbreakers through the various institutions of law enforcement and justice.

Although much very good and very important work has been done on frontier violence, there are obviously major gaps that need to be filled. Until they are filled, scholars will be unable to assess with certainty the frontier's contribution to the violence and lawlessness that plague American society. I hope that this book will fill some of the gaps and provide greater insight into the frontier experience and its meaning for Americans.

BIBLIOGRAPHY

MANUSCRIPTS

Mono County, California. Calendar of Criminal Cases, Superior Court.

———— . Criminal Calendar, Dep't No. 2, Superior Court.

———— . District Court Calendar.

———— . Great Register.

———— . Jail Register: Bodie Branch Jail.

———— . Justice Court Record.

———— . Marriage Certificate Record.

———— . Mining District Records.

———— . Minute Book, Criminal, Dep't No. 2., Superior Court.

———— . Minutes, Criminal Cases, Superior Court.

———— . Record of Town Lots.

———— . Records, A, County Court.

———— . Records, A, District Court.

———— . Register of Actions, Superior Court.

———— . Register of Deaths.

Nevada. Unsorted Territorial Correspondence, Nevada Division of Archives, Office of Secretary of State, Carson City.

Whitney, George A. Letters and Correspondence, 1862–1887. No. 2363. Nevada Historical Society, Reno.

Youngs, Samuel. Journal. Private collection of Robert E. Stewart, Carson City, Nevada.

GOVERNMENT PUBLICATIONS

California. *Appendix to Journals of Senate and Assembly of the Fourteenth Session of the Legislature of the State of California.* Sacramento, 1863.

————. *Appendix to Journals of Senate and Assembly of the Fifteenth Session of the Legislature of the State of California.* Sacramento, 1864.

————. State Mining Bureau. *Eighth Annual Report of the State Mineralogist.* Sacramento, 1888.

————. Historical Records Survey Project. *Inventory of the County Archives of California, No. 27, Mono County.* San Francisco, 1940.

————. *Journal of the California Assembly.*

————. *Journal of the California Senate.*

————. *Records of California Men in the War of the Rebellion, 1861 to 1867.* Sacramento, 1890.

————. *Report of the Adjutant-General of the State of California for the Year 1863.* Sacramento, 1864.

————. *Report of the Adjutant-General of the State of California from May 1st, 1864, to November 30th, 1865.* Sacramento, 1866.

————. *Report of the Superintendent of Public Instruction for 1864–65.* Sacramento, 1865.

————. *Statutes.*

Nevada. *Journal of the Nevada Assembly.*

————. *Journal of the Nevada Senate.*

————. *Journal of the Nevada Territorial Council.*

————. *Laws of Nevada Territory.*

————. *Statutes.*

————. *War Claims of the State of Nevada Against the United States.* Carson City, 1882.

United States. Congress. *Congressional Globe.*

————. Congress. *House Journal.*

————. Congress. *Statutes at Large.*

————. Department of Commerce. Bureau of the Census. *Statistical Abstract of the United States: 1981.* Washington, 1981.

————. Department of the Interior. Census Office. *Statistics of the Population of the United States at the Tenth Census.* Washington, 1883.

————— . Department of the Interior. *Eighth Annual Report of the U.S. Geological Survey, for 1886–1887.* Washington, 1889.

————— . Department of the Interior. Geological Survey. *Aurora Quadrangle.* Washington, 1956.

————— . Department of the Interior. Bureau of Indian Affairs. *Report of the Commissioner of Indian Affairs for the Year 1863.* Washington, 1864.

————— . Department of the Interior. *U.S. Coast and Geodetic Survey Report, 1899–1900.* Washington, 1901.

————— . Department of Justice. Federal Bureau of Investigation. *Uniform Crime Reports.*

————— . Department of the Treasury. *Report on the Internal Commerce of the United States for the Year 1890.* Washington, 1891.

————— . Department of War. *The War of the Rebellion: A Compilation of the Official Records of the Union and Confederate Armies.* Washington, 1897.

NEWSPAPERS AND PERIODICALS

The Argonaut.

Aurora *Esmeralda Herald.*

Aurora *Esmeralda Star.*

Aurora *Esmeralda Union.*

Aurora Times.

Bishop *Inyo Register.*

Bodie Chronicle.

Bodie *Daily Free Press.*

Bodie Evening Miner.

Bodie Morning News.

Bodie Standard.

Bridgeport Chronicle-Union.

Bridgeport *Mono-Alpine Chronicle.*

Carson City *Daily Appeal.*

Coloma *Argus.*

Gold Hill *News.*

Los Angeles Times.

Reno Gazette.

Sacramento Bee.

Sacramento Daily Union.

San Francisco *Bulletin.*

San Francisco Call.

San Francisco Chronicle.

San Francisco *Daily Alta California.*

San Francisco *Daily Evening Post.*

San Francisco *Examiner.*

Tombstone Epitaph.

Tybo *Sun.*

Virginia City *Territorial Enterprise.*

Virginia City *Virginia Daily Union.*

Visalia *Delta.*

BOOKS AND ARTICLES

Adams, James Truslow. "Our Lawless Heritage." *Atlantic Monthly* 142 (December 1928): 732–40.

Anderson, Harry H. "Deadwood, South Dakota: An Effort at Stability." *Montana: The Magazine of Western History* 20 (January 1970): 40–47.

Angel, Myron, ed. *History of Nevada.* Oakland, 1881.

Ashbaugh, Don. *Nevada's Turbulent Yesterday.* Los Angeles, 1963.

Athearn, Robert. *Westward the Briton.* New York, 1953.

Axelrod, D. I. "Mio-Pliocene Floras from West-Central Nevada." *University of California Publications in Geological Sciences* 33 (1956).

Bancroft, Hubert Howe. *History of Nevada, Colorado, and Wyoming 1540–1888.* San Francisco, 1890.

———. *Popular Tribunals.* 2 vols. San Francisco, 1887.

Barth, Gunther. *Bitter Strength: A History of the Chinese in the United States, 1850–1870.* Berkeley, 1964.

The Bay of San Francisco: The Metropolis of the Pacific Coast and Its Surburban Cities. 2 vols. Chicago, 1892.

Bourke, John G. *On the Border with Crook.* New York, 1891.

Brown, Ralph H. *Historical Geography of the United States.* New York, 1948.

Brown, Richard Maxwell. *Strain of Violence: Historical Studies of American Violence and Vigilantism.* New York, 1975.

Browne, J. Ross. *Adventures in the Apache Country: A Tour Through Arizona and Sonora, with Notes on the Silver Regions of Nevada.* New York, 1869.

———. *Report of J. Ross Browne on the Mineral Resources of the States and Territories West of the Rocky Mountains.* Washington, 1868.

Buckbee, Edna Bryan. *The Saga of Old Tuolumne.* New York, 1935.

Bunnell, Lafayette H. *Discovery of the Yosemite and the Indian War of 1851.* Los Angeles, 1911.

Burns, Walter N. *The Saga of Billy the Kid*. Garden City, 1926.

Canlis, Michael N. "The Evolution of Law Enforcement in California." *Far-Westerner* 2 (July 1961): 1–13.

Cawelti, John G. "Cowboys, Indians, Outlaws." *American West* 1 (Spring 1964): 28–35, 77–79.

————. "The Gunfighter and Society." *American West* 5 (March 1968): 30–35, 76–78.

Chalfant, W. A. *Outposts of Civilization*. Boston, 1928.

————. *The Story of Inyo*. Bishop, 1933.

Chang, Hsin-pao. *Commissioner Lin and the Opium War*. Cambridge, 1964.

Clarke, H. G. "Aurora, Nevada: A Little of Its History, Past and Present." *School of Mines Quarterly* 3 (January 1882): 133–36.

Clemens, Samuel L. *Roughing It*. New York, 1913.

Colcord, Roswell K. "Reminiscences of Life in Territorial Nevada." *California Historical Society Quarterly* 7 (June 1928): 112–20.

Collis, Maurice. *Foreign Mud*. New York, 1947.

Connelley, William E. *Wild Bill and His Era*. New York, 1933.

Coolidge, Mary. *Chinese Immigration*. New York, 1909.

Coy, Owen C. *The Genesis of California Counties*. Berkeley, 1923.

Crampton, C. Gregory, ed. *The Mariposa Indian War, 1850–1851*. Salt Lake, 1958.

Custer, George A. *My Life on the Plains*. New York, 1874.

Daughters of the American Revolution. *California: Fifty Years of Progress*. San Francisco, 1900.

————. *Records of the Families of California Pioneers*. San Francisco, 1957.

Davis, Reda. *California Women: A Guide to Their Politics, 1895–1911*. San Francisco, 1968.

DeQuille, Dan. *The Big Bonanza: An Authentic Account of the Discovery, History, and Working of the World-Renowned Comstock Lode of Nevada*. Hartford, 1877.

Dimsdale, Thomas J. *The Vigilantes of Montana*. Norman, 1953.

Dodge, Richard Irving. *The Hunting Grounds of the Great West*. London, 1877.

Drago, Henry Sinclair. *The Great Range Wars: Violence on the Grasslands*. New York, 1970.

Dykstra, Robert R. *The Cattle Towns*. New York, 1968.

Elliott, Mabel A. "Crime and the Frontier Mores." *American Sociological Review* 9 (April 1944): 185–92.

————. *Crime in Modern Society*. New York, 1952.

Fairbanks, Harold W. "The Mineral Deposits of Eastern California." *American Geologist* 17 (March 1896): 144–58.

Farquhar, Francis P. "Lee Vining." *Sierra Club Bulletin* 13 (1928): 83–85.

——— . *History of the Sierra Nevada*. Berkeley, 1966.

Farquhar, Francis P., ed. *Up and Down California in 1860–1864: The Journal of William H. Brewer*. Berkeley, 1966.

Fay, Peter Ward. *The Opium War, 1840–1842*. Chapel Hill, 1975.

Ferdinand, Theodore N. "The Criminal Patterns of Boston Since 1849." *American Journal of Sociology* 73 (July 1967): 84–99.

——— . "Politics, the Police, and Arresting Policies in Salem, Massachusetts, Since the Civil War." *Social Problems* 19 (Spring 1972): 572–88.

Fernandez, Ferdinand. "Except a California Indian: A Study in Legal Discrimination." *Southern California Quarterly* 50 (June 1968): 161–75.

Frantz, Joe B. "The Frontier Tradition: An Invitation to Violence." *The History of Violence in America* (New York, 1969), pp. 127–54.

Friedman, Lawrence M., and Percival, Robert V. *The Roots of Justice: Crime and Punishment in Alameda County, California, 1870–1910*. Chapel Hill, 1981.

Geis, Gilbert. "Violence in American Society." *Current History* 52 (June 1967): 354–58, 366.

George, Henry. "The Kearney Agitation in California." *Popular Science Monthly* 17 (August 1880): 433–53.

Heizer, Robert F., and Elsasser, Albert B. *The Natural World of the California Indians*. Berkeley, 1980.

Hittell, J. S. *Mining in the Pacific States*. San Francisco, 1861.

Holden, William C. "Law and Lawlessness on the Texas Frontier 1875–1890." *Southwestern Historical Quarterly* 44 (October 1940): 188–203.

Hollon, W. Eugene. *Frontier Violence: Another Look*. New York, 1974.

Hutchinson, W. H. "Wilding the Tame West." *Westways* 70 (February 1978): 21–22, 80.

Jackson, Helen Hunt. *A Century of Dishonor*. New York, 1881.

Jackson, Joseph Henry. *Bad Company*. New York, 1949.

Johnson, Edward C. *Walker River Paiutes: A Tribal History*. Schurz, Nevada, 1975.

Kauer, Ralph. "The Workingmen's Party of California." *Pacific Historical Review* 13 (September 1944): 278–91.

Keith, Elmer. *Sixguns by Keith*. New York, 1961.

Kelly, J. Wells. *First Directory of Nevada Territory*. San Francisco, 1862.

Kersten, Earl W., Jr. "The Early Settlement of Aurora, Nevada, and Nearby Mining Camps." *Annals of the Association of American Geographers* 54 (1964): 490–507.

Kroeber, A. L. *Handbook of the Indians of California*. Berkeley, 1953.

Lake, Stuart N. *Wyatt Earp: Frontier Marshal*. Boston, 1931.

Lane, Roger. *Policing the City: Boston, 1822–1885*. Cambridge, 1967.

———. *Violent Death in the City: Suicide, Accident, and Murder in Nineteenth-Century Philadelphia*. Cambridge, 1979.

Lawton, Harry W., et al. "Agriculture Among the Paiute of Owens Valley." *Journal of California Anthropology* 3 (Summer 1976): 13–50.

Lillard, Richard G., ed. "A Literate Woman in the Mines: The Diary of Rachel Haskell." *Mississippi Valley Historical Review* 31 (June 1944): 81–98.

Lord, Eliot. *Comstock Mining and Mines*. Berkeley, 1959.

Lyman, Stanford M. *The Asian in the West*. Reno, 1970.

———. *Chinese Americans*. New York, 1974.

MacManus, Seumas. *The Story of the Irish Race*. Old Greenwich, Conn., 1979.

Madis, George. *The Winchester Book*. Dallas, 1961.

Marshall, S. L. A. *Crimsoned Prairies*. New York, 1972.

Marshall, Thomas M. "The Miners' Laws of Colorado." *American Historical Review* 25 (1919–1920): 426–40.

Maule, William M. *A Contribution to the Geographic and Economic History of the Carson, Walker and Mono Basins in Nevada and California*. Berkeley, 1937.

Merriam, C. Hart. *Studies of the California Indians*. Berkeley, 1955.

Mighels, Ella Sterling. *Life and Letters of a Forty-Niner's Daughter*. San Francisco, 1929.

Miller, Nyle H., and Snell, Joseph W. *Why the West Was Wild*. Topeka, 1963.

Mondy, R. W. "Analysis of Frontier Social Instability." *Southwestern Social Science Quarterly* 24 (September 1943): 167–77.

Monkkonen, Eric. *The Dangerous Class*. Cambridge, 1975.

———. *Police in Urban America, 1860–1920*. Cambridge, England, 1981.

Mooney, James. *The Ghost-Dance Religion and the Sioux Outbreak of 1890*. Chicago, 1965.

Murray, Keith A. *The Modocs and Their War*. Norman, 1959.

Myatt, Frederick. *The Illustrated Encyclopedia of Pistols and Revolvers*. New York, 1980.

The National Cyclopaedia of American Biography. Vol. 8. New York, 1924.

Paine, Albert Bigelow, ed. *Mark Twain's Letters*. 2 vols. New York, 1917.

Parr, J. F. "Reminiscences of the Bodie Strike." *Yosemite Nature Notes* 7 (May 1928): 33–38.

Paul, Rodman W. *California Gold*. Lincoln, 1947.

———. *Mining Frontiers of the Far West, 1848–1880*. New York, 1963.

Perrigo, Lynn I. "Law and Order in Early Colorado Mining Camps." *Mississippi Valley Historical Review* 28 (June 1941): 41–62.

Pitt, Leonard. *The Decline of the Californios: A Social History of the Spanish-Speaking Californians, 1846–1890*. Berkeley, 1970.

Prassel, Frank Richard. *The Western Peace Officer*. Norman, 1972.

Rister, Carl C. *Border Command: General Phil Sheridan in the West*. Norman, 1944.

Roberts, Gary L. "The West's Gunmen." *American West* 8 (January and March 1971): 10–15, 64, and 18–23, 61–62.

Rosa, Joseph G. *The Gunfighter: Man or Myth?* Norman, 1968.

Royce, Charles C. *Indian Land Cessions in the United States.* Washington, 1899.

Russell, Carl P. "Bodie, Dead City of Mono." *Yosemite Nature Notes* 6 (December 1927): 89–96.

———. "Early Mining Excitements East of Yosemite." *Sierra Club Bulletin* 13 (February 1928): 40–53.

———. *One Hundred Years in Yosemite.* Berkeley, 1947.

Russell, Don. "How Many Indians Were Killed?" *American West* 10 (July 1973): 42–47, 61–63.

Russell, Israel C. "Quaternary History of Mono Valley, California." *Eighth Annual Report of the U.S. Geological Survey, for 1886–1887* (Washington, 1889), pp. 228–79.

Shuck, Oscar T., ed. *History of the Bench and Bar of California.* Los Angeles, 1901.

Sinclair, C. H. "The Oblique Boundary Line Between California and Nevada." *U.S. Coast and Geodetic Survey Report, 1899–1900* (Washington, 1901), App. 3, pp. 265–315.

Smith, Grant H. "Bodie, Last of the Old-Time Mining Camps." *California Historical Society Quarterly* 4 (March 1925): 64–80.

———. *The History of the Comstock Lode, 1850–1920.* Reno, 1943.

Spicer, Edward H. *A Short History of the Indians of the United States.* New York, 1969.

Steckmesser, Kent Ladd. *The Western Hero in History and Legend.* Norman, 1965.

Steward, Julian H. "Irrigation Without Agriculture." *Papers of the Michigan Academy of Sciences, Arts, and Letters* 12 (New York, 1930): 149–56.

Steward, Julian H., and Wheeler-Voegelin, Erminie. *The Northern Paiute Indians.* New York, 1974.

tenBroek, Jacobus, et al. *Prejudice, War and the Constitution.* Berkeley, 1954.

Utley, Robert M., and Washburn, Wilcomb E. *The Indian Wars.* New York, 1977.

Wallace, Anthony F. C. *The Death and Rebirth of the Seneca.* New York, 1970.

Wasson, Joseph. *Account of the Important Revival of Mining Interests in the Bodie and Esmeralda Districts.* San Francisco, 1878.

———. *Complete Guide to the Mono County Mines. Description of Bodie, Esmeralda, Indian, Lake, Laurel Hill, Prescott, and Other Mining Districts.* San Francisco, 1879.

Waters, Frank. *The Earp Brothers of Tombstone.* New York, 1960.

Wellman, Paul I. *The Indian Wars of the West.* New York, 1954.

Winther, Oscar O. *Via Western Express and Stagecoach.* Stanford, 1945.

Zimmer, Ethel. "Colonel Samuel Youngs' Journal." *Nevada Historical Society Quarterly* 2 (Spring 1959): 27–67.

INDEX

Designer: Steve Renick
Compositor: Wilsted & Taylor
Printer: Vail-Ballou
Binder: Vail-Ballou
Text: Goudy Old Style
Display: Copper Plate Gothic